George Bell

Rough Notes by an Old Soldier during Fifty Years' Service

George Bell

Rough Notes by an Old Soldier during Fifty Years' Service

ISBN/EAN: 9783337307011

Printed in Europe, USA, Canada, Australia, Japan

Cover: Foto ©ninafisch / pixelio.de

More available books at **www.hansebooks.com**

ROUGH NOTES

BY

AN OLD SOLDIER,

DURING FIFTY YEARS' SERVICE,

FROM ENSIGN G. B. TO MAJOR-GENERAL, C.B.

Man plods his way through thorns to ashes!

LONDON:
DAY AND SON, LIMITED,
6, GATE STREET, LINCOLN'S-INN FIELDS, W.C
1867.

DEDICATION.

To the Young Officers of the British Army.

Stick to your trade, young Gentlemen.

The wheel of fortune is always going round, and every spoke comes uppermost in its turn.

I was SIXTEEN years a SUB.

G. B.

PREFACE.

I FOUND my bundle of Notes, closed up in my knapsack, so much defaced and worn by long travel, that I was very much inclined to throw them all into the fire, when I was stopped one day by an old *camarada*, who persuaded me to link them together and send them to the press. I protested, having no ability for book-making, not being an enthusiast or a novel reader, and to come out as an *Author* appeared to me to be worse than to hear the "tir-whit" of a shell from the *Redan* into one's tent. "Never mind," he said, "try your luck; don't say too much about the R— T—; the truth is not always to be told, you know, and as for the critics and reviewers, you need not fear them: they are considerate and kind to old soldiers, who sit down in the evening of life by the fireside, without pretension, ostentation, or dash, to talk of old campaigns, and fight their battles o'er again." These few words gave me some little encouragement. I condensed my bundle of notes into the smallest space I could, and they will be found in the following chapters without any varnish!

G. B.

CONTENTS.

CHAPTER I.

Farewell to Home.—The Route.—Marching and Dining.—A Serious Loss.—The Lazy Lieutenant.—Arrival in Lisbon.—Paterfamilias.—My Billet.—The Route, March, Arrival.—How we Fared.—Subaltern Life.—Roughing it.—In Pursuit.—First Blood.—Victory..................................*page* 1

CHAPTER II.

After the Battle.—Albuquerque.—Merida.—Ciudad Rodrigo.—The Assault.—*Bone* Soup.—Horrors of War.—Badajos.—Preparations......................................*page* 17

CHAPTER III.

The Assault.—Fall of Badajos.—After the Assault.—The Sacking of Badajos.—Neglect of the British Government.—Departure from Badajos.—Discipline.—Jollifications.—Castle Mirabete.—Forts Napoleon and Almaraz.—Disappointment.—Chivalry.—Flat Burglary.—Quill to the Rescue.—Leonora.—Estramos.—To Lisbon on Leave ....*page* 29

CHAPTER IV.

Better Times.—A Night Adventure.—Lisbon.—Caveat Emptor.—Military Discipline.—Toledo.—Salamanca.—Heroic Conduct.—After the Battle.—Yepes.—The Route.—The Parting.—A Surprise.—A Retreat.—Madrid ....*page* 50

CHAPTER V.

The Retreat.—Ready for Action.—Adventures.—A Surprise.—Hard Lines.—A Godsend.—Female Insubordination.—Mrs. Skiddy.—Short Commons.—Fever.—Theatricals.—1813.—Campaigning.—Destruction of Burgos.—The British Soldier.
page 66

CHAPTER VI.

Battle of Vittoria.—Victory.—The Pursuit.—The King in Danger.—A Night Auction.—Narrow Escapes.—Curious Booty.—The Wounded.—Maurice Quill.—Masterman.—Sir William Stewart. — The Basque Provinces. — The Alarm. — Warm Work.—The Wounded..*page* 85

CHAPTER VII.

The Valley of Bastan.—Sharp Affair.—Sauve qui peut.—A Ride for a Doctor.—Wellington and Soult.—Affair before Pampeluna.—The Colonel of the 34th.—A Chance Lost.—Roncesvales. — Foraging. — The Lost Sentries. — Unrequited Bravery ....*page* 102

CHAPTER VIII.

Ghostly Quarters. — Hard Lines. — A Snow-storm. — Corporal Punishment.—Kindness is Better.—Tom Eccles.—Nivelle.—Victory.—Individual Bravery.—Spanish Ladies.—A Bull-fight.—Short Commons.—Maurice Quill's Wager.—Maurice wins. — The French fraternize. — How we got Cognac. — Paddy Muldoon.—Passage of the Nive.—Bayonne ....*page* 116

CHAPTER IX.

Soult's Tactics.—Villefranche.—St.-Pierre.—A Bayonet-charge.—The Gordon Highlanders.—The Wounded.—After the Battle.—Vieux Monguère.—Spanish Ingratitude.—Orthes.—Soult's Effort.—Its Failure .... *page* 136

CHAPTER X.

The Duke of Richmond.—Discipline.—Combat at Aire.—Victory.—Vic Bigore.—A Turn of Luck.—Tarbes.—The Combat.—Major Dogherty.—The Three *Generals*.—Adjutant Peckett.—A Cheated Stomach.—Toulouse.—Deserters.—Fighting with Stones. .... *page* 149

CHAPTER XI.

Battle of Toulouse.—The Retreat of Ten Thousand.—The First Act.—Progress of the Battle.—A Bird's-eye View.—Entry into Toulouse.—Peace Prospects.—" The Duke."—The Duke d'Angoulême.—Route for Bordeaux. — My Billet.—Rather in Luck. — Freemasonry. — Private Hostilities. — The Duello.—Home, Sweet Home.—Mrs. Commissary-General Skiddy.

page 164

CHAPTER XII.

Adieu to Bordeaux.—On Board Ship.—Welcome Home.—Hero-Worship.—The Huntingdon Peerage.—Life in Ireland.—Sounds of War.—The Castle Guard in Dublin.—Tipperary.—Peace.—Life in Scotland.—A Prize in Life.—The Baby Major.—The 45th..*page* 184

CHAPTER XIII.

At Sea.—Mutineers.—Breakers ahead.—Shark-fishing.—Crossing the Line.—The Trade Winds.—Trincomalee.—Its Scenery.—Landing at Madras.—Fort St. George.—A Journey.—Palankeen-bearers.—Negapatam.—The Cobra.—Back to Madras.—The Route.—My Wife's Diary ....*page* 198

CHAPTER XIV.

Embarkation.—At Sea.—Rangoon.—The Great Dagon.—The Burmese.—Goose Eggs.—Burmese War-boats.—Tiger-traps.—Palmyra Toddy.—Sandford and Bennett.—The Rhahams.—Sagacious Elephants.—Tactics.—Mal du Pays ....*page* 217

CHAPTER XV.

Bandicoots.—Celebrated Mosquitoes.—Ants.—Rat-catching.—My Cuisine.—Burmese Customs.—The Great Bell.—Burmese Law.—Mandamar.—Jungle Fever.—Cholera.—Burmese Honey.—The Climate.—Burning a Priest.—I Exchange.—A Thunderstorm.—Adieu to Ava...*page* 233

CHAPTER XVI.

At Sea.—Arrival at Madras.—A Severe Tea.—Summary Punishment.—The Bag of Rupees.—March to Bangalore.—A Curious Idol.—Damul-Wallagahnagur.—Arcot-Vellore.—Pallicondah.—The Moharum Feast.—The Ghauts.—Rice-fields.—A Surprise.—Arrival at Bangalore ....*page* 250

CHAPTER XVII.

Bangalore.—Its Garrison.—Amusements.—The Cobra.—Its Bite cured.—A Snake-charmer.—Devotees.—Sir Thomas Munro.—En Route encore.—Brahmin Women.—Naikanairry.—My Friend the Colonel.—Guzaron.—Vellore.—Mauvais Temps.—Affliction ....*page* 267

CHAPTER XVIII.

An Old Friend.—Affair with a Tiger.—At Sea.—Diamond Harbour. —Land again.—Calcutta.—Our Ménage.—Calcutta.—Fort William.—Barrackpore.—Serampore.—Kidderpore Orphan School.—A Nautch.—An Apostate.—A Christian Prayer.—A Fakeer .... *page* 283

CHAPTER XIX.

Mortality in India.—Mirzapore.—The Races.—Stewart's Museum. —Hindoo Deities.—Ceremonies.—Beast-worship.—Summary Punishment.—A Monster Banyan.—Converts.—Leave Calcutta.—A Night on the River.—En Voyage.—Masulipatam.— On Shore.—Football.—Madras .... *page* 300

CHAPTER XX.

St. Thomas's Mount.—Wallajabad.—Conjeveram.—Wild Fowl.— Arcot.—Chittoor.—Palamanair.—Moolwaugum.—The Burial-ground.—En Route.—Arrive at Bangalore .... *page* 318

CHAPTER XXI.

An O'er-true Tale.—Murder.—Remorse.—Court-Martial.—The Defence.—The Sentence.—The Criminal.—Repentance.—The Scaffold.—The Execution.—"*Otium cum.*"—A Youthful Débutante.—Bal Costumé.—A Durbar.—The Rajah of Mysore. —Fighting Men.—Their Presents.—A Courtier Elephant.— Cheetah-hunting.—The Death.. *page* 329

CHAPTER XXII.

The Rajah's Carriage.—A Procession.—Seringapatam.—Tippoo's Tomb.—Hyder's Palace.—A Pagoda.—The Dussorah Festival. —A Drunken Donkey.—Novel Tiger-hunting.—The Rajah's Review.—A Durbar.—Falls of the Cauvery.—On the March.— A Canny Elephant.—Fine Waterfalls.—'Ware Tiger.—Buried Alive.—Closepet.—Welcome Home .... *page* 349

ROUGH NOTES BY AN OLD SOLDIER.

"Man plods his way through Thorns to Ashes."

CHAPTER I.

Farewell to Home.—The Route.—Marching and Dining.—A Serious Loss.—The Lazy Lieutenant.—Arrival in Lisbon.—Paterfamilias.—My Billet.—The Route, March, Arrival.—How we fared.—Subaltern Life.—Roughing it.—In Pursuit.—First Blood.—Victory.

THE *London Gazette* of the 11th March, 1811, proclaimed "George Bell, gentleman, to be Ensign in the 34th Regiment of Foot, by command of His Majesty King George the Third." On the 11th of March I was at a public school, when some one came and gave me the above information.

So soon as I collected my senses, I jumped up, broke my way into the presence of the great Dominie; bid him a hasty farewell, shook hands with my class companions, and bolted out of the house, no one seeming to know what it was all about until I was clear away, and sent back a newspaper with the Gazette, which fully explained my hasty retreat from thraldom.

Six days after the 11th of March I was just seventeen years of age, an independent military gentleman, let loose upon the world with the liberal pay of 5*s.* 3*d.* a day, less income-tax, which has never been increased from that day to this.

I had an official letter very soon to join my regimental depôt without delay, signed

HARRY CALVERT, *Adjutant-General.*

So I went off that night by the mail a hundred miles' journey, to bid them farewell at the beautiful paternal residence on the banks of Lough Erin. Here I only remained two days: there was weeping and lamentation over-much at my departure; but it was the tender custom in Ireland long ago. The family circle saw me off, at the end of the long avenue, all pretty cheery until we heard the mail-coach horn in the distance, when the ladies began a fresh lamentation, which set me going until I nearly cried my eyes out.

I was now fairly off, and with my pocket full of money, so I began to brighten up by the time the coach stopped for the night, for this hundred-mile journey occupied two days.

This royal mail-coach was horsed with a pair of old Irish hunters, carried four passengers inside, and two guards in royal livery behind, with a box of blunderbuss firearms and pistols, to protect themselves and the mail-bags; the roads in those days being swarmed by highwaymen. We had no adventure.

After being well furnished with a good kit, and supplied liberally with everything I required, I sailed in the mail-packet for Liverpool, which I reached the third day, after a stormy voyage. It was then the custom for each passenger to carry his own prog; my hamper never was opened, I was so desperately sea-sick, consequently the steward came in for nearly all the good things, and might have set up a cookshop for many a day afterwards.

Safely on English ground for the first time, I enjoyed myself for a couple of days, and then took coach with four spanking horses for Beverley, in Yorkshire, where I joined my depôt, and went to drill under the command of an old sergeant, who used to say that he was preparing me for a great general some day, if I didn't fall on the bed of honour before my time.

At this time the Peninsular war was being carried on with desperate strife: there was a continual demand for men and money; the former were engaged at eighteen guineas bounty, while the Spaniards were supplied most liberally with English gold, our army being half-starved, and Lord Wellington snubbed by the Government, and every obstacle thrown in his way towards success.

I now mounted my uniform for the first time, and when full dressed was ashamed to appear in the streets. I fancied all the people would be laughing at the raw Ensign, with his cocked hat and feather, jack boots, white breeches, sword, and belt; then the sword was always getting between my legs, trying to trip me up as I cautiously went along, not daring to look at any one. I thought myself the observed of all observers, being just bran new out of the tailor's shop. We were encumbered with many sorts of regimental useless dresses, such as long black cloth leggings, with about two dozen of bright buttons up the outside of each leg! Then, for the evening, tight-fitting white kerseymere pantaloons, and Hessian boots with black silk tassels in front; and, when on duty, a gorget hanging under one's chin.

I was a right jolly fellow when I got all this toggery off my back, and enjoyed myself to the full. We had no mess, lived in lodgings, no restraint on us young fellows, and had, with the 5s. 3d. a day, 6s. a week lodging money, to provide ourselves with respectable quarters.

I found the pretty town of Beverley a most agreeable residence, and never dreamt of leaving it, until one fine morning we heard of the battle of Albuera, in which my regiment was engaged, and suffered severely: the gaps of death must be filled up; the route came upon us suddenly, and I was one of the number ordered out to fill a vacancy.

Albuera may be considered amongst the great and bloody battles of the Peninsula. At the conclusion of the day, 1,500 unwounded men, the remnant of 6,000 unconquerable British soldiers, stood triumphant on the fatal hill!

I am not going to write any descriptive account of battles, nor am I at all qualified to write a book, or turn author; I have but a few rough notes and a bright memory, and if any one should happen to fall in with this manuscript, he will only find the relation a truthful statement of simple but stirring facts of the day.

The route came upon us all of a heap, in the midst of fun and frolic, to march for Portsmouth, and embark for Portugal. It was twenty-two days' march; and away we went, thoughtless jolly dogs, living at hotels on the road, which astonished the 5s. 3d. a day! The marches were long at times, and many a day

I almost dropped footsore and weary, which I never confessed. We always had breakfast at the half-way house, ordered by one of our men sent in advance; halted and formed up in military order before we marched into the town or village, swords drawn, and our drum and fife playing martial music. We had all the little boys and girls half a mile round pressing into the ranks to hear the *band*, as they said, and see the soldiers. After one hour's halt, and 2*s.* worth of a first-rate morning meal, leaving the jolly landlord very little profit, we continued our march, the same orderly going on to announce our approach at the billeting town, and to order dinner for the *army!* The march from Brigg to Lincoln I shall never forget,—twenty-four miles of a straight line, the steeple that held Big Tom always in front,—only one other march in all my campaigns knocked the life so much out of my feet, and that was a forced night march to Madrid, which I may record hereafter.

The landlords of the hotels always waited personally on us, to know our pleasure about the dinner hour, and what wines we liked best, &c. For my own part, I would have been perfectly satisfied with a beef-steak and a pint of ale, but dared not express anything so *infra dig.* with a red coat on my back; so left it all to my *superiors*, and paid my share of the bill with the best grace I could, not being a wine drinker, and finding the 5*s.* 3*d.* only about equal to satisfy the servants and some minor things by the way. At Oxford we were met by another detachment of different regiments on the same route, going to the wars; here we amalgamated and had a great jollification dinner-party. I could only consent to any proposal, having no voice of my own in the matter, paid three times the amount of the usual bill, and had a crashing headache next morning to cheer me. I was astonished to see what some of those fellows could drink, and not seem to feel the worse; one lad of my own age and standing got "screwed" every night—but he did not last long! I gave him many a lecture, being his "senior officer" by one week, but could not make any impression on a lad that "sucked the monkey," *i.e.*, going to bed with a bottle of brandy.

We had charming weather all the way,—old women came toddling out by the wayside as we passed, crying out—"There goes a few more lambs to the slaughter, poor things!" which only caused some merriment amongst the soldiers, who were the most thoughtless set of dogs I ever saw since or before— not one of them ever returned to England!

We finished our march at Portsmouth, and were billeted at an hotel called the "Blue Posts." I was very tired and very *green* in those days; I went to bed early, left my door unlocked, threw my clothes on a chair, and was soon in my dreams. I had £25 with me—all I was worth in the world; my pocket-book contained this treasure—it had many folds, in which my money was divided. When I turned out in the morning, I was nervously horrified at seeing my clothes scattered about the floor; I approached the examination, with dread and saw at once the shadow of, to me, a great calamity. Some very unkind but thoughtful person had entered my bedroom while asleep, to count my money and square my accounts, extracted a ten pound Bank of England note, for the trouble and risk, and left, but perhaps overlooked, the balance of £15 which lay in another part of the book, so that I was not altogether bankrupt. I had a very good guess who this wretched robber was, and might have put my hand upon him, but I had no proof. I made my report to the commanding officer of our party; but he seemed to doubt my tale; nor would he make any inquiry, which nettled me more severely than the loss I sustained.

A week in Portsmouth reduced my £15; I had £7. 10s. to pay for my share of sea-stock; the balance I changed into dollars, and embarked, in light marching order, on board the *Arethusa*, a rotten old transport of 300 tons. We had a gale of wind, of course, in the Bay of Biscay O, and put back to Falmouth for some little repairs and more prog. We all subscribed and laid in a few sacks of potatoes, flour, and fresh meat. I took a Sunday walk in the country, strolled into a farm-house, while the jolly fat landlord and his dame were at their roast beef dinner and ale; they looked a little surprised at seeing a young fellow in a red coat at the door in that part of the country, but asked me to come in and taste their roast beef. I was always hungry in those days, and took my seat at the little round table, in the neat, clean, well-furnished kitchen; there was an air of comfort about it one hardly ever sees in any other country; they asked me a great many questions, every one then being interested in the war; I told them all I knew; and when I was going, they both shook my hands with some interest. I gave them thanks, bid them good-bye, left half-a-crown on the table, and went back to my den upon the waters. Our commanding officer had a cabin about the size of a coffin to himself; thirteen of us commissioned officers of different corps messed, and slept in the cuddy, a sort of dog-kennel, where we washed by turns in the morning. One very lazy fellow, a lieutenant of the 39th regiment, who swung in a cot over the table, never could be got up in time to have the *saloon* swept and garnished for breakfast. I told him that the next time I was on duty as the orderly officer, if he was not up at the first bugle sound I would cut him down. The weather now was very warm, and this Paddy from Cork slept without any shirt, whether from long habit or economy I did not inquire. However, as usual, he could not be roused up, so I cut the head-rope of his cot, and down he came whop on the table; then arose a whillaloo of "my neck's broke," &c.; he was furious, grasped a knife and chased me up on deck. I ran into the rigging like a cat; he flourished his knife, the people stared and thought him deranged. I explained in four or five words, "I cut down Mr. Lazybones." Then there was a general yell of laughter; he dived below; I had only obeyed orders; so he dared not dispute the matter, and was never late again.

The voyage was a long one, owing to a convoy of all sorts of small craft going to Lisbon. "What have you on board?" said our skipper to a wretched-looking tub from Cork. "Fruit and timber," says Pat. "What sort are they?" "Birch brooms and praties, admiral," speaking through an old tin pot with the bottom knocked out of it, and then a roar of a laugh on the potato barge. We were on short commons before we made the land, and our potatoes were counted out every day until we entered the Tagus. A joyful day it was to get out of prison. Ten miles up the river, and we anchored off the Block Horse Square. The scenery all around the country is beautiful—very beautiful. The city stands on the north bank of the Tagus, here nine miles wide, and could shelter ten thousand ships. No end to the multitude of churches, chapels, convents, and monasteries. What a good people these ought to be, with so many friars, priests, and nuns scattered amongst them to look after their morals!

We landed under a broiling sun. The men were sent into an old monastery, and bivouacked in the corridors; the officers got billets in different parts of the city; mine was in a very ugly quarter of the town, and had a cut-throat-like entrance, through a long dark vaulted passage. I made my way up a long flight of dark stairs, knocked at an iron portal very like a prison, presented my billet, which was examined by a Portuguese nigger, with a grin. The door closed until "Massa see ticket," when, after some delay, I was admitted, and shown into a small room with a wee sleeping-cot in the corner, and there left in solitude. Not knowing three words of the Portuguese lingo, and no one coming to pay me a visit or give me a welcome, I went out for a ramble, lost my way, and wandered about until ten o'clock at night, when I most fortunately met an officer going to our ship, who took me on board for the night. Next day I found my quarters, took the bearings, and went in search of my party, but could not find one of them. The weather was broiling hot, the market full of the choicest fruits—oranges, grapes, melons, peaches, green-gage, an abundant supply of all sorts, enough for an army. Like a very imprudent young spoon, I went right at them all, and feasted too freely, then made my way out of the town into the country, about half a league, to enjoy the breeze. Seeing a fine vineyard, and the gate open, I went in without ceremony. The Señor was there, recumbent in a beautiful arbour, while his people were busy making wine. He very politely asked me to be seated, talked a great deal, I supposed about the army of England. All I understood were a few words, as Wellington, and the guerre, and Marshal Soult. I felt myself very small, not being able to speak to this gentleman; but there was no remedy, so I resolved at once to learn the language, and thus quieted my mind. He ordered one of his men to present me a goblet of wine, which I drank off to his health. He returned the compliment, only tasting his cup, and we parted, my host accompanying me to the gate, hat in hand. I found my home, went to roost early, was taken seriously ill in the night, and lay there for many days. No one of my party knew where I was; I could not speak, and the only person I saw was a little black maid, who brought me some rice-water daily, and put it down by my bedside. The fruit and the wine nearly finished me. Had I been in the hands of a doctor, he would most likely have put me under the sod—particularly a medico of this country, who are celebrated for their ignorance in the profession. Ditto in Spain, where they continue the old Sangrado system, phlebotomize nearly to death, shut you up tight in a dark room without a breath of fresh air, and give you plenty of hot water to drink. The patient dies, of course!

When I was able to crawl, I went out in search of the monastery, met one of my men, who conducted me to it, and there found all my people; some thought I was kidnapped, others that I had deserted, and many were the surmises what had become of G. B. The old captain, our commanding officer, never troubled himself about me. I found out for the first time now, that we were all entitled to rations, and that Captain B——— had been drawing mine and making use of them like an honest fellow. He was our Paterfamilias, an old soldier who had been at home on sick leave, and knew the country and its ways and means, up to every dodge, and how to take precious good care of himself. He told us many stories about his former campaigns, and how he leathered the French. Subsequently we were informed it was but his playful way of amusing "Johnny Newcomes," as he had never yet had the good fortune of slaying a Mounseer in battle. He had the soubriquet in the regiment of "Bloody Mick, who killed all the French with his great big stick."

I went back to my billet with my servant to take away my few traps, and settle down in the old monastery with my companions. I was met by the padrone, who inquired after my health, and asked me to dinner at two o'clock with his family. This was done by the aid of a Portuguese and English dictionary. I made my appearance, and got Benjamin's portion the first course—that was, a plate-load of rice and oil, chopped onion and garlic, too savoury for an invalid. I put it gently aside, which rather astonished the landlady, who was evidently taken aback that I did not relish this part of her dinner. However, there was something else without that most delicious flavour of Portuguese garlic—good bread and palatable wine and fruit; and so I finished my first and last meal in the house of a Portuguese gentleman.

I gladly embraced the opportunity of housing myself now in the monastery amongst the monks and friars—a lazy, indolent crew, with their bull-necks, bare shaven crowns, sandals, cowls, and white rope girdles and rosary. They lived in their cells, or very comfortable little rooms, while we occupied the corridors and galleries. I slept on the flags with my martial cloak around me! It was all the bed and bedding I had; the climate was blazing hot, and the broad flags kept me cool.

We had a camp-kettle in which we cooked all our rations together; there was an abundance of the finest vegetables, very cheap, so that, with some rice in addition, we turned out excellent soup and *bouilli*. Each of us had a tin dish, an iron spoon, knife and fork, without any other incumbrance of this kind. Sometimes we got a bullock's head to add to the rations, which when cold also gave us a breakfast.

I joined another lad in the purchase of a *boura* to carry our baggage, *i.e.*, in English, a donkey. My camp equipage was small when the broadside of a donkey carried it all. This purchase cleared me out. I had not a dollar left, and had no opportunity of seeing any of the sights, or enjoying any of the pleasures of a Lisbon life. I became a sort of a monk myself, visiting those old crows every day. They supposed me a good Roman Catholic, because I spoke a little Latin to them, and confessed myself an Irishman. One question they never forget to ask, "Are you an Irishman?" They consider all Irishmen Roman Catholics; regarding myself, they were quite out of their reckoning, for there never was a more stanch, loyal Protestant subject of the Queen of England than G. B.

The route came for us at last, and all the convalescent men from Belem depôt joined us for the march, and away we went in the middle of the night, to get it over before the burning early sun of the morrow. It was weary work ploughing through the deep sands all the way. How I looked back to home, sweet home! and to the noble horses I used to ride there at pleasure. Any money now for "Billy Button," the orderly pony, always ready saddled in the stable for general use.

The marches were sometimes very long, and dreary, and provoking. No one knew the distance; meeting a solitary peasant now and then we would ask, "Quantas leaguas, Señor, a Sacavem?" Answer, "Dos leaguas e pokito, Señor" (two leagues and a bit); march on another league and meet pizano the second, and ask the same question, "O Señor, Sacavem, *tres* leaguas e no mas" (just three leagues)! No milestones, no hotels, inns, or refreshment houses; we knew, however, that there was a town in the distance somewhere, and that we must reach it. Our Captain, commanding officer, was well mounted and always had some grog, &c., in his haversack, which he seemed to enjoy at the usual halting-place half-way, under a shady tree, all alone! Sergeant Bolland, a fine old soldier of our regiment, returning from Lisbon, aided us in many ways, gave us good advice in the arrangement of our future campaign and as to how to take care of ourselves, for as he said, "this is all pleasure to what is before us, if I may judge of the past;"—he had been wounded at Albuera.

We went merrily on for many a day, living on our rations, until we arrived at Portalegre, the head-quarters of the 34th, and such a nice handy well-disciplined corps, with high-caste officers, all well seasoned and experienced in the late campaigns.

I had letters of introduction to Colonel Fenwick and other officers of note and standing, all of whom received me cordially, and I was no longer a stranger. The Colonel asked me to breakfast on arrival, when I gave him my history from the starting-point, and a sample of such an appetite that must have astonished him, and I feared would prevent him from showing me any more such attentions; but he was always kind—an amiable man, a good and gallant soldier, decided in character, just and impartial.

I was appointed to the company of "Moyle Sherer," then a lieutenant, a gentleman, a scholar, an author, and a most zealous soldier.

I now settled down in my billet, commenced my orderly duties, and endeavoured to make myself comfortable and to prepare for the storm of war, then sweeping over unhappy Spain. I had nothing to trouble me but a big appetite, for which my ration was quite insufficient: three-quarters of a pound of lean beef, half bone at times, a pound of brown bread or biscuit, and half a gill of rum; I often finished the whole *dish* at a sitting, and got up from the noble repast very hungry. The beef or the bread never was weighed; a certain quantity was served out to each company; say the company was fifty strong, the meat was cut into fifty pieces, and spread on the turf. One man turned his back on the rations not to see them, another called out, "*This*—say Tom Johns," and Tom picked up his morsel of beef; "*This*—Jack Simmons," and there was a great roar of a laugh, for it was nearly all a marrow bone! "*This*—Mr. G. B.," and so on, all fair play between officers and men.

I had a chair and a table, and a sort of a bed in my little room on which I slept soundly—dogs always go to sleep when hungry!

I had no books and was very idle; it was not customary in those days in the army to read the Bible; I don't think that I saw one for three years, so that Portugal or Spain had no fault to find with us on this score! However, there were some good and pious men to be found, who were not ashamed to

> Kneel, remote, upon the simple sod,
> And sue, *in formâ pauperis*, to God.

We Subs were a sociable class of bipeds; we had dinner

parties, and evening parties, and dancing parties, and horse-racing parties all very simple in their way, and not attended with any expense; for instance, "Come to dinner to-morrow in camp fashion," that meant, send your rations, your servant, chair, knife, fork, spoon and plate (not plates); three or four rations of fresh beef made better soup than three-quarters of a pound with a bone in it; then there might be a bit of liver and bacon, and some roast *taties*, and roars of laughter and fun; so much for subaltern dinner in service fifty years ago.

Those who could afford an evening party, had brandy and cigars, or wine and crackers for their guests, plenty of chat about the past, the present, and the future; and some comic songs. The bottles being all drained, the evening closed, and good night was said; some one of the guests adding, "You will all come to me to-morrow night."

The girls were very fond of dancing; we sometimes all joined for a *ball*, and invited young ladies and their mammas to look after them. We had no band; a flute and guitar filled the orchestra; there was some lemonade and cakes—to refresh the Señoritas—all they wished for; all they expected. The priests were always reluctant and jealous to see any of their fair flock mixing with *heretics*; the ladies quite differed in opinion!

The Derby never created more fear or excitement than our race-ground on the olive plain; all the Tats in the garrison went to the post very smart, and ready to win the bag of dollars hanging on the big olive-tree; first away often last in the race,—the real winner sometimes losing his race by dismounting before coming to the scales to be weighed,—one or two disappearing as *bolters* amongst the trees. A jockey with perhaps a red *night*-cap going right off to his stable in the town, and knocking down two priests in the gateway. Then the donkey race; every Jock, sitting with his face to the tail, a smart fellow running in front with a bunch of carrots; a so we passed our time.

I had a letter from home now, and no little sympathy expressed for my loss at Portsmouth. I might draw for my allowance in advance; it was enough for me—more than I deserved; but far away less than the young gentlemen of the present day in the army receive, or demand, or cannot do without! I never went into debt in all my life—I knew that it was dangerous; and, not being able to pay, dishonourable. I had recourse to my old commanding officer, Captain B——, for some money—he was the only one who seemed to understand those pecuniary affairs with advantage. He charged me six shillings sterling for every dollar he gave me, a dollar being worth 4*s*. 2*d*.! I was now rich for the present, and fared well, and had an evening party—no very great enjoyment to me, for I detested brandy and cigars. The latter has had no fellowship with me all my life, nor was I ever a dead hand at the bottle.

I made myself happy in a way until October, when there was a flare-up with the French. General Girard made too free with our side of the country, and began to poach on our ground. The 2nd Division, commanded by Lieutenant-General Sir Rowland Hill, was let loose to hunt him out of our district. The rainy season had commenced, and the weather was dreadful. We marched all the day, and lay down on the wet sod by night, which rather surprised and alarmed me, expecting to be under cover in some civilized way after our day's work, instead of herding with the beasts of the field. I had an old boat cloak and a blanket for my bed and bedding. I never had more, but sometimes less, for the next three years. "We have made a raw and rainy beginning of our campaign," said Richardson, my chum; "how did you sleep?" "Slept like a fish," I said; "I believe they sleep best in water." "Bravo!" said he; "you'll do." I thought in my own mind I might *do* for a night or two more, but I would soon be done in a bivouac in such weather; however, I kept that secret to myself. David Richardson was an old soldier, and passed through a campaign. "Come over to my *quarters*," he said, "and have a cup of tea; it will take the chill out of your old bones; you look blue in the face." Near at hand his kettle was boiling under an olive tree, and a pork chop in the frying-pan—very savoury. "Shake a little pepper on it, Ned, and be quick; the bugle will sound directly, and get the other plate." "There's only one, sir," replied Ned; "you know we left in light marching order." "You have the advantage of me, Davey," added I, "having seen service, and knowing how to forage; as for me, I am indeed in light marching condition, and have nothing but my haversack, containing my three days' rations cooked,—but where in the world did you fall in with this savoury meat?" "Well," he said, "my man Ned there has a sharp eye and a sharp bayonet, and if those pigs will intrude upon us at night, it is at their own risk; you will learn more about these little private affairs time enough." Bugle sounds. "There, Ned, get your breakfast quickly, and throw that leg of pork into the bag, and load the donkey."

We continued our march in this way for a week. Our ration of rum at night kept the life in us. There were no tents in the army in those days; it was all bivouac, pleasant enough in hot weather and dry ground; but this was an exceptional case, and not meant to continue. The rain kept along with us. I was never thoroughly dry, yet there is nothing that keeps out wet like a blanket; there was no such thing as an india-rubber or a macintosh A.D. 1811, and as for anything else called waterproof, it was all fudge. We never undressed of course, but just pushed on, apparently having the right scent, as the men would constantly say, "I smell those *crappos*, they can't be far off." They had been keeping one day ahead of us, and left behind them a perfume of tobacco, onions, &c., that could not be mistaken. On the evening of the 27th of October we got close to their heels; it rained all the day, and in the dusk we halted on ploughed ground. "Pile arms; keep perfectly quiet; light no fires; no drum to beat; no bugle to sound," were the orders passed through the ranks. I was very tired; threw myself up against the side of a bank ditch, dived into my haversack, where I had in reserve a piece of cold bullock's liver and salt, some biscuit, and a very small allowance of rum, so I was not so badly off. All was still, and cold, and cheerless, until about two o'clock in the morning of the 28th, when the word was gently passed through all regiments: "Stand to your arms!" The whole division was now in silent motion, and moved on to the plain some few miles, pretty close to the enemy, who were quartered and encamped in and about the little town of "Arroyo-Molino." The division was now divided into three brigades, cavalry on flanks and centre. It was just the dawn of day, with a drizzling rain. We could just see our men to call the roll.

> The regiment now was mustered,
> And ready on parade,
> Every man was present,
> And none of them afraid.

Our gallant and worthy general, riding along our front, said, "Are you all ready?" "Yes, sir." "Uncase your colours, and prime and load." All this looked very serious, and I began to have a queer feeling of mortal danger stirring my nerves. As I took the king's colour in charge, being senior ensign, the major said, "Now my lads, hold those standards fast, and let them fly out when you see the enemy."

Away we went now across the plain to be baptized in blood. Our skirmishers in advance had come upon the French outlying pickets, and had begun operations. A cannon-shot came rattling past, making a hissing noise, such as I had never heard before. Four sergeants supported the colours in battle; my old friend Bolland was one of them. I said, "What's that, Bolland!" "Only the morning gun, sir; they're just coming on them now." A little onwards, and I saw two men cut across by that last shot, the first I had ever seen killed. I was horrified, but said nothing.

The French were getting ready to be off again when our advance got up to their pickets and began the quarrel. Their horses were saddled and tied to the olive trees, infantry gathering from different points for their alarm-post—artillery taking up position,—all getting on the defensive, when they were skilfully hemmed in on three sides; behind the little town the 71st and 92nd regiments brought up their left shoulders, and came pouring into the streets with a destructive fire; the French were now falling by fifties, but fighting and struggling hard to maintain their ground. We had lined the garden walls, and kept pitching into their ranks while our cavalry cut off their retreat; they formed squares, but our artillery mashed them up and the cavalry gave them no time to re-form; a thick mist rolled down the craggy steep mountain behind the town; there was a terrifying cheer, such as is not known except amongst British troops on the battle-ground; it drowned the clatter of musketry, while the driving storm carried with it the enemy up this sierra, the 28th and 34th regiments at their heels; we pressed them so closely that they threw off their knapsacks, turned round, and fired into us; still our men pushed on until this body of Girard's brave army dropped their firelocks, dispersed, and as many as could got clear away over the mountains; below, the 50th and 39th regiments were tormenting the unfortunate French with the bayonet and making prisoners; the 13th Dragoons captured their artillery as they made a dash for escape, which was simply done by shooting a mule in each gun; the 9th Dragoons and German hussars charged and dispersed their cavalry with great loss, taking many prisoners; Prince D'Aremberg, making his escape in a light carriage, was followed by a few of our dragoons; one of them rode up to the door and desired him in English to halt; the reply was a bullet through his head—a useless and rather cowardly endeavour to save his liberty, for instantly one of his mules was shot, which brought him to a single anchor, as the sailors say; he was then handed out of his coach, not by a powdered footman, but at the point of an English broadsword, and his comfortable nest immediately plundered, the soldiers being exasperated for the untimely death of a comrade while doing his duty. Girard was wounded, but fought nobly until he saw that any further resistance was useless; then, having gaving his men the order to disperse—"*Sauve qui peut*"—fled and saved himself; 600 men, the remains of 3,000 of the most valiant and chosen troops of France, saved themselves by flight.

Our trophies this misty morning were General Le Bron, the Prince D'Aremberg, 40 officers, 1,500 men, all their artillery, baggage, and commissariat stores. I was very proud of having unfurled the colours of my regiment before the French for the first time, and cheered loudly with the rest when I saw them run! Our loss did not exceed 70 men left *hors de combat*—not many killed.

CHAPTER II.

After the Battle.—Albuquerque.—Merida.—Ciudad Rodrigo.—The Assault.—*Bone* Soup.—Horrors of War.—Badajos.—Preparations.

IT was a little remarkable that the two regiments—34th English and 34th French—happened to meet face to face in mortal combat. The *Parley Vous*, as our men called them, had no chance against the old Cumberland infantry. We took very many of them prisoners, with all their band and drums and the drum-major and his long cane. They are still, or part of them, in possession of the regiment. I know of only one officer now alive who was present on that day, and he bought from a soldier a very valuable diamond crescent for three dollars, taken out of the Prince D——'s carriage. There were many valuables for sale at a low figure that day! I had not a dollar left, or would have given it cheerfully for a loaf of bread, little expecting that I would soon have one for nothing. Our commissary bought plenty of flour at the mill, "Arroyo-Molino," and set all the bakers to work to give the troops a ration of fresh bread and an extra ration of rum after their morning's amusement. I was drying my wet duds in the village when my eye caught the sight of a cart-load of bread going by, and a Portuguese soldier behind in the act of stealing a loaf. I watched until he performed the successful operation, when I gave such a yell and a rush, he thought me the provost-marshal, dropped the loaf, and ran for it. I continued the cry of "Halt, Ladrone" until he was too far gone to see or know what use I made of it!

Lieutenant Strenowitz, an Austrian officer on General Hill's staff, always too dashing, was made prisoner. He was brave and enterprising, useful, and very clever in reconnoitering the enemy at any time. He had been dodging the movements of Girard all along, and was well known, having abandoned the French army in Spain to join the Partidas, and liable by the laws of war to death. Sir Rowland, anxious to save him, frankly applied to General Drouet, who, although smarting under his late disaster, released him. A noble generosity, worthy of being recorded in letters of gold.

The 34th now took charge of all the French prisoners, officers and men. The former accepted parole; the latter we locked up in the church, a goodly congregation for the old padre. Yesterday, perhaps, they were robbing his hen-roost, and to-day certainly teasing his church-toggery — indeed, before the day was closed, they had arranged a theatrical troop, and were performing a play, all rejoicing in the expectation and hope of being escorted to their future banishment by British troops, being under bodily fear of the Spaniards, who would, as they well knew, have bayoneted every man of them that fell out of the ranks; for they had a long account to settle with these French marauders. The following day we had a rest, and the prisoners opened a bazaar in the church to dispose of, "perhaps," all their unlawful gains. It was a great day for the church and for the priests when those fellows departed; every one of them seemed to have a watch for sale, gold or silver, and a great variety of bijouterie; there were some great bargains going, but I had not a dollar to get a single kind remembrance of those dear departing friends! My regiment escorted them down to Portugal. By the way they were very cheery, and went to church every night for safety!

On a pinch we always turned the churches to useful and good account. The commissariat, mules, and stores of biscuit and rum were lodged there for nights, weeks, and months, as required, the padres looking in now and then, crossing themselves right-centre and left, with a wailing sort of grunt, seeing their confession-boxes filled with sacks of barley and kegs of rum, the mules picketed on one side, big cooking-fires on the other, and a pleasant smell of fried pork and garlic! The only priestly sound left in the temple was the bell-ringing, every mule having a dozen or more of them as part of his trappings; and pleasant music it was to us many a starry night on the lonely march to hear the muleteers coming along through the cork woods, singing plaintive strains, accompanied by the light guitar. The muleteer is a fine, honest, independent fellow, well made, quaintly dressed, always gay, strong and active, and very fond of music and dancing when time admits; but he never neglects his work, carries his guitar, sits between two bags of biscuit, both legs on one side, singing a serenade, and twitching his own heart with something plaintive, or perhaps with a fandango, the Castilian Maid, or a bolero.

The French officers, being all on parole, conducted themselves with great propriety. They messed with the colonel, major, and one or two of the senior officers who had means of adding something to the rations. They were under no restraint, and their old soldiers were very careful in not attempting to straggle or fall out by the way, knowing what a sharp look-out the Spaniards had after their liberty. We delivered them all over in safety to another escort in Portugal, returned to Estremadura, and took up quarters in the old town of Albuquerque, with the 28th Regiment, or "Slashers." Every regiment and division had its cognomen; the 2nd, Lord Hill's division, was called "the Surprisers," after the affair of Arroyo de Molino; 3rd, or Buffs, "the Resurrection Men," so many of them returned to the ranks after Albuera. They had been returned missing, but the truth was, having taken a brilliant part in that day's big fight, and finding the French retreating through the woods and forest, they pursued them until night, and many of the old Buffs who lost their way in the dark, bivouacked, and came carelessly back to their old ground the next and following days, sat down upon the sod, and went to work to clean and polish up their old flint firelocks for another day; and then inquired after yesterday's rations; for they were very hungry after hunting "them frog-eaters through the woods—bad luck to them!" The 50th always went by the name of the "Dirty Half-hundred"—they had black facings; 34th, "the Cumberland Gentlemen." We had certainly some of the most select and high-caste officers I ever met in the army—such brave and zealous men too; such as Colonels Maister and Fenwick, Willett, Wyat, Fancourt, Egerton, Sherer, Baron, Worsley—Jolliff, the most liberal paymaster, and the clever surgeon, Luscombe; Sullivan and Eccles, bravest of the brave; Norton, Day, *cum multis aliis*. I love to record their honoured names, being myself, I believe, the last man of that generation that I know of living, unless it be Captain Norton, the inventor of an exploding shell, about which he hoped to gain a name and some emolument, after many years of incessant toil. Not being in the dress circle, I believe all his labour was in vain, and his talent pooh-poohed.

At Albuquerque we got the English newspapers with an account of our exploit at Arroyo-Molino, and wasn't I proud to see Sir Rowland Hill's despatch in print, with the few words, which never escaped my memory, viz., "where the 28th and 34th Regiments eminently distinguished themselves"?

Albuquerque was a very old town, at one period of some importance. It was walled all round, and had a castle of defence, crumbling away like the old walls. In the castle, which stood high, there was a square tower standing still much higher, commanding a most extensive view of the country on towards Badajos (pronounced by the Spaniards Badahos). On the top of this tower there was always an officer on the look-out, from before daylight until ten o'clock, with telescope in hand, to watch any movement of the French coming over the plain, a duty not very agreeable to early risers! On many a cold morning I have got up to take this duty for one of my own brother officers better off and more provident than myself, with the understanding that I was to breakfast with him when relieved; for the truth may be told, I had not myself a breakfast to eat, and really nothing at this time but my one scanty meal per diem, and that was my bit of ration beef, which I fried in a pan with *water* for want of a spoonful of oil. My money was all expended long ago. Our pay was months in arrear. My time was not come to draw for my home allowance, and I would not ask for a penny in advance, although I knew it would have been cheerfully granted.

About this time, Drouet came down to forage the province with 14,000 men, and to throw supplies into Badajos. We left our dry quarters, and sallied forth to meet him, Sir Rowland

Hill intending to give him battle. On our way to Merida we fell in with a battalion of French infantry in a fog, who were out foraging. We could see nothing. They *felt* our advance guard as we came up, and left some few wounded prisoners, who told the tale. As the fog rose, we saw them retiring over the plain in the greatest order. Having a good start of us, our cavalry were called to the front, and slipped at them; the French retiring double quick in quarter-distance column. On the near approach of the 14th Light Dragoons, they formed square, and waited the charge, which was repulsed by a volley, leaving some empty saddles. While the cavalry were re-forming for another charge, the French again formed quarter-distance column, and went off at the double. The 14th went at them again on two sides; for they whipped into square in a moment, but as unsuccessfully as at first. This play was repeated three times without any success, when our guns came up from the rear, unlimbered, and sent a few round shot into their ranks, which left them short forty men; but the rest got clear away into Merida. I don't remember our loss; but I saw many of our men and horses killed and wounded as we passed by. Nevoux, which was the name of the brave French colonel who commanded, was decorated with the Legion of Honour for his gallant conduct on this occasion.

Honourable retreats in war, they say, are in no ways inferior to brave charges, as having less of fortune, more of discipline, and as much of valour.

'We marched on and took possession of Merida, driving the chief and head-quarters of his army out of this fine old town. It stands on the Guadiana, had a bridge of sixty arches, said to have been built by the Romans, as well as the town, which was partly of very great antiquity. Here we were quartered for some time amongst pretty girls and burly priests, who kept a sharp look-out upon their intimacy with British *heretics*. This was all jealousy; for I think I had cause to see and believe they were the most immoral and irreligious part of the community. Lazy, indolent, useless cowls, and their name was Legion. The señoritas were generally very pretty, very graceful, ladylike, and extremely correct in manner, morals, and conduct, although at times there was an elopement with some wild handsome young fellow who know the soft language, which cannot be surpassed in love-making. How many of those poor girls were forced into convents by the aid and advice of crafty priests, where their young hearts were blighted for ever! I often had conversations with them through their iron grating, hearing them wailing and lamenting their unhappy fate, and pining for liberty. "We are here," they would say, "like birds with clipped wings, powerless;" then a little noise perhaps, and they would fly like a chamois, with an "adeos, adeos, caballero. Otro tiempo."

Monsieur le General Drouet gave us a great deal of bother at this time, marching and counter-marching across that great plain to Almandraleho, a little town some five leagues distant. There he assembled his army, took up position, inviting a quarrel, but always declining to fight. When we got within reach of a nine-pounder gun, he was off in retreat, leaving no chance of giving him a checkmate. Here we halted, generally for a couple of days, and returned to Merida. This game was played so often, I was thoroughly acquainted with every big tuft of grass and swampy pool over that dreary plain ploughed up by wheels, cavalry, and baggage animals. The object of the French was to harass our troops as much as possible, and to keep us away from Ciudad Rodrigo, a great fortress, which he knew would be attacked by Wellington before we could advance up country.

Settled down once more in Merida, *pro tem.*, we tried to be happy. I was now pretty well broken into harness, learned something, and began to like my trade, seeing all my comrades as jolly and fearless as if they were foxhunters. We were soon, however, on the trot again. Our division was separated, and placed in different towns and villages near Rodrigo.

In January, 1812, Wellington (as I may now call him with great respect) laid siege to Ciudad Rodrigo (city of Rodrigo), and now for the horrors of a siege, and the double horrors of another near at hand; this one lasted twelve days, the city being stormed on the 19th January. Wellington's morning order on that day was laconic and to the point, understood, and nobly responded to; it was this, "Ciudad Rodrigo *must* be stormed this evening."

All the troops reached their different posts after dark; the storming-parties—volunteers and forlorn-hope—foremost; as they advanced, they were ravaged with a tempest of grape from the ramparts, which staggered them; however, none would go back, although none could get forward, for men and officers falling fast from the withering and destructive fire choked up the passage, which every minute was raked with grapeshot. Thus striving, and trampling alike upon the dead and the wounded, these brave fellows maintained the combat. The stormers of another division, who had 300 yards of ground to clear, with extraordinary swiftness dashed along to the glacis, jumped into the ditch, eleven feet deep, and rushed on under a smashing discharge of musketry and grape, gaining the ascent; the foremost were blown to shatters, their bodies and brains plashing amongst their daring comrades behind, which only stimulated their determined exertions and doubled their strength. Supports came forward, all the officers simultaneously sprang to the front, when the herculean effort was renewed with a thrilling cheer, and the entrance was gained. The fighting was continued with fury in the streets, until the French were all killed, wounded, or prisoners; the town was fired in many places; many were killed in the market-place; our soldiers were desperate, really mad with excitement, furious; intoxication, disorder, and tumult everywhere prevailed; discipline and restraint disregarded, the troops committed most terrible deeds; they lighted a fire in the middle of the great magazine, when the whole town would have been blown into the air but for the courage and immediate exertions of some officers and soldiers who were still in their senses, and sensible of the awful gulf around them.

Our loss was, I think, 1,400 soldiers and 90 officers,—60 officers and some 700 men fell in the breach. Generals McKinnon and Crawford, two noble and gallant soldiers, were killed; and along with them many stoutly brave, fell that day, who feared no danger, and whose lives were more precious than fine gold.

The great obstacle in the advance of the siege was caused by the useless and most disgraceful tools furnished by the Storekeeper-General's office in England. The contractor's profits seemed to be more attended to and respected than our chance of success in taking this fortress; and so it has been the case, again and again, even on to the siege of Savastopol, forty-two years afterwards, to my knowledge.

300 French had fallen, we had 1,600 prisoners, immense stores of ammunition, 150 pieces of artillery, and Marmont's battering train. On the following day, when the escort with the prisoners were marching out by the breach, somehow or other an explosion took place and numbers of both parties were blown into the air!

Wellington was now created Duke of Ciudad Rodrigo by the Spaniards, Earl of Wellington in England, and Marquis of Torres-Vedras in Portugal. Thus ended this chapter of the war.

From this time until the middle of March, 1812, we were kept roving about the country to pot the French, kill them, and cook them in our own fashion: all was lawful in war; but they were very sharp and always slept with one eye open: we had to do the same. It was like deer-stalking at times,—a glorious thing to whack in amongst a lively party with their flesh-pots on the fire of well-seasoned wood. A chest of drawers, perhaps, or the mahogany table of some *Hidalgo* in the middle of the street blazing away, and the *crappos* calling out, "Bonne soupe, bonne soupe." " *Bone* soup," says Paddy Muldoon one day; "those vagabones live on bone soup: I *blive* they would make soup out o' an owl gridiron that once fried a red-herrin'. But we're purty near them now, I think, to have a crack at their *bone* soup." Paddy, a front-rank man of the Light Company, was in advance, as we cautiously moved along under cover of some of the ever-green olive-trees and stone walls. He was brave, but nervously irksome to be at his work whenever he smelt a Frenchman; and here he spoiled our fun and a capture. As we approached the head of the village, Paddy let fly a shot into the middle of a *covey* who were in reality cooking their dinner, as I have said. Then a general rush on both sides; one party to grapple their arms and run, the other to pursue, slay, or capture. But the French Light Infantry run very fast when there's powder and lead at their heels; and no blame to them. Paddy was called to account for breaking the peace without orders. "I couldn't help it, sir, you see, for I had a fine rest for my firelock on the wall, and was sure of one on 'em, bein' in line sittin so close; but they've left their kittles behind, and o' course their *bone* soup, packs, and all." We gave them chase a little way, and captured a few, who Paddy said had corns, for the rest got into a wood and cleared out of sight in no time. The kettles were left and examined: some contained bits of pork and vegetables, or a gallina or old hen, but no fresh meat. "'Pon me conscience," says Muldoon, "that's the cook I knocked over, for there's the bullet-hole right through his pot, and I'm sorry for him; but he kept a bad look-out."

This was merely a small advance picket of the French. Such things happened almost every day, and there was nothing more about it.

War for three years was spread over unhappy Spain; battles were fought, men were slaughtered, the country ravaged, houses robbed and burned, families flying to the mountains to escape the horrors of licentious soldiers. The terrors of a marauding army are little known. Legions of low-caste, vulgar men, all loose amongst the people,— always for evil, never for good. Then the guerilla bands for ever watching the French, intercepting their convoys and detachments, and pouncing into them from the rocks and mountain passes, dealing fearful death to every victim; and this continued for six years in a charming country, amongst a formerly happy, contented, and amiable peasantry. I have been at the heels of a French party as they escaped from a sweet little country town, leaving their camp kettles on fires in the street, lighted (as I have said) by household furniture, and sometimes one or two members of a family lying murdered on their own hearth-stone! This was but too common a tragedy, and repeated very often to my own personal knowledge.

We again returned to our quarters at Albuquerque early in March, and I made my acquaintance once more with the look-out tower, where the order was vigilance from dawn to dark.

The British army now began to concentrate their forces in Estremadura; a great battering train was moved up from Elvas, a large fortified town in Portugal, about three or four leagues from Badajos; this was a laborious, slow-coach affair, the great guns were moved slowly along, with only a cavalcade of bullocks the whole length of the *natural* road that never felt a stone on its soft surface; hundreds of the Spanish peasantry were employed carrying the shot and shell. All the engineers, sappers, and miners were called to *attention;* groups of officers at every corner with unusual solemnity talked of the coming storm, when ground would be broken, who were to lead the way, what divisions to be chosen, and who would describe the fall of Badajos to friends at home.

No one doubted the success of the enterprise, but no one ventured to say that his life was his own after the first gun was fired; there was a terrible day approaching, but nobody afraid, even bets being frequently made on the day and hour of the opening ball.

I had no particular nervous feeling now; men stand together and encourage each other in the hour of danger; but I can't understand the man who would openly express himself callous to all feeling under a shower of lead, or before the mouth of a cannonade. A common saying was, "every bullet has its billet," and all seemed outwardly serene.

Badajos, which stands on the river Guadiana, in a plain, is about the strongest fortress I had ever seen; but there was nothing proof in those days against British valour. Here were two of the most warlike nations on earth armed against each other in deadly strife. "Vive Napoleon! vive l'Empereur!" was the exciting cry on one side;—on the other, "Hurrah for old England,"—a flourish of drums, with the "British Grenadiers," or "Garryown," set our fellows wild for a dash at any time. Both were so badly armed that I wonder how we killed each other at all; but the distance was very short at times, and the bayonet did a great deal of the work,—the French never liked the steel; still they were brave, very brave.

The days rolled away quickly as they do at present; we got a small advance of pay; the 16th was my birthday, and if I had no salutations, gifts, or a home jollification, I had a good loaf of Spanish bread, a pork chop, and a bottle of country wine, all alone in my billet, and was content. The battalion was so scattered, that few of us *subs* could form a little mess to put our rations into the same pot to make some "bone soup." My billet was on a very respectable family,—the patrone, his señora, and two daughters, both "hermosa." We sat of an evening over the *brazero*, or brass pan, filled with charcoal, red cinders, which kept life in our finger-tips; it was renewed occasionally, and we conversed about the coming storm, for they had many friends in Badajos. I had picked up the language pretty well for my time, which was a great advantage; it is a sweet and expressive language and easily learned.

The Duke had now arranged his plans. Patrick's day came round as usual, and on that fighting festival-morning the band and drums enlivened all Patlanders with the national tune. The same night 1,800 men broke ground 160 yards from the out fort of Picurina, protected by a guard of 2,000; so that some of the Irish soldiers were not altogether disappointed in having a bit of a shindy before they went to sleep. There was a call for some volunteer officers for the engineer department, and to superintend the work in the trenches; two from the 34th,—Lieutenant Masterman and G. B. I was very much attached to poor M.; he did me a service once, and I never forgot the smallest kindness in all my career, which has been a long one. The trench work was as dangerous as it was arduous; all those who served before Sebastopol will understand this—and now the work of death began in reality.

Generals Picton, Colville, Kempt, and Bowes, commanded alternately in the trenches. All the arts of war then known were brought into play on both sides, for the attack and defence; every man carried his life in his hand; hope lived in the hearts of all. The whole world at this time could not produce a nobler specimen of a soldier than the British;—quick to orders, calm and resolute in danger, obedient and careful of his officers in all peril; he will go to the front, even to the muzzle of the gun, fighting his way until blown to eternity. And what is that fearful word? It is the lifetime of the Almighty!— Many were our difficulties: torrents of rain at nights poured upon the working parties, shot and shell continually striking down the men, provisions scarce, our pontoon bridge carried away, artillery and engineer officers being killed and wounded every day, but no suspension of the fiery trial.

About nine o'clock on the night of the 24th the assault was made on Fort Picurina. The distance was short and the troops quickly closed on their game—black and silent before—now one mass of fire. The depth of the ditch baffled them; also the thickness of the poles; the quick shooting of the enemy, and the guns from the town, rendered the carnage dreadful. Rockets were thrown up by the besieged; the shrill sound of the alarm-bells, mixing with the shouts of the combatants, increased the tumult; still Picurina sent out streams of fire, by the light of which dark figures were seen furiously struggling on the ramparts, fighting hand to hand with the enemy; none would yield until but eighty-six men of the fort and the commandant were left. Our loss was eighteen or twenty officers and some three hundred men killed and wounded. This was only clearing the way a bit; a frightful and destructive havoc was carried on inside and outside (in particular) the town until the 4th of April. Time being now a great object, and Soult advancing with a large army to relieve the city, the breach being reported practicable, eighteen thousand of our daring British soldiers burned for the signal of attack.

The assault was arranged and ordered for the next evening, and eagerly did the men make themselves ready for a combat so fiercely fought, so terribly won, so dreadful in all its circumstances, that posterity can scarcely be expected to credit the o'er true tale; but many are still alive who know that it is true.

CHAPTER III.

The Assault. — Fall of Badajos. — After the Assault. — The Sacking of Badajos. — Neglect of the British Government. — Departure from Badajos.—Discipline.—Jollifications.—Castle Mirabete.—Forts Napoleon and Almaraz.—Disappointment.—Chivalry.—Flat Burglary.—Quill to the rescue.—Leonora.—Estramos.—To Lisbon on leave.

THE night was dry and cloudy, the trenches and ramparts unusually still—lights were seen to flit here and there, while the deep voice of the sentinels proclaimed " All well in Badajos." The British, standing in deep columns, as eager to meet that fiery destruction as the French were to pour it down, were both alike gigantic now in terrible strength and discipline, resolute, and determined to win or die. The recent toil and hardship, the spilling of blood, the desire for glory, an old grudge and a dash of ferocity, not omitting the plunder and thirst for spoil, and pride of country and arms, caused our men never to doubt their own strength of arm to bear down all before them, and every obstacle opposed to their furious determination. At 10 o'clock the Castle, the San Roque, the breaches, the Pardaleras, the distant bastion of San Vincente, and the bridge-head on the other side of the Guadiana, were to have been assailed at the same time, and it was to be hoped that the enemy would quail and lose some of their strength within this girdle of fire; but many are the disappointments of war, and it may be taken as a maxim that the difficulties are so innumerable that no head was ever yet strong enough to forecalculate them all.

An unforeseen accident delayed the attack of the 5th Division, as at first intended, and a lighted carcass, thrown from the castle, falling near, rendered it necessary to hurry on the attack about half an hour before the time which was subsequently arranged; and so all being suddenly disturbed, the 4th and Light divisions moved swiftly and silently against the breaches, and the guard of the trenches rushing forward with a cheer, encompassed the San Roque with fire, and broke in so violently that little resistance was made there; but a sudden blaze of light and the rattle of musketry indicated the beginning of a frightful conflict at the castle.

General Kempt fell here wounded; General Sir Thomas Picton took his place. The men dashed forward under a terrible fire, spread and raised their ladders against the castle walls, and with unexampled courage ran up under a shower of shot and shell, stones and small arms, while a fearful fire was kept up on the Red-coats from flanks and centre. The leading men on the ladders were met by pikes, bayonets, and musketry, and their ladders pushed from the walls. Now the deafening shouts, crashing of broken ladders, and the shrieking of the crushed and wounded men, became loud amongst the din of war, and excited to madness the comrades of the undaunted brave below, who swarmed again round the ladders, swiftly ran up, and were tossed over from the enemy above, who cried, " Victory ! " and " Why don't you come into Badajos?"

The brave Colonel Ridge, with a voice like thunder, called to his men to follow, raised a ladder to the wall a little further off, and met but little opposition until he got in. Another ladder was raised, and our men went pouring in, took the enemy in the flanks, and delivered a volley which very much astonished and staggered them. Here another fight commenced, and here poor Ridge fell—no man died a more glorious death in battle, although multitudes of brave men fell who deserved great military glory.

The frightful tumult at the main breach all this time, the incessant roar of cannon, musketry, bursting of shells, yells of the wounded, and cheering of those who had so short a time to live, rent the air in a fiery lava of exploding shells and barrels of powder.

Every flash showed the French ready and prepared on the ramparts—showed their glittering arms, dark figures, heaps of live shells, and an astonishing amount of artillery, every man having three loaded muskets beside him—and yet our men leaped into the ditch, of whom five hundred volunteers, being foremost, were dashed to pieces with shot, shell, and powder-barrels. The Light Division stood for a moment in horror at the

THE ASSAULT.

terrific sight; then with a wild shout dashed with one accord into the fiery gulf, and, with the light of a blaze of fire-arms from above, the 4th Division followed in an excited fury,—100 men were drowned in the inundation (for at this time the sluices were opened, and the water let into the ditch from the river). They now turned off to the left, seeking for the main breach, and got crowded and mixed together; the only light was that of the flashing guns, pouring death and destruction among them. The confusion was great, but all cheered like thunder; the French cheers also were loud and terrible,—the bursting of grenades, shells, and powder-barrels, the whizzing flight of blazing splinters of barrels, the loud voice of the officers, and the heavy groans of the dying, were sufficient to create a terror indescribable. Now they found the way, and went at the breach like a whirlwind. Sword-blades, sharp and pointed, fixed in ponderous beams, were in their front as they ascended; planks, too, filled with iron spikes; while every Frenchman had three or four loaded muskets at his feet, with leaden slugs over the usual bullet. Hundreds of our men had fallen, dropping at every discharge, which only maddened the living; the cheer was for ever on, on, with screams of vengeance and a fury determined to win the town; the rear pushed the foremost into the sword-blades to make a bridge of their bodies rather than be frustrated in their success. Slaughter, tumult, and disorder continued; no command could be heard, the wounded struggling to free themselves from under the bleeding bodies of their dead comrades; the enemy's guns within a few yards, at every fire opening a bloody lane amongst our people, who closed up, and, with shouts of terror as the lava burned them up, pressed on to destruction—officers, starting forward with an heroic impulse, carried on their men to the yawning breach and glittering steel, which still continued to belch out flames of scorching death.

About midnight, when 2,000 men had fallen, Wellington, who was looking on, sent an order for the troops to retire and re-form for another attack. In the retreat from the ditch there was great confusion and terrible carnage under the continual fire of the French; the groans and lamentations of the wounded trampled on, and expecting to be left to the mercy of an exasperated and ferocious enemy, were awful. Who could explain their feelings? The bitterness of death to them was past. The 3rd Division had gained the Castle; the 5th Division also was engaged at another point—the town was girdled with fire—General Walker's brigade was escalading—the Portuguese troops were unnerved, and threw down the ladders. Our men snatched them up and raised them against the walls nearly thirty feet high; the ladders were short, yet the men clambered up. The fire of the French was deadly; a mine was sprung under the soldiers' feet, live shells and beams of wood were rolled over on them with showers of grape; man after man dropped dead from the ladders. Other points were attacked and won; the French fought like demons,—a death-struggle of fiery antagonists took place at every corner, while our men most thoroughly maddened with rage and excitement, dashed at the breach with wild resolution; for is it not recorded, " Who shall describe the martial fury of that desperate soldier of the 95th, who, in his resolution to win, thrust himself beneath the chained sword-blades, and there suffered the enemy to dash out his brains with the ends of their muskets."

Here now was a crushing and most desperate struggle for the prize; the bright beams of the moon were obscured with powder-smoke,—the springing of mines, powder-barrels, flashing of guns and small arms, rendered our men marks for destruction—death's grasp was just on the remnant of the brave, a total annihilation of humanity on our side, when the troops who had escaladed the Castle made a dash at the breach, and, with one loud cheer for England, and a sweeping volley, and another mad shrieking yell, rushed on with the bayonet, and cleared the bloody gap for those below, who now rushed in, driving the French from every point,—and *Badajos was won!*

Let any one picture to himself this frightful carnage taking place in a space of less than a hundred yards square; let him consider that the slain died not all suddenly, nor by one manner of death; that some perished by steel, some by shot, some by water, some crushed and mangled by heavy weights, some trampled upon, some dashed to atoms by the fierce explosions, that for hours this destruction was endured without shrinking, and that the town was won at last. Let any man consider this, and he must admit that a British army bears with it an awful power. No age, no nation ever sent forth braver troops to battle than those who stormed Badajos. When the extent of the night's havoc was made known to Lord Wellington, the firmness of his nature gave way for a moment and the pride of conquest yielded to a burst of grief for the loss of his gallant soldiers.

For two days the town was in possession of the victorious, and it may be as well to draw a veil over the misdeeds of men stained with the blood of their comrades, now excited to very frenzy. A siege is always terrible, but the sacking of a town is an abomination; here the inhabitants suffer the terrible vengeance of all the ferocity of the human species.

I remember two sisters, beautiful daughters of Spain, who made their escape from the town when the soldiers spread for plunder and mischief; they made their way into our camp outside, and threw themselves on the protection of the first British officers they met (two of the — Regiment). One of those ladies married her protector; I knew them both; he became a distinguished general officer, and now lies in Westminster Abbey; she is still living. The scenes that took place in the town were frightful, not fit to be recorded. The priests took refuge with the fair sex in the great church for safety, and barricaded the doors; there was no safety anywhere, the maniacs "for the time" loaded their firelocks and let fly a volley into the lock of the door, which opened it quickly enough, and then——

The wine-shops were all in demand; if the men were not all drunk, there were none of them quite sober, but very able to go on with the plunder. One fellow might be seen with a bag of dollars; another cove would take him into a wine-house, make him stupidly drunk, and carry off the *douros*; one or two more working in concert would knock this chap down, and rob him of his treasure. They brought all sorts of things into the camp, until the tents were supplied with furniture such as was never seen in a camp before. One fellow with a tattered red coat, grasping his firelock, was groaning under an old-fashioned eight-day clock; while another had a broad looking-glass on his back; chairs and tables, priests' vestments, ladies' dresses, beds, blankets, and cooking-pots, with sausages, and pig-skins of wine. "Stop, Jack, and give us a *dhrink* ov that wine," some fellow would say (dressed in his half-bloody uniform, and on his head the *sombrero* of an old priest). "Devil a drop, now; it's going to the camp." "Faith an' I'll tap it for myself, then;" and slap goes his bayonet into the skin, and out flows the wine. Then there is a wrangle, and then they are friends, and both get jolly drunk, and lie there helpless long enough. There were watches amongst them, gold and silver, some valuable ornaments, doubloons, and dollars; they were fond of parading their treasure, and more fond of drinking to excess; consequently these articles changed hands frequently as they got drunk, and the sober ones saved them the trouble of looking after their stolen goods; but still the truth must be told, the besieging army were promised the sacking of the town when taken, and, notwithstanding all the devotion and bravery of the British soldier, this promise of pillage adds to his courage and determination. Therefore it became their reward, and as all the Spaniards in the city had timely notice of the siege, and were offered a free and safe escort away to any place of safety, those who chose to remain stayed at a fearful risk; very many went away at the beginning, but many who favoured the French party remained to their cost. There was no discipline as yet amongst the *stormers;* all was riot, confusion, and drunkenness. The officers had no control over their late devoted and obedient soldiers; they were mad, and went about with loaded muskets and fixed bayonets, to the terror of each other and everybody else. The Duke rode into the town with his staff, on the evening of the second day, and was immediately recognized. "There he comes, with his long nose," said one old warrior who knew him well; "let's give him a salute." A dozen or so of half-drunken fellows collected, fired a volley of ball cartridge over his head, with a cheer, saying, "There goes the *owl* chap that can leather the French!" and then they all cut away and hid themselves out of his sight. It was rather a dangerous *feu-de-joie;* for the commander-in-chief, who did not seem to like it, went off directly and gave orders for a gibbet to be erected in the great square, and had it proclaimed in camp and through the town that any man found in Badajos the next day would be hanged! This seemed to sober the drunken and curb the passions of all; fatigued almost to death with fighting and excitement, riot and drunkenness, they were glad of some rest, and, gathered in now to the camp, became obedient to orders, and got ready for any future emergency; and many a bloody, hard-contested battle-field was still before them, which I intend, in my poor insignificant way of writing, to record, but only what I saw and shared in.

Badajos had now fallen, and with it five thousand of our bravest men; and, to the discredit of the English Government, no army was ever so ill provided with the means of prosecuting such an enterprise. The ablest officers trembled when reflecting how utterly destitute they were of all that belonged to real service; without sappers and miners they were compelled to attack fortresses defended by the most warlike, practised, and scientific troops of the age. The best officers and the finest soldiers were obliged to sacrifice themselves in a lamentable way, to compensate for the negligence and incapacity of a Government always ready to plunge the nation into a war without the slightest care of what was necessary to obtain success. The sieges carried on by the British in Spain were a succession of butcheries, because the commonest materials, and the means necessary for their art, were denied the engineers; and this liberal and generous Government and their noble successors took *thirty-six years* to consider whether the men of Badajos and those who fought their way from Torres Vedras to Toulouse, in victorious conquest for six long years, were yet worthy to wear a medal!

Napoleon's troops *fought* in bright fields, where every helmet caught some beams of glory, but the British soldier *conquered* under the cold shade of aristocracy; no honours recognized his daring, no despatch gave his name to the applause of his countrymen; his life of danger and hardship was uncheered by hope, his death unnoticed; he endured with surprising fortitude the sorest of ills, sustained the most terrible assaults in battle unnerved, overthrew with incredible energy every opponent, and at all times proved himself to be a soldier worthy of England.

Poor old Badajos was awfully battered about; the steeple of the church in the Plaza-grandé stood so very much in the way of our shot, going up to the breach, that it came down by the run, and the ball made a bed for itself below the level of the flags. The houses, balconies, churches, convents, and monasteries all suffered severely. None of the multitudes of saints came to protect their *sacred* possessions, though invoked by chanting priests, *holy* friars, religious nuns, ringing of bells, and tubs of *holy* water. All the miracles of priestcraft ceased for a season; the saints all ran away, and those burly priests who remained in the beleaguered town were sorry enough they did not run after them. I was greatly surprised at the size of the guns and mortars used in the fortress—some of the latter were wide enough to admit my head and shoulders; and often when the shot and shell fell and exploded in our lines, they left holes wide enough to bury a horse.

The wounded, amongst whom was my friend Masterman, were sent to the hospital at Estramos, in Portugal, established there as the grand depôt for sick and wounded; and now we all broke up from before the shattered town, and went our different ways. Soult had made a forced march down country with a great army to relieve Badajos, and got as far as Merida to be just too late, for our people had blown up two arches in the fine old bridge to delay his progress, and on finding, while within hearing of our guns, that the place had fallen, he retired. Lord Hill went back to Merida; we crossed the bridge, it being repaired in a temporary way by our own engineers, the men passing over by files, the baggage animals one at a time, while great caution was used in getting over the guns. It was melancholy to see the two centre arches had gone, but still there were left fifty-eight in glory.

The French army had divided, and so we had to give them chase. We had a variety of marching and counter-marching, stopping here and there in nice Spanish towns, billeted for a week or two, and then off like a shot when in full enjoyment of rest and peace. Zafra, Fuente del Maistre, Malpartida, Caceres, and *otras pueblas*, were familiar to us all, having visited them so often; but still it was a weary and hungry time with most of us. The army was long unpaid, and our credit low. I found favour in the eyes of the brigade butcher, himself a private soldier of my own regiment, who gave us tick for a bullock's head, heart, or liver—sometimes a sheep's head and pluck—until we got our pay. These, to us luxuries, were his perquisites, for three of us were now messing together, adding any little additions that fortune might throw in our way into the camp kettle. There was a positive general order against plunder, and of course no officer would be guilty of such an act. Our rations were short at times, yet we fed the Spanish troops; and *their* generals purloined the English gold, robbed and plundered, and sold the very arms supplied them by England for their own defence; yet if a soldier of ours was caught picking up an old hen or duck, or a stray goose, he was at once tied up, and got six dozen. If a very grave offence—such as robbing the person—he was tried by court-martial, and, if found guilty, hanged upon a tree, and no mistake. I remember seeing three soldiers hanged one morning on the long projecting arm of a cork tree, for robbing some muleteers; men who would have fought to the death in the battle-field. It was a most melancholy and touching sight, as we marched away, to see three redcoats dangling in the air, awaiting the vultures which generally followed on the army.

The Spanish muleteers were the very life and sustenance of the Peninsular war; we could not have existed without them. Everything was conveyed by them for the army—provisions, ammunition, rum, &c. Their patience, hardiness, and fidelity to the British army were remarkable; but, on the contrary, the men high in rank, generals, governors, diplomatists, hidalgos, the Spanish Junta, and Portuguese leaders, such as the ambitious and intriguing Bishop of Oporto—commonly called the Patriarch—the Sousas—were contemptible, selfish, cowardly, ignorant, fraudulent, faithless, and cruel. These were the worthies Wellington had to contend against while fighting their battles—always contentious and deceptive.

Our next exploit was to take and destroy the stronghold of Almaraz, a fortress held by the French on the Tagus. General Sir Rowland Hill assembled his corps of the army in and about the fine old town of Truxillo in the middle of May, 1812. My regiment happened to be billeted in this city of Pizarro; his birth-place, his house, still a noble building, gave good cover to our soldiers; altogether a likely place to look at for one's dinner; but there was no hospitality. So we determined to get up a big mess dinner for the whole regiment once for all, to celebrate the battle of Albuera! A celebrated sutler, one Tamet, a Turk, always followed our division with a supply of good things; such as English hams, tea, sugar, pickles, and a variety of other luxuries, all at famine prices; but Señor Tamet was a good-natured fellow, and gave some people tick until the next issue of pay, and continued to give credit to those who paid according to agreement. He now furnished our regiment with what we required for our banquet. We selected a pretty spot outside the town, under some cork-trees, marked out the size of our table on the green sod, and cut a trench all round. Our legs in the trench, we sat on the ground, with the *table* in front, but without a table-cloth. This was our arrangement.

We were like school-boys about Christmas, looking out for a jollification dinner; but all was rough, and nothing at all smooth in these days. However, the 16th of May was to be a day of festivity.

There had been a great many auction sales of late, so many officers being killed at Badajos; it was usual to sell their effects, and remit the amount of sale to the agents at home. In this way most of us got our supply of clothing. I bought a pony saddle and bridle. Always fond of horses, being light in weight and a good horseman, I was now a sort of mounted officer, and a great don in my own estimation. I was in demand for riding races, too, an amusement manly, cheerful, and always present where there is a British army. While preparations were being made for the 16th, which was the following day, we got orders to cook three days' rations, and march the same night! A sad disappointment—no baggage to accompany the division, so that our return was pretty sure, at least that of the living; but of course we were obliged to postpone our dinner *sine die*. Three of us jolly subs messed together, called the "Tria juncta in uno;" and our motto was, "Toujours prêt." I gave up my pony to carry our three days' prog, tied up in our haversacks, and slung across the saddle, with *three* distinct orders to my servant to be careful and follow the column and not lose sight of the troops.

We marched away by moonlight; the men slung their arms, to prevent the enemy seeing our line of march and calculating our numbers, for the barrels were bright in those days and might be seen glistening a long way off by moonlight. The daily polishing of the old flint firelock gave the men an infinity of bother and trouble; rainy days and night dews gave them a rust which was never permitted on parade, as we were more particular about clean arms and powder dry than anything else. We moved on all quiet, the muleteer alone singing a serenade to beguile the passing hour. We marched through rugged mountain passes nearly all the night, halting about every quarter of an hour, in consequence of the many obstacles in front; and at every halt I was fast asleep on the sod, and everybody else also perhaps;—but let every one write a book for himself, and tell his own story. I can't undertake it, but may say in truth that twenty men of any perception or interest in their *trade* might write a history of a campaign or a battle, each one clear in his story, yet all differing in narrative.

About four o'clock in the morning my regiment was ordered to halt, the rest of the division pushing on, and now Colonel F—— explained *our* plan of attack in a few words. On the top of a mountain, just above, stood the castle of "Mirabete," garrisoned by 1,000 French soldiers and eight guns, with a rampart twelve feet high; to storm this place by coup-de-main, by an escalade in the old style, and as quickly as possible, was our part of the night's amusement. Volunteers were called for the forlorn hope, and they jumped to the front in a minute, with an officer, Lieutenant Sullivan, at their head. Being myself orderly officer for the day, I was detailed to go in front with the scaling-ladders to place against the walls, a position I considered at the time equal to a wooden leg; but it never can be too often repeated that war, however adorned by splendid strokes of skill, is commonly a series of errors and accidents. We crawled up this steep ascent with great caution and silence; but just as we approached the tower, a solitary shot was fired at the foot of the hill, and the next moment the castle was in a blaze. Luckily for us it was not yet daylight, and that a cloud of mist hung over the castle top; we could not be seen, but the garrison kept up a random fire, all their shot passing over our heads as we lay on the heather. It was now too late to surprise our friends, as they rather surprised us with their *feu d'enfer*, and so we retired a little way down and got under cover before dawn; there we lay all the day waiting for fresh orders. General Hill, too, was discovered, and lay *perdu* with 6,000 men until nearly daylight on the morning of the 19th, when he let loose his troops upon Forts Napoleon and Almaraz; sharp work and severe loss in the escalade; but our men went there to win, the forts were taken and destroyed, guns spiked and sunk in the Tagus, and all material rendered useless. We lost 2 gallant good officers and 180 men, captured 17 officers and 250 men of the French, besides the number killed, one stand of colours, a large amount of ammunition, stores, &c., opened the passage of the Tajo, and went back to Truxillo. When the day closed, my regiment retraced their steps, and joined the main force all safe and sound. A little thing deranges the best-laid plans; when leaving Truxillo, as I have stated, I gave my servant his orders, he dallied, and kept too far in rear of the column, in company with a groom of General C——, who was leading a spare horse. They missed the turn in the road, dawdled on until they popped on the sentry of an outlying picket, who popped on to them at once; the General's groom was killed, my fellow was unhorsed, the pony ran away and kicked off saddle, haversacks, prog, and all; that single shot awoke up the garrison above, the whole expedition was deranged, and many lives were lost in consequence; but many, too, were saved, for we left the tower and its garrison for another day, and I cannot say that this grieved me *very* much!

My pony was found, with his back bare. After having countermarched, three of us found ourselves likely to starve for two days, unless that other *coves* could spare part of their common cold ration—Colonel Fenwick kindly spared me a bit of his cold beef and biscuit to keep me alive, just at a time when a quartern loaf, a pound of ham, and a quart of brown ale would have tempered my appetite while dinner was being prepared! However, we looked joyfully forward to the coming big dinner at Truxillo. We did return victorious, but not to the banquet. Alas! in our absence a foraging party of French dragoons entered the town and carried off all our larder, with all the baggage they could grasp. The wines were overlooked, and, fearful of another foray, our doctor, who had been left behind unwell, got up a ration dinner with a few other friends, took the chair, represented the whole corps, drank to the success of the war, the memory of the brave who fell at Albuera,. a safe return to the regiment, and other toasts, until he got so merry he bolted off to a convent to release the nuns like a gallant knight! Many of the fair señoritas he knew were there pining for liberty; but the watchful and wily priests came to the rescue; there was a shindy of course, a few officers of the baggage-guard, who had shared in the toasts, collected their forces and joined the *medico*, assailed the convent again, and had nearly forced an entrance, when the second in command received a wound on the head and tumbled down the stairs. The doctor called off his troops to see after the wounded, and dressing the *cabeza* of the only one, made an awkward incision on his *corona*—the *sangre* began to flow, and the *holy* priests made their escape, satisfied in preserving the dark-eyed maidens from the hands of such heretics, and keeping perdu lest they might get into a scrape for wounding one of H. M.'s officers in uniform. After this Quixotic deed the dinner-party retired to their siesta, and I believe all got up sober.

Great ferocity existed at this time amongst the guerilla chiefs, and indeed at all times. Mina was cruel and revengeful;

the curate Merino, too, was revolting in cruelty; he took some hundred French prisoners on one occasion, and hanged fifty or sixty of them in cold blood, deliberately butchering them in order to avenge the death of three of his men, although he had no proof of their being killed at all. Then there was counter-retaliation, and so the blood work went on continually, both parties to be condemned. Yet, make the case our own, and ask, if an enemy landed on our shores, killed, burned, and destroyed all before them, what would *we* do? how would we feel towards such an enemy? The poor Spaniards had very great provocation; but still no one could approve of the ferocious conduct on either side.

There was at all times a chivalrous feeling between the English and French in all their quarrels. We respected each other when prisoners of war, and sometimes in deadly strife I have known some instances of such generous conduct. For example: at Elboden there were some days of hard fighting, and some brilliant examples of skill and bravery. In a cavalry charge, a French officer, in the act of dashing sword in hand at the gallant Lieutenant-Colonel Felton Harvey, of the 14th Light Dragoons, saw, just in time, that he had but *one arm*, and with a movement as rapid as his horse brought down his sword into a *salute*, and passed on. Nothing on military record more manly, or more beautiful than this!

About this time I was ordered away, in charge of a convoy of sick and wounded, to the grand depôt at Estramos, in Portugal. I sold my pony to raise the wind and pay my debts, and prepared for my long journey. I had about ten dollars over, and my donkey, which was now all my own. I bought him out and out; he carried all my world's treasure on his broadside, and might have carried myself at times, for he was not overloaded. An old leather trunk, containing my kit on one side, balanced by a sack on the reverse, which held the frying-pan, camp-kettle, reaping-hook, and some odds and ends, with my servant's knapsack, a privilege which he claimed when away from the regiment. Tom Tandy, who was a good forager, always left room in the sack for anything Providence might send on the way, as he said, " to help the rations." He drove the willing donkey before him, and we commenced our journey.

My troop were all mounted on commissary mules, one muleteer having charge of three or four. Taking sick and wounded down to the depôts, they always returned to the army with a cargo of rum and biscuit. They were constantly employed.

My companion, the assistant-surgeon in charge, was a joyous fellow, full of Irish wit and humour, and all sorts of quaint sayings and drollery. His name was Maurice Quill. Any old soldier still in the land of the living, who served in Spain, would remember something about Dr. Quill and his exploits. We marched away from Truxillo without much regret. Quill stated that he had never had a decent dinner since he came into the country, and could not be worse off on the line of march, although he did not consider it his turn of duty for such *practice*. The weather was very hot, and the marches sometimes long to some town or village, where, according to route, there was to be cover for the night. A billet, with fire and light, was all that we could demand. If the people were kind, and gave us a welcome, we were soon very good friends, and gave them no trouble. This was generally the case; but they seldom attended to one's appetite, and we really had to forage a bit privately about the roadside, it being considered no man's land, not that I remember personally breaking the law, but I believe I may have said to my Sancho, "How nice *one* of those ducks, or that little pig, would fit into the sack, and roast for supper at our next billet." Somehow or another, Tom had a magic knack of inviting these innocents in a playful way into his big wallet, for a ride on the outside of a donkey never agreed with them!

We always called a halt about a mile or so from our next resting-place for the night, to look about us and do a little business, to save our *patrone* any trouble. Tom took out his reaping-hook, stepped into the next field of standing green corn, and bundled up a ration for the gentleman who carried his knapsack. Never forget the poor dumb animal, he must live as well as his master. As for the muleteers, they were at home, and took good care of themselves, and so we snailed along until we came to Badajos, the mutilated and battered old town. They were building up the walls and ramparts, and cleaning away the débris out of the ditches as we passed in. All the tools were laid down as they scanned the cavalcade with sympathy, and with a " Viva los Engleses" and " Via vm. con Dios." Having first housed my troops and left Quill to look after their health, I went in search of my billet, and to arrange for our dinner. The great event of the day is a good dinner, here and there and everywhere, with cheerful company, and we fared very well; a gallina and sausages, salad, bread, and good country wine, formed no bad repast after a march of seven leagues. The Spanish bread is the finest in the world, the pork in its season most excellent, and the sausages, with the little tinge of garlic, the best I ever tasted. Quill was very tired with his long tramp, as he called it, and retired early. I was fairly knocked up myself with the march, and a broiling sun beaming on my head all the day. I had comfortable quarters in the square—two rooms and a decent kind of bed. The windows below were all guarded by iron gratings. My bedroom was decorated by an iron balcony, from which I looked out on the poor, desolate, shattered city, hardly a house visible without a smash, Spaniards still coming in looking for their old habitations, others mending, patching up temporary dwellings, and looking patiently bewildered.

The seven-league march sent me early to roost. Tom picked out a soft plank for himself on the floor outside my door. I left my window wide open to see the dawn and be early away, tumbled in amongst the fleas, and was soon insensible to their claws. I will back Spain and Portugal against the world for the breed of this very lively creature. Like the dogs in Constantinople, I believe they are encouraged to live and multiply. Always early, I jumped up about five o'clock, rather late for me, and to my horror found nothing in my room but an old shooting-jacket, a pair of trousers to match, my cocked hat and feather, my sword and shoes! I opened the door and found Tom Tandy asleep, gave him a kick to open his eyes, and then asked if he had been in my room.—" No Sir." The whole thing now flashed before my eyes, the open window invited some Ladrone to walk in and inspect my kit. It was easily done, like crawling up a ladder—everything valuable was gone: my trunk and its contents, red coat, boots, trousers, and all—with the few dollars I had in reserve for hard times coming—all this to me just now was a great calamity. I flung myself into the tattered garments left, and ran off to tell the Medico, still hoping it might be some trick of his; but, soon undeceived, I related the sad tale, of which he knew nothing, but kept saying, "I'll get your traps for you." When dressed he said, " Now, come along, and show me your Patrone" (landlord). I saw that he was screwing himself up for a charge at the Patrone. I said, " He knows nothing of the robbery; Tom was asleep, with his head to my door, all night."—" Never mind, I must see him." I sent Tom down for the Señor; and, so soon as the poor gentleman appeared, the Doctor made a spring, and fastened in his collar, saying, in his own native language and excitement, " If —you—don't—get—this—officer—all—his—things—which—you—stole—I'll—cut—your—Spanish—throat," laying an emphasis on every word, that the Spaniard might not misunderstand him! The poor man was dreadfully alarmed; there was a noisy row—his daughter, a pretty black-eyed maid, rushed in to the rescue, at the time the Doctor was making signs of an incision across her father's throat. I tried to drag him off; the young lady screamed, but the medico declared it was all sham, and he *would* have my traps restored. However, I got the Señor released from an iron grasp, and his daughter in tears took him away. Quill at the same time took his leave, saying, " If I chose to submit to be robbed at every billet in Spain, not to call upon him for any advice or assistance!" He could not speak a word of Spanish, and was much prejudiced against the whole race, believed every man in the country to be a public robber, and looked sharp after his own kit. He was not very far wrong, but still there were honest men and women too, and plenty of them, who loved " los Engleses " as well as their own bright land.

Time being nearly up, I ran off to the office of the Alcalde to report my misfortune, not expecting much redress there. "Give me a list of your losses," he said, "and I will make inquiry after them; you must wait the result here." I gave him the list in writing, and my address, name, regiment, and division of the army, and there it ended. Going back with all my dander up and a melancholy phiz to move off my traps, I heard a sweet voice from a balcony call out, "Señor George." I looked up, and saw a fair lady whom I had known formerly in my old quarters at Albuquerque. She called me up, and, quite rejoiced to see me again, asked a hundred questions all at once—where was the regiment? how were all the officers? how came I here in this queer dress? and where I was going. When she gave me time to speak I told her all, which greatly distressed her. "To be robbed," she said, "amongst my own people;" and, "Dios mio, yo siento mucho,"&c., and "I'm grieved that I cannot help you. I am only here to see some friends who stood out the siege; we are all poor now. Our property destroyed and pillaged, and Spain ruined. You must have some chocolate and something to eat by the way, and two of my brother's shirts, and——." "Oh no," I said, "I can't take anything. I must be off; my people are waiting;" but the chocolate came in with some toast, the almuerzo (breakfast) of all the better class of Spaniards. I parted from her with great reluctance, and with what is called a tender good-bye too. She saw me to the door, slipped two dollars into my hand, and ran up-stairs with a "povorasito" on her lip, and a "viva mil años, caro amigo, á-Dios, á-Dios." Dear, sweet, gentle, kind-hearted Leonora! I never saw her afterwards to return a hundred-fold her generosity. I would have walked a long day's journey to have met her again to show my gratitude—so much was I touched with this disinterested loving-kindness.

I found my troops all present, and in the saddle—" a pack-saddle." "Nobody dead, *sir*," said the medical officer; and took his usual place in front, and away I went from Badajos in very light marching order, never to see it again; the doctor as mute as a tombstone for two leagues, when I called a halt, and sat down by the side of a clear nice fountain, while the mules had their refreshing beverage. Quill now came up and sat down beside me, with a laughing face and admonition for not permitting him to " choke that rascally Spaniard who stole my traps." "I hope he didn't steal the *frying-pan*." " I have all the cooking traps," says Tom, who was sitting beside his donkey at the fountain, gnawing a bone. "*All*," says the doctor,—" a tin pot and an ugly frying-pan." " All we want, sir," said Tom, " where nothin's to be got without money, and I haven't seen a dollar of *my* pay for five months, and nuffin' to eat but the rations." " What are you eatin' now, then ? " said Quill. " Just pickin' a sheep's wag, sir, I got at the last billet." " Or the hotel, say, where you paid for everything, and two sheep and a pig into the bargain." " Sir, you're hard upon the patrone; he couldn't get into master's room, yer see, the door being shut and my head up again it all night; it was some ladrone that climbed up and got in at the window, which was wide open and easy as a stair. They're not bad people the Spaniards, sir, if you could speak to them like me, sir, and not meddle with anything about their doors ; you see, sir, when the old fox wants a goose or a duck, he always goes away from home to forage, and never touches a chicken near his own den." "Vamos, señor," said the leading muleteer, and we moved on. The doctor came up to me and said that he had a few dollars in his pocket, and would divide with me the last pisetta (1s.), and made himself very agreeable until we crossed the border and entered the little kingdom of Portugal, put up at Elvas, a strongly fortified town, met an officer, Lieutenant Bowers, of the 50th, stationed there, an old acquaintance, and passed the day with him. I had no occasion, I said, to lock my door to-night, for all my wardrobe was on my back, which astonished a well-dressed military officer of the British army, until I explained the cause. " Why," he said, " if you were not so very young, you would be taken for some guerilla chief, and all the convoy for prisoners of war, only that the guerillas are on our side." " Just so," I said, " and that makes all the difference."

We passed on our way without any adventure until we

sighted Estramos, the end of our journey. It was a bright sunny day, hot as you please. About noon, as I headed my long line of mules bearing the lame, and the sick, and the sore, the battered trunks of brave men representing many corps, a general officer and his staff, with their cocked hats and fine plumage, stood in the middle of the square and caught my eye at once, as I marched in at the head of my troop. With open mouth and eyes they all turned towards this spectacle, particularly the commanding officer in the fancy dress. Up comes an aide-de-camp directly from the General, to inquire who *I* was, where I came from, my name, "*and about your dress, sir.*" I thought I would have a rise out of this well-dressed gentleman, so sleek and so well fed. "Just from the fighting army above," I said, "we are not over particular in dress; hard times too, little to eat, and plenty of field exercise in the *fire-away-style;* here's a sample of our trade behind me." He went off to make his report to his master, who sent him back for a more direct reply, particularly about my uniform. I then told him the whole story, and my duty being discharged when I had delivered my *troops* at the general hospital, requested permission to proceed to Lisbon to get a new rig out.

The General gave me two months' leave at once, but forgot to ask me to dinner! Quill wished me a safe return through Badajos, and desired me to be sure to call and apologize to my old patrone! and ask him for my toggery, particularly the *douros!* We shook hands and parted mutual good friends,— more of him again.

I went in search of my good friend Masterman who had been wounded in the siege; he was nearly recovered. I passed the day with him; he gave me an old military blue coat and two dollars, all he could spare, and with this I began my journey over a whole kingdom on foot. Tom had his red coat; and so we could not be mistaken for any other than true British soldiers. I knew that there were bandits on the road, but consoled myself with the truth that they would not disturb a couple of English red-coats, driving an empty donkey before them. Tom had his brown bess, and sixty rounds of ball cartridge; he kept his flint well fixed and his powder dry. We had a ride on the donkey, and carried the gun turn about; I was commanding officer, and Tom as respectful as on parade, *while sober*. The firstnight on our new line of march he got right jolly on wine; he had no money nor credit, but a winning way at the wine-house, and a singular way when he lost his balance. I found him in heavy marching order, firelock in hand, when I thought him in bed for the night. "Ho, Tom," I said, "where are you going?" "Back to the regiment," he said; "I go no further: no service on this road." I gave him a punch that floored him right into his little den, where he lay as quiet as a turtle until I took away his gun, knapsack, and ammunition, then locked him up a close prisoner till morning, when he turned out quite fresh and as penitent as priests, who'll never do it again until the next time! And so Tom worried me all the way, but only at night, when I usually locked him up. I had no other adventure on this line of march. Rations were provided by the head man of the village to all who had a route to show, and were paid afterwards by our commissary.

CHAPTER IV.

Better Times.—A Night Adventure.—Lisbon.—Caveat Emptor.—Military Discipline.—Toledo.—Salamanca.—Heroic Conduct.—After the Battle.—Yepes.—The Route.—The Parting.—A Surprise.—A Retreat.—Madrid.

IT was a long, weary, hungry walk over a little kingdom; but I had a stout heart then, a pair of very active legs, an iron constitution, an appetite too big for my means, a devil-me-care way of my own, always merry and ready for any sort of fun or frolic. I rejoiced to see "Aldea Gallega;" and here I crossed the Tajo, nine miles to Lisbon, and made my way to Belem, the English depôt, where an officer of my own regiment was stationed. Lieutenant R——n was a kind, hospitable fellow, glad to see me and to give me a room in his quarters, as well as a hearty invitation to be his guest while I remained in Lisbon; and here I did enjoy myself full measure: very opportunely, too, a box of clothing had just arrived in the river for me from home, with a permission to draw for *the ready*; in addition, I was now all right again, and went to work quietly to equip myself out like a campaigner for rough days before me. I got up a canteen, bought a silver spoon and fork, a *new* fryingpan, tin plates and dishes, and tins for salt, pepper, tea and sugar, &c. A tailor made up my uniforms, riding-jacket, and cap for racing, and other habiliments. All this was going on while I was enjoying myself. I had a good horse to ride, and dined out often; old starvation ration days were forgotten, and I became a great swell. At this time our old friend Dr. L——, who played the part of Don Quixote at Truxillo, arrived in bad health, with a home certificate for six months' leave. He came out to dine with us one day, when we observed by his singular manner that he was not just all right in his pericranium. Dinner was being prepared and

wine on the table; he walked in, and was helping himself to a
goblet of sherry, when I interposed and requested him to wait
a little; he put down the decanter, took up a carving-knife
and made a rush at me; I ran round the table, he after me,
when I jumped out of the window, which fortunately was
open, and made my escape. I turned round and spoke to
him; he flourished his *cuchillo* and told me not to come back,
or he would stop my promotion! We found that the poor
fellow had gone a little crazy; he had cut half the tail off
his red coat, and had played some queer pranks in Lisbon.
We had him carefully looked after, and I saw him safely on
board a ship and placed under the special care of the captain,
who took him safe to England. He was considered a very
clever man in his profession; he never rejoined the regiment,
but we shall meet him again.

Major B—— of ours was promoted into the 77th regiment,
now only seven miles from Belem. He asked us to dine at
the mess which they had established; we rode over to have a
jollification, for it was almost necessary at that period to drink
wine for *three hours* after dinner; then supper, and finish off
with spiced wine and a stirrup cup. I saw that my friend R——
was getting top-heavy, very loquacious, speaking like a senator,
and getting very valiant. He was invited to a shake-down
for the night. Oh, no! his gallant grey was at the door and
would take him home in no time; so we mounted and rode
away quietly about one o'clock in the morning. We had not
gone far when my companion fancied he saw a regiment of
French Dragoons in his front, and ordered me to charge.
He dashed away at full speed, swaying from side to side in
the saddle, so that the right or left spur was always in the
flank of the poor horse. The moon was bright, and the perfume along the hedges sweet as honey. Such a climate at
that hour was meant for the thoughtful, the gentle, thankful,
weary traveller on some errand of mercy, not for Don Quixote
and Sancho. I am sure if R—— had met a windmill in his
flight he would have made the fatal charge; as it was, I found
him in a ditch by the roadside about a mile on, and his horse
standing gently beside him. I jumped off my nag and roused

him up. Finding no bones broken, I got him once more into the saddle after a great struggle; for people in their cups are always very wise and very obstinate! No sooner firmly seated than he gave one wild whoop and was off again, full speed. No use in following, I thought; it would only urge on his horse the faster. I rode on quietly, watching both sides of the road for this wild fellow, but never saw him or his horse. I arrived at home about six o'clock in the morning and sent his servants in search of him along the road that we came; but no tidings until mid-day, when he came riding home quite jolly, as if nothing had happened, and blew me up for leaving him alone in a quinta! Poor R—— was a very sober fellow at all times, but addicted to gambling, which ultimately ruined him.

I had no desire to dine out again with such-like hospitable friends; a simple repast under a tree suited me better, and I do not remember being at any sort of a mess dinner again during the war.

I saw a good deal of Lisbon this time and the beautiful country around it; as for the city itself at that period, it was the most filthy town I had ever seen: it was dangerous to walk the streets by night. No end to the slops coming from the top windows whop into the gutters below; the dogs ever on the alert at night, prowling and fighting,—a community of scavengers without owners, rejected and kicked about; existing in mangy wretchedness, and dying in the streets. As for beggars, they were as plenty as paving-stones—lazy, indolent, and filthy, they lay on the hot flags, stretching out the long bone of an arm for an alms, but would not rise for it; they lived in the sun, half-naked; but as a shirt and trousers were quite enough for any Señor Englese, they required few garments—it was awfully hot.

The churches are always open; they have so much to do in the way of confessions and funerals, fast-days and feast-days, high mass and low mass, processions and exhibitions of saints' bones, and all the paraphernalia of deceit practised amongst this bigoted people, who are kept in perfect submission to the Church; but still I like to see the doors open.

Many a weary, oppressed, humble penitent finds refuge there in time of trouble and affliction; though unfortunately their prayers are more addressed to saints and images, and to the tawdry-dressed doll over the altar in that glass-case, than to the Almighty, through the merits of His most blessed and exalted Son, the only Saviour of man.

No town could be better situated for drainage than Lisbon, but they seemed then to rejoice in its nastiness. I have always remarked that nothing goes right in those bigoted Roman Catholic countries, where the people are kept in darkness and overwhelmed in idolatrous priestcraft. So much of their valuable time, too, is deducted for penance, gabbling long prayers, counting over a string of beads, confessing their peccadilloes, and worrying themselves doing *works* for their salvation!

My time was now up, and we started—a large detachment of many corps—to join the army. I got charge of a spare horse going up to a field officer of the 2nd Division, so I was in luck. Tom and the donkey in good feather and high condition for the road; Tom was two months under garrison discipline, and sober as a judge; and very glad, as he said, to go home again. We halted at Elvas *en route*. I called on the commandant, and found that officer dressed in part of my late wardrobe. I said to him, "Might I ask who is your tailor?" "Why do you ask?" he said. "Oh, just because he made for me as well, and my things fit you so nicely. That silk riding-jacket is mine; I had it for riding races. I can't swear to the trousers, but the vest I would know anywhere." He seemed very much taken aback, and explained how he had bought several things ready-made from a travelling pedlar, which no doubt was the fact. When I explained the Badajos tale, it was all clear that the pedlar was the ladrone (thief), and he had purchased stolen goods, not knowing that they were stolen from Ensign G. B——, when in the performance of his duty in the service of King George III., of gracious memory. He offered to restore all he had at half the price he paid for them, but I declined his offer, saying that I had a full kit, and really wanted for nothing. Between this little unexpected surprise and excitement he forgot to ask me to dinner, so we parted, and never met again. I was satisfied that I did not awake when the wretched thief was in my room, or I might have felt the plunge of his cuchillo under my fifth rib, to keep me quiet. I got *home* safe, and was welcome; there was no fighting in my absence, so I lost nothing.

I found my young friend P——, who used to drink more than his allowance of grog on board the *Arethusa,* missing, and was informed that, on one unlucky morning for him, the brigade was roused up suddenly to disperse some advance troops of the enemy, who were poaching upon our grounds. They were being followed up close by the infantry when the word was passed to the rear to send up the guns, as they were rattling past, and our men closing to the left. Poor P—— lost his balance, tumbled over, and a gun-carriage ruffled his legs, with one of the colours in hand. There was an inquiry, and it could not be denied that he had been indulging as *usual* in too much of the strong waters, so he got leave to go home for an indefinite period, which meant to say that his military career was at an end.

The other gentleman, Lieutenant S——, was found one night while on duty mortal drunk, and got leave to quit also. It was this unfortunate fellow who chased me up on deck with knife in hand for cutting him down on board the old transport.

Commanding officers had almost unlimited power in those days to dismiss officers without court-martial for grave offences like the above: it saved a great deal of trouble and inconvenience, and kept young fellows and old ones *in terrorem;* the men were being flogged every day for drunkenness, and it was right that there should be no partiality between officer and soldier for this crime.

Wellington about this time ordered Sir Rowland Hill to give battle to Drouet, Count D'Erlong, who was roving about *our* part of Spain with a large army, feeding and foraging upon the unhappy Spaniards, who received nothing but blows and abuse for feeding their enemies. We hunted them all over the country, and from town to town, but they would not have our acquaintance on any terms. We drove them from Toledo and Valladolid, two cities of Spain celebrated in story. I did so enjoy a short stay in the former; the French were hardly gone when we marched in, and the same evening a ball was given at the Palace in honour of the English general and his officers, the first British troops that had been here. These Spanish balls and parties are not attended with any expense beyond the refreshment of country wine, lemonade, and cakes. The Bishop was present; many Grandees, poor and proud, assembled there, and the gentle Señoritas, so neatly and so simply dressed, looked pensive and beautiful. They move about in the dance so gracefully, while generally their feet and figures are perfect. There is a very fine cathedral here, and a magnificent organ, on which I helped to perform a grand piece of church music in the way of blowing the bellows—a simple process. 'Tis not done by hand, but by the feet. You walk up and down the great double bellows behind the organ; as one exhausts, the other fills, and so 'tis a walk up and down hill while the music lasts. Toledo was celebrated for sword-blades, as it is now for priests and friars. It stands on the Tagus, in New Castille.

We started in chase once more, and they led us a dance at their heels into Leon, declining to enter into any personal gunpowder quarrel with us for the present. We had very long marches and very hungry soldiers, no money and no credit, six months now in arrears of pay, the muleteers twelve. What could one expect in the trail of a French army? I paid *six shillings* for a loaf of bread, my daily pay being five shillings and threepence, less income-tax! Soldiers without money become robbers almost everywhere; but our men behaved admirably. Bad ones were to be found in every corps, because we got the sweepings of jails at home to fill up our ranks, recruits were so scarce at *eighteen* guineas bounty; but they were all game cocks at fighting; never was such an army, and Wellington knew it.

At this period, our noble Duke and the French General Marmont were dodging each other, and manœuvring about Salamanca, both on the *qui vive* some days before the 22nd of

July, 1812, on which day the great row began. The battle was fought and won by the noble army of Old England, a day of victory garnished by the blood of thousands. Many a time that day did the battle change its very doubtful position. Wellington was here and there and at every point at the right time. The men went down by hundreds; but won their way by desperate courage through such a fire as British soldiers only can sustain. Onwards they pushed through gloom and blood and powder smoke, which rolled along the field, and clothed the scene in partial darkness. In sounds of terror, the battle raged, volley following volley with deafening rapidity, while charges of cavalry and the booming of great guns swept off the warriors, on both sides brave and bold. They fell in soetions, crying victory before the fight had half begun. The French reserve came quickly on upon our front and flanks; their great masses closed on us in clouds of smoke and streams of fire. The hill-side was soon covered with the dead and dying. The battle-ground was shaking like an earthquake; for the French rapidly followed up their advantage, and their fire sparkled along the line with terrible effect, as the many gaps in our ranks clearly showed. The crisis was at hand, and victory awaited the general who had the best and largest reserves.

The 5th Division now met the enemy with a shower of leaden hail in their teeth, a cloud of dust blinded their vision, and in that cloud a tremendous charge of cavalry, swift and sure, sword in hand, broke in upon them in full tilt, trampled and cut them down. They lost both nerve and courage, and upwards of a thousand men threw down their arms, while the glittering swords of our heavy dragoons, all powerful, cut down all before them; but not before a hundred saddles or more were emptied by a flank fire. The French left was now broken, Marmont was wounded, and some of his generals, amongst others Desgraviers, killed, the batteries still ploughing through each other's ranks. On our side a sheet of flame advanced in front, men only thinking of victory. A few more desperate conflicts took place along the lines; the French, drunk with excitement, staggered, were beaten, and having lost two thousand prisoners, retreated in the dusk of evening, with our dragoons at their heels, made for the Tormes, and crossed that river by night. The Duke, always wide awake, left the Spanish General Carlos d'España at Alba de Tormes to intercept the French in case of retreat; but, as usual, he paid no respect to his orders. He left his post, and so let the defeated enemy escape across the ford! Trifling actions often mar great combinations; if this valiant Spaniard had obeyed his orders, at least a third of the fugitives would have been captured. As it was, the victory was great and decisive. Many stories might be told of noble deeds of valour done that day, every tale a true one,—of how the gallant soldiers of 1812 fought for Albion, and sent their laurels home. A 43rd man, shot through the thigh, lost his shoes in the marshy ground; refusing to quit the battle-field, he limped on under fire with naked feet and blood streaming from his wound, and thus marched on for several miles over a country covered with a small flinty stone. Kit Wallace, a private in my company, a simple sort of fellow, who had no friends and was always a butt, and often called a coward in joke, said, "I'll not fire a shot, a single shot in the rear rank" (his proper place), and rushed to the front, expended his sixty rounds of ball-cartridge, and calling for more, said, "Now, am I a coward?" A man who fought beside Wallace was struck with a ball that passed through his body on the right side; you might have put a ramrod completely through the hole. He deliberately took his last shot, walked to the rear, lay down under a tree, and went to sleep in death.

The delicate and beautiful wife of Colonel Dalbiac braved the dangers and privations of two campaigns with the fortitude and patience of her sex. In this battle of Salamanca, forgetful of herself, supported by strong affection for her gallant knight, irresistibly impelled forward, trembling at the fear of death, she rode amidst the enemy's fire, exposing herself to imminent peril. There was no man present that day fighting the battles of his country that did not fight with more than double enthusiasm seeing that fair lady in such danger on the battle-field.

Wellington was hit by a spent shot in the leg, but pushed

on early next day after his friends, when there was another row and some slaughter. Poor General Forey had died of his wounds, and was buried by the roadside. The *brave* Spaniards found the spot, and tore up his body from his humble grave to mutilate and dishonour the shattered shell, when our soldiers came up, and rescued it from their unholy grasp, buried it afresh, and covered it over with large stones for greater safety. The French lost in this day's sport one field-marshal, seven generals, 12,500 officers and men killed, wounded, and taken prisoners, two eagles, several standards, and many guns (when we talk of *guns* we always mean cannon). We lost 6,000 killed and wounded, with four generals. Our troops marched one hundred and fifty miles in twelve days, just before the battle. Some regiments suffered severely; but the 11th and 61st could not muster at the end of the fight over 150 or 160 officers and men—all that were left to tell of noble deeds done on that hot day. Some 6,000 men lying in the hospitals of Salamanca, besides French prisoners also suffering from their wounds, rendered it the abode of extreme misery. Officers sold their horses and what they could get a few dollars for to sustain life, and many died of want and wounds—in plain language, starved to death from neglect, the reward of devotion and courage unequalled in the annals of Great Britain!

There was no getting quit of these Frenchmen, they multiplied and formed new armies, always on the trot, like locusts, eating up all before them. The order of the day with them was free quarters. They paid for nothing, and it was always an unlucky time for us when we got in their wake, for they cleared out the whole country as they went along, the poor Spaniards hiding out of sight all they could put away. Supposing a brigade of French troops on the march to a certain town, where they would arrive on the next day, they sent an armed escort in advance to the alcalde, or head man there, desiring rations to be ready for, say 500 or 1,000 men next day; there was no alternative but that of providing for these plunderers, or taking the chance of their being let loose to help themselves. "Ye gentlemen of England, who sit at home at ease," how would you like such visitors along the coast of Kent, or in your snug little country towns?

We passed nearly the month of September in the pretty town of Yepes. It was the vintage season, and all were busy gathering in most delicious grapes and making their wine; the people were very kind, simple, industrious, and happy. My regiment and the 28th were the first British troops that had ever paid a visit here, and we were welcome. The town was divided between the two corps for their separate quarters in this way: the quartermasters went on in advance, looked into each house, and chalked upon the door, "Grenadiers, 34th, ten men," more or less according to size and convenience, and so on until the whole corps was disposed of. All this was done without asking the proprietors a single question. The best of the houses were marked for the officers, one or more in each house, as there was room. The commanding officer had the best quarters of course, and went there at once. When the men were put up, all the officers assembled to choose their quarters by seniority. They were not particularly choice when my turn came. Once in possession, good or bad, no one's senior could turn you out if you selected your house according to regulation.

I had an excellent quarter (that had been overlooked) as far as rooms went. My patrone was one of those old grandees of Spain, advanced in age, as well as his señora. I very seldom saw them, but the servants had orders to look after my comfort, which they did in their own way. My table was served with grapes and sweetly-preserved melons. A loaf of bread and a big sausage would have been more in my way; but I fared better than usual. There were many pretty girls in the town, all fond of dancing, in which we often indulged of an evening, until we became almost as one family; in fact, every young fellow had his sweetheart. The young ladies were charming, barring education; the priests took care to keep them in ignorance, and free from the trammels of overmuch learning, so that they were generally very idle, but fond of music, dancing, gossiping, and eating grapes and chocolate. However, we thought our fair friends here of a superior race, and indulged them in every way we could. It was a terrible blank to those who could not speak their beautiful language.

Our little evening dancing parties were not expensive; lemonade, fruit, and cakes was the usual refreshment,—all that we could afford, all that was expected. I was a great don in the dance; knew all the figures and all the boñitas.

The weather was beautiful, and after morning parade we had nothing to do but enjoy life in this paradise. With my rations and half a cow's head once a week I made out a living.

I walked into the coach-house one day to look at two curiosities in the shape of the Spanish carriage of the olden time, and found on the seat of my host, the grandee, a hen's nest with seven eggs, which I put by for breakfast, leaving a white stone in their place, which the good old hen was kind enough to consider sufficient security, and called there every second day.

Wellington all this time was laying siege to Burgos, and although not so strong as Badajos or Rodrigo, he was obliged to abandon it after thirty-three days' pounding and five assaults, with a loss of more than 2,000 men, thanks to the home mis-government not supplying him with the guns he asked for and required. Surprising difficulties met this great warrior at every corner in his every-day arrangements, while straining every nerve to accomplish the very-work cut out for him by an English cabinet. He was always active, vigorous, firm in all his arrangements, with a wonderful foresight and conception, admirably formed for success, but he must have found a certain bad Government a scourge with a double thong. What a man of patience and perseverance!

This failure at Burgos knocked all our charming little arrangements to bits; we thought we had taken root in Yepes, being nineteen days undisturbed.

An unexpected order came to "march to-morrow." It came as an order never came before—most unwelcome. All was now hurry and bustle, to get the donkeys ready, and go and see our hermosa Castilian maids, and feel there was a farewell to peace and pleasure whilst a Frenchman remained in Spain. My washwoman, Mrs. Skiddy, came in with my two shirts, &c. "No money yet, Mrs. Skiddy; I owe you a long washing-bill." "Och, never mind that, jewil, if you never paid me; sure, you're always mindful of Dan on the march, and carry his firelock sometimes a bit when the *crather's* goin' to drap wid all the leather straps on his back, and nearly choked wid that stock round his *thrapple*." "Well, we march to-morrow, and so go and get ready." "O worra-worra, march the morrow, and not a shoe on me wee donkey. The curse o' the crows be on the French; may they niver see home," and away she went, storming *agin* the French.

When the unwelcome news spread over the town, the young ladies seemed to feel it most, and many of them, indeed, sadly grieved. However, we got up a dance the same evening, as a farewell party. I well remember it was not so joyous as usual. Before the evening was over, many a sigh and gentle tear was heard and seen sliding over pale cheeks. I passed very little of my time in the house of my grandee patrone. I was welcome in another quarter, and my comrade and self promised our fair friends to come back and see them from Aranjucz (pronounced "Aranwhays").

In the morning early the windows were crowded with our sweet young friends. "Adios, Señores! adios, Vi vm. con Dios!" was heard till far away. I believe there were some very tender partings, for we never left a town in Spain with such regret. Our march was over a plain, about six leagues, to the nice town of Aranjuez, on the Tagus, where the country palace of Spanish kings has stood for centuries. Fine gardens and pleasure-grounds, and fishponds and statuary adorned this royalty; inside the palace all those charms in which kings and queens luxuriate. We had permission to see everything. One room was occupied by mirrors from top to bottom, in which, if any person was shut up, he could never find his way out, so curious was the construction. Another room had its walls entirely covered with paintings—the exploits of Don Quixote, and so on.

A few days passed here, when three of us young fellows

agreed to go over to Yepes next morning at daylight, to pass the day, and see our young lady friends once more, according to promise. I was at my post in good time; there was a rumour of a move, and so my two coves backed out of the trip to Yepes. Nothing daunted, I started off alone, and found a joyous welcome after my long walk across a burning plain. My dress was a scarlet jacket and white waistcoat — the Spaniards liked it, and I did not care a rush who did not. I made for the Caza Don Chaves, and ran upstairs without ceremony. There was a great welcome, and, I believe, some kisses, and a hundred questions about Señor S. and twenty others, and why they did not come, &c. &c. I was almost swallowed up with kindness. Maria sat before me, with her raven hair so nicely turned back from her snow-white forehead, her ivory teeth seen through her smiles, and her beautiful speaking eyes, listening to all I said so imperfectly. All the people in the town seemed to be attached to our men, who behaved so well amongst them; they understood each other by a few words and more signs. An early dinner was being prepared, I was in the midst of enjoyment, and going out to pay another visit, when some one came rushing in, in great fear, saying, "Los Franceses! los Franceses! O, per Dios, Señor George, via vm." (The French are coming! For God's sake, escape for your life — we are all ruined.) Another messenger—"La caballeria, la caballeria viene!"

All was now hurry, scurry, and excitement in the house to secure valuables, and hide themselves. I tried to compose the ladies by an assurance that they were safe, but their fear of the French, of whom they heard so much, gave them great alarm, and they would not be comforted. I have found ladies in general everywhere much alike in this respect, and I might add that the civillest person I ever met was a woman in a fright. A hasty "Adios, caras amigas," and I bolted out of the house—just in time, for the advance guard of a cavalry regiment sounded a halt at the top of a long street leading down to my friend's caza. In any other dress than a red jacket, I might have approached near enough to count their numbers and make a report, but my object now was to run for it, and escape. I went off at a good round trot for a league or so, and then, wet as a sponge, broke into a smart walk. I might be seen at any distance on this wide plain, and kept both eyes open. Here I met a pizañno going to Yepes with a mule laden with wine. The wine in Spain is carried in pigskins, tanned, dried, and prepared or the purpose, as in days of old Bible history (Matthew ix. 17). The bottles might have contained ten or twelve gallons each. I stopped to tell him the news, which seemed to stagger him exceedingly, knowing very well that the French were not in the habit of paying for their wine, nor drinking to the health of the Spaniards. The salutation of our allies, I well remember, was always, "Viva los Engleses." He said," Is there any of your army in Yepes?" "None," I said; "I am the last to leave," and explained as well as I could. "Lo siento mucho, Señor," he said, and began to open a bottle, the mouth of which was a leg of the skin, tied by a string. He had a tin measure, and filled me a bumper. "Drink," he said; "you seem hot and tired;" and I did with gusto toss off a pint of his *bueno vino*, and bid him God-speed.

I got *home* just in time to join my regiment crossing the Tagus—one bridge on fire, and the other about to be blown up—a little later, and I should have been on the wrong side! The two bridges had not been destroyed more than an hour or so when the French cavalry approached, and sent their videttes down to the river to look after our locality. It might have been very inhospitable, but they received a very ugly discharge of musketry from our riflemen, who lined the banks under cover of the evergreen shrubs and bushes. I was in no good humour with them myself for routing me out of Yepes, and so I paid into them some shots from a rest which, I fear, told what I intended at the time, although of all the sports in the field that of man-shooting I like the least. There was a good deal of pot-shooting across the water from our amateurs out of sheer spite, for we were all very angry at being disturbed from our royal quarters. Our troubles were only beginning, but we were in happy ignorance of all before us. When night came on, we all moved off silently from before Aranjuez, across some newly-ploughed lands, wherein I sank to the ankles, until my short boots got full of sand and dirty water. When we did get into the Camino Real, or "royal road," there was a halt to let all stragglers come up. Fires were soon lighted and blazing bright. I pulled off my Wellingtons and my socks to get them quickly dry, and fell asleep, so dreadfully tired as I was after the long day's work. I never awoke until the whole army had moved away, and there I was all alone in the darkness of solitude. The fire had nearly burned out; my socks pretty dry, but the boots very damp. I pulled one on after a painful difficulty—the other foot would not go home on any terms. Half on and half off, I limped on until I came up with my regiment at the next halt, fairly knocked up, but continued on till morning, when we pulled up at Madrid; and there, on the bridge leading into the great city, I dropped like a stone, where I lay for two hours unable to move, footsore and weary. The day was fine, and a general rush was made into the town, when the bugles sounded the assembly. A general order was issued to serve out three days' rations and have them cooked immediately, and then to be ready to march at a moment's warning. The butchers were very expert at their trade; the oxen and fatlings (without any fat) were slaughtered, cut up, divided, served out, and in the camp kettles in less than two hours. I dragged myself down to the river, got off my boots, washed my socks, got up a fire, and fell asleep. Tom roused me up with, "The rations, sir." "What have you got, Tom?" "Somewhat of three pounds of beef with a big bone in it, orders to cook and be off again—sharp. I suppose them *Franceses* are coming after us—the d—l's luck to them!" If my feet sometimes failed me, my appetite never did; the dinner was not at all inviting when turned out on a tin plate, but it was all gone in twenty minutes, barring the bone, and I got up rather hungry, and put two pounds of the biscuit into my haversack for the next two days' subsistence.

Fancy being in Madrid without a dollar in one's pocket to buy a loaf of bread or a sausage, all that I desired or cared for at that moment. However, I was now refreshed; the bugles sounded, I rolled my blanket, strapped it on my back, and waited for the assembly call, when the 88th regiment, or Connaught Rangers, passed by as merry as larks, singing and cracking their Irish jokes, regular bronze fellows, hard as nails, and as ready for a fight as for a ration of rum. One fellow took a side glance at me and said, not in a very under tone, "I think that young gentleman would be better at home with his mother!" I was very indignant at this remark, and kept it to myself; I knew they were a *crack* regiment, and esteemed them for their remarkable bravery at all times.

CHAPTER V.

The Retreat.—Ready for Action.—Adventures.—A Surprise.—Hard Lines.
—A Godsend.—Female Insubordination. — Mrs. Skiddy. — Short
Commons.—Fever.—Theatricals.—1813.—Campaigning.—Destruction
of Burgos.—The British Soldier.

IN Madrid was a junction of the whole British army. Soult and his best generals were at our heels with 58,000 fighting men, 84 guns, and 8,000 cavalry, a sad turn of affairs as we all thought at the time, and so began the grand retreat from Burgos and Madrid; a frightful scene of misery and death, continual slaughter, privation, and cruelty. Men, women, and children crowded around us, bewailing our departure, moving along with us in one great mass for some miles.

We passed the Escurial, that celebrated palace, built by Charles V., where his bones and those of so many kings of Spain were deposited with regal pomp. The great passeth away in his greatness, and a bit of a churchyard fits everybody!

Many peasants lay dead by the roadside, murdered, but by whom we did not know, and I doubt if any one cared, for death was so familiar in all shapes at that time. We crossed the Guadarama mountains, and a splendid sight it was to see so grand an army winding its way zig-zag up that long pass, as far as the eye could see from the top step, in the far distance. The old trade was going on, killing and slaying, and capturing our daily bread. When we got on to the plains on the other side, and crossed the Tormes, we expected some rest, a bit of sleep, and better rations, or some improvement in the foraging department; but things got worse and worse. I had been feasting the last few days on some bullock's liver without salt, and hard biscuit, abominable feeding until people come to know what hunger really is. We got near to Salamanca, and bivouacked in a cork wood; the oak trees too were large and numerous, and the acorns ripe and dropping from the branches. We were gathering, and roasting, and eating them all day, for the commissary failed in issuing our common ration of biscuit, serving out instead, a quarter pound of raw wheat to each man; this we pounded on a stone, and threw into the camp kettle with our beef, which thickened the soup! There was a little bit of growling now and then, much laughing and joking, but no complaint. Queer music it was to see and hear an army sitting on the sod, each man with two big stones grinding his dinner; but everything was sweet that came out of a camp kettle. It must be remembered that the British army had no tents, it was all bivouacking, *i. e.*, lying out on the sod in all weather, like any other wild beasts, and always up and armed ready for anything one hour before daylight, and never dismissed until we could see a white horse a mile distant. This was always a very long hour, just unrolled from one's blanket to stand shivering in the early chill of a drizzly morning.

We had to be always ready for a move, or a march, or a change of ground, or a fight, as the bugle sounded; always on the *qui vive*, night and day, and much need too, for we expected the army of France to be upon us at any moment. I bought a pony on *tick* just now, *i. e.*, to be paid for by instalments as we might get our pay; this was the practice, and the price I paid was eighty dollars, being glad of anything to get my feet off the ground; I was so much knocked up. As for forage, my *caballo* was not entitled to forage, or anything but what he could pick up for himself; he would eat acorns like a pig, and lie down by the camp fire like a Christian at night. "Yonder they come," is echoed by a hundred voices; the bugles sound, and the old word runs along, "Fall in."

The French now are seen in dense dark columns, crossing the Tormes by the fords,—the train of artillery miles long, cavalry in front and on the flanks,—all move on quietly towards us for a while, when they bring up their right shoulders and sweep along the base of the Arapiles out of our sight, but right under the eye of Wellington and his guns; and from this point he offers to deliver battle to the French Marshal; but that crafty general will not accept the challenge. He had made an effort to get us into his net by a combination of movements, but would not fight. It is a great thing to fight an important battle against such a general as Wellington, and such troops as the British, and to win. But Soult might have been excused, if he thought twice before putting the life and fame of so many thousands upon the event of a day, for here, on this very ground, *three* months before, General Marmont was beaten, and his army nearly destroyed. Wellington now courted a battle on the Aripiles, or on the Tormes; he opened a cannonade, did all he could to invite them on; but no go, they declined to quarrel.

My regiment was formed in quarter-distance column at this time on the breast of the hill ready for action, all the French on the other side out of our sight; anxious as we were to get a peep at those ugly customers, we could not see one of them. An aide-de-camp came riding down the hill now, and asked our colonel if he had a mounted officer. "Yes, I believe there is one." "Please send him up to the crest of the hill there, where the Duke is with his staff, and let him report himself to the Quartermaster-General." "Always in luck," said a few of my comrades, as I jumped on my dirty white steed. "Yes," I said, "but there is bad as well as good luck at one's heels everywhere." "Never mind; come down and tell us, if we are going to fight to-day, for it is getting late."

When I got up and swept my eye over the plain below, what a grand spectacle! The massive dark columns of the whole French army standing at ease or with arms piled; dragoons alongside their horses, and the guns limbered up, our artillery pounding at them without provoking a return shot. I saw they were beginning to move, so asked for my orders at once. "Go off," he said, "as fast as you can to Algiho, and order the baggage of the 2nd division to push on to Ciudad Rodrigo." "I don't know the way, sir; how am I to find the place? nor do I know the distance." "Right in that direction," he said, pointing with his glass, "and the first village you come to ask for a guide; now be off, quick." I could now see that instead of a fight we were likely to continue our retreat.; so I jogged on to the first village to get my guide. The town was empty and pillaged, inhabitants all gone, night was on me, I got bewildered, but rode on in the direction I was told as well as

I could remember. As the dark clouds left the bright moon clear, I got a glimpse now and then of the skeletons of man and horse lying where they fell in the great battle of July, looking grim and ghastly.

How soon one loses his way if he shuts his eyes for a hundred yards! I ought not to have been here at all, the first hours of darkness put me all astray, and so I wandered on, not knowing where I was or where I was going, until I saw in the distance a corps of cavalry coming towards me. There was no cover on the plain where I could hide; my pony white, and so I had no chance of escape, I could not evade the enemy. To France I must go a prisoner of war, and no mistake, if they thought me worth catching for the pony. As to my pockets, they were empty; I had not a dollar, and was altogether nothing of a prize. I kept edging off on the flank, when I heard a loud English laugh. Oh, what a relief, how cheering—a regiment of our own cavalry! "Where are you going?" I said. "Up to the army; where are you bound for?" "Can hardly tell; to look after baggage in some forest, perhaps ten leagues off; you'll find the army in retreat from the Aripiles,—good night."

I went on my lonely way until I fell in with a Portuguese regiment in bivouac, close to a large town. I asked the name. "Salamanca, señor." *Prodigious*, entirely out of my line of march. However, I thought I might be still in luck, for our kind and generous paymaster I knew was here, and having been to see him a week before, I remembered his quarters and made my way there in the middle of the night, made a thundering noise at his door with a big stone, when he popped his nightcap out of the window in alarm, with "que quiera vmd?" "Oh, never mind talking Spanish to me, dear Señor Pagadore; let me in, for I'm half dead, and my pony ditto." Kind, amiable, good fellow, he came down directly, in amazement to find me so far away out of my place. I soon told him all; the pony was brought into the house and got some provender. "And now," he said, "go off to the alcalde and get a guide for to-morrow, while I am getting your dinner, tea, and supper ready, for you look starved." There was a great stir in the city, of course, and the chief office of police open all the night. I asked for a guide in the name of Wellington. The chief man present, an uncouth-looking savage, said, "Take that fellow beside you;" pointing to a pizaño in the dirty crowd. "I don't know the way, señor." "Take him away," he said, "he's a ladrone, and knows the country well." So I drew my sword, and walked him off to the paymaster's, and locked him up for the rest of the night. I had a most excellent feed, and had my haversack stored for the march next day, lay down for three hours' sleep, my very kind friend keeping watch to have me up in time, and not letting me go without a few dollars in my pocket. I was away early with my guide, who was very loquacious and very hungry, as he said, and I believed him, but declined allowing him to go home just for ten minutes, to *comer* (to eat). I gave him a piece of bread and beef out of my wallet, and we became great friends until we arrived at the next village, when he gave me the slip; he doubled round a corner with an "Adios, señor," and I saw no more of him!

I got another vagabond guide here, a piece of pork, four potatoes, and two loaves of bread, and took my journey onwards without the slightest knowledge of where I was going. It appeared that this fellow was taking me to his own native village, and when we got there he bolted off like a shot, and left me on the road. On foot I might have kept him beside me, but on horseback I had no chance. So it is between cavalry and infantry; vain and fruitless to match the sabre with the musket, to send the charging horseman against the foot-soldier. I have seen the squadrons cheering on loudly, and at full speed closing on the infantry squares, when they were instantly scorched and scattered by the peal of musketry. As the smoke cleared, the British bayonets glittered and the regiment came forth unscathed as from a furnace.

I rode on a few leagues farther in a mysterious jumble of thought about responsibility, and the wild orders I had received, when I met a multitude of the peasantry, men, women, and children, all laden with their little household goods and traps, the matrons marching erect with babies in little cork baskets balanced on their heads. "Where are you all going?" I said. "O, señor, come back with us to Salamanca; the French are behind us, our town pillaged, the English all killed, and you will be a prisoner." Poor people, I was sorry for them, but thought I would not give up my wild-goose chase upon this report, and rode on. I soon met another batch with the same tale, and turned back with them, being satisfied that I really was on very dangerous ground, and as it happened met with my own regiment crossing my path, and joyfully did I fall into my old place, after making a full report of my journey to the good Colonel F——. My haversack was soon lightened by a few of my hungry comrades, but still I held on to the pork and potatoes with a loaf of bread in reserve!

The whole British army was now in full retreat; the rains had set in, the weather had became dreadful, and we were sorely pressed by the enemy; all dreary and desolate, marching and fighting all day, tired and hungry but not desponding. My regiment being in its turn one day on the rear guard; we halted by the edge of an oak wood to cook, and I rode over to a cottage a little way off very wet, and asked the patrona, a poor old woman, to make up a good fire, and give me a little pot to cook my dinner, which being done *con amore*, I then pulled off my boots and socks, and put them to the fire. "And your coat, señor," said the good woman. I made room for that too, put the piece of pork and the potatoes in the one pot, and sat there in great luxury, everything going on as nice as in a restaurant, and getting so dry; my *landlady* heaping on sticks and the pot boiling, when she came bustling in, greatly alarmed, with "O, señor, los Franceses—los Franceses!" I heard a distant shot and looked out; sure enough, and to my horror, there was a French cavalry corps feeling their way up to the wood, where the smoke of our fires told them a tale. A few more stray shots; I looked out; the bugle sounded; there were men falling in after upsetting their half-cooked rations and shoving the beef part into their haversacks; all hurry-scurry and long shots at the cavalry. I got on my toggery, pretty well dried, and bolted out of the cabin just in time to fall in while my corps was forming square against those bold dragoons; they were very plucky, but great spoons to match themselves against a regiment of infantry without support; we emptied some of their saddles, when they retired to re-form, and wait for their advance-guard of foot-soldiers coming up. In the mean time we got into the wood and continued our course. I lamented all the day for the loss of my dinner, which I carried so far and left at last to be devoured by a Frenchman; how the men did swear at them! "If the *vagabones* had come on after dinner, sure they'd be welcome, but just as our pots were on the boil—O, bad luck to them, and may they niver see home!"

The enemy followed, and pressed us hard until night, when they bivouacked; we did the same, after a good start in advance; it rained hard, and the ground was in one great swamp; we had no baggage, it being all in front, as is usual in retreat. I got up into a cork-tree, amongst the thick branches, and balanced myself there until we moved on, about four o'clock in the morning. This was a hard day upon the men, from the heavy rains; many fell out, some sick, others disabled and footsore; hundreds broke down overcome by the great weight they had to carry, in addition to the wet clothes on the back—viz., a knapsack, heavy old flint firelock, 60 rounds of ball cartridge, haversack with sometimes three days' rations, wooden canteen, bayonet, greatcoat, and blanket, —half-choked with a stiff leather girdle about the throat, and as many cross buff belts as would harness a donkey—it was wonderful how they moved along, and more surprising that they were not all left on the line of march; as it was, the French were picking them up in scores as they dotted the cheerless route.

We gained our bivouac at a late hour, made our fires, and prepared for *supper*—a hard biscuit and the remnant of a carrion ration of beef, no rum—we finished the little we had by the way; our commissary (Brook) came up now with the mules and stores, pitched his tent beside us, and looked so comfortable, that three of us cast lots as to who would go on a sort of forlorn hope and ask or beg of him to give us a ration of rum to keep *in* life till morning. I braced up all my courage, went forth, and demanded an audience. "Hard times, Brook (no preface), three of us here beside you, famished; will you give us a drop of rum?" "And then," he said, "I will have the whole camp on the top of me, and my supply short already." "Honour bright," I said, "close as a pill-box." He called one of his people and told him to fill my flask; my flask happened, luckily for me, to be my wooden canteen, which held about three pints, and the generous muleteer filled it up to the brim, and away I went joyful; and little as this trifle may appear, it was more than gold could purchase, and raised our barometer amazingly. Our luck was not yet over, the moon came peering through clouds of rain, when a herd of innocent, friendly swine wandered in amongst us, crunching the acorns as they delicately passed amongst the men. This was tempting beyond all endurance; thousands of hungry soldiers by fires blazing bright, hundreds of well-fed pigs at the very point of the bayonet, the camp already yielding in anticipation a perfume of pork chops, who could let these wanderers of the dark forest pass away without further acquaintance? It would not be etiquette; but now, against all military discipline, a hundred shots were fired almost simultaneously, the *mudlarks* were knocked over right and left; the bivouac all in alarm, the drums beat to arms, bugles sounded the assembly, the men groped their way to their alarm-posts, every one supposing that the enemy were upon us (barring the pig-shooters). The general officers kicked up a frightful dust about this unaccountable midnight row; *nobody* did it, it was all the fault of intruders; however before morning there was a savoury smell of roast pork about our fires, and no further inquiry. I found a small joint beside me, left there by the fairies, not over nicely dressed, the bristles like porcupine quills, but well fed.

The Duke made a great fuss about all this insubordination; but it is to be remembered that the line of march from Salamanca was through a flooded and flat clay country, that the troops, ankle-deep in mire, mid-leg in water, had lost their shoes; and with strained sinews had heavily made their way upon *two* rations *only* in *five days,* feeding on acorns, when

Wellington supposed that the commissaries were supplying the army with their usual rations.

The great commander, in whom we had the firmest reliance, was unrivalled in skill, vigour, and genius, but could not see at once into the wants and necessities of 70,000 men. The pursuing enemy captured much of our stores and baggage, and our loss of seasoned British soldiers on this retreat, in killed and wounded, and prisoners, according to the returns, came up to 8,000 men. War tries the strength of military framework, and hunger will not resist a pork-chop fried on the top of a ramrod. "The pigs," men said, "had no right poaching on our grounds, and we *had* a right to our ration of acorns."

When we came to rivers, there was no halting or hesitation; the men walked in and over, as if on parade; when pretty deep, they linked together to break the stream. In fording the Duero, near Toro, we found it so deep and rapid, that the men slung their ammunition on the back of their necks to keep it dry. Our baggage being in advance, it made one wince to think of the chance of the poor little *donkeys* crossing this gulf with all our treasure on their back, and it was many a long day before we heard the fate of our respective quadrupeds; many were lost with their precious load, and there was no compensation.

A multitude of soldiers' wives stuck to the army like bricks; averse to all military discipline, they impeded our progress at times very much, particularly in this retreat. They became the subject of a general order for their own special guidance. They were under no control, and were first mounted up and away in advance, blocking up narrow passes, and checking the advance of the army with their donkeys, after repeated orders to follow in rear of their respective corps, or their donkeys would be shot. "I'd like to see the man that wud shoot my donkey," says Mrs. Biddy Flyn; "faith I'll be too early away for any of 'em to catch me. Will you come wid me, *girls?*" "Aye, indeed, every one of us;" and away they all started at early dawn, cracking their jokes about division orders, Wellington, commanding officers, and their next *bivouac*, Mrs. Skiddy leading the way on her celebrated donkey called the "Queen of Spain." She was a squat little Irishwoman, and broad as a big turtle. "Dhrive on, girls, and we'll bate them to the end ov this day, at any rate," says Mother Skiddy. "An' the morrow too," says Mrs. Flyn; "An' the day after," cried Betty Wheel, and then a chorus of laughter by the whole brigade (those three industrious women will be remembered by any old 34th man still alive). Alas! the Provost-Marshal was in advance—a man in authority, and a terror to all evil-doers; in his department the Habeas Corpus Act was suspended throughout the war, and he was waiting here in a narrow turn of the road for the *ladies* with an advance guard, all loaded. He gave orders to fire at once on the donkeys, killing and wounding two or three, *pour exemple.* There was a wild, fierce, and furious yell struck up at once, with more weeping and lamentation than one generally hears at an Irish funeral, with sundry prayers for the *vag⸱bone* that murdered the lives of these poor, darling, innocent *crathers!* As we came up, the cries of distress echoed in the hollow trunks of the old cork-trees; it was "Oh, bad luck to his ugly face—the spy of our camp—may he niver see home till the vultures pick his eyes out, the born varmint," and so on. They gathered up what they could carry, and marched on along with the troops, crying and lamenting their bitter fate, with not a dry rag on their backs. It was wonderful what they endured; but, in spite of all this warning, Mother Skiddy was foremost on the line of march next morning, as she said, "We must risk something to be in before the men, to have the *fire* an' a *dhrop* of tay ready for the poor crathers after their load an' their labour; an' sure if I went in the *rare*, the French, bad luck to them, wud pick me up, me an' my donkey, and then Dan would be lost entirely." She was a devoted soldier's wife, and a right good one, an excellent forager, and never failed to have something for *Dan* when we were all starving. Dan Skiddy was not much bigger than his wife—short and stumpy, but with great bone and pluck, and of good character. I carried his firelock for him at times many a mile, when he was ready to drop, as he said, with rheumatiz pains.

Our long and weary wet march of seventeen days came to an end at last; during all the time I don't think I was perfectly dry for twenty-four hours. Our Brigadier, General Wilson, an old man with a grey head, who rode a blind horse, was always very plucky in showing the men how to cross a stream. When they hesitated on its brink, he would dismount, walk in with the greatest nonchalance, and remount with his boots full of water; but this practice did not agree with his years or constitution, "and *he* died." The French did not get fat on our trail; heaps of heavy baggage and broken-down soldiers fell to their lot, but little to eat. Our good paymaster, J———, offered a poor peasant one day a doubloon (sixteen dollars) for a loaf of bread. He said, "Señor, I can't eat your gold; I am starving myself"—so hard were we pressed at times for food. But these little incidents in a campaign were soon forgotten, and never entered into the columns of an English newspaper.

We got into the mountains bordering on Portugal, and the army was soon distributed amongst the towns and villages in Estremadura, very celebrated for fever and ague. The little village of Caza-don-Gomez sufficed to give covering to my regiment; bad as it was, we rejoiced at the change. I lodged with a very poor peasant in a very humble dwelling. He herded goats all day on the hills, was dressed in sheep-skins, and returned at night to the family meal, which he always prepared himself. It never varied; a loaf of brown bread sliced into a wooden bowl, some olive-oil poured over it, then some hot water, and mixed up. He and his wife and children sat round with their spoons and kept time till the dish was cleared out. None of the party ever spoke a word until the evening meal was finished. In this humble way they lived and seemed contented. In their simplicity and poverty there was a courteous hospitality, such as never sitting down without asking me to partake of their supper. I had a little sort of a bed in a recess in the kitchen, near the fire, where we all sat of an evening by the light of some sticks, a very taciturn party. I was hardly domiciled here when I was taken ill of a fever, accompanied by total prostration of strength and physical power. I don't remember how long I lay in the corner. The regimental surgeon came daily to see if I was dead or alive. He had nothing to give me but a kind and encouraging word. Men died here by the score for want of care and medical comforts.

Poor Robert S—— and I were very great friends, but he had nothing but his *carving tools*, blue pill and salts, and his good name, which carried him through an honourable life with success. I met him accidentally long afterwards in India in a *choultry* by the wayside, and years after I returned from the Burmese war we were stationed in the same beautiful cantonment at Bangalore.

We got a little of our back pay on account at this time, and I was able to provide some tea, sugar, and bread for myself,—all that I cared for. I got some of the goats' milk for my tea, which I considered a perfect luxury. The rough edge was wearing off the winter, brighter days shining through dark clouds. Change of quarters and returning health cheered me up a bit when I thought I was left here forlorn to die in a hovel, but I was never forsaken; there was a bright star above to guide and protect even the thoughtless and unworthy, and so far strength of frame and energy of mind had borne me scathless and uninjured through scenes of fatigue, and danger, and blood, and death. I had been pining after home in my long illness, but as health came gradually rolling back, and rousing me up, I soon forgot the feeling.

I had sold my pony to pay for himself, and was again on my pins, a foot-soldier. There never was any objection to an officer keeping a horse and riding on the line of march, but he got no forage beyond the usual allowance—that is, *two subs* were allowed forage for *one* baggage animal. When we came to a *scrimmage* on the line of march at any time, we quickly dismounted and sent our steeds to the rear; if they were killed in action we bore the loss, besides having a better chance of being killed also.

My regiment moved to another little village, just able to hold us all, and no more; so we had it all to ourselves, and a pretty, cheerful little place it was. The people were poor, but very simple, honest, and kind in their way.

We got clear away from the Spanish army for a time. They were incapable of any dexterous movement. No master spirit was amongst them, and they continually worried our great chief with their apathy, intrigue, and dogged habits of indolence, faction, and violence; their insolence and ferocity at Salamanca were infamous. One instance is well known: a horse, led by an English soldier, being frightened, backed against a Spanish officer, commanding at a gate. He caused the soldier to be dragged into his guard-house, and there destroyed him in cold blood with bayonet-wounds! There was nothing for it but counter-violence.

Another Spanish officer wantonly stabbed at a rifleman, who shot him at once. A British volunteer slew a Spanish officer at the head of his own regiment in a sword fight, the troops of both nations looking on; but here there was nothing dishonourable.

Our kind, good, and amiable soldier chief, General Sir Rowland Hill, had a little pack of hounds sent out from England at this period to afford some field sport to his division. There was no lack of the sly fox; plenty of red-coats in the field, and good horsemen too. Crossing a plain one day in full chase, Reynard disappeared all at once; the foremost horseman had but just time to pull up at the edge of a rocky precipice, when they discovered poor Reynard and nine of the hounds below, all dead!

The General's head-quarters were at Coria, about two leagues from us; he encouraged any amusement likely to afford pleasure to his officers, and now he patronized an amateur theatre, which was very well got up. We had amongst so many regiments capital actors, scene-painters, and really a first-rate company. The delicate-looking, pale-faced, slim ensigns, distinguished themselves in petticoats, and right well they played their parts. All we wanted was an audience! We had some very handsome Spanish señoras, who looked on and laughed through their bright eyes, but understood nothing. There was one fair and beautiful Englishwoman always present, joyous and happy, a charming representative of those bright stars of Albion, whose presence was always cheering amongst so many red coats, the only lady at head-quarters, wife of

Colonel C——, Hill's first aide-de-camp, who afterwards fell
at Waterloo.

After the play we all went in our stage dresses to the
General's supper-table, where we *did* enjoy ourselves to the
full, a singular-looking group of painted actors and actresses.
I can now see his good, honest, benevolent face shining with
delight at the head of his table, enjoying the *scene* and the
songs that went round until a late hour. He was the man who
never could say an ill word to any one; the Duke's favourite
and most successful general. His sobriquet was "Farmer
Hill," while another was called Tiger C——, and so on; every
General, as well as regiment, had a nick-name; but there was
a mutual confidence that could not be shaken between the
parties, and they, one and all, had the firmest reliance on
Wellington. He never came near us without a cheer from the
men that made the woods ring. When he appeared, the men
would say, "There he comes with his long nose, boys; you
may fix your flints."

My captain, Egerton, or, as the girls called him, "Señor
quatro-ojos," or four eyes, as he wore spectacles, was a fine
specimen of a Cheshire gentleman and a brave soldier. He
had gone on General Hill's staff as chief aide-de-camp, and was
always my friend, until he finished off his campaign, a general
officer on his native ground.

1813.—We were very busy with parades and drills and field-
days, and some little horse-racing in April. Large reinforce-
ments of cavalry and infantry arrived from England, and the
whole British army was being reorganized by the great chief
for the coming struggle. Our ranks were filled up by officers
and men, all "Johnnie Newcomes" of course, but were soon
drilled into a new form of discipline, which rather astonished
some of their backs. They were men, chiefly volunteers from
the Militia, who seemed to have had a *leetle* too much of their
own way; but that was soon drilled out of them, and they were
taught that the first duty of a soldier is "to obey orders."
Amongst the officers, a nice-looking lad, named Phillips, about
seventeen, with June roses on his cheeks, stuck to me, and we
ran in couples very happy during his brief campaign, which

ended on the battle-field in less than four months. I grieved after this lad very much, so young, so brave, so full of life and joy.

Since we finished off the retreat from Burgos and Madrid there was great mortality amongst the troops, fever and ague prevailing; I caught both, and suffered severely. There was no cure; all the *charms* the doctors got from the medical department at home was some rotten old bark intended to be mixed with some country wine, to dose the soldiers. Some fusty sawdust would have had the same effect! Lives were held cheap, but they cost money, nobody cared; "things will last my time," and the national debt will probably last a while longer!

On the 1st of May Wellington mounted his gallant steed, took a last look across the hills, and saying, "Farewell Portugal!" headed his grand army to do or die in this campaign.

Three of us young fellows clubbed up a little mess. I was the best provided of the party with everything, as my baggage got safe over the retreat. I bought another donkey on the strength of all *subs* being allowed forage for *one* animal; and our kind and generous paymaster made me a present of a very pretty Spanish jennet; and now I was all right and ready for the road, barring the ague, which left me prostrate every second day. The cold shivering fit first came on, nothing would warm me, then after a few hours the hot or burning fever fit succeeded, with a splitting headache that nearly drove me crazy; the next day I was *quite* well and fit for anything.

We now broke up from our cantonments, and the very first day was my ague day, and somehow doubly severe. I suffered dreadfully; unable to keep my saddle, I tied my horse to a tree, lay down beside him until the last fit passed away, and then followed my corps to the camping-ground; sometimes detained until long after dark, when my messmates were sure to have something for me along with the tea, always a stand by and a luxury.

We commenced this compaign with tents for officers and men. The mules that formerly carried the camp kettles now carried the tents; the old large *iron* cooking-kettles were put *hors-de-combat*, and replaced by smaller tin kettles which were carried by the men in addition to their usual load. Captains had a mule allowed to carry a tent (and some company books, &c.) for himself and his subs. I had the fortune, good or bad, to be once more in the company of "*Bloody Mick*" of former days; he had the politeness to say at the start that I *might* occupy a corner of *his* tent at *night*. I knew very well I had as much right there as himself; but the invitation was not so hospitable as to induce me to sleep in the same house with my gallant captain. I preferred the outside, and slept under a tree on the sod for two months, when I was transferred to the Light Company, one of the subs thereof being taken prisoner in a *scrimmage* with the French. My captain (Fancourt) was a first-rate fellow, a fine and gallant soldier, always generous, hospitable, and kind. I never left him afterwards; he was the best dressed man in the army, very fond of horses, and always well mounted. Joking one day with our Commissary B——, he said, "I wish you would give me a little barley for my horse, I am very hard run over for a feed." "Do you see that sack-full there? It contains rations for three mules for ten days; if you will carry it to your quarters on your back you may have it; mind, no help." Fancourt peeled off his red coat, made one great effort, got under the sack and carried it out of the store, through the town, to his quarters amidst hurrahs,—and "Well done, old fellow, you have done the Commissary." He dropped his burden at his stable door with a face as red as a peony with laughter and exertion! He would have shared his rations with his horse at any time if hard pressed. Commissary B—— never made him a similar offer, although they were ever good friends.

The weather was very fine and very dry, it was rather agreeable sleeping under the trees at night although the dews were heavy; to keep dry I generally cut a bundle of fine branches to lie on, rolled myself in my blanket, put my saddle under my head, tied my bonny black jennet to a tree, gave him the length of his tether to feed, and went to sleep myself until the bugle sounded before dawn, when I had the night dew shaken out of my blanket, placed it as usual under my saddle, and marched away. The men were generally cheerful and full of mirth for the first few leagues, when they began to labour along in silence until they reached the next lodging-ground to shake off their load for the night.

Wellington led on his brave army with confidence to a succession of victories. We crossed the Douro and the Ebro in our line of march, the army divided into many columns, and were not long in scenting out the enemy. I went on the Burgos road with General Hill; his orders were, I believe, to fight there or take the fortress. It cost us 2,000 the last visit, and here we fully expected another slaughter; but King Joseph B—— had not the master-spirit of Soult, whom he disliked; as we advanced, he retreated from Burgos. The castle had been prepared for destruction, and I was not sorry at being awoke one night out of my tired slumbers on the green sod by an awful explosion, like an earthquake; I drew myself up, half-asleep, into a sitting posture, and said, "Thank God! there goes Burgos," and lay down again to finish my slumbers. But with the castle three hundred souls were blown into eternity! At the moment, I cared little for that; such is war! From hurry or neglect, the mine exploded before its time, several streets were laid in ruins, thousands of shells ignited and exploded and rolled about with destructive power; and so this great impediment in our way was finally removed, just as we could have wished, except the terrible death of three hundred of our enemies. In war, nothing so bad as failure or defeat, and this must have damped the King's courage a bit. His brother, the great Napoleon, they say, used to tell him that if he would command, he must give himself up entirely to business, labouring day and night, just the thing; he never was cut out for, as will be found recorded in his history; indeed, his cognomen was "Roi de Bouteille." He had a fine command, a great and brilliant army, an obedient army; but that soul of armies, the *mind* of a great commander, was wanting; *it* was all on our side, in Wellington's knowledge-box! and nothing now retarded his progress. With an eagle's sweep he poured his columns through all the deep narrow valleys and rugged defiles, gullies, ravines and passes, amongst the rocks. Nothing even retarded the march of the artillery: where horses could not go nor draw, the soldiers did their work; and when the wheels could not roll, guns were let down or lifted up with ropes; and bravely did our rough veteran infantry work their way for six days, with unceasing toil, through those wild and beautiful regions.

Our army, swelling in numbers, came rushing in from hill and vale and valley, like roaring streams from every defile, foaming into the basin of Vittoria. When the King was conjecturing about the quickest way to put the English army *hors-de-combat*, and at what hour he might consistently partake of the banquet he had ordered in Vittoria, Wellington was making *his* arrangements to cook him before sunset. The 20th of June was my ague day; I was wearied and worn with this horrid complaint persecuting me every second day for the last two months, but I was not singular; however, I stuck to my *trade* and resisted being left in hospital at any of the depôts formed in our rear,—perfectly well to-day, to-morrow in torture, dejected and cast down. I lay under a tree, seeing my comrades pass away over the plain. Night came on, I rose like one from the dead and followed in their wake; my chums had some tea ready for me, with something in the frying-pan, when I got into camp.

We knew little or nothing of what was to come off the following day, except from our men, who were fixing their flints, chaffing and talking of the "frog eaters" who could not be far off. They said they *nosed* them from their *backie* and *inions!* I declined the tent accommodation, and slept soundly on the sod. We were all under arms right early in the morning, the rolls were called, all present, and nobody afraid! It was a bright, warm, and beautiful day—the longest day—and a long day's work was before us, before the sun was to set on so many of the brave. We had scarcely advanced a league across the plain when we heard the riflemen on our left beginning the work of the morning; cheers through the ranks, many jokes and quaint sayings; there was great hilarity, buoyant spirit and cheerfulness, a determined resolve to fight to the front, and never say die. When the British soldier is let loose in the field with all his steam up, the difficulty is to keep him in check, to stop his onward rapidity. When he sees the enemy in his front, he fights for his Queen, fights for old England, fights for victory, and always wins. The British soldier is a queer sort of biped, fierce in battle, full of a child's simplicity and kindness when over; he will tear the shirt off his back to bind up the bleeding wounds of his fallen foe, carry him away on his back to some quiet spot for medical care, lay him gently down, and divide with him the contents of his flask.

CHAPTER VI.

Battle of Vittoria.—Victory.—The Pursuit.—The King in danger.—A Night Auction.—Narrow Escapes.—Curious Booty.—The Wounded.—Maurice Quill.—Masterman.—Sir William Stewart.—The Basque Provinces.—The Alarm.—Warm Work.—The Wounded.

TWENTY soldiers may give a descriptive account of a battle, all different, yet all correct; it is impossible for one man to see the entire of a battle-field ten or fifteen miles in extent, even on the swiftest horse. One intelligent, active mind can gather in a great deal from personal observation, and collect from other sources much information and *truth*, and unless a truthful narrative is recorded in a journal like this, it is not worth the printer's ink. There was no man of our day could give a more thrilling descriptive account of a battle-field than the brave and gallant veteran Sir W. Napier.

The river Zadora ran through the whole line of the battle-ground for many miles, and was spanned by seven bridges. It was about ten o'clock before we (2nd Division) got into action. General Hill had 20,000 men, and moved them on the left of the French position, when we began with a sharp skirmish, and renewed the old quarrel. We soon began to warm to the old work, and matters looked serious. We won a hill on which the enemy were strongly posted; but at a severe loss. The Hon. Colonel Cadogan, commanding the 71st regiment, was killed here, with many other valuable officers. We were gaining ground along the side of the mountain, when we met with a biting fire, and the battle here remained stationary for some time, until our General sent us more aid; then, passing the Zadora, we won the village of Subijana-de-Alava, in front of General Gazan, and maintained our ground in spite of all opposition. There was a good deal of fighting in the church-yard, and some open graves there were soon filled up with double numbers; indeed, churches and churchyards were always a favourable resort for this peculiar amusement; they were places of strength, and contended for accordingly; and here *our* battle raged with more violence and contention. We had possession—nine-tenths of the law in battle—but, hardly pressed front and flank, I thought we had killed more of our French neighbours here than was needful; but as they cared little for life in their excitement, they would be killed; and, as Colonel Brown said, "If you don't kill them, boys, they'll kill you; fire away."

There were three great battles going on. The curling smoke in the far away distance and booming of guns showed that our comrades were deeply engaged with all the destructive power at their disposal; our wretched old flint firelocks would not burn powder at times until the soldier took from the pocket in his pouch a triangle screw, to knock life into his old flint, and then clear the touch-hole with a long brass picker that hung from his belt. Many a fellow was killed while performing this operation; but the French had no better fighting tools than ourselves, so in this respect we were not unequally matched; however, the red-coats got impatient and excited to be at them with the bayonet, and when the word was delivered, "Prepare to charge," the very hills echoed back the mighty cheer of thousands with an overwhelming terror, for the charge was irresistible.

Upon all favourable occasions our men were let loose in this way to complete a victory. Our opponents never liked the steel, it was so indigestible, and at this part of the play the "*En avant*" was never heard, but rather "*Sauve qui peut.*"

It was now about one o'clock; the whole line of the battle-field was in a blaze—guns, mortars, cavalry, and infantry displaying double exertion and courage to win the day. Seventy thousand brave men, not fearing death nor danger, on each side were contending for a kingdom that must be lost or won this day. Yes, this 21st of June, 1813, must decide the fate of Spain.

"Morillo's" Spaniards displayed unusual courage, and fought well, himself wounded, but "Longa" would not move his troops when they were required at a very critical moment, just like the old mule. Our troops plunged into the village of Arinez amidst a heavy fire of musketry and artillery. This was an important post. Fresh French troops came pouring down to the bloody work. The smoke, dust, and clamour, the flashing of fire-arms, the shouts and cries of the combatants, mixed with the thundering of the guns, were terrible; the continuous cries of the wounded for water were piteous, while the horses, distracted and torn with cannon-shot, were hobbling about in painful torture, some with broken legs, and others dragging their entrails after them in mad career. It was indeed a sickening sight I never wished to see again, but my heart and eyes were since in time to be tortured with more dreadful scenes. As we gained this village and advanced, many guns were captured. It was a country of high corn, vineyards, wood and plain, ditches, villages, hamlets, and the river winding right away down to the Ebro. We had now fought over about six miles of country, yet the French were not quelled nor beaten. General Reille maintained his post on their last high ground, and made his muskets flash like lightning, while *fourscore* pieces of artillery, nearly all fired together, made a furious uproar that shook the earth, and ground our men to pulp before they had time to make the dash. Amidst the fire and smoke, the dark figures of the French artillery were seen bounding about, and serving their guns with frantic energy. This terrible cannonade and fire of small-arms checked our troops until the 4th Division came up; they needed no introduction to General Reille. With one long loud cheer, an electric shock to Frenchmen's nerves, this important position was won at a rush.

In other places the battle was waged with fury and great energy on both sides. The day was not yet won; it was the longest, and in every respect the most bloody day, that many of us had ever seen, but I had little time to think about it.

A Spanish pisaño told Lord Wellington that one of the bridges was undefended, and offered to lead any troops to it. A brigade was immediately sent forward, and while passing over it at the double, the poor fellow at their head was killed by a cannon-shot.

About six o'clock the whole of the French army was beaten back to their last defence, about a mile from Vittoria. Behind them was the plain, and beyond the city; thousands of non-combatants, carriages, men, women, and children belonging to the host of the great army, were crowded together in wild terror; our cannon-shot went booming over their heads, which threw them into a convulsive movement of distress; they swarmed together, swerved, looked about for safety; but there was no hope now for the multitude or the army. They lost the day. It was now the wreck of a nation—of a great army in all its power and pride and glory, led by a king, and the most efficient and accomplished generals of an emperor. Twelve hours ago the balance of military power on the plains of " Old Castille " was about equal; but there was a confiding reliance throughout our ranks in the skill of our great chief that never was shaken, and defeat was never named. Yet we *did*, if the truth must be told, get rather a severe kick in one month after this by these very well-beaten Frenchmen, or by some of their relations or friends.

The British army closely pursued the flying and shattered columns of the French, now broken and dispersed, until night stopped the chase. Never was there a more complete victory, and, as General Gazan said, " They lost all their equipages, all their guns, all their treasure, all their stores, all their papers —so that no man could prove how much pay was due to him."

Generals and subordinate officers were reduced to the clothes on their backs, and most of them barefooted. The trophies were very numerous. Marshal Jourdan's bâton, a stand of colours, 140 brass cannon, all their stores, carriages, and ammunition, their treasure, and prisoners too many to enable us to pay attention to their wants and safety. They lost 6,000 men; our loss was nearly equal, 5,176; of these, according to returns, 1,049 were Portuguese, and 553 were Spaniards, our loss being more than double that of our two friendly powers. In fact the red-coats were always expected to do the real fighting business. British troops are the soldiers of the battle.

The spoil was very great; it may be said that the fighting men were marching and fighting upon gold and silver, without helping themselves. *Five million* dollars, abandoned by the French and left upon the ground, were picked up by non-combatants and camp followers. There were little barrels of doubloons and Napoleons in gold, for the picking up, but rather heavy to put into one's haversack. The chase was so swift, and the men so excited, that but a few just stumbled over this treasure, nor would any man be permitted to stop a moment if observed, yet a great many did fill their pockets, and haversacks, and *holsters* with loose treasure just *en passant*, and kept on blazing away like fun. Not a dollar ever came to our treasury as prize money, which the Duke complained of; but, as for this, it was no great loss to us *subs*, for we were always cheated of all but one-tenth of our share, and received that *six* years after the *Peninsular* war, and *fourteen* years after the first Burmese war. However, I only speak for myself; I know the time, and place, and amount I received, and the sum total did not come up to £20! My losses were more than five times as much.

But to continue our pursuit: the wreck of the army was in full retreat, *their* contest ended; the allies being now advancing on every point, caused their confusion to increase, the guns were abandoned, the drivers rode off the horses at speed, the soldiers pressed wildly through a road half-choked up with the unfortunate refugees from the capital, and the vast number of vehicles which moved along with them in their flight. A scene of the most frightful disorder ensued; the sun now began to sink below the western hills, and the last rays of golden light fell upon a spectacle not easily described. Red columns of infantry were advancing steadily over the plain; the horse artillery were galloping to the front to open a fresh fire into the fugitives; the *cavalry* charging along the Camino Real; while the 2nd (Hill's) Division, which, overcoming every obstacle, had driven the enemy from its front, was extending along the heights and lower ground, on the right of the British army, its arms flashing brightly in the fading sunshine of this ever-memorable day (our arms now are brown; in former days they were bright and glittering in the sun or moonlight march).

Never was a victory so complete, nor an army so very well thrashed and disorganized as this great French host. The bright and warm sun of a June morning rose on three united grand corps, all speaking the same language, perfect in every arm, admirably combined, and placed in a position of battle well selected and defended with batteries and breastworks, a river in their front, and all the chances of war in their favour. Night closed upon a pitiful and helpless, broken-down, dislocated, and shattered rabble, hurrying away from the fatal field of their defeat. The day was ours, but one could not help feeling deeply for the helpless multitude when our cannon-shot plunged amongst such a crowd of humanity trying to escape. "Like the Scottish monarch at Flodden (just three hundred years ago, 1513), King Joseph remained to witness the ruin which his rashness wrought, but not to expiate his folly with his life." He effected his not very glorious retreat with difficulty. Our dragoons overtook and fired at his carriage, out of which he escaped by jumping, mounting a horse, and riding, harder than ever John Gilpin did, for life and liberty, guarded by a strong escort. He made "Pampeluna" that night without the value of a horn spoon of all his treasure.

I happened to be marching along in his track, and came upon his carriage upset in a ditch, and also seven waggons loaded with his personal baggage jammed up in a heap; the mules all gone, soldiers excitingly engaged, their muzzles black with powder from biting the cartridge, and perspiring like hunters, all busily employed stripping the carriage even of its lining in search of something portable in the shape of the image and superscription of Napoleon. I never saw such handy fellows, so expert were they, that the whole contents were laid before the *public* in about fifteen minutes for selection, or, as a *Paddy* of a Grenadier said,—" Come, boys, help yourselves wid anything yes like best, *free gratis* for nothing at all! The King soon made his will and left all you see *behind* him for our day's *throuble*. He's away to France, an' the de—l's luck to him! Who'll have a *dhrink* o' wine?" And so they cracked their jokes at the expense of his Majesty. Another party were actively engaged *unloading* the waggons, pitching into the whole contents—trunks, boxes, great bundles of papers, letters private and confidential, charts, pictures of great value, which had been cut out of their frames, best French wines, brandy, beds and bedding, portable furniture, a whole library of books, everything in the cuisine department, camp equipage, and lots of grog corked and ready for this fatigue party; with skins of Spanish wine, and a multiplication of other things which had belonged to this robber king, too tedious to be inserted in this bill of fare! I picked up hastily a big sack, a cold fowl, a few maps, and a flask of wine, the sum total of all the plunder I touched that day, and rode on.

Wellington went back to Vittoria about nine o'clock, still daylight, where all was panic and confusion; every door closed, every lattice darkened, the streets funereal and deserted, where two nights before all was brilliant and gay. The game took an unlucky turn for all Spaniards of the French party; many of whom went off with the retreating robbers. The loyalists now began to crow, and received Wellington with welcome cheers. During the progress of the battle, over three leagues of difficult country, the long summer's day was spent in an unremitting succession of laborious exertions to attain this great end. It was not generally a night of repose. There was a grand general auction in the camp of every brigade; the great variety of articles for sale was far beyond anything ever heard of, and if one was to attempt to enumerate them, would be beyond belief; how they were picked up so quickly by fighting men, who kept their fighting place, would astonish the reader; but when an army finds itself beaten and receives the word "sauve qui peut," away they go, d—l take the hindmost; and as "light marching order" is the swiftest retreat, they cast away everything as they run, arms, ammunition, firelocks, knapsack, and an accumulation of plunder, which our men picked up in their advance. When they stumbled over a cask of dollars, in went the head with a punch from the butt-end of a firelock; the cask then rolled over, an inviting spread, and every one helped himself and pushed on.

At this great night fair dollars were sold eight or nine for a guinea, or a Napoleon—too heavy to carry! In Spain the British army were paid in old English guineas and dollars. The 21st was my good day. I had no ague, but felt tired and excited after such a fight and a chase, for my horse was in the rear until the grand retreat began. It being now late, we halted for the night. I rode into a field of corn, so very high I could not be observed; here I dismounted, sat down and ate my supper, provided by the cook of his Majesty or some of his people! I tied my gentle little horse to my leg, gave him a long tether, lay down upon my sack, and fell asleep, *tout de suite*. Now and then "Sancho" would get too far nibbling at the corn and give me chuck. I pulled him in by the rope close to my bed, and soon fell over again in dreams of peace and home. I was very early astir, and found my companion, *cheval noir*, lying beside me; he was a great pet and a handsome fellow. Saddled, mounted, and away to look for my regiment which was scattered about without any regularity in bivouac; but *Freeman's* bugle, so well known to every 34th man, soon brought us all together,—no, not *all*, the prison of many a soul was broken up.

My servants were generally in great luck, having their legs and arms broken by musket-shot, and none of them killed outright except Tim Casey, and he was only *kilt*; but he made a most horrible whilalaloo about it, crying out, "Oh, *murdher*, I'm kilt entirely; I'll never see home—I'm ript up!" holding his bloody hand to his stomach. "Let me see where you're *kilt*, Casey; there is no *murdher* here; everybody kills everybody—that's the order." A ball struck one of his buttons, turned off, and ripped open the surface of his bread-basket from right to left without in the least spoiling his appetite.

Andrew Orrell, one of my chums, was playing "hide-and-seek" with a French voltigeur amongst the trees. I told him he would get a lump of lead that would stop his rations if he exposed his long legs to this rifleman any longer (he was all legs and a long Lancashire tongue), and very soon was he hit something like poor Casey. The ball broke a trousers button, turned off its course, which was intended for the "bull's-eye," went through his flank, and lodged at the backbone. I took out my penknife to cut it out, but he made such an oration, I knocked off surgery, and went to my own business. He was carried away, and came back all right in three months.

Lieutenant Ball had a narrow escape; a ball meant to go right through his head, was turned by the scale of brass on his cap, opened a furrow across his forehead, baring the bone and passing away on the other side. Poor A. B. C. (Allen Bellingham Cairns) was wounded, not badly; yet he died afterwards. I got his watch and key—the latter as a remembrance—no reminder like a watch-key. I have used it ever since, upwards of fifty years, and it is as good as new still; and, I may say, it has ever since been a nightly remembrance of my old comrade.

It was wonderful the multitude of extraordinary wounds that men received. I felt a curiosity in their examination, attending with the surgeons at times (it was the profession that I was first intended for, so many of my name being eminent men in Scotland); wounds in the feet and in the groin were the most painful and dangerous. Lieutenant G—— had both his eyes shot out. Lieutenant C—— narrowly escaped the same dreadful calamity; the ball passed close under the eyes, breaking the bridge of his nose, and spoiling his beauty. I have seen men wounded in every part of the human frame—some wounds most extraordinary and severe—and yet the men recovered I should hardly get credit for the relation, if I enumerated them here.

The morning of the 22nd of June displayed the extent of the spoil which the runaway Frenchmen left behind them; there was a scene rarely to be equalled for many leagues about Vittoria—the wreck of a mighty army, and plunder accumulated for years, torn with rapacious and unsparing hands from almost every province in Spain.

Waggons, and cannon, and caissons, tumbrils and carriages of all descriptions, upset and deserted, a stranger *mélange* could not be presented to the eye. Here the personal baggage of a king—there the scenery and decorations of a theatre—

war stores and china ornaments, all sorts of arms, drums, trumpets, silks, jewellery, plate, and embroidery mingled in strange disorder; wounded soldiers, deserted women and children of all ages imploring aid and assistance and seeking protection from the British—here a lady upset in her carriage —in the next an actress or a *femme de chambre;* sheep, goats, and droves of oxen roaming and bellowing about, with loose horses, cows, and donkeys—everything in lamentable confusion.

Camp followers were dressed up in the state uniforms of the King *Joseph's court;* the rough class of women-kind, drunk with champagne and Burgundy, and attired in silks and Paris dresses—once envied, perhaps, in a palace. The pride of France was, indeed, levelled with the dust after this signal defeat.

The greatest part of the enormous baggage and plunder was grabbed by the people who had the best right to it, viz. the Spanish peasantry following up our army. The sword of the king was secured, and a marshal's bâton was sent by Lord Wellington to the Prince Regent, who returned the compliment by sending him a bâton of a marshal of England. *Occa's* of women—wives, actresses, and nuns—were captured, but no *padres* that I heard of; all of them were treated with respect, and allowed to follow their husbands and sweethearts as they found opportunity.

A week or ten days were wholly occupied collecting the wounded and burying the dead, in a fashion, just as they fell. Men were found alive on the wide field the *ninth* day, where they dropped in obscure places: having crawled to some water-pools, they existed; but they were few. Carts were in constant motion carrying away from the hospitals dead men and amputated limbs—a scene of anguish to look on—the pale, shattered, desolate, blood-stained, helpless forms of soldiers, so very lately in fine health, marching along for six weeks in joyful glee to meet a sudden death and no grave. Our sawbones were not prepared for so much practice coming on them all of a heap, and hundreds died for want of medical care and hospital comforts—no fault to our medicals; they worked away day and night at their trade like good ones.

When the battle began, my old friend Doctor Maurice Quill was in his proper place in the rear of his regiment. He deposited his *carving tools* under a tree in charge of his hospital sergeant, and crept along in rear of the troops until he saw the men begin to fall, when he ran away back as hard as he could tear to bring up his mule and the apparatus. Doctors wore at this time cocked hats and feathers, and were not easily distinguished at a little distance from the general staff. As he went at speed on one side of a hedge, a general officer with his aide-de-camp came galloping up the opposite way. The General cried out, "There's an officer running away; stop him. Halloo! sir; where are you going to?" No answer. Both wheeled about their horses, and called loudly to stop. "Stop, sir!" cried the General, "and give an account of yourself and your name."

"No, no," said Quill; "I'm off; seen plenty of fighting for one day," and ran on. The General got furious; a court-martial at least crossed his mind as he pushed on after the *fugitive*, the stiff fence between them.

"Give your name, sir!" "Oh, never mind my ugly name; everybody knows me,—your life's not worth a dollar this blessed day. Go to the front and be killed if you like—every-one's being killed but myself—oh, such slaughter!" speaking all this time over his shoulder and running like blazes. On he went at full speed, pursued by his enemies until he came up to what he called his tool-box (the hospital panniers), told his hospital sergeant to load the mule and move up quickly to the front, while he got out a few things for immediate use, and then right about face and away back as hard as he could tear.

"Oh, I see it all now!" said the aide-de-camp; "'tis that wild fellow Maurice Quill—always up to some drollery in camp or quarters;" and with a hearty laugh they galloped away.

At early dawn on the 22nd, our bugles sounded the assembly, when men and officers might be seen emerging from ripe wheat-fields nearly as high as one's head, and from behind hedges and ditches and trees, until all the living got under arms to pursue the retreating enemy. About mid-day, as we were marching over the hills, there commenced a fearful thunderstorm. I was riding alongside of my friend Masterman (who gave me the two dollars at Estramos when I was so hard up on my way to Lisbon). Poor fellow! he was struck dead in a second of time by the lightning—his horse was also killed, the hair of his head was scorched, his watch-chain cut in two, and the little steel screws inside were extracted. The full force of the forked thunderbolt passed right through him; I was so electrified, that I lost all power of holding my horse, which ran away with me downhill in fright; my knees shook and trembled, my hands were useless. I lost all power of holding or guiding my little jennet, although I managed to keep the saddle, and gradually recovered. The glittering arms of so many men, no doubt, was a great conductor for the lightning—several were knocked down, but none killed; the regiment halted for a melancholy hour, the pioneers dug a grave under a big olive-tree.—Poor dear Masterman was rolled up in his blanket, and left behind! Awfully sudden: on this summer's morning to lose his hold of life, and pass away!

Alas! poor Masterman, so kind, so gentle—such a favourite with all of us—mourned for and deeply regretted—escaped from the battle of yesterday—to-day snatched off in a moment —but in those days nothing more sure than "battle, murder, and sudden death."

We followed after the runaways, leaving the great fortress of Pampeluna blockaded by the Spaniards. It was the key of the kingdom; had a garrison of 3,000 men, and an able commander, but was not victualled for a very long siege. When the French got well into the hill country, they gathered up some pluck, rallied, and contested every mile of ground: by this time they had lost *all* their guns, 150 brass cannon. We had many sharp affairs with them—so very unwilling were they to leave Spain, but never let them out of sight until we drove them right over the Pyrenees. They robbed and plundered everywhere *en route* to make up their losses; but murder and even worse crimes were combined with plunder. Our own men were very expert at times, just looking into houses along the way for a *parlez-vous* or a loaf of bread. On one occasion, opening a press, the poor man of the house fell over on the top of a big grenadier, quite dead; perhaps he had taken refuge in the press from the marauders, who, as they looked in, found the poor fellow hid there, and ran a bayonet through him.

Women and young girls were found on their own hearthstone, outraged and dead; houses fired, and furniture used for hasty cooking, as our army passed along. Such is war! We had the last brush with these vagabonds on the 30th June, *i.e.* on the Spanish side of the Pyrenees, while skirmishing in the wood up the hills. General Sir William Stewart, a brave and gallant officer, who had been wounded in the leg at Vittoria, was at our head, with a pillow between his leg and the saddle; he was here wounded again, for there was no keeping him out of fire—just like Picton, that old hero, always foremost in the fight—and so he now passed us, going reluctantly to the rear, held on his horse by two soldiers. "Sorry to see you wounded again, Sir William," we said. "Never mind—never mind me, gentlemen; take the hill—take the hill," was his reply. He had a lisp, and spoke quick; I can see him now, distinctly the bravest of the brave, cool and collected; he was always cheered by the men when at any time riding through the camp. We took the hill, of course; in doing so, Brigadier Sir William Pringle was badly wounded, shot right through the body, but he ultimately recovered. Our major (Worsley) tumbled over; some wag cried out, "There goes a step in the regiment;" but he was out in his reckoning, for the gallant major was on his legs *tout de suite;* his horse was shot in the head, and dropped like a stone; a bullet ruffled one of his epaulets, but left him all right for another day.

One of our sergeants, a fine young fellow, said, "We must not leave the major's saddle and bridle behind; I would rather carry it on my back." While stooping to unloose the girths, a French rifle-bullet hit him in the mouth, and took away his lower set of teeth quite handy; no dentist could have done it in half the time. It was an ugly wound, and deprived him of all acquaintance with hard biscuit for many a long day. I do not know what forty or fifty thousand of our men were doing at other points on our left; they may give an account of themselves, or some clever cove may do it for them; I must stick to my own people, General Hill and his division, and endeavour to *immortalize* myself by writing a book. There are, I believe, different ways of leaving a name in remembrance, and I honestly confess that I have no talent for book-making, and am one of the least qualified for such an attempt, and therefore ready to be "kicked, cuffed, and disrespected" by the press and by the public for such presumption.

At sundown, on the last day of June, we fired our last shots into the skirts of the *Parley Vous*, as we slashed them over the hills into their own country, while they carried along with them the curse of a whole kingdom!

We went down and encamped in the beautiful valley of Bastan to have some rest after our two months' *frolic* across the country; the men wanted washing, and shaving, and patching, and darning, scrubbing up, and a bit of polish for the next fight. I continued to sleep under a tree, my bed was the royal sack filled with ferns, dried grass, chopped straw, or anything soft that came to hand. In my good days I rode about the country, into the town of Alizondo, and made my acquaintance with the mountain passes, hamlets, and houses of the Basques—a quiet, primitive, honest people, like the Swiss, fond of their native hills, and speaking a language distinct from Spanish or French, very active and intelligent, detesting their French neighbours, who plundered them as they did every one else. They wore wooden shoes, and a *fac-simile* Kilmarnock bonnet.

Three of us chummed together; having a horse, I was considered the grand forager for the mess. I sometimes got a loaf of bread for a dollar; some milk and honey; the chestnuts were large and ripe; they flourished on great shady trees above head; my horse eat them raw; we preferred them roasted or boiled; they filled up chinks, and were a good stand-by, better than the acorns in bivouac at Salamanca. The Basque lingo was most difficult to get hold of; the only word I could retain in memory was "housequack," *i.e.* the bellows, which I often borrowed to blow up our fire under the chestnut tree. I

drilled our servants to be very civil to those people; they
would lend us anything they had. "Well, Tom, what did you
say to the lady of the house?" "O sir, I just seyd, plase
mam, will you lend us the housequack, an' she handed it out
at onst; but I forgot the name av the fryin'-pan, *ours* is goin'
in holes, an' *beint* of any much use." In fact, Tom was always
brushing the bottom of this old frying-pan with a sprinkling of
water to burnish our shoes, which had a wonderful effect on
leather, and was a tolerable substitute for Day and Martin. Try
it, gentle reader, in your next campaign, and you will see Tom
Shandy's receipt for polishing boots of a Sunday morning before
church parade! A chaplain was now in reality sent out from
England, and attached to Farmer Hill's division. My regiment
was here alone, and his reverence came to perform Divine
Service; twenty minutes was the regulation time. A square
was formed, the big drum placed in the centre to do the duty
of a reading-desk; the parson entered, made for the drum at
once, got one leg up, when the big drummer made a rush,
caught him by the tail, and pulled him nearly over, saying,
"You'll be through it, sir; the only parchment in camp." The
poor padre thought, he said, it was to *elevate* him in reading the
service. No one, of course, could keep his gravity during this
scene. I remember the text very well—in St. Luke iii. 14.
There went a buzz through the ranks. The men knew very
well they were six months' pay in arrears, and their daily bread
was killing and slaying their neighbours!

The 7th of July was one of my very worst ague days; but
turned out afterwards a day of rejoicing, thanks to our enemies.
I was lying under an apple-tree in the beautiful valley, *hors-
de-combat*, in a hot fit, my head splitting open, as I thought,
with pain; the day was extremely hot, which only aggravated
the malady, and increased my sufferings. All of a sudden the
drums beat to arms, the bugles sounded the assembly, and the
men hastened to the alarm-post, and the order of march was—
up the mountain as fast as we could go. I joined my company,
and *dragged* myself along with difficulty, faint and weary with
pain and debility. There was in those days a chivalry, an
esprit de corps amongst officers and men never to be absent if

possible when there was a chance of a brush with the enemy; it was a point of honour not to be detained by any trifling illness, and so I stuck to my trade as usual. When we got up to the table-land, we met the French advanced skirmishers, and renewed our acquaintance in a very unfriendly way, by knocking over a few of their riflemen; the compliment being returned, both sides went to work, and the matter was who would live longest under a shower of lead. Their supports came rapidly up, swelling their ranks, while our brigade, 28th, 34th, and 39th, decreased in numbers. We fired kneeling, to take down all the birds we could; still, so overmatched were we, that the combat became extremely doubtful; plenty of help *was coming* to us, but never came. A whole division of ours was lost in a fog, crawling up hill in another direction to take the enemy in flank. Wellington and his staff came up; but the fire was so brisk, and the heather about their horses' heels so torn up with musket-balls, he said, "This won't do, we must get away; these regiments will be sacrificed." The fog saved us; it came on so thick we were all soon rolled up in a cloud of darkness. The fire continued at random, the French still groping their way; we heard them distinctly talking and getting nearer and nearer. Being formed in line, both ranks kneeling, we gave one loud cheer and a volley, which took the shine out of them for half an hour, when they commenced another fire at a greater distance, all their shot passing over our heads. This waste of powder and ball lasted till eleven o'clock; but we never arose from the sod until daylight next morning. The fog then cleared away, and we saw the strength of our opponents far below, going home to breakfast!

When the fog rose in the morning under a bright sun, we discovered the extent of our loss. Lieutenant Ball, who was hit on the head at Vittoria, was here badly wounded. Some fellows were always being hit, while others—a few others—went through all the war without a scrape; the wounded were groaning on the heather all night, and not a drop of water within our reach. They always suffer extremely from thirst, and their cry is, "Water for God's sake!" I remember drinking more water on an occasion of this kind than I had done for a month previous. My servant followed me yesterday to the fight, seeing I was rather shaky at the start, and got his arm broken by a musket-ball; my two left-hand men had their legs broken. We had many wounded; the dead were left where they fell, and being myself first for escort duty, I got charge of all wounded in the brigade to take them to the hospital at Alizondo. The only conveyance for these poor cripples, with broken legs and arms and shattered shells, were some mules sent up by the Commissary. Two men were placed on each mule, with their broken limbs bandaged up in a way and dangling down. No help for it; no cart-roads in the Pyrenees, and the poor fellows were groaning with their sufferings all the way. When night came on I got my cavalcade under cover of an old cattle-shed I happened to spy out a little out of my way. The assistant-surgeon got them dismounted as quietly as possible, and laid upon some dry ferns. We had nothing to eat or drink; not a spoonful of water for the dying men. I could not sleep for their moaning and groaning all night. I could not see them nor help them in the dark. When the morning was welcomed in, I found that many had passed away to the promised land; the mortal part was left where the spirit took its leave. We had no means here to bury the dead. We got to Alizondo on the second day of torture and suffering, and glad I was when I delivered over my charge to the chief *saw-bones* and was allowed to depart for my home, which I always considered to be under the colours of my gallant corps.

On the 7th I was roused up in a fit of ague; I went into fire unexpectedly; in the excitement I forgot everything. I lay out under a cold damp fog all night; the ague took flight and *never* returned during the war!! Some fellows said that it was frightened out of me! May be so. I wish it had been frightened out of me sooner. I have had some severe shocks of it afterwards in the East and West Indies, and other climates; but I know how to treat it without any medical advice,—*quinine!*

I found my old corps with the flags flying on a table-land half-way up the Pyrenees, and they were here 8,000 feet high.

CHAPTER VII.

The Valley of Bastan. — Sharp Affair. — Sauve qui peut. — A Ride for a Doctor. — Wellington and Soult. — Affair before Pampeluna. — The Colonel of the 34th.—A Chance Lost.—Roncesvales.—Foraging.—The Lost Sentries.—Unrequited Bravery.

GENERAL HILL settled his head quarters in Alizondo. I was invited to dine with him by my old Captain E——, his chief aide-de-camp. A *great day* for G.B.! I had a better dinner with him afterwards in Belgrave Square! But he was always so kind and hospitable, so desirous to make one at home and talk over *the* old campaign, it doubled the agreeable pleasure of meeting him when Commander-in-Chief, with Egerton as his private secretary. I lost two good friends when they finished off their campaign.

The 2nd Division was encamped in the valley of Bastan, detaching a brigade in advance up the hills; from this brigade a regiment went forward a long way up (relieved weekly). This advanced corps gave the pickets and outposts, which were planted on the very tip-top of the Pyrenees. The view was very grand, and the climate up there charming. France lay right in our front, and as we looked down below, there was the French army in camp quite visible, and their drill going on as in a barrack-yard. "Plenty on 'em (as one man said) arter all the whackin' of late." To the left the sea and the ships—a glorious sight once more; on the extreme right the "*magnum mare,*" but quite out of view.

The 34th being the advance corps for the week, gave the pickets on the 24th July, commanded by Captain Moyle Sherer, a vigilant and distinguished officer. He had three subalterns, H——n, R——l, and P——s. On Sunday morning, the 25th, at dawn of day, the picket and outposts were suddenly attacked by an advance of French sharpshooters. The signal-gun was fired, when we got away up hill as fast as we could (the men never went on a parade at any time but in heavy marching order, just as if they were never to return to the same spot); but the pass up was narrow, steep, and tiresome, the loads heavy, and the men blown. We laboured on, but all too late,— a forlorn hope; our comrades were *all* killed, wounded, or prisoners. The enemy had full possession of the ground; some ten thousand men were there, nearly all with their arms piled, enough of them arranged along the brow to keep us back. It was death to go on against such a host; but it was the *order*, and on we went to destruction; marching up a narrow path in file, with men pumped out and breathless, we had no chance. The Colonel is always a good mark, being mounted and foremost; he was first knocked over, very badly wounded. The captain of Grenadiers (Wyatt), a very find handsome man, being next in advance, was shot through the head; he never spoke again; my little messmate, Phillips, was also killed. I thought at the time, what a sin to kill such a poor boy. Seven more of the officers were wounded, the adjutant, severely hit, tumbled off his horse and was left for dead (more about him hereafter). We persevered, pushed on, and made a footing notwithstanding our disadvantage, for the men were desperately enraged, and renewed all their exertions to be at them with the bayonet, but in vain. We kept our ground until we were minus, in killed and wounded, some 300 men and nine officers; some slight wounds were never returned. We did not think it very warlike to notice every *skelp* one got when little harm was done; but this little point of modesty was a mistake, found out too late, for at the conclusion of the war every officer who had been returned as wounded, was compensated from a great fund raised by the usual liberality of the English people, and many were well recompensed for the loss of a little *claret* or broken bone.

Different regiments scrambled up the hills to our relief, as fast as they could. The old *half-hundred* and 39th got a severe mauling; then came a wing of the 92nd and opened a flank fire on the enemy, while we moved over to another hill, got all our men left, and commenced a cross fire. The 92nd were in line pitching into the French like blazes, and tossing them over. They stood there like a stone wall overmatched by twenty to one, until half their blue bonnets lay beside those brave northern warriors. When *they* retired, their dead bodies lay as a barrier to the advancing foe. O! but they did fight well that day; I can see the line now of the killed and wounded stretched upon the heather, as the living retired, closing to the centre. Every regiment that came up lost its quota, and the French increased as the battle went on. We had two six-pounder guns up here for signal, to give warning. Richardson, self, and two other lads made an effort to turn them to salute the French, but a few rifle-shots stopped our play; so, for fear they should go over to the *other side*, we wheeled them round, and at the word "Let go," away they went rattling down the mountain with great velocity, perhaps never to be seen again. We 34th for the last hour had been amusing ourselves in comparative safety, picking off our *friends* in the distance, when a very large column came down upon us to stop our play; there was but one escape for us now,—to run away, or be riddled to death with French lead. The officer commanding, a brave man, saw how useless it was to contend against such a multitude, gave the word to retire at the *double*, and away we went down hill at a tearing pace. I never ran so fast in my life! Here the French had another advantage, rather a cowardly one; they kept firing after us for pastime; every now and then some poor fellow was hit and tumbled over, and many a one carried *weight* over the course, *i. e.*, a bullet or two in the back of his knapsack.

We were now broken and dispersed. Our bugles sounded, few heard them—some too far away! the old corps severely handled. We hoisted a flag at the bottom of the hill, *Freeman* blew his well-known blast, and all that heard the sound rallied here. Up another hill we scrambled, and passed the night "among the heather;" hungry, cheerless, and thirsty, I would have given a dollar for a drink of water. Lieutenant Simmons had his horn full of brandy slung on his back going into action, and was about to rejoice over it just now, but alas, the *bottle* was empty. A musket-ball played one of those practical tricks one hears of after a big fight. One passed through the horn during the row, and let off the brandy without any notice; Simmons knew that he had been slightly wounded in the side, little knowing it was a cow's horn saved him! Our sergeant-major found his arm very stiff about the *crook*, as he said; no blood, nor mark of a shot-hole; he pulled off his jacket, and found a ball lodged in his elbow-joint, which had run up his sleeve in this playful way. A young officer was shot through the nose, which, as he jocosely said, made him sneeze a bit! Every part of the human frame in one or other was riddled with shot, and many wonderful escapes were talked of that night,—were there any thankofferings?

In the middle of the night, a horseman nearly rode over me bawling out for a doctor. "What's the matter now; who's dead, that you want a doctor in the dark?" "Sir W. Stewart bleeding to death, they say." "Sorry for it; he's always getting bled by Frenchmen's lead; call louder, all the sawbones are asleep;" and he passed on. Soon after an orderly dragoon came thundering amongst us in our feather—no, in our *heather* beds, calling out for a guide (all such orders in the dark were circulated by a loud call). "Where to, France or Spain?" "No, sir; Alizondo." "Well, I know the way, I think, in the dark, if that will do." "All right, sir; will you come with me to the Quartermaster-General." "Yes, lead on, I want to warm my legs, the dew is heavy, and I feel stiff and powerless; I feel very like the Irishman's gun, that wanted a new stock, lock, and barrel, all in rags, and my barrel empty. Have you got any water in those holster-bags of yours?" "Not a drop, sir; not a grain of barley for my horse all day, nor a pick of a ration for myself, being the whole day mounted and riding about with orders." "The men got a great slashing to-day, sir; I see them coming down the mountains in hundreds wounded, for by what on 'em were left behind doubled up, an' the whole country below like a mixed fair. The commissary, artillery, baggage, and wounded all jammed in that narrow road, trying to get away; but we're near, sir;" and he called out, "The Quartermaster-General said that Sir Rowland Hill wished to get his division out of the hills the very shortest way into the valley by daylight." "Do you know any path?"

"O, yes, I think I will steer the column out of this darkness," and took my place, led the way down curving goat-paths, clear away into Bastan before sunrise. I had the personal thanks of the dear General, and moreover dined with him, had a sheep's head for dinner, the first I had ever seen decently cooked, a dish I have patronized ever since, as it makes a first-class curry.

A month had only passed away since the battle of Vittoria, and here the French stood triumphant on the Pyrenees, for all the passes were forced on the same Sabbath day! The truth was, the Emperor superseded his brother Joseph (it was but mockery to call him King), gave the command of the army to Soult, with orders to reorganize it, and, when prepared, force all the passes in the Pyrenees, assault Wellington, drive him back into Spain, relieve Pampeluna before it fell, and be quick about it! It can't be denied that his first efforts were successful; we all felt it to the bone, and the men were vexed and disappointed.

The French army came down after us very cautiously on the 26th, but declined battle, endeavouring to get round our flank, a movement well watched by General Hill. We retired and took up position on the 27th; they came on, looked at us, but would not engage in any war game that day either. Our great chief was engaged during all this *row* with the siege of St. Sebastian, which he left in a hurry, and came up to us in the nick of time, always the right man in the right place; all honour to his glorious memory. He saw at a glance the object of his adversary, and put his army in motion. Soult was pushing on for a great victory to restore the fortune of France. At a racing speed Wellington rode for Sauvoren, and seeing the enemy close at hand, is said to have dismounted, taken a look at Soult, as pointed out to him by a Spanish spy, pencilled a note on the parapet of the bridge, despatched it by his only staff-officer present, the late lamented Lord Raglan, then Lord Fitzroy Somerset, and rode up the hill alone. He was at once recognized by our troops, who raised a triumphant shout of gladness. The cheering swelled out loud and long as it ran through the line from corps to corps, and became that appalling shout which the British soldier is wont to give upon the day of battle, and which the army of France never heard unmoved!

Our field-marshal stopped in a convenient spot, conspicuous enough to be seen by his troops, so as to let them know that he was on the ground. It is said that he fixed his eyes on his formidable enemy, and speaking as to himself said, "Yonder is a great commander, but he is a cautious one, and will delay his attack to ascertain the cause of these cheers; that will give time for the 6th division to arrive, and I shall beat him."

The Marshal Soult made no attack that day. Nevertheless, there was some hard fighting at different points between the detached divisions of English, Portuguese, and the French, but now for another battle, which caused mourning and lamentation, pain and sorrow.

Early on the morning of the 28th July, our chief formed his army in order of battle in front of Pampeluna, in the midst of rugged hills, craggy rocks, and rivulets, and there waited the pleasure of the French field-marshal, who sent on his legions with all the ardour and determination of a warlike people, to win this day and let his troops once more into Spain to regain their reputation. Both sides were soon engaged, and under a biting fire. Both fought bravely, but nothing could stand against the ragged red-coats of old England, when they met their late acquaintance on fair honest ground, with any sort of equality. Both armies were jealous and vexed, the French having been whacked out of Spain, and the allies having met with some reverses of late. Now was the time, this was the day to decide a great and final triumph—ay, for a kingdom.

For two miles and more a storm of fire raged along the line; the ground was uneven, rugged, and hilly. Strong posts were taken and retaken with the bayonet. It was what the Duke called "bludgeon work." Charge succeeded charge; each side yielded and recovered ground by turns, yet all the noble valour of French effort was of no avail.

Wellington brought forward, at a critical moment and at full speed, the gallant Enniskillen and the Northampton regiments

(27th and 48th), who came with a rush from the hills, against the crowded masses of the French, rolling them backward in disorder and throwing them down the mountain side; and, with anything but child's play, these two regiments fell upon the enemy *three* separate times with the bayonet; and although their charge was irresistible, lost more than half their numbers. A great slaughter was going forward along the whole line of battle, the cannonade furious; every man held his life in his hand, to dispose of it to the best advantage for his own country. A French brigade made a great dash up a connecting hill. Our gallant Somerset regiment (the 40th) waited in stern silence, and with unwonted patience, until the enemy planted their feet (with their " En avant ") on the very summit, when the *war whoop of charge* was given. The whole mass was almost instantly broken to bits. Away they went at the double, a tempest of lead following their heels. *Four* times this assault was renewed, the French officers, caring for nothing but victory, dragging and driving on their weary and exhausted men to win or die! The thundering shock and cheer of the British soldier ever prevailed in these days; and at last, with their ranks thinned, heartless and fainting, hopeless from failures, the French gave way, having lost two generals, a great many brave officers, and 1,800 men in this part of the battle-field.

We had less sanguinary play against Count D'Erlong in another position. Every regiment drew a prize that day. The British soldier is a disciplined biped. Discipline is the sure means of conquering, without which bravery is useless; and ours was an army always ready to go into action, not to be driven. It was the difficulty to keep them back and restrain their impatience, game-cocks as they were, and as they proved themselves this day, and every day.

Soult was still very powerful, and kept up the *ball* day after day, hoping still to gain some advantage against Wellington. Of the danger and intricacy of this hill country, in manœuvring and fighting an army, no one can form anything like a true idea. A formidable enemy might be concealed within a mile and the sharpest eye not know it. The great chief, with an escort, I believe it was said, of the 43rd, went out to reconnoitre in the hills, and dismounted to examine his maps. A sergeant, who was sent up the hill to look out, had not been there long when he discovered the French winding round the side of the hill, where our Welling*ton* was sitting. (The Spaniards always laid a weighty emphasis on the *ton*.) One of the men holding his *caballo* (horse), Sergeant Blood, as his name was recorded, came flying down the rocky hill like a deer, calling out, "The French! the French!" He might have called out "The Philistines are upon you, and what a prize!" But the Duke was mounted and away at full gallop in a moment, not without a shower of bullets after him by the disappointed Frenchmen. There were spies in both camps, and they well knew the whereabouts of the grand prize! There was hard fighting and plenty of broken bones on the 29th and the following day. Then Soult went off in retreat the way he came, the whole British army at his heels like terrier dogs, snapping at him round every corner.

When our colonel was wounded on the 25th, shot through the knee-joint, the agony was so great he was put into a house by the road-side; his servant and the doctor (Murray) alone remained with him. The French advanced that day, and hearing that an English officer lay wounded here, Count D'Erlong, the general commanding, went in to express his regret and to assure him of protection and quiet; he placed a guard at the gate and a sentry at the door, with orders that no one should be admitted while his army was passing that way—a noble trait of generous feeling; but the Count was always a kind-hearted, good soldier, and respected his enemy. It was said at that time that he and Sir Rowland Hill, now in direct antagonism, had been at one time school-fellows.

It so happened that my regiment, in following up the retreating French army, passed along the same road over which we had retired, and coming to the little house in which the colonel had been left, and hearing from his servant at the gate that he was alive, the men gave one unanimous cheer, which so unnerved him, that the doctor came running out to stop a repetition of such kindly feelings. He said, "The colonel is doing very well; with the only help I had (one servant), I cut off the leg to save his life; the French behaved admirably, only asked the colonel's parole, would not take mine; the Count saying I had only done my duty. And now keep quiet," he said; "he knew the cheer came from his own men, but another like it might destroy life, he is so nervously excited."

In due time he recovered, went home, and was exchanged for a colonel of the French. He was appointed Governor of Pendennis Castle, married a wife, and had three sons in the army, all colonels.

We pushed on to the pass of "Donna Maria," where the French made a stand, and we had a big fight, the 34th leading; a thick fog prevented our pursuit, there was a small victory, and a loss of 400 left *hors-de-combat*. Soult kept on his retreat through the mountains, and Wellington kept his eye upon him like a hawk; but there is nothing certain in war— a great chance was lost, and here it is recorded. The French Marshal had got into a deep narrow valley and halted. The Duke gave strict orders to prevent fires being lighted, the straggling of soldiers, or any indication of the presence of our troops; placing himself amongst the rocks from whence he could observe every movement of the enemy. Our troops were ready to cut them off, when unluckily a few marauders entered the vale, and were instantly carried off by some French horsemen, when their whole column beat to arms and marched away; and thus a few plundering vagabonds deprived the great chief of the splendid success he had in his eye, and saved the French from a terrible loss. However, they were pressed hard, and although they got out of this prison, their chains hung round them; the pass was narrow, the beaten army was great, vast numbers of the wounded were carried by their comrades on their shoulders, while their baggage impeded the march, and all got mixed in extreme disorder. Prisoners and baggage fell at every step into our hands; men fled from their broken and confused ranks up the hills for safety, being all sorely crippled before they got out of this *trap*, to fall into another where they were wedged in a narrow road with steep rocks on one side, and the river on the other. Indescribable confusion followed;

the wounded, thrown down in the rush and trampled on by the cavalry, were calling out to our people for quarter, while very many were supported along, carried on branches of trees, on great coats clotted with blood, and gory stained sheets taken from the cottages,—wretched sufferers! brave men would not, did not fire upon them, and so they straggled along out of this labyrinth. The Spanish General Longa, as usual, did not attend to his orders, or the retreat of this part of the French army would have been entirely cut off,—but the prize was lost.

General Hill pursued his old friend D'Erlong to the pass of Maya. Pitching into his people as we went along, we helped them over the hills here, 8,000 feet high, and halted on the old battle-ground on the 1st of August, being absent only eight days! Our dead lay there just as they fell, only most of them stripped naked, decomposed, and swelled up to a vast size. Some had the appearance of being dressed in fine white muslin shirts, the skin inflated and raised up, from long exposure to the air—the *medicoes* may understand it, I don't. The vultures had been here, they always followed the armies—dirty birds of ill omen—they begin their feast with the eyes, and sometimes leave bare bones!

I was for picket, and had to pass the night in the midst of this loathsome company of horrible perfume and decaying humanity. Going my rounds I was continually stumbling over old comrades, and would then roll my head up in my cloak, and lie down amongst them for half an hour or so, jump up, and tumble over another ghost!

Next day we had all the dead covered with sods,—graves impossible on that rocky ground.

The second division now encamped on the tip-top of the Pyrenees, along the ridge from Maya to Roncesvales. Sir Rowland Hill pitched his tent amongst us and kept a sharp look-out against another surprise; for a surprise it was in July, and no mistake. I lost two of my messmates for whom I was very sorry, particularly for the joyful, rosy-faced lad Phillips; but there was no real grief for any one beyond a week or two,—all a shadow that passed away. Their effects were sold by auction. We bought their clothes and wore them, and they were sold again perhaps in a month, being once more part of the kit of deceased officers killed in action.

The mountain sides about the pass of Roncesvales were covered with thick woods, trees were felled, and log-houses built at every point where an enemy might approach, and we slept with one eye open. I formed a new alliance, got into another mess of three, our assistant surgeon, Robert S——n, president! A fine, handsome, clever young fellow, and a general favourite in and out of the regiment; he was afterwards surgeon of the 13th Dragoons and 7th Fusiliers. I was still the active forager for the mess, being mounted; our batman always took good care of my horse, which, with others, was always kept with the baggage when there was any fighting going on. Poor Tom Tandy, my old servant, was killed in one of the late battles; he knew my ways and winks, he knew how to forage in safety, and just the sort of fellow who, if hard up, could live on the smell of an oil-rag for a day or so. I got another intelligent sharp fellow, who knew a sheep's head from a carrot, was only sober when he could get nothing to drink, but never got into a scrape; along with the rations, he sometimes had a *present* of a duck, or an old hen from the "valley below." Pigs were few hereabouts, but the fairies would be kind at times and shove a little joint under the walls of our tent after night!

I used to ride into Alizondo, and get back the next day with anything I could pick up. A *dollar* a loaf for bread was the usual price asked and given, sausages and pork were scarce and dear, and no wonder after a French army passing twice through this little pretty town. Every man in a French army has the organ of destruction just over his eye; what he can't use he will destroy from pure mischief.

The weather was charming; we had little to do, little to eat, no books, and led a monotonous life. We would pass hours rolling stones down the mountains; it sometimes occupied three or four of us for an hour *engineering* at a great rock to get him up on the right end for a start; once in motion, nothing could stop its heavy velocity, it dashed through the forest trees amputating great limbs and branches, making such a row as it passed away, and leaving an echo which traversed the forest and deep glens even into France.

We had very advanced pickets posted in chain-links down the hills on to the French border within pistol-shot of the *Parley-vous*. I always led my horse down to keep me company, and get him some good grass feeding, when on this duty. There was a picket-house, where the men kept up a roaring fire. I took the sergeant out in the middle of the night to visit the outposts. One of the sentries was gone; we halted to listen for any sound or voice. We knelt down and put our ears to the ground, when we heard voices in the distance and gradually approaching us. It was dark; they knew where our pickets were posted every night, and thought to catch us asleep. I said, "They may make a dash. Fire at once in the direction, and alarm our men at the house." "Wait, sir," he said, "a moment. Let them come a bit nearer. Now, I hear them pushing through the bush;" and he fired. All the other sentries immediately fired at the moment. There was no other result that we could tell than the words "*Ah, grand diable !*" and all was quiet. My horse lay down beside me at the fire amongst the men, like a Christian, and we had no other adventure that night.

At one of these outposts our sentries had disappeared in the night three times, and always at the same place; good intelligent soldiers not at all likely to desert. Many surmises and opinions were advanced about this mystery. I recommended double sentries one night to be planted close to each other—one of them to have his ear to the ground frequently, to catch any sound or movement. The place was very quiet and retired, by the side of a goat-path amongst the rocks, and the night was dark and late. One of the sentries jumped up from the ground, where he had been most attentively listening, and whispered to his comrade that he heard a little rustling amongst the leaves and low brushwood. There was no wind, all else was calm and quiet. They now stood together a little more retired, round the edge of the rock breast high, and waited this coming ghost, as they said, with their flints fixed.

The men's names were Murphy and Styles. "Don't you hear a noise, now," said Murphy, "just like a pig *smellin'* for acorns?" "I do, and I think I see something crawling up here, like a bear. Will you cover him, and fire? I'll keep my shot in reserve—hush! It approaches slowly, on all fours, and crouches down." "I see it," says Styles; "it's a bear. Cover him well, and knock him over." And over he went at the instant. Both men waited a little—one to reload, and then cautiously advanced with fixed bayonets. The game was dead as a door-nail,—and what was it? A Spanish spy (perhaps) in the French service, dressed up in an old bear-skin, armed with a sort of tomahawk, short spear, and a *cuchillo* (Spanish knife). No doubt the same wild beast that carried off former sentries, who might not have been so watchful on their solitary outpost. We supposed this *wild beast* might have had a reward for every red-coat he caught alive. It is certain none of our men were found, dead or alive, after we missed them; and, again, the French had too much of military honour to engage in anything so unworthy of their noble character. The advanced sentries were always doubled in future.

Twelve battles had been fought within the last seven or eight weeks, in which the French lost 15,000 men, and the allies 12,000; and the streams of blood were deep, and everything seemed to recoil at death but the soldiers in this war. There were deeds of valour achieved by hundreds of British officers, within the last few weeks, that would astonish the soldiers of any other nation in the world. Wellington himself declared that "he could go anywhere and do anything with the army that fought at Vittoria and in the Pyrenees." Yet those officers were entirely neglected by the influence of cold aristocratic pride, injustice, and partiality. Promotion went too often by favour, *Court* influence, political intrigue, or Horse Guards interest.

I remember riding sixteen miles one day, through slush and mud, over the fetlock at every step, for no other purpose but to get a real dinner at St. Juan de Luz, and bring *home* something for our mess. The posada was crowded; horses and mules stood jammed together in the stable as close as they could pack. I bought a good bundle of forage for my poor tired horse, but his neighbours right and left had eaten two-thirds of it, for they had nothing provided for them. I had myself a wretched apology for a dinner, and a corner of the floor to lie on, without bed or blanket—neither of which one would desire if he meant to have a snooze; a soft plank is preferable to a *lively* mattress.

This was the Duke's head-quarters. My companion on the ride down to the coast was the *senior* lieutenant of the 11th Regiment, a man of long and good service. There was a death vacancy, and so fearful was he of being passed over, that *his* object was to see the Duke and to present his letters of recommendation to secure him a step which was his legitimate right. Many brave men were driven out of the service by tyrannical injustice. They could not brook the system of being passed by and purchased over by boys from the nursery, who stayed at home and never smelt powder. Army tailors had wonderful interest in those days!

CHAPTER VIII.

Ghostly Quarters.—Hard Lines.—A Snow storm.—Corporal Punishment.—Kindness is Better.—Tom Eccles. — Nivelle. — Victory. — Individual Bravery.—Spanish Ladies.—A Bull-fight.—Short Commons.—Maurice Quill's Wager.—Maurice wins.—The French fraternize.—How we got Cognac.—Paddy Muldoon.—Passage of the Nive.—Bayonne.

ALL military men who have seen much active service, have no doubt had many opportunities of witnessing the dash and courage of the British soldier; how, when the hour of danger approaches, his anxiety to meet it increases, and how, still more, he will court danger, although duty does not call on him to face it. I remember one striking example of the latter.

It was a practice permitted in regiments to send a steady non-commissioned officer down to the coast to bring up what good things he could purchase for the officers. He had his list, a bag of dollars, and a couple of mules, with a pass from the commanding officer. On one occasion, when the great siege and butchery was going on at St. Sebastian, a sergeant named Ball, belonging to the 28th, or "Old Slashers," was on his way with a party for this purpose. Hearing the guns, he pricked up his ears like an old hunter, persuaded his party to follow him, lodged his trust—some 2,000 dollars—with a Commissary, took a receipt, dashed on, joined the storming party, survived, reclaimed the money, made his purchases, and returned to his regiment without any boasting or bravado. Insensible to fear or danger, this was the stuff our men were made of!

We changed our quarters or camp from Maya to Roncesvales. It was late when we pitched our tents in a beech wood; all tired, we lay down upon the sod, and were soon asleep. The first object that caught my eye in the early dawn inside our dwelling, close to my nose, was the two feet of a dead man with his toes up.

"Hallo!" I cried; "whose ghost are you, my friend? and how came you here?" "O, begad!" says my comrade, "here is a fellow's head under my pillow of ferns! We are in some graveyard where they don't bury the dead; we have pitched our tent in the dark on the late battle-ground, amongst the dead." "By Jove!" says Captain Darcy, a rollicking Irishman, "I didn't pitch at all. I saw a fellow snug asleep in his blanket, and lay down quietly at his back to keep myself warm. When I cleared my eyes this blessed fine morning, who was it, do you think?—don't know? A dead man, sir, without a rag on his back, enough to frighten a donkey!" Many of the old Buffs and 20th had fallen here on the 25th of July; we knew them by their buttons. They had not been buried; we had them all covered up and changed our ground.

We led a monotonous idle sort of life here; we had no fine view into France, as at Maya; it was a thick wood before and behind us, outlying pickets were our only amusement!

At Roncesvales, a very small town on the highway from Spain into France, there was a posada, a sort of inn or caravansera, full of muleteers and ladrones, followers of the army. I rode down there one day to dine at the *table d'hôte*, put up my horse and stopped an hour to regale the inward man on a sausage and some rice, oil, and *vino tinto*. I smelt strong of garlic for three days afterwards—so I was told. Going into the stable for my horse, he *was* there, but the saddle and bridle absent without leave. I called out the patrone, kicked up a dust, but the *innocent* landlord knew nothing about it. I persevered in my search, twenty or thirty fellows watching me; at last I discovered the treasure up in a loft, covered over with chopped straw. I saddled my jennet, rode away in triumph, but never to return to dine at Roncesvales.

Our brigade returned to the Maya pass, and we had the pleasure of looking down upon the French army in the distance becoming again organized and getting ready for action. We overlooked their camps and saw their drills going on; they could only see our flags flying above them, the old "flag that braved a thousand years the battle and the breeze."

October came on, and with it the snow, which buried us all up for some time. We were frequently dug out of our tents of a morning by the pioneers. My old captain, who never loved fighting, had gone away somewhere to take care of himself, and I had no one to cash a bill for me at thirty per cent.! My best donkey died in the snow, and my mule was stolen one night when I was on outlying picket. I sat down now in real grief, and could have cried with vexation. Misfortunes seldom come alone; here was I in a fix; I had paid sixty dollars for the mule and forty for the donkey; there was no remuneration, a dead loss of one hundred dollars to be made up from my pay, six-and-sixpence a day, minus income-tax, which was never forgotten to be deducted from our paltry pay, which was now again five months in arrear. I could not bear this double misfortune with a patient endurance, and fear that I was very stormy about it; but, *cui bono*, what can't be cured must be endured; it might have been worse; had we got a sudden order to move, I should have had no choice but to leave my little baggage behind me, but the snow kept us fast. Provisions became very scarce; bread, six pounds, thirty reals, or about six shillings a loaf, when we could get one; anything else to be had was equally dear, and no wonder, when such a multitude of *locusts* were on the ground; towns, and villages, and hamlets of white *canvas* to be seen everywhere, all alive with red-coats and blue. The Spaniards were not particular in *their* dress—a coat, like *Joseph's* of many colours, seemed most in fashion—and with a ration of beef (raw), or any bit of plunder, stuck on the bayonet, they passed on in their own rollicking, independent way, more like banditti than soldiers.

There was always some officer being killed, or disposed of, which caused an auction sale of effects, and so I bought another stout baggage animal on *tick*—we always got credit until the next issue of money, or by a bill on home, which was more acceptable—somehow, my money never lasted its *natural* time! As Paddy said who lost the despatch on the road, "It eloped out of his pocket."

We had many severe snow-storms at night, and one day in particular, a hurricane that floored every house in the town, church and all. The commanding officer's marquee was called by the wags the church, the rest of the tents the town. Huge branches were torn from the trees and whirled through the air like feathers; thin streams swelled into torrents, and dashed down the mountain ravines, rolling great stones with a mighty clatter; the melting snows increased into rivulets and waterfalls, where so very lately we could not get so much as would fill a teapot; in the distance, we could observe the sea, in terrible commotion about Bilboa and Santander, where many fatal disasters occurred. This very rough weather did not last long, and glad were we to see the heather green once more. I always had a good bed since I picked up the *royal* sack at Vittoria; stuffed with leaves or chopped straw it was invaluable; yet I was doubled up with rheumatism for nearly three weeks, and unable to run in a foot-race, sweepstakes, a dollar each, ready money, the second in to save his stake. Very few could beat me in this sport, and none with the pole.

Pampeluna was still holding out; being the centre of a ring no one could get out, no one get in; and so the question was only a matter of time, and many were the bets about its fall; the most common was, "Give me ten guineas* and I will give you a guinea a day until the town falls" or, as the case might be, five, six, or seven guineas.

Pampeluna, the key into Spain, did fall; not before the garrison had eaten up all the prog in the city, as well as every horse, dog, donkey, cat, rat, and mouse that they could catch; they held out bravely until starvation compelled a surrender, and no fortress being now in our rear, Wellington prepared to enter and visit our old *friends* in la belle France. We left our snow-capt mountain homes on the 9th of November, and descended the hills to cross the border, just to see what the *parlez vous* were doing there so long, and soon found that they had been very industrious since July last, fortifying an immense position on the Nivelle, extending all the way to the seacoast, about sixteen miles.

* The British army was paid in guineas.

We were, under General Hill, on the right of the army, the Duke on the left, fighting in the mountains. For weeks past there was a continued struggle going on to dislodge the French from strong posts they had occupied in the intricacy and labyrinth of this hill country. Other generals, brilliant and brave, commanded the centre, and there lay the promised land before our eyes; who will cross the border and live?

Few people, I fear, ever thought of danger or death, heaven or hell; death was too familiar to be looked on with terror, and made no impression. I never saw a Bible nor do I remember ever seeing any one read the Bible, although that is *the* book, a sure guide on our way to eternal life. We never thought that the time was short and the soul precious, where the man spared in the battle of to-day was killed on the morrow. I don't say that men did not pray, but I never saw but one on his knees. Yet here was a palace for prayer—pray in the open air, " 'Tis God's palace."

> To kneel remote upon the simple sod,
> And sue *in formâ pauperis* to God.

What could be more acceptable? or what place more appropriate for a soldier? But soldiers were not looked upon in those days as parts of humanity, although wasting their lives to keep the people of England in possession of their wealth, their homes, and firesides.

Corporal punishment went on everywhere the whole year round. Men were flogged for small offences, and for graver crimes flogged to death—*a thousand lashes* were often awarded by court-martial. I have seen men suffer 500 to 700 lashes before taken down, the blood running down into their shoes, and their backs flayed like raw red-chopped sausages. Some of these men bore this awful punishment without flinching for 200 or 300 lashes, chewing a musket-ball or bit of leather to prevent or stifle the cry of agony; after that they did not seem to feel the same torture. Sometimes the head dropped over to one side and the lashing went on, the surgeon in attendance examining the patient at times to see what more he could bear, and I *did see* with horror a prisoner receive *seven hundred* lashes before he was taken down. This was the sentence of a general court-martial, carried into effect in the presence of a brigade, for an example.

We had certainly some very bad characters sent out to fill up gaps in the ranks of the army, sweepings of prisons in Great Britain and Ireland; but such punishments were inhuman, and I resolved in my own mind if I ever had the chance of commanding a regiment I would act upon another principle. The time *did* come, and I *did* command a gallant corps for eleven years, and abolished the lash. Kindness is the key to open the human heart, and with that key I reformed the worst characters. It does not always tend to reform a man by bullying and abusing him before his comrades. I often made a deeper impression by taking a bad character into my room privately, speaking to and admonishing him in a sort of friendly way, appealing to his better feelings, and with a promise to forget all the past. In this way I reformed one of the most drunken characters I ever met wearing a red coat. He became the quartermaster of a militia regiment afterwards, a teetotaller, and a most intelligent, useful officer. His name was Murray.

On the evening of the 9th of November we bivouacked on the broadside of a heather brae (out of sight of the French outposts not far away) to eat our supper off whatever might be found in the old haversack; little and good would have been acceptable, but it was generally less and bad. We lay in groups and talked of the morrow, and of a great battle sure to come off, for which the two game-cocks of England and France were long preparing.

"Now Tom Eccles," I said, " good night, and mind that if you run your jolly red nose into danger, as you always do at the first flash of fire, we will miss you to-morrow evening." This was a most excitable, young, thoughtless Irish officer, who had fought through the whole way up to the present Lord Mayor's day. He had nearly lost one of the colours of the regiment in Albuera by running far in advance of the battalion while fighting in line; the staff of the flag was cut by a shot in his hand, while he was loudly cheering on the men. Nobody could hold him, he was always in the front of the battle. When the morning signal-gun fired for our advance, the whole army already being under arms, loaded and ready for action, we went forward by divisions, brigades, and regiments, according to the nature of the ground and previous arrangements. Skirmishers to the front. In ten minutes or so the dawn was lighted up by the flashing of great guns and small arms. The fusilade ran down the line like wildfire. Poor Eccles, always foremost, was riddled to death with French bullets. We never saw him more.

Several points of the enemy's position were assailed at the same time, and some of their intrenchments and redoubts taken at the point of the bayonet; but these were minor works in advance, which were only taken after a sharp resistance and loss on both sides. They were beaten back to their stronger position, well defended and guarded by batteries, breastworks, and plenty of cannon, with brave men and gallant officers ready for death or victory. "En avant" was their continual cry, and "Vive Napoleon," "Vive l'Empereur." Our shells and round shot kept them uneasy on their ground, while our men were advancing in their old formidable way of renewing acquaintance with "Johnny Crappo," as the soldier red-coats so often called them. It was hard work charging up these sloping hills, receiving a heavy fire in the face, and losing men at every step; but if a certain number were destined to fall, the survivors only got the more excited in strength, agility, and resolution, feeling determined to win, and never looking behind. Oh! how clearly I can look back and see that day and the noble deeds of valour displayed on both sides. That gallant *chef de bataillon*, leading on his men, waving them forward with his cocked hat at arm's-length high in air. He rode far in front and cheered them on, while our shot were rattling amongst their legs, our men saying, "Well, I'm blowed if I like to knock him over, he's so plucky." "Ay, Bill, but you see he must come down, for he wants to be killed." "Faith, and I'll make him leave that," says a big Irish grenadier, "or he may be riding over us," when down he tumbled off his charger as dead as a stone. I was really sorry for him at the moment, but he was madly brave. All this was but a preface to the great battle of the day then only beginning.

Ninety thousand of our troops, with ninety-five pieces of artillery and 4,500 cavalry, descended to fight this great battle. I believe the French army were less in numbers; they had more cavalry; they were of one country and one language, while the allied army were a mixture of English, Spaniards, and Portuguese, the Spaniards never to be relied on in the moment of trial and danger. The French too were fighting *in* France, *for* France, and on a very strong position which they had been fortifying for three months, so they had no disadvantage.

The river Nivelle formed a semicircle; both flanks of the French army rested on that river. In the centre of their commanding position many hills and mountains were strongly fortified with all the skill and ingenuity of Frenchmen. I believe such defensive posts could not be wrested from our old red-coats, but our fellows took them all that day under a most tremendous fire, and an avalanche of great stones which rolled down the hills amongst them and made them jump about like buck-goats, as they expressed it.

General Hill, with 25,000 men, threw himself on the left flank of the enemy, and made his attack. General Sir John Hope assailed the right, while the great Duke forced the centre after a most severe conflict. We had redoubts—batteries, abbatis, and deep intrenchments in our front, with a determined and most formidable foe well planted behind them, shooting fast and thickly, as we advanced—their skirmishers all driven in by this time;—the battle now thickened fast, but no one could see very much of this brilliant fight beyond his own regiment or brigade; indeed, at times I could see nothing from the obscurity of powder-smoke.

As we advanced, the red-glare flash of the cannon, the bellowing of the guns, and the white puff far to our left, showed us that death and destruction were extremely busy, but that the fight was going on in our favour.

I was on the right, with Lord Hill, and when the moment arrived to make the grand *coup*, he made a flank movement, getting on the French left, while the centre of their position was penetrated by one grand and tremendous effort. The day was ours—they began to retire; and once the chain was broken, nothing could stop the current of their speed. Away they fled; d—— take the hindmost; nobody wished to stop them! Our fellows forgot their fatigue in the moment of victory, hurried on and after the enemy with a cheer and a volley, and many fell at the eleventh hour. I confess I was not sorry to see them give way; for we had enough blood and brains on the sod for one day, our loss being 2,690 officers and men, 2 generals, the late Lord Strafford and Sir James Kempt, wounded. The loss of the French: 4,260 men and officers, 1,200 prisoners, one general killed; 50 cannon and their field magazines taken, to swell our triumph; and great *swells* we thought ourselves that day!

We passed on through their lines of defence, where they had been so long domiciled; their huts were extremely neat and comfortable, many had their green blinds over their little lattice windows; their neat little fireplaces, bedsteads of green boughs, shelves for their prog, and arm-racks, so like the natty Frenchman in camp. We found their rations uncooked, and plenty of onions and other vegetables, which were transferred *tout de suite* into our haversacks *en passant*. We pressed on with a running fire after them until sundown; then gave up the chase, stretched our weary limbs on the November sod, turned out the contents of our larder—a Dutch cheese, onions, biscuit, cold ration beef, and a little rum—and finished off the breakfast, dinner, and supper all at a go, went to roost, and thus ended another chapter of the war, as recorded in history.

It was marvellous how quickly the dead, and often the wounded, were stripped on the battle-field by the camp-followers of the two great armies,—an unhallowed trade, and no stopping it. I remember nearly stumbling over the bleeding body of a young French officer rolling in the dust, speechless in agony, and stark naked! He was very handsome, well formed, and from his light moustache he had not numbered twenty years. A ball had passed right through his body, poor fellow, and his end was near at hand. I had wished him out of pain before I passed on. Close by him lay one of his rough soldiers, also stripped naked, showing a terrible and fatal wound, and rolling over and over in the dust, for the November day was warm, and the ground very dry.

Many young officers have an opportunity at times of distinguishing themselves in battle, while others are more careful of life, or may not have the chance. Two or three I may name whose memory will never die as long as the history of the Peninsular War is read. Lieutenant-Colonel Thomas Lloyd was killed to-day at the head of the 94th regiment; he was a valiant officer, skilled in knowledge and of great experience; he predicted his own fall, as many often do before a battle, without any abatement of courage; when he received a painful and mortal wound, he remained on the ground watching the fight, and making his own observations, until death closed his eyes where he fell, at the age of thirty years.

Another young fellow, a simple lieutenant, about nineteen, bearing many wounds, in person very slight, and so very handsome that the Spaniards thought him a girl in disguise, fell on that day; so vigorous, active, daring, and brave was he, that the old soldiers watched his looks on the battle-field, and followed wherever he led, and obeyed his slightest signal in any difficulty or danger. Edward Freer was well known; one of three brothers, who all died in the service; he had also that presentiment of death in the coming battle so often felt and expressed by military men; he was pierced by several balls in the early part of the morning while storming what was called the Rhune rocks amongst the hills. Old soldiers wept for him, even on the battle-ground, when they heard his fate!

After five hours' hard fighting about the above rocks, where poor Freer was killed, the Spaniards cowed, and hesitated to attack an outwork, or abbatis, behind which a very strong regiment of French were firing as hard as they could load. Lieutenant Havelock, of the 43rd, who was then on the staff, a young officer of a brave and fiery temper, could not resist this opportunity of showing the Spaniards the shortest way how to quench this murderous fire. He took off his hat, called upon them to follow him, and putting spurs to his horse, at one bound and a dash cleared the fence, and went headlong amongst the enemy; the Spaniards followed, shouting and hurraing for " El chico blanco." This one shock broke the spirit of the French, and sent them flying down the hill, the Spaniards in their turn paying them off as fast as they could load, and crying out, " Viva el chico blanco ! " (Long live the fair boy !) for he was very young, very fair, and very brave. The Spaniards would have fought well had they been led in this gallant style; but their chiefs were too haughty, proud, and selfish to admit English officers to command in their service. Not so the Portuguese; every regiment, I believe, was commanded by an English officer, who obtained a step of rank as he passed from his own corps into the other; so a captain in my regiment became a major, with major's pay in the Portuguese service, and his superior rank was confirmed after the war. The Portuguese army was always well and gallantly led, fought well, and ranked next to the English troops in all ways.

Marshal Beresford was their chief, and he sent his troops into the field well disciplined and well clothed, with an *esprit de corps* not so well understood amongst the Españoles. There was more genuine heroic pride amongst the ladies of Spain than in the ranks of the army. I remember a beautiful Castilian maid looking from the balcony of her house on to the square where some Spanish troops were again preparing to take the field after a severe defeat and a run for it. She said, " Los Engleses son bravisimos, pero nuestro general es una vieja " (" The English are very brave ; but our general is an old woman "), and concluded by saying or speaking through those bright expressive dark eyes, " I will never marry a man who will not distinguish himself in the army of Spain and for the honour of his country ! "

" Bravo, Señorita," I said ; " you are worth fighting for."
" Gracias, Señor ; " she replied, " á-Dios ! hasta la vista," and she tripped lightly away.

I saw her afterwards enjoying the fashionable but barbarous

delight of a bull-fight, in the square where all the beauty and fashion of the town were assembled, seated in the balconies, and eager as we are on our race-course to see the " Derby."

There were a multitude of people below enthusiastic for the *sport*. The different entrances into the square were secured by wooden bars fixed into the grooved stone sides. A bull was driven in, who faced the audience with dignified simplicity; he was hooted, jeered, pricked with spears, and taunted for his patient forbearance, but declined a quarrel with his adversaries on any terms, and was turned out in disgrace. Another of the tribe was driven into the arena, a very stout, fierce-looking fellow, with short, sharp horns, a fiery eye, and full of mischief; some one gave him a prick of a lance behind, when he made a sudden rush forward, caught a fellow on his horn, and pitched him up in the air like a sheaf of corn, then stood with a defiant look, pawing up the ground, undecided what to do next. I was in the crowd, expecting safety amongst so many, and, as I supposed, out of horn's length, when this wild beast made another charge, cleared all before him, and took a bit out of my best holiday white trousers behind with the tip of his horn. My conscience! if I did not run for it, and soon found myself high up in a balcony, never to be seen again amongst such wild beasts in a bull-fight!

This poor beast was now driven to utter madness by his tormentors. Several men were carried away wounded, perhaps dead; two horses were killed, and dragged out of the square amongst the cheers of the people above, the ladies waving their handkerchiefs. This was quite delightful!

The square was now clear of all but two expert horsemen with spears and scarfs, and two or three regular professed bull-fighters on foot, armed and dressed in the same way. They were the most expert, active fellows I had ever seen; when the bull made a charge at one of them, he threw a red mantle over his head, and slipped aside. Now a horseman attacked him with his spear, and there was another rush head foremost, horns nearly touching the ground; it was surprising the dexterity with which the horses were managed so as to escape; however they were occasionally ripped up! The poor beast was foaming at the mouth, with wild bloodshot eyes, but still powerfully strong, when the matador, the great leader in these *games*, jumped on his back while a mantle had been thrown over his head and horns, and gave him the "*coup-de-grâce*," and 1,000 voices gave consent to this finale with no end of bravos, and the now happy bull was dragged away. This is the national sport of Spain; so enjoyable by all classes of the people, from the grandee to the pisaño; and is it less cruel than the cock-fighting of England, now happily abandoned?

Our supplies now became very scanty indeed, and there were symptoms of discontent in the camp, for it was reported that some commissaries had a league with speculators down at Bilboa and St. Ander, and used the public mules for getting up luxuries for sale at a fabulous cost; but our great chief appealed to the military honour of the army to be patient and firm, and the supplies would come in as usual in a few days. The Duke had only to make an appeal at any emergency to his ragged red-coats, and they would go through fire and water for him, ay, to the death. It was hard on those fighting fellows to be so long in arrear of pay, and to have their rations cut short. I paid myself sixteen dollars for a pair of boots, brought up from the coast; and everything else was equally dear.

Sir Thomas Picton told his commissary one day, that if he did not find rations for his men, he would hang him on a tree. The commissary became very indignant at this insult (as he termed it), and went off to Lord Wellington to complain. After hearing the whole story with wonderful complaisance, he said, "Did Sir Thomas *really* say so?" "Yes, my Lord, those were his very words." "Very well, you had better get the rations, or you may be sure he will keep his word. I can do nothing for you; good morning!"

The commissary returned and found the rations for his brigade.

Maurice Quill, joking on the parade-ground one day after the men were dismissed, said, "Who will ride over to headquarters and smell out some prog? I used to get a sheep's head upon *tick* once a week from our butcher, but I never see head nor horns now." "O," says Tom Higginbottom, "I suppose you're going to dine with Lord Wellington." "Well, I might do that same and do worse. As for you, Mr. Higginbottom, you begin to crow very loud that you have got the use of your Irish pin again; the next time you get a crack on the leg perhaps I may give you the chance of a pension by taking it off! *I am* going over to head-quarters; and if any of you sporting fellows are inclined for a bet, I'll stake ten dollars that I will see Lord Welling-*ton* (as Tom Higgy takes the liberty to call him), and borrow ten dollars from him before I come back, and more than that too, I'll bet other ten dollars I will dine with his Lordship." "Done, done, done," shouted (with loud laughter) many voices. "Win or lose, my coves, the money to be paid the next issue of pay;" and the bets were booked.

Sawbones, as the subs called him, was full of adventure, and loved a joke whatever it cost; but this day's excursion and his bets would have shut up any common-place man in the camp. However, he mounted his mule in a most confidential *cut*, as they said, and we saw him really off; whistling along to bear his courage up, turning over in his mind, no doubt, the sort of reception he was likely to meet from so great a man as we all justly thought the Grand Duke to be. Riding up valiantly to the quarters of his Lordship, he gave a thundering knock with a big stick at the door, and asked if the Duke of Wellington lived here. "Yes, sir," said the orderly, "here is an aide-de-camp coming. May I ask your business, sir?" "I wish to see Lord Wellington, if he is at home." "His Lordship is in the house, but too much engaged to see any one to-day; I will take your message to his Lordship." "No, I thank you, if I can't see him to-day, I will wait until to-morrow." "Something particular, perhaps, you wish to say in private." "Precisely so." "Well, step in, and I will see what I can do for you." Away he went and told his Lordship that "a Doctor Quill was below in a state of anxiety, and would not take any denial, came a long way to see your Lordship, and could not go back until he delivered his secret."

K

"Well, well, show him up." After some bowing and scraping—"My Lord," he said, "I am the surgeon of the 31st, and have come over to pay my personal respects, and to *see* your Lordship, and——"

"Yes, yes (cutting him short), how are you all getting on in the second division, many men in hospital? You must get them out, we will want them all by-and-by." "Indeed, my Lord, I was going to say, that we are badly off for hospital supplies, and no money to be had; I think I could get many restoring comforts for the invalids that would put them on their legs if I might make bold enough to ask your Lordship for a loan of ten dollars until the next issue of pay, when I will return it with a thousand thanks." "Very well, very well, Mr. Quill, you shall have it; how far have you come to-day?" "O, indeed, I have rode seven long leagues on an empty stomach, and there's not a bit of an inn over the whole country where a body could get a morsel of dinner." "O, well, if not too late for you, stay and have some dinner before you return, we dine at six. Good morning, Mr. Quill."

Quill's eyes opened wide and joyfully at this invitation. He was punctual to *the six* as he said. All his wit and humour came to the surface. He kept the table in a roar of laughter all the evening until he retired with his ten dollars and his Wellington dinner, got a shake-down with his friend the aide-de-camp, and his whack of brandy and cigars; got safe home next day and claimed his bets. He told his story honestly, and gave his reference; but there was no question about it, every one knew him to be as upright and honourable as he was eccentric and surcharged with mirth and glee when others were desponding.

Some impudent fellow asked him one day why he had exchanged into the 31st. "O, just because," he said, "I wanted to be near my brother who was in the 32nd." That man was shut up, and asked no more questions.

The weather became very wet and rainy about the end of November, but we happened to get under cover in some hamlets near the Nive, hard up too for provisions, and no money; the French had cleared the country of everything as they retired, like so many locusts. I had three articles that I could pawn, or pledge, or exchange, and they must go : an old half-crown, and the silver fork and spoon I bought in Lisbon. The half-crown had been given to me when a lad, by a kind, good old lady who said at the time with great simplicity, " My dear, as long as you keep that, you will never want money ! " She was right; but I thought I had kept it long enough, and exchanged it for an old hen, the mother of many a brood. The fork went for one loaf of bread, and the spoon followed in a few days. An iron fork was always my abhorrence, but there was a necessity. Bread was dear; when an old Spaniard said to our paymaster, "I can't eat your gold, Señor, I'm starving myself." The money offered was sufficient to buy a baker's shop well stored.

The French crossed the Nive,—it was now our line of demarcation. We planted our line of pickets along the left bank, while they did the same on the other side, with an understanding between us that there should be no hostilities without due notice. The river was narrow, but rapid in the rains; we kept watching each other carefully day and night, yet were good friends.

We conversed with the French officers across the stream; they told us of their many escapes in action, pointing to bullet-holes in their *head-dress*, and why they had retired *just now*, "just to collect all their forces and be ready to return to Spain when the Emperor came down to take the command personally." In reply, we told them how happy we should be to meet them all in *Paris* soon. This little badinage went on with good humour; we exchanged newspapers occasionally, rolling up a stone in one and throwing it over, and getting one in exchange.

On the very day that we entered France, the Spaniards lost no time in beginning their foraging excursions amongst the people and spreading themselves over the country, committing all sorts of villany on their murdering excursions. They considered marauding, murder, and plunder their chief duty, now that they got into an enemy's country; the poor French people fled from their homes in terror after witnessing the frightful excesses of those wild and reckless fellows, whose country, no doubt, had suffered most fearfully for many years under the dominion of the soldiers of France—not from the peasants of Gascony.

Wellington marked his lofty character of justice in putting to death all the marauders he could grasp, and sent back into Spain their whole army, save that of Morillo's division. Thus confidence was restored, everything was paid for, and a friendly intercourse established—much to our satisfaction and advantage.

Our men made acquaintance, too, with the French soldiers across the river. This being a permanent picket station, they built a hut here, which was added to daily until it became a water-tight, snug little dwelling, and a shelter from the rains. It stood just opposite a ford, with the entrance facing the French picket on the other side. There were stepping-stones of large size across, which were used by the country people when the river was low—one day they were all dry above water, and the next covered, perhaps, by a torrent.

Our fellows knew there was *brandy* in France, but the matter was how to get it. They made themselves very agreeable to their neighbours, calling out at times "*Bono-frances*," *Fromage*, *Cognac*, and *Tabac*, which seemed to be understood over the way, so they established a telegram when the river ran low, they subscribed their coppers, put them into a mess tin, gave it a rattle to draw the attention of the sentry; and, without any arms in hand, one of the picket stepped down to the water, gave his tin another rattle, placed it on the centre big stone, calling out "*Cognac!*" and retired. By-and-by it was taken away, and returned in the evening full of brandy (not likely of the best quality). The relieving picket was let into the secret, and the trade went on for a while, but not so smooth as the stream, for the brandy-pot forgot to come back one day. One Paddy Muldoon, a big Irishman—always very fond of a *dhrop*, as the boys said—was very indignant at this *thratement*, and watched an occasion to square accounts with the *robbers acráss* the *wather*. Seeing the sentry put down his firelock for a few minutes to go into the hut, he dashed across, laid hold of his arms; and, as the rogue of a *parlez-vous* stepped out, he gave him a *clout* on the head and brought his firelock over to his own side in pledge for the brandy-pot.

Soon after this feat the French officer on duty came down to the bank and called over for the officer of our picket, told him the true tale, and requested that the firelock might be restored, or the young fellow, who was but a conscript, would be tried for leaving his post, and severely punished.

A search was made in the hut, the musket found and restored, the French officer returned thanks, and Paddy was sent back a prisoner to the camp, where he was tried for the offence, found guilty, and sentenced to a corporal punishment. He was a brave, dare-devil soldier, and his defence was honest and truthful. He said "he only wanted back the money or the brandy, an' did not want to be done by any ov them frog-ating fellows, who he was chasing all over Spain for three years, and hoped the *coort* would consider his good service, and the next time he met this fellow, he might rely on it he would never see his firelock again." The punishment was remitted, and the brandy trade stopped.

The weather was now mild, but very damp and rainy; the winter had really set in and kept us under cover until the usual time of turning out, one hour before daylight, when all the troops were on their respective alarm-posts until dismissed, and we could see a white horse at a mile distant, was the most disagreeable part of our war game. On the 8th of December there was a great stir of cocked hats and orderly dragoons galloping about—a sure indication of a move. The men dived into the secret at once, and began to fix their flints and look to their ammunition. In the middle of the night we received orders to be on our alarm-post earlier than usual in the morning. The women were all astir in a moment, lighting their fires "to have a *dhrop* ov tay for their respective warriors, jist to warm their *harts* before plunging into the river, bad luck to the French." Well did they know our line of march, and were always in the way; but this intended advance bothered them. How were they to cross the river and follow the troops, against a positive general order? The *ladies* assembled around a big fire on a dark winter's night to discuss this point; Mother Skiddy, Brigadier-general of the Amazons, so called, addressed the meeting. "I have the wceest donkey of you all, an' I'll take the *wather* if I'm to swim for it, and let me see who's to stop *me*, Bridget Skiddy, who *thravelled* from Lisbon here into France; if Dan falls, who's to bury him? God save us!—divil a vulture will ever dig a claw into him while there's life in Biddy, his *laful* wife. Now, girls, you may go or stay;" and so she began to saddle her ass.

The troops were now assembled in perfect quiet; no drum nor bugle beat was sounded—not a word was spoken—all as still as death, waiting the signal-gun to make the rush. The outposts on the river-side had their orders not to take any advantage of the enemy; when just at dawn bang went the first cannon. The French were under arms in a moment; our pickets on the river-bank gave them the signal to clear off. They took the hint, got out of the way a little, halted, and formed up on the defensive. Bang went another gun, and now the field-day began. Our men had slung their pouches behind their necks, resting on the pack, to keep their powder dry, as the river was swollen, and the grand rush was now being made under cover of our guns. We took the stream; some killed and wounded went away with the current, for the French kept up a fire on us now, which was quite lawful. We made good our footing on the right side; fought on all the day, and calling the roll at night, we found there were many widows.

The passage of the Nive being successfully made by our Division on the right, there was hard fighting along the left of the entire position, and a desperate attempt made to repulse our whole army. It was known at the time that Soult had written to the Minister of War to expect good news very soon, Wellington's army being divided by the river Nive. Lord Hill's Division being now situated in an angle between the "Nive and Adour," was cut off from Wellington. It was very unpleasant, to say the least of it, and required great caution and brave hearts, resolute and determined, to keep our ground. On the 10th Soult attacked Wellington in front of Bayonne with *fifty-five* thousand men and thirty-seven guns. The ground was very unfavourable for fighting—ugly weather and swampy land, rough and rugged—it was always cheery enough fighting over grass fields and churchyards on a sunny day. The Light Infantry and Rifles liked the *tombstones*, they said they were such a steady rest for a *pot-shot*, and a good shield!

The great marshal, Soult, got a thrashing to-day after all his boasting and expectations, but it cost the Duke 1,200 men, two generals *hors de combat*, and 300 prisoners. However, to balance the account, the French loss was considerably more; moreover, a whole regiment of Nassau and Frankfort came over to us, their Prince having abandoned the Emperor Napoleon in Germany. But there was no end to this quarrel; we were all fighting again the next day, when there was a trifling loss of some 600 men a side. The 12th was also a bloody day in our army; death was busy from dawn to dusk, and that was only preparatory to the following day, the 13th December, 1813, when Soult tried his grand coup upon General Hill.

CHAPTER IX.

Soult's Tactics.—Villefranche.—St.-Pierre.—A Bayonet-charge.—The Gordon Highlanders.—The Wounded.—After the Battle.—Vieux Monguère.—Spanish Ingratitude.—Orthes.—Soult's Effort.—Its Failure.

ON the night of the 12th, the rains swelled the Nive, carried away the bridges, and left us cut off from the rest of the army, between the two rivers, with less than 14,000 men and officers, and 12 guns. We had a front of less than two miles of ground, which was rather in our favour, the enemy not being able to deploy their overwhelming force. We (28th, 34th, and 39th) occupied a plateau on the left, the Château of Villefranche being just in our rear. The morning was ushered in with a wet, misty fog; we had no time for a mouthful of breakfast, shook the rain out of our blankets, and stood to our arms. The fog continued heavy, covering the vast masses of the French dimly seen; now and then, they appeared in solid columns like black thunder-clouds, as the mist rose spreading over a mile of ground. Soult expected to trap our *Farmer Hill* and his little force by marching out from Bayonne and his intrenched camp with 35,000 fighting men, quite fresh, and 40 guns, early in the day. The sparkling fire of the riflemen spread far and wide over the low grounds, and gradually crept upon us, while the thundering of parks of artillery shook the ground from river to river, but never shook the nerves of a British soldier. The French General Abbé pushed on his attack against our centre, with a force and determination difficult to resist, and gained upon us rapidly. The musketry and cannonade rolled for hours in our teeth. Regardless of all danger, the two armies now met each other; neither would yield, and the artillery tore the ranks on both sides fearfully. We had hard work to keep our own against such long odds, 35,000 versus less than 14,000! besides their 40 guns against our *one* dozen of nine-pounders! Our brigade was let loose early, and we soon separated, on account of the ground, as we could thus do more work independently. Colonel Brown said to the old "Slashers": "There they come, boys; if you don't kill them they'll kill you; fire away." This was the longest address he ever made to his men; he never had but one book, and that was the "Army List;" he was a great soldier, very popular, and survived the war.

The Château of Villefranche, which was in our rear when we commenced operations in the morning, was well in our front before twelve o'clock; *i. e.* we had to abandon it to a superior force, and this caused our fellows to get furious; it had been taken and retaken several times to-day, but we held it at last. It was one of those fine old French family mansions that one sees sometimes peeping out of a wood elevated amongst the trees; it had been deserted, and left by its owners, well and substantially furnished in old style. The old ladies' arm-chairs, the library of the landlord, the young ladies' nick-nacks, with all the beautiful china ornaments, &c. &c., were mashed up together; the feather beds, down pillows, mattresses, and ottomans were stuffed into the windows for defence to resist incoming shot, and very sensible barricades they made. The cellars were not overlooked, and many thirsty souls were all ready to do full justice to the wines of Bordeaux, although preferring, as they always do, "strong waters;" however, in this department they were generally disappointed, for some prudent officer was always at hand to knock in the heads of wine and brandy casks and let them run.

We left this château now to camp-followers, the worst of all enemies (as it was no longer of use to us), and took ground to our right, to help a brigade of Portuguese who were fighting bravely; we were just in time to strengthen their hands to fight it out. Before we got up, we saw them *twice* charge their adversaries most gallantly with the bayonet. We pitched a flank fire into the *Parlez-vous* and made them "*leave that,*" as Paddy said, when he fired at the French sentry. "Did you hit him, Pat?" "No," he said, "but I made him leave *that!*"

The enemy now concentrated all their force towards the centre, to make the grand coup, and so we took that direction, keeping up the ball as we moved towards St.-Pierre. This was a hamlet on the main road, leading from the bridge at Cambo (across the Nive) into Bayonne. The French now attacked this point with three strong columns,—the very key of our position; whoever kept this key was pretty sure to be master. We formed in reserve, a couple of regiments behind the houses, with a battery of three guns and a howitzer; a good deal of pounding went on below, and on both our flanks; every point was attacked to weaken our force and keep us separate, their guns keeping up a terrific fire, knocking the dust out of St.-Pierre, and ploughing up the side of the hill, thinning our ranks, and playing Old Harry, having no regard for life or limb.

We were now on the *highway* for a retreat or a victory; the latter was the choice of the British army, and nobly did they win it. Facing Bayonne, and on our right, an old British regiment was firmly placed in a very strong position, the right of that regiment resting on the Adour. As the enemy's main column advanced up the hill to the hamlet, they were annoyed by a flank fire from our left; but they persevered and approached within pistol-shot of the key of our kingdom! Just then our little battery opened a fire of grape into their ranks, which made a lane through their column. A few volleys of musketry, in their confusion, staggered them grievously, and sent them pell-mell on top of their reserve, our guns plunging their shot into their ranks until there was a flow of blood down the great road: yes, the blood was *running* in a stream!

A tremendous fire of artillery now covers the advance of another great column of the French, who are determined to have Saint-Pierre at any cost. With a cloud of voltigeurs in front and on both flanks covering their deep and dark masses, they steadily move up the incline. We are prepared by order to be steady: "Dead or alive, my lads," said our chief, "we must hold our ground." Every eye is fixed on this deadly mass, every nerve is strung. Like the gallant steed as he champs the foaming bit, ready for the charge, so was every man of ours in pain to be let loose. A howitzer, with a double charge of grape, went slap into their foremost ranks; then one tremendous cheer, that only British soldiers *can* give with electric fire. "Hurrah for old England!" "Ireland for ever and the Limerick lasses!" "Bonny brave Scotland, hurrah!" "Hurrah!" from a thousand voices, as they dashed with the cold steel bayonet into the solid mass of human flesh before them. Writhing and quivering humanity lay over each other now in mortal combat, steeped in blood; the cannon-shot from each side crushing up the living with the dead and dying. It was a horrid sight, but not yet over. This broken column retired, and on the way lost considerably from our guns, which banged into them as fast as we could load. They went far away to the rear before they could re-form, while another massive column took their place and came on. The French always attacked in column. I think they were wrong, but they know their own business best, and upon this occasion gave us an opportunity of showing them an error, which they never acknowledged to this day. This last black, dense, great body of troops came steadily on, encouraged by seeing our troops on *their* left give way, and losing their grand position, which might and ought to have been kept against very long odds. Lord Hill saw at once this alarming turn in affairs, and despatched part of his force to retard the progress of the enemy there or drive them back. We had not a man to spare. Another frightful and uncommon event occurred which nearly damaged our day's work. A brigade and a regiment were commanded by two nervous old officers who had no wish to be killed; they had most likely been reading that *couplet* in Hudibras—

> "He that fights and runs away,
> May live to fight another day;
> But he that's in the battle slain,
> Will never rise to fight again."

Cowards die many times before their deaths—the valiant never taste of death but once.

They had a *ticket of leave* next day from the Duke, and were no more seen. I need not mention their names.

As this great column of France came up, they were first met by a discharge of shrapnel shells and canister shot, which did not slacken their pace over the dead bodies of their comrades that lay in their way. St.-Pierre was the key, still in our hands; to lose it all was lost. The Highland Brigade was under cover, in waiting for them, headed by the gallant 92nd "Gordon Highlanders," who led on the charge, colours flying, and their piper blowing out his national music to cheer them on. He was soon floored by a broken leg, but would not be moved, playing "Johnny Cope" with all his might, while the blue bonnets, well supported, went into this mass with the bayonet and sent them back in utter confusion. This was to understand war.

We were also successful on our right and left. The French couldn't do it; they had enough for one day, and did not renew the attack. Two divisions which had been on the line of march since daylight now made their appearance in our rear, and formed in line of battle, but were not required. Our ranks were terribly wasted, nearly all the staff had been killed or wounded, as also three generals.

Lord Wellington had been riding hard from the time he heard the first gun in the morning, and only arrived at the very close of the battle, and declared that he had never seen a field so thickly covered with dead. It was Lord Hill's own day of glory, and it was recorded by the celebrated historian, Colonel W. Napier, that "five thousand men were killed or wounded in *three hours*, upon a space of one mile square."

When the Duke rode up, he shook our chief by the hand, and said, "Hill, the day's your own."

Our men threw up their caps in the air, and gave one long, loud, thrilling cheer, that echoed down the valleys amongst the retiring foe. And so ended the battle of the Nive, which lasted five days, from forcing the river on the morning of the 9th to the evening of the 13th.

The days were short, and night closed upon the saturated field of blood, before we had time to light our fires and cook the wretched ration dinner; but still, with our half-gill of rum, after so long a fast, exercise, and excitement, it was an acceptable banquet. It came on now to pour rain like fury, and the bivouac was anything but agreeable, particulary to the wounded, among whom there was a multitude of *hurts* (as the doctors called them), great and small, from the amputation of limbs to the scalping of heads! I don't know if I was thankful enough for my escape; I was not hit very hard and got off cheap. Three inches taller and it was all up; an inch makes a wonderful difference they say in a mans nose,—life or death was today in the *height* of many a British soldier!

14th December.—We sent in a flag of truce to the French general to say they might carry away all their own wounded men from off our ground, and we would bury their dead; we had no hospitals nor medicos to care for them, and as prisoners of war they were not worth their rations.

All was friendship and politeness now; our offer was accepted, and a line drawn out between us. Some trees were cut down and laid across the high road into Bayonne; our men collected all the wounded of the French, carried them down in blankets to this point, and handed them over. The sentries of both armies were planted along the line, not over six or seven yards from each other, as quiet and gentle as lambs! The hill-sides were perforated with cannon-shot, some places like a rabbit-warren, and dyed with blood. Our little hamlet of St-Pierre was knocked inside out; but if ever the French got a decided thrashing, they might have boasted of it yesterday, in sight of one of their own chief towns. This "labour of love," in presenting so many disabled and useless soldiers to their country, lasted some days, and no end to groaning and moaning until we had them all removed. Two or three nights exposed to the rains left many of the unfortunates in a pitiable condition, for they had fallen in sand-pits, amongst brushwood, and in nooks and corners out of sight. The rains continued to overshadow the scene of desolation all about us, and not a blink of the sun to cheer or warm the bivouac for many days, our baggage not having yet come up. We had no feather beds; the old pound of lean beef, a hard biscuit, and ration of rum our banquet; a cold sod and a shower-bath our dessert; hard times; but we survived them, to tell of yet more battles. Our sentries, and the French ditto, paced at the distance of a few yards from each other, trying to converse a little in their respective lingo's

The officers kindly proffered their services in sending into Bayonne for anything for us that we required; we took advantage of their civility. I got a piece of cloth to make up a new Sunday pair of inexpressibles, very much required, and a bottle of brandy, for which I invested the few dollars in hand. The tailors were not all killed, and so I turned out very respectably dressed, but rather out of the fashion, in a week or so. We paid in advance; there was no mistake, everything came to hand about the hour appointed, and delivered at the outpost picket. The officers showed us the bullet-holes in their shakos and clothes; I believe we could do the same. They said we would all be back into Spain very soon; the reply was, " Not before we see a little more of la belle France ;" and really there was not the least animosity between us, and I thought it very unkind and inhospitable to have any more of a quarrel; but the two great chiefs of the fighting cocks thought otherwise.

The truce ended, sentries withdrawn, we gave our friends warning to be on their guard, as we intended to pursue our campaign; they took off their hats with an " Adieu, messieurs; au revoir!" and it was not long before we met again in mortal combat. My regiment was left in the shattered hamlet of St.-Pierre, to take care of itself and keep a sharp look-out to our front. Bayonne was just one league distant, full of French troops, and a whole army was concentrated in and about the city, holding fast their intrenched position, Sir John Hope in command. Vieux Monguère, a little town on our right, on a hill just above the Adour, where Lord Hill quartered himself and his staff, all jolly fellows; they were not long there before they got up an amateur theatre, and the drama went on as in Estremadura in Spain; our dear, rosy-faced Farmer Hill entertaining the whole *dramatis personæ* at supper after the play. There was nothing about the war, except in some comic songs composed for the occasion, of how "He (Lord Hill) *leathered* the French." I had to walk *home* in the middle of the night, up to my ankles in mud, after the fun; but I had a pair of wonderful legs for hard work day or night. We had little to do now for a long time, but listen to the attack and defence about Bayonne—bellowing of guns and waste of gunpowder.

We had quite gained the confidence of the people: everything was paid for; they were permitted to go into Bayonne with their sheep or their cattle as they liked, and soon found that the English were as equitable as brave, and that the word of a British general was sacred. All we seemed to want now was money, and a dollar was worth eight shillings.

The battle of the 13th was hardly over, when Mother Skiddy came into camp, mounted on her wee donkey, calling out for Dan, "Has any ov yer seen Dan Skiddy? he's not killed or wounded is he by them vagabones, bad luck to them; sure I'd been up two days ago, only I was drowned *crassin' that bit* ov a *sthrame*, an' sure I've niver been dry since?" "O, then, you're welcome home, Misthress Skiddy, how did you lave all behind you?" "Och, is that you, Paddy Muldoon? *avourneen*, it's me that's glad to see ye on your two Irish legs; I'm thinkin' you paid them off for the brandy." "Bedad, we gave them a great slashin', and not many ov us killed after all; will you let me take ye off your *charger?*" "Is *our* captain safe, and our two officers?" "O be gar they are, only Mr. B—— had a bit ov a scalp and a bullet through his cap in San Pierre there, but they can't touch him, or Mr. Norton in all the fights and scrimmages we have." "But where's Dan, tell me at ons't?" "O, indeed, he's run away wid a French lady he tuck in the battle." "An' he'll spake Irish to her," says Mrs. Skiddy; "but no more ov your blarney, where'll I find him?" "Well, he's up there in the hospital-tent wid a broken leg, and got off chape if they cure him; and there's Mr. Higginbottom wid another *cropper* beside him, and there's Sergeant ——" "O, worra, worra, that'll do, let me go; they're all kilt;" and away she went bellowing to the shambles.

We lost 300 officers the last five fighting days. Some of them had cut their way from Lisbon to be buried in France, but they were soon forgotten; they had their day of glory, and a bit of a churchyard fits everybody.

Wellington had his hands quite full. The intrenched camp before Bayonne was very strong, the weather rough and rainy for troops on the *qui vive* day and night close to a watchful enemy playing the sortie too often for one's comfort and patience, a game which ended by Sir John Hope being grabbed, wounded, and carried off to town-quarters. A terrible slaughter of officers and men took place also on both sides, without any advantage being gained.

It was said, and I believe it was very generally recorded as true, that our patient, scientific, and gallant chief was abused and libelled by the Spanish Government, with all his army. Their hostility and growing enmity were no secret; we were all considered as invaders rather than friends; the insolence and duplicity of their Minister of War were obvious. All this ingratitude and savage conduct troubled the Duke's temper a bit. In fact, he had good reason to rebuke Morillo for allowing or permitting the Spanish soldiers to plunder in France, and to commit violence on the people, which he encouraged, from his savage, untractable, bloody disposition, hating English, Portuguese, and French equally. The poor French peasantry would have been entirely ruined without our protection. Sometimes they would take refuge in our camp or quarters with their bundles, even to escape from their own soldiers, and many of our own men were hanged for plundering them. I never could excuse our soldiers for committing any such excesses. But 'tis true that they never saw their pay, and were half starved at times. Morillo, of course, sent a sackfull of lies by every post to his corrupt, imbecile, prejudiced, ungrateful Government in Madrid for the snub he got from his superior. Spanish pride was touched with the pen of justice and equity, and Spain is jealous and revengeful.

No one complained if the Duke was severe in our own ranks, it was never without cause; it was said that he was cold and careless of his officers. Some discontented men may have said so, but the truth was, no one expected reward for doing his duty, unless for some very gallant and extraordinary conduct—such as the leading a forlorn hope, when a step of rank was expected; but there were a hundred chances to one against the daring heart that tried this game;—yet they were never wanting to lead the way when required.

I sold my only donkey to raise the wind, and bought two nice little horses, on tick, at the sale of the effects of officers killed in action. A bill on England was always acceptable payment, or the *next* issue of money the same. This traffic always went on briskly, and in this way were we supplied with second-hand clothes! I was now ready for the road; my head-gear had something of a warlike appearance all right for a five-foot-nine man—a six-foot fellow, and he was a gone coon.

We sent our wounded to Cambo, on the Nive, where an hospital was established. My poor friend Allen B. Cairns died there; he had been wounded, but not badly—what the doctors called " a hurt " cost him his young life. I got his watch-key; I have had it, and that of another friend, in use for fifty years, and might say with truth that I never used them without thinking of the poor fellows.

We had a weary time of it now, since the December day that St. Peter declined to help the French to kill all the *heretics* in the British army. I have observed in all Roman Catholic countries where we carried on war, that saints were invoked in vain to aid our enemies. It seemed as if they were ashamed of the rags of Popery, false doctrines, purgatory, penance, &c., and all such absurd darkness. No, no, the saints don't hearken to such priestcraft. We had now done watching these *vagabones*, as the old woman warrior called them. They never came out to pay us another visit, so we went away to look after the grand army, and another fight up the banks of the Adour; and somehow we always got on the right scent like foxhounds, and never gave up the chase until the whole pack was in at the death, Wellington being huntsman.

On the 25th and 26th of February, our chief was examining Soult's position, which was a right good one as usual. It had the bend of a reaping-hook, and it was difficult for cavalry to

L

approach from swamps and rocky ground. It was high ground above the "Gave de Pau," and near to Orthes, where our friend Soult received battle. He had a fine army, and his best generals commanding them, such as Drouet, Reille, Clausel, Villatte, Paris, Harispe, &c. There was a very handsome old bridge across the river at the town, fortified and mined. Above and below the bridge it was deep, and full of jagged rocks, and altogether a very formidable and dangerous place to run one's nose into without leave. There was some little fighting in the advance towards it, just to keep up the steam. We lost twenty or thirty men, but that went for *nil*. Early on the 27th the great row began. Wellington delivered battle (as old chroniclers used to say) to his warrior antagonist Marshal Soult, the favoured and favourite lieutenant of the Emperor. There were two valiant armies in the field, of some 40,000 men a side, besides cavalry and guns. Our approach to the French position on the heights was marshy and difficult, in some places our troops sinking up to their knees, and the enemy above pounding at them in the mire—painfully provoking. But still this only braced their nerves, and made them more savage. Just now there was more swearing than fighting, for this part of the force were struggling to get out of the mud, unable to use their arms. The cannonade and flashing of small-arms had now begun in earnest to echo down the river, through the town, and over the hills—all was in full play about nine o'clock, and continued all the day. The bold French rushed upon our columns with a wasting fire, and forced back our inferior numbers with unusually desperate valour, but our supports came up and shattered their masses. The nature of the ground would not permit very many to be engaged at this point; so that little progress was made, except in deadly slaughter, in which the French had the best of it.

Soult put all his reserves in motion, to complete what he supposed must be a victory all *but* gained, and 'twas said that he exclaimed aloud, "I have him at last." The moment, no doubt, was very dangerous, but Wellington's head was clear, and he had the most devoted hands and hearts to aid him, in the full assurance of another victory for old England.

Amidst all this thundering din of battle, which shook the earth with violence, the Duke ordered Hill's division to ford the river on the French left, and get on their flank. It was deep to our loins. We slung the cartridge-boxes on top of the knapsacks, to keep our powder dry. The men linked arm in arm, to support each other in a very strong current. Some cavalry formed in the river above us, to break the force of the stream; and so we all passed over unmolested, and marched on without halting for a moment, our shoes full of water, and our nether garments clinging to our bones, for none of us were very fat, but still in good working condition. The 4th Division gained ground, and secured a good position in the church and the graveyard (all ready for its victims). The French marshal now rallied all his forces to make the grand *coup* that was "at last to have him." The thunder of the guns on both sides made the very hills quake. Our grand chief was wounded, with two other generals, Ross and Walker. After fording the river, we drove back the troops there, seized the heights, cut off the French from the road to Pau, and turned the town of Orthes, menacing the only line of Soult's retreat. When his troops began to yield, our army advanced with an incessant and destructive fire of musketry and cannonade, losing men very fast, for the French saw their own danger, and fought like devils. But, seeing their retreat being cut off by Lord Hill, we hurried on until both sides began to run. They ran for dear life, and we kept to their heels, until coming up pretty close, down went their arms, after that their knapsacks; they got into racing order in no time, and endeavoured to make good their escape. But our fellows got amongst a regiment with long great coats, and now Paddy Muldoon had fair play at last, as he said. I don't know how many of these "*Parlez-vous*" he had caught by the tail, giving each of them a "crack on the *lug*," as he termed it, pulling him down upon the sod, and telling him to *stay there* while he was hot after another, but never firing a shot at those unarmed.

Sir Stapleton Cotton with his cavalry got amongst them in another quarter, and cut them down by scores. Upwards of

2,000 threw down their arms, and their whole army now dispersed, *sauve qui peŭt,* leaving nearly 4,000 killed and wounded on the field of battle.

When the French broke, they made a rush for the bridge, which was soon choked up with baggage, broken gun-carriages, waggons, dead men and horses, thousands pressing forward to this point of escape, our troops in full pursuit, and cheering them on to destruction, while a brisk fire of artillery mixed up the living and the dead upon it. Our guns soon got the range, and kept it up, tearing to shatters every living thing attempting to escape that way. The skeletons of late strong fine regiments dashed into the boiling river on both sides, amongst the jagged rocks (peeping above the current), hoping thus to escape; but they only met another grave, nearly all perishing. It was an awful sight, as we passed that fine bridge, to see it covered with dead bodies and the *débris* of an army; the wounded groaning in torment, supplicating for water, and it so very near. The Duke was so hurt, he could not ride without pain, and so the pursuit was relaxed at sundown, when we gave up the chase, and then, weary enough and nothing in the *larder,* lay down on the sod, to dream of weeping and lamentation in England and France, our loss being 2,500 killed and wounded! *Cui bono?*

CHAPTER X.

The Duke of Richmond. — Discipline. — Combat at Aire. —Victory.—Vic Bigore.—A Turn of Luck.—Tarbes.—The Combat.—Major Dogherty. —The Three *Generals.*—Adjutant Peckett.—A Cheated Stomach.— Toulouse.—Deserters.—Fighting with Stones.

AFTER the affair at Orthes the medicos had great practice in carving. Maurice Quill was engaged with the French wounded a good deal, and while extracting a ball from the left side of an old veteran, he said, "I hope you don't feel much pain." "Ah," he said, in deep emotion, "cut deeper, sir, and you will find the Emperor; he's buried in my heart!" I was looking on while he was taking off the arm of another old soldier; when done, he laid hold of it, and tossed it up in the air, crying out "Vive l'Empereur! Vive Napoléon!"—Such was the enthusiasm of those brave men.

The Duke of Richmond (then Lord March) had served on Lord Wellington's staff during the whole war without a scratch; he was a captain in the 52nd regiment, and, like a good and gallant soldier, joined his corps the night before the battle, to be shot through the body at the head of his company, thus learning by experience the difference between the labours and dangers of staff and regimental officers, which are in the inverse ratio to their promotions! We never got a step but by a death vacancy; the cold-hearted, ungenerous, self-interested, arrogant directors of military affairs at home threw a wet blanket over young officers, unless there was a handle to one's name, court interest, or a hat-full of votes for a Tory minister!

"What can ennoble knaves, or fools, or cowards?
Alas! not all the blood of all the Howards!"

The Duke of Richmond was ever the friend of the old Peninsular army; he was a true and gallant soldier, brave and generous, and to him the remnant of the officers of that unconquerable army, so glorious to the arms of England, were indebted for the distinguished medal, bearing on clasps the names of numerous battles in which we were engaged; he represented the tardy justice to our Queen, the fourth crowned head for whom this army fought so many battles; and this noble and generous sovereign, best of all monarchs that ever filled an English throne, granted the request for all those victories achieved before she was born! The Duke of Richmond himself had ten clasps, and we gave him a splendid piece of plate to keep in continual family remembrance our love and respect for his manly and soldierlike bearing in behalf of the just claims of his comrades in war.

The battle of Orthes added another laurel to Wellington's name; it was another Sabbath-day's slaughter: somehow, most of our quarrels happened on Sunday; but I do not think that one in a hundred knew Saturday from Sunday, or Sunday from Monday, when in the field.

We followed up our friends the next day as close as we could, sticking to them like a bur to a sheep's tail. They made every effort to shake us off with a forced march and in light order, having left their arms behind them.

We had something to do as well in tinkering up our own broken ranks for the next scuffle, which was not far off. I believe, to do the thing well, an army ought to march twelve miles, fight a battle, and follow up the fugitives twelve miles farther to gain a great victory! I think we accomplished this more than once; it was surprising to find how soon the French troops rallied and made another stand after being dispersed and scattered like frightened sheep all over the country.

The weather was now very fine, which was always cheery in the field, and we had some pleasant marching over la belle France, falling in at times with some of those domestic birds about barn-doors and farm-yards that will not get out of one's way; it was a serious matter to meddle with them or ruffle their feathers. A farmer did complain one day, after passing his gate, that he was *minus* a goose; a halt and a search was made, quite satisfactory to our honesty; but these gobblers make such a fuss when out of their own element, *goosy* was heard skirling and clapping her wings most violently, there was a *tittering* laugh amongst the men, and an *oho!* Another search-warrant, and the farmer's goose was discovered in a drum! A drumhead court-martial on the spot, and the drummer got goose without sauce for breaking the law, all the people about looking on in amazement with their mouths wide open at the severity and justice of our discipline in an enemy's country. Our military law was severe but necessary; hanging on a tree for theft and violence was not uncommon, the dead bodies being left there for the vulture.

Lord Wellington's wound towards the end of the battle of Orthes saved the hostile army, and so they showed front again very soon at Aire. They always met us like lions; but in the end it was like hare-hunting; it may be that the French soldiers have a little more science in war than the soldiers of our country. The French look about them, and if they see their flanks being turned, or anything adverse to their forward movement, they consider it necessary to give way; while the ragged old red-coats always fought away right to their front, so long as they could see a Frenchman before them, leaving their officers to do the rest. This "grand Welling-ton" of ours, as the Spaniards always talked of him, had a conception for arrangement and promptness never surpassed, decision and immediate action in all his preparations. The best generals oftentimes grope in the dark, but Wellington's head was never under a cloud; he was a *born* soldier, while others were educated for the trade; it is one thing to fight a battle without fruits, another thing to fight a battle with success!

We came up with the enemy again on the 2nd of March, General Hill in command of our division as usual. We fell on them at once; the action was sudden and severe, and was nearly lost to us at one moment when General Da Costa, a man of no ability, attacked with his corps of Portuguese in such a slovenly, unsoldierlike way; he was repulsed and driven back in a charge by the French; as usual, we had to go to their aid. We had won the high grounds by this time, and spared two regiments, 34th and 39th, to tinker up the damage. Our men got savage at the Portuguese for giving way, and I believe would have fired into them at the moment as heartily as into the French. With one vehement cheer, with one powerful charge, they went slap-dash into the enemy's columns, and drove them back on their reserves; but still they rallied, and renewed the battle with singular courage for fellows who had been whacked so often; but it was all in vain, the blood of the old *bricks* was up, and having now done so much, the whole division entered on the play, and with one great rush upon the poor French, General Harispe at their head, their ranks were broken, and we drove them into and right through the town of Aire. They crossed the Adour, broke down the bridge, and made their way into the clouds of night, leaving us their dead to cover up. About one hundred prisoners and a vast number of conscripts threw down their arms, and went away to their respective homes. They got very much into this practice when the army of France passed their doors, and was not likely to return that way. They lost some valuable officers. Our General Barns was wounded, Colonel Hood killed, and some inferior officers, *i.e.* some captains, lieutenants, and ensigns, small fry not worth talking of! It was not the fashion in those days to regard the death of a poor subaltern more than that of a cavalry charger, yet many of the small fry lived to be great fishes; as to private soldiers, thousands upon thousands that joined the army from England were never heard of by their kindred or friends, dead or alive. They fought and they fell and were forgotten!

Before going into the town of Aire, I stepped into a house by the roadside to look for a drink of water, the day being very hot. The only tenant I could see was a very handsome young cavalry officer of ours, elegantly dressed, lying on his back, and quite dead; he had been recently killed in an affair with French cavalry thereabouts by a shot from a rifleman; the fresh blood was oozing from a bullet-hole in his *forehead*, and, like so many of his brave comrades, he died *facing* the enemy. It was a charming day to spatter the early flowers of spring with human blood.

In sixteen days we had marched nearly one hundred miles, passed over five large rivers, forced the enemy before us, captured over a thousand prisoners, six or seven guns, and magazines, and been everywhere victorious; let us now have a little rest to patch up our *duds*. I got into a very respectable house, where the good dame had some knowledge of humanity, and must have seen a starvation-looking face every time she said to me "Bon-jour." I had not a franc in my pocket, and was too proud to ask for anything to eat. I had my rations, which did keep me alive, and one day a ham was sent into my room for my acceptance, which I finished off for breakfast, even polishing the bone; but I may as well explain that it was a *goose*-ham well cured, smoked and bronzed, the first I had ever seen; but they are common in that part of the south of France.

The English army became popular in time; all the supplies were paid for in gold by us, while their own army did not respect property. It was said at the time that Soult remarked, "I may expect to find by-and-by that the inhabitants will take up arms against us." I could see that the people rather liked the red-coats now, old prejudices were wearing out, our discipline was more perfect than the French, and everything was paid for; but there was no resting-place for the soles of our feet, and so we took leave of goose-hams, and a quiet rest of a few days, to look after our fighting friends, and found them as usual well posted, and ready for action, at Vic Bigore, on the Adour, General Paris at their head, where he fought a vigorous little battle without any advantage. We soon slashed him out of his fine position at a loss on our side of 260 men and officers. Colonel H. Sturgeon, a skilled and accomplished officer, was amongst the slain, a great loss to our service, and much regretted by all who knew his worth.

My comorado was out on picket to-night. I went to see him in the evening at his *country* house, just for the purpose of knowing personally if we might eat his share of the ration dinner or send it to his post. I found him in a comfortable château, with a jolly gentleman landlord, who was preparing to make him very snug for the night. The cloth was laid for dinner, plate and wine on the table; it was a beautiful sight and made me ravenous. I required no second invitation to be seated and wait for what was coming. I supposed the good host considered me a reserve or support to this outlying picket, sent there for his protection, as *he* thought, and gave me a welcome. My poor friend Mr. Simmons, the real officer on this responsible duty, went out every now and then to visit his sentries, being not very far from the enemy. However, we had a real dinner and very good wine, so good that an extra bottle or two were discussed after the cloth was removed, and while the interesting subject of the war was talked over.

The landlord was all on our side, perhaps from policy; but it was all the same to us which battle he fought for this evening; his cheer was good and we had no bill to pay. We praised his wine; it pleased him, so that he begged us to take a magnum bottle of his best to our camp in the morning, which he brought up from his cellar at once, and planted on the mantel-piece in full view. He then showed us into a handsome bedroom, with everything complete for two, and bid us " bonne nuit, messieurs." My chum could not indulge in the *state*-bed, of course, being on duty, so I volunteered to occupy it for him. He slipped out and away to the barn to keep watch with his men, and I peeled and slipped into bed quite bewildered. A grand French bed, damask drapery, fine polished furniture; a swing glass, six feet high; and such lots of nick-nacks and china ornaments; a toilet, also, that could only be arranged by the fingers and taste of a French lady, but yet we never got a glimpse of a petticoat. I knew that I was safe, having an *officer's guard* over my slumbers, so I tumbled into such a bundle of feathers I was nearly suffocated. I had not been in such a civilized apartment, or in a bed at all, for two years and more; *i.e.* such a thing as they call a bed in England!

I thought the night passed away in about ten minutes. I was called at early dawn to have some coffee. I sometimes allowed myself five minutes to dress, but just now I was in a hurry to be off, and might have taken three minutes and a half for washing and all, all the time having my eye on the magnum of wine which I had in charge. Some one now bawled, " The French cavalry in the long avenue." All the house astir and in as much commotion as if the Russian army was upon them. I told them not to stir; my friend outside soon stopped their progress, and having emptied a few saddles from behind the barn wall, the cavalry took the hint. A few shots after them put them full speed, and they never again returned to the " Château de la Reine." There was some brisk firing near at hand.

I was rather out of place, so I buckled on my sword, jumped out of a back window in a violent hurry, and away to my regiment, which I found ready to move, having just given some French patrols notice to quit! In my hurry, alas! I forgot the *magnum*, a source of deep regret to us for many a day. I was well chaffed, and deserved to have my grog stopped, but consoled myself in the charming thought of having passed a night of luxury in a château where I had no right to be at all, and the remembrance of the finest omelet I ever tasted. I believe it is only in France they can make omelets and coffee.

We called in the picket *en passant*. The château and its people were respected and cared for, which was acknowledged by the kind landlord, and I have no doubt but that he lived free and easy ever afterwards from such visitors, for neither party ever returned that way.

We had a respite now for a long time, *i.e.* from the smell of gunpowder, gradually feeling our way after our unsubdued friends. Some shins were cracked and heads broken here and there, little *affairs* of no importance, too small for the butcher's bill! The weather was fine; no place more charming than the south of France for a fight or a bivouac. On the 20th of March we came up once more with the *" Parley vous,"* as our men continued to call them.

My regiment halted in the pretty town of Tarbes, piled arms in the street, and waited for orders. The cracking of rifles was heard pretty sharp outside in the vineyards; but here comes a cocked hat in a gallop, so we may as well "fall in." " Colonel W——, your regiment is to halt here till further orders. The men may get under cover and be ready to turn out at a moment's warning on their alarm-post." A gentle hurrah went through the ranks, every one happy but the

Colonel, who wanted another fight and to be killed, and the most singular part of the play was that he never was killed, but died in his bed like his grandmother.

I was welcomed into a nice house in the street. We all divided, and were received with much civility, it being our first appearance on this stage. A kind Frenchman brought me a large metal basin of water and a napkin to wash the dust out of my eyes. I thought the introduction very agreeable, and a preliminary of something for the interior department, as I fancied I smelt an omelet. The day was young, and the people here dine early. I had my horse put up and *saw him* fed, and now for a peaceful and a pleasant day, as I rubbed my hands with delight, when that in——l bugle of ours, as all called it, joining in the naughty word, sounded the assemblée. There was no appeal against this music; there was a thundering cannonade going on not far distant, and so we were all out of the town in a crack, and killing each other in the usual way, *secundum artem*.

The French had been driven out of the town in the morning by the 95th Rifles, the most celebrated old fighting corps in the army, or perhaps in the world. They retired to their position to receive battle once more and try their luck, and bad luck attended them as usual, as Mother Skiddy predicted.

The action really now began, about twelve o'clock. Hill's artillery thundered away on the right, Clinton's on the left, Baron Alten attacked the centre. The French General, Harrispe, was posted very strong on a hill, but was assailed most gallantly by some rifle battalions. The fight was brief and violent, a fiery combat muzzle to muzzle. Of course our men would not give way, so the French did. Meantime we forced the passage of the river and sent Villatte and his troops away double quick. The country was now covered with confused masses of prisoners; some tried to escape or hide themselves, others had thrown down their arms, crying out for quarter, while the wounded on both sides lay patient and still in all their agony.

This part of the country was flat, covered with vineyards,

farm-houses, deep ditches, and inclosures, not at all suitable for cavalry. But our pursuit was stopped by General Clausell, who had four fresh divisions drawn up in our front right in our path, and all ready for battle. He lost no time in opening upon us all his batteries. However it was now late, and night closed the scene upon all the combatants. Fighting for this day ceased, and in the morning the stage was clear, and not a Frenchman to be seen. We had lost a great many good soldiers, and a dozen valiant and most excellently brave officers. When the prison of the soul was broken up, the poor shattered shell lay there without burial, no kindred friend to close the late brilliant eye, or say the last leave-taking words—" *Requiescat in pace.*"

I lay down under a fig-tree very tired with the day's excursion (my horse, of course, being in the rear, as usual on all fighting days), and disappointed of enjoying the hospitality ready for me at Tarbes.

We pushed on the next day after our beloved friends over the green hills of la belle France. Soult, we understood, was making for Toulouse, losing his young soldiers by the way; for, as soon as a conscript passed his home, he deserted. However, every bit of ground was disputed on our line of advance. Fighting was our daily bread, and I believe that officers and men went at it "*con amore,*" as they would follow a pack of harriers.

When we came up with their cavalry yesterday, old Major Dogherty, of the 13th Dragoons, might be seen charging at the head of his regiment, supported on his right and left by his two sons. Was not this a glorious sight of war and chivalry? deeds of daring and of victory too, bequeathed as an inheritance to the future armies of England. A new race of younger men soon stepped into their saddles and their shoes because they had no friends; no reward for the many and great achievements of this war. That terror of all tyrants, the *press*, had not the power, nor the pen, nor the freedom, nor the courage to speak out for the army as they have in the present day; so all heroic deeds were forgotten and left in abeyance, and clouds of darkness overshadowed the lives of hundreds of brave men who died in obscurity, many of them personally known to myself.

Our line of march was now directed on Toulouse, fighting our way and driving the rightful owners of the soil before us. A long wet day found myself and two messmates in a very comfortable and well-furnished château, of which we took possession for the night; the lawful owners having run away in alarm, the house now fell into the hands of three lads of different nations. We held a council of war how it was best to proceed with honour and justice. It was quite out of the question to starve in a cook-shop, or go without dinner in such fine quarters. A couple of old servants had been left in charge, so we thought it best, like gentle visitors, to ask them politely to prepare some supper for three generals! "*O mon Dieu!*" they began both together, talking threescore to the dozen, keeping time with a jerking of the head, shoulders, arms, and legs; in fact, there was nothing in the house to eat or drink; but it was out of the question to take the word of an old French butler, so we began the evening's amusement in our own way to forage. *General* Thomson and his servant took the outside of the dwelling, including the hen-roost; *General* Russell the interior; while *General* G. B. got up a good fire, collected feather-beds and blankets, and made a grand shake-down for three on the hearth of the library, where he lay in luxury awaiting the foraging party. By-and-by the two *Generals* and their *staff* appeared with a very good supply. The cook and butler got out of their alarm, and busied themselves, like good allies, in helping to prepare the evening meal. The library was a large room with a wide fire-place, and good enough for all we required. A couple of fowls were soon roasting before *our* fire, a flagon of wine on the table, and sausages, with a yard of bread! They make bread by the yard in this part of France, and sometimes in a ring as large as a horse-collar.

We all lay down by the fire now, quite cosy, our wet clothes hanging at the sides to dry, my little horse provided for, and all as happy as three kings, when that bird of ill omen, "our Adjutant," raised the latch and walked in, opened his roster-book, and warned me for outlying picket *immediately!* "The men have fallen in and are waiting, please look sharp, sir; I thought I would not have found you out to-night." "Well, I'm very sorry you did find me, but you are always in luck finding *me* when you want an officer in a hurry for duty; besides 'tis not my tour for picket to-night." "No, it is not," he said, "but Mr. W—— can't be found, and you are next on the roster—you shall have an overslaw." No use battling with an old adjutant like Peckett; precise and correct in everything regarding his duty, he had been an excellent sergeant-major, and always gave the *time* to a second. "What time is it, Peckett?" "Ten minutes and a half-past one, sir." He carried a load of a big silver watch as large as a turnip, which regulated the whole regiment!

Casting one glance at the fowls as they began to brown at the fire, I turned out in the rain, and banged the door after me like thunder. I suppose I was in a thundering bad humour, but away I went in the dark about two miles with my good orderly men who never complained; reconnoitred the country as well as I could see, planted my sentries, and got the picket under cover in a brick-shed. There was a village in front, occupied by our cavalry. If I had been in my proper place, I ought to have been in advance of this village; but that was no business of mine. "Obey orders," was the order of the day, and the night too.

I groped my way down to this cavalry quarter, called and requested to see General Long, in command of all the advanced posts here. He and his staff had just done dinner; I touched at once on the valour of his cavalry by saying, "I am sent here, sir, to support you,—my men are close by, what are your orders?"

"I don't require your aid at all," he said, "you may go back if you wish." "Very good, sir, I will return, for my men are wet and weary after a long day's march." "But you had better have some dinner before you go, 'tis getting late." I hesitated a moment, thought of *home*, and the pair of roast fowls and fire-side! declined the General's offer with all due thanks, made for my post, called in my sentries, and away we went quite jolly for our own quarters at a quick march.

All this took up as much time as would roast a sheep, but still I did not despond, but kept my eye on the mess dinner, in the luxurious hope of coming in for a bone. But, alas! when I got back, the *two generals* were asleep by the fireside where I left them, and the *debris* of the dinner on the table— some bones, a piece of bread, and the tail of a bottle of wine. I was horrified, and called myself a stupid donkey, anything but an old soldier for not sitting down and eating my dinner at the table of a real general, when I had the blessed opportunity. I have not forgotten or forgiven myself yet, and thought,—

> Who fights to the end may win, but doubly wise,
> Who knows the moment when to compromise,
> And for a bird in hand, forbear to push
> A doubtful search, for *two* inside the bush!

A ham and cold roast turkey just going from the General's table as I went in—dry bones, the tail of a sausage, a morsel of bread, and a driblet of wine was all I found on my return.

When dogs are hungry they go to sleep,—and so did G. B——!

Off again the next cock-crow, dodging our Gallic friends across the country. They roll people up in wet sheets in Germany, and put them to bed to make them warm; we are generally kept warm on the line of march, trudging along in our wet shirts, which dry on our bones when a blink of the sun favours us; we had got into a rainy week.

Our General now crossed the Ariège river; and of course we never did pass a river, or could walk peaceably over a green sod in France, without being insulted by a shower of musket-balls, cannon-shot, or a dragoon sabre, ready to cut off a fellow's nose. *Vide* poor Captain C—— of the Buffs, who lost his *nose* and an *arm* on the same day! Our dragoon sabres were sharp too, and left their mark behind them.

We were now approaching, at the beginning of April, the famous town of Toulouse, where Marshal Soult had pitched his tent, and hoisted his colours to make another stand, and another grand effort to beat Wellington; but six years of almost uninterrupted success had engrafted a seasoned, warlike strength and confidence into the very heart and muscles of our soldiers that made them invincible; they would willingly fall under their colours, and die in battle, but they would not be conquered at the eleventh hour, and so here was another pretty quarrel just going to begin.

My corps was distributed in some hamlets convenient to the river, where we kept watch, and kept ourselves warm for a few days, when the brilliant sun of France came forth to pay us a long visit, a most agreeable change which made us all very cheery. We had the big town before us; conjectures were innumerable; a thousand opinions *issued* every day from all ranks.

Our baggage was up; commissariat supplies enough to feed the troops. We had *wine*, rations, and everything but money; still kept six months in arrear of our pay. But we knew that England was a good paymaster, and it would all come in a heap some day, *if* one lived to see it.

The river Garonne, as every one knows, runs through Toulouse; the position was a valuable one for the French Marshal. A town, not regularly fortified, but made very formidable by batteries, redoubts, intrenchments, loop-holed houses, an ancient wall, the river, and a canal; all these places were *ornamented* with cannon, ready to salute the British General on his first appearance before the city. The suburb St. Cyprian was protected by an old wall, very thick, with towers and intrenchments, loop-holed houses, and batteries in the streets, all very nicely arranged to stop the progress of Lord Hill and his division; this was our allotment in the part of the play which was to come off very soon, in the teeth of General Reille and two divisions of the French army. On the 27th of March our brigade was ordered up from Murat to get over a pontoon bridge at midnight; found the river too wide for our number of boats, so gave that up; tried it again on the 30th, when a new bridge was laid—crossed and recrossed, and yet that did not answer. I don't know why, I was not in the secret. It was a laborious work throwing over this bridge on a dark night. I was very tired; about two o'clock in the morning, the open door of a house which was close by invited me to look in; an old rickety straw bed, looking very *lively*, stood in the corner, upon which I lay down to have forty winks, positively no more, but was fast asleep in the crushing of a musquito. Unlawful slumbers are never refreshing; I had no business to be there. One is always jumping up and saying, where am I? what brought me here? I opened my other eye (soldiers sleep, or ought to sleep, with one eye open), by the glimpse of a rushlight and found myself hemmed in against the wall by our Brigadier-General, the Honourable Sir Robert O'Callaghan, the biggest man in the whole division, snoring like a windmill. "All right, *little Bob* (as he was sometimes called), if I have no business here, I'm sure you haven't, unless the pontoons are gone down with the stream. It is the first time I have had the honour of sharing a bed with any of the Lismore family. Bad luck to the fleas and all backbiters!—Sleep on till I call you," saying which I cautiously crept over the giant, to put my wet boot upon the face of another *deserter*, and to tumble over a third on the floor. They both jumped up in alarm, and roused *little Bob*, who thought the French had him pinned up in a corner. I knocked over the glimmer for safety, leaving the trio in the dark to explain, if they wished, how they all got there while on duty!

I told this little anecdote to the dear old General long afterwards at one of his dinner parties at Madras, when he was there as Commander-in-Chief, which made him laugh heartily, and introduced many of the old stories and anecdotes of the Peninsula—not in an old tent, but in a splendid palace. He was a brave soldier, and a powerful Irishman; carried a big sword, and used it at times with great effect, slashing the heads of Frenchmen in the "Donnybrook Fair" style; he would cut them down right and left, and upon one occasion, when his sword was shattered in his hand, he got hold of a big *shillelah*, and laid about him like a thresher with a flail, and never afterward gave it up—it answered so well, he said. But like the rest of the gallant band, he dropped into his narrow cell, and was soon forgotten.

There were many ways of meeting the enemy in combat, but who ever heard of an officer going into battle with a pocket full of stones? It was a sort of pastime with a Captain Irvine, of the old " Slashers." He was a capital shot with a stone, and a very strong, able, active man, left-handed, who delivered his *shot* with such force and accuracy that he would knock a fellow into next week. He never minded meeting two or sometimes three Frenchmen, when they were detached; pretty sure of knocking one down with a stone, he sprang upon another like a leopard, and knocked him on the head with his own firelock, and with one great, thrilling shout he paralyzed the third, and if he did not trip him up he frightened him out of reach, pelting him with stones as he ran. All this gymnastic play created at times roars of laughter amongst the men, for it never was done in a corner, nor for bravado. This brave Irish gentleman and soldier survived the war, but never reached any rank beyond a captain.

CHAPTER XI.

Battle of Toulouse.—The Retreat of Ten Thousand.—The First Act.—Progress of the Battle.—A Bird's-eye View.—Entry into Toulouse.—Peace Prospects. — "The Duke."—The Duke d'Angoulême. — Route for Bordeaux.—My Billet.—Rather in Luck. — Freemasonry. — Private Hostilities.—The Duello.—Home, Sweet Home.—Mrs. Commissary-General Skiddy.

OUR men began to fix their flints and examine their powder on the 9th, as we approached the town, and took up our quarters in front of St. Cyprian; weather very fine, every one jolly, and the *Patlanders* in particular cracking their jokes. "How the d—— are we to get over that big *sthrame* av a river to leather them vagabones out o' that?" says Paddy Muldoon, for he wasn't kilt yet. "O, niver mind," says another old cripple, who lost an eye on the Nive; "that countryman av yours wid the long nose will show you the way when he's riddy." "O, be gar, then, we'll not wait very long, for I seen him over here this morn wid our *Farmer Hill*, spying them wid his long eye-glass, an' he won't keep us waiting. But there's oceans on 'em down there in the town pickin' holes in the wall, and *fencen* all the houses, so mind that other eye av yours!" They were ever laughing and cracking their Irish jokes at the worst of times.

The Duke crossed the river about fourteen miles below the town, on his pontoon bridge, with the Light Division; and early in the morning he had formed his army. On Easter Sunday morning, the 10th of April, 1814, I was very comfortably seated in the library of a château belonging to some stupid fellow who had run away in alarm, leaving his hall door open. We were preparing a breakfast of fresh eggs and bacon, which were quarrelling in the frying-pan outside in the sunshine, when bang! went the signal-gun, and Freeman, our trusty bugleman, sounded the assemblée at once. Whilst the men were getting on their packs and their arms ready, we gobbled up the contents of the frying-pan, left our traps in charge of our servants, fell into our places, and marched down to join in the bloody fray of another Sabbath day's unholy work. It was very handy for us, not far to go, and all fresh as young colts. In twenty minutes we came to the scratch, and were hard at work fighting in the town, on the suburbs on the left bank of the river, where the enemy had two divisions under the command of Count Reille. It is always ugly, dangerous work fighting in a town; so many holes and corners, hiding-places and loop-holes, where one may be picked off by an unseen enemy. This was just our case, fighting from house to house and from street to street, our men having their bones cracked, and dropping off at every corner. As the enemy retired, or were driven back, they fired the houses they left, to arrest our progress, not sparing their *own* property. We found in many houses the furniture piled up in rooms, ready for the torch. The streets were barricaded, and cannon planted at every entrance, pounding away at the first blink of any red coat; but our men dashed on through fire and smoke, and carried on the work surely and gradually, for we lost nothing that we gained. Our senior Captain, Baker, had that morning got his majority, and was one of the first killed. He had come all the way from India to join our battalion. Other officers had been with the regiment in all its battles, and had never been hit for five years—such is the fate of war!

There was a furious row going on across the river, a tremendous crash of great guns and small-arms. The two Marshals had met, with their two valiant armies, and quarrelled; they were always fighting and quarrelling. Saturday or Sunday was all the same to them, and here they were at it on an Easter Day, a festival of solemnity in all Christian lands, but not the least regarded on the banks of the Garonne. The battle went on with desperate fury, both sides determined to win the fight. It was a charming day, and worthy of better deeds than destroying life. We had *the* bravest, the best, the finest-disciplined and well-seasoned army in the world; fighting was their daily bread—it gave them an appetite. No other soldiers on earth had a chance against them in fair and open ground; the Duke knew it, and let them loose this morning.

There was *pounding* on both sides of the river in full force about noon, the French having all the advantage; their two miles of position along Mont Rave being defended by intrenchments, breastworks, redoubts, and immense batteries bristling with cannon. Our side, too, looked as formidable. I never had, personally, any taste for fighting in the dark, or in the streets, although we used to practise the art of "street-firing and retiring." All fudge!

The advance towards the French position was very swampy and unfit for cavalry or the passage of guns. This alone would shake the nerves of any other man than Wellington, but, always confident, he relied on his own British soldiers.

General Freyve, a Spanish leader, asked permission to have the honour of leading his troops first into battle. Granted—and away they went, 9,000 strong, with a good reserve, very resolved to have all the victory to themselves. The French began to torment them, as they advanced, with a shower of lead; they wavered, and rushed for shelter into a deep hollow. The French, now taking the advantage of war, turned out of their breastworks and poured volley after volley into the poor Spaniards, the bullets hissing through their quivering flesh and bones, until some 1,500 of them were slain. The rest fled as hard as they could tear, the enemy at their heels, until too near our cavalry, when they returned to their trenches. All this was very mortifying to the Duke, but the only remark he made was—

"Well, I have seen some curious sights, but I never saw 10,000 men running a race before!"

Sir Thomas Picton failed in his attack at another point, entirely from disobeying his master's orders; turning a false attack into a real one, and losing thereby his chance of success, and 400 men and officers. Poor Sir Thomas never could bridle his ardour when he had a chance of a dash at the French. But dashing in war means courage without prudence.

We had now forced the first line of intrenchments and barricades on our side. The second we looked at; but it had such a very angry appearance that we slackened our fire to bide our time and listen to the music on the other side. The crisis was approaching with some good promise to the French, the Spaniards being utterly routed. General Picton had been repulsed, and our men, frightfully reduced in numbers, were making their way to the French position through a deep swamp tangled with many other obstacles, a heavy fire of great guns and musketry being poured into their teeth the whole way, they not returning a single shot. What other troops in the world would have faced such a storm of death? But they did advance, and met Taupin's whole force rushing down upon them. At this moment some rockets were discharged from our side, got amongst the Frenchmen's legs with an unheard-of hissing, curving, serpentining, biting, and kicking noise that they never saw or heard of before. It staggered their courage and steadiness long enough to let General Lambert's brigade make a rush with a cheer amongst them, with such irresistible power that they went to the right-about and fled. Taupin was killed, and our people gained the platform.

Soult, seeing this danger, brought up all his artillery to make a clearance of this little force, aided by double numbers of infantry. But the domineering courage of British soldiers overcame this obstacle, and decided the first act of the play. The Scotch Brigade and the Portuguese, with Marshal Beresford's division, dashed on next, scrambling up the hill; all the breastworks and batteries in their front, pouring a wasting fire into their face, did not stagger their courage. The French yielded here for a little, but rallied and returned with their reserves, and there was an awful struggle. General Harispe encouraged his men, and fought with them with great vigour, surrounded the redoubts we had taken, and broke in upon the 42nd Highlanders; this gallant corps fought so bravely against such long odds that there were but few blue bonnets left in half an hour. The fighting was desperate here; our men fell fast and were soon reduced to a "thin red line" of old *bricks*. The French had the advantage from numbers and position, but the British, regardless of numbers at any time, go in to win. Harispe and another general had now fallen, fighting like game-cocks. Our 6th Division rushed on madly for a victory, and kept the ground until the French left the platform. Soult, seeing that the red-coats had won the day, abandoned the field, covered with slain, relinquished the whole of Mont Rave, further resistance being useless, and retired into Toulouse.

This was what I would call honest good fighting, face to face, hand to hand on the open field, the usual practice in the Peninsula. On the other side we had gained a good many streets, and kept them; wherever a head appeared from under cover it was in danger of being cracked with a dozen bullets. I had myself some providential escapes. Passing into a long, narrow, shady street, very quiet, and no one visible, a cannon-shot came whistling past my head so close, I felt the wind of the ball on my cheek, which *whift* me round. I darted into a house in a jiffy, when another came bang after me, passed through the room, and fell from the opposite wall. My captain had just turned the same corner, when I warned him to look out, and only just in time to save his life, for which he blew me up, saying, "You never keep your eyes open, or you might have seen that gunner at the top of the street, just waiting to crack your wild head." I peeped out at the door, and, sure enough, there he was, standing by his gun, ready to blow the match. I rolled his own shot out into the street, keeping my eye on him; but he fired no more. One of our men saw him, and "made him lave that sure," as he said; for "I saw him fire on the captain, and only waited to creep near enough to pitch him over!"

Curious to see how the battle was going on over the river, I *invited* our Colonel, Worsley, to accompany me for a belle-vue quite at hand. "Where are you going to take me?" he said; "remember every house is full of sharpshooters, and if I follow you, it will surely be into their company." "Oh no, 'tis all safe; I have got a ladder here; we will top this house and see a bit of the fight on the other side. Did you ever hear a more terrific fire? Like the Kilkenny cats, there will be nobody left soon." "What about the cats?" he said. "Were you ever in Ireland?" "No, never." "Well then, the cats in Kilkenny fight with a ferocity as savage as cannibals. To try their metal two big tom-cats were tied by their tails, thrown across a rope in an empty room, and the door locked. Next morning when Paddy went in to see which of them had won the battle, he declared there was nothing left but the tail of the one and a bit of the *flue* of the other."

"Well done," he said, "that's one of *your own*." "No, indeed it is not; it was recorded in Kilkenny before I was born, and they believe it there to be a true *tail*." By this time we had clambered up to the top of a house, keeping a big brick chimney in our front, just high enough to look over to see some of the murder over the way, but had not long enjoyed the view when the brick-dust was knocked out of the chimney by a shower of bullets, we not having calculated that our heads were not only visible, but the very shell of humanity exposed to be cracked like an egg.

When the ostrich is pressed hard in the chase he runs his head into a bush or into the sand, and considers himself safe! I don't think we much exceeded the wisdom of this stupid bird upon this occasion of our curiosity. The next volley, which came fast, sent us away double quick rolling down, ladder and all, and nearly broke our necks. I got off cheap enough with a slight wound; Colonel W—— had his epaulet spoiled with a shot, and a ventilator made in his shako.

We kept pounding away until night drew the curtain over a wide scene of painful misery. Multitudes of wounded lay scattered over miles of ground; the agony and torment and shrieks and helpless condition of thousands found no relief for a long time; hundreds died in the night for want of care; it was impossible for the medicos to attend to half the wounded; the living had a heavy day of fatigue and fighting with great excitement, but their hands and their hearts were up to their work, in spite of any reaction.

The programme of the Easter Sunday was now closed; the men lighted the camp-fires and sat round them cooking and chatting over the ration dinner and *absent* comrades.

Next day was a *dies non, i.e.*, we had no fighting worth talking of. We kept all the town we gained, and the French kept the rest. We buried the dead in shallow graves. Both parties kept a sharp look-out on each other all day. I went on outlying picket at night with instructions to be wide awake, and feel my way at the dawn of day towards the bridge if I met with no opposition.

On the morning of the 12th, at grey dawn, I was feeling my way with the picket without opposition; arriving at the fine stone bridge, I found it barricaded all the way over with hogsheads filled with earth and stones and gravel; walking over these, I came to the ponderous iron gate, locked and fastened with heavy chains. When the people saw me advance with my party of red-coats, they came down with good will, with crow-bars, and forced the gate open, and gave us a cheer and a welcome, so that I had the honour of being the first British officer that entered Toulouse. Here I halted until my own corps came up; we then marched in, colours flying, drums beating, all very jolly, and halted for an hour in the street waiting for orders. In the mean time most of the officers popped into a café to get some breakfast. The windows and balconies were soon crowded with ladies, waving their white kerchiefs, and throwing down amongst us bouquets of fresh flowers, as if they had sprung up spontaneously. The white cockade appeared as if by magic everywhere, although the French army had not been out of the town twelve hours.

We *fancied* that we were now to be left here in this garden of Eden amongst sweet flowers and pretty girls that were smiling down upon our tattered red coats—vain imagination! An *atrocious* cocked hat of an aide-de-camp came riding up with a smirk, saying, "Colonel W——, you are to follow up the enemy on the Toulon road with your regiment as quickly as you can. You will receive subsequent orders," and away he went, after destroying all our hopes and pleasant waking dreams. I believe our fighting colonel was the only one who wished to advance in such a hurry; and not to retard our progress a moment, he paid the breakfast at the café and hurried us off.

The whole French army had taken to their heels in the night and filed through the town. As they passed on they broke down the bridges over the canal to impede our line of march; but we never came up with them again, nor smelt the perfume of tobacco and onions which tainted the air behind them. We halted at the little town of Villefranche, and there we heard by an express from Paris that Napoleon the Grand had abdicated, and that the Allies were in the capital of la belle France, and all the rest of it. This was all very serene, and I believe joyful news to most of us, for in reality we had enough fighting and marching and starving for a long time to come. At all events I thought so, and was quite content with the little share and small part I had in the campaign, having marched through Portugal, all over Spain, and well into France; having been in thirteen engagements with the next best troops in the world, and escaping for three years out of the hands of the Philistines without any broken bones, a providential and rare occurrence in those days, when one considers the rough usages of war, and that we left in Spain and France the bones of nearly *one hundred thousand* men; most of them bleaching in the sun, after being picked bare by the vulture and the wolf.

We now considered the war at an end, and began to enjoy ourselves in a fashion, proud of our conquests and the glory of our arms, a stirring sound amongst all ranks; but war is never far away; from man to the very smallest insect, all are at strife.

After conquest one begins to count the cost. War is a great evil, and a very expensive trade. In this one England expended more than a hundred millions sterling money on her own operations, besides an immense expenditure on Spain and Portugal. Her land forces fought and won eighteen pitched battles, besides *affaires* and combats without number, took four great fortresses by siege, and sustained ten others. *Two hundred thousand* of the enemy were killed, wounded, and prisoners.

It was said the Duke of Wellington committed faults. Who ever heard or read of a great commander making war in all things faultless? He was a great general, with a patient foresight, a clear judgment, prompt and decisive, insuring the whole confidence of his army, and yet had to contend against the Governments of England, Spain, and Portugal; all retarding his progress and casting dust in his eyes. All those to whom he looked for support were jealous and vindictive, even the Cabinet Ministers of his own country; and they say he committed faults,—what were they? England had no army until *he* made one. He landed in Portugal with 9,000 men, and beat back the armies of France to their own firesides. He had rare qualities as a commander; he overthrew the great conqueror Napoleon, the swell and dash of a mighty wave, before whom kingdoms fell. If you fight for England you should *always* win, and what English general was ever so victorious as Wellington?

In summing up accounts and returns for the last few days, it appeared that we had lost 4 generals and 4,659 officers and men, killed and wounded: total loss of the French, 5 generals and 3,000 officers and men, ditto; a useless and lamentable sacrifice of life, Napoleon having abdicated before the battle. A Colonel Cook and a French Colonel, St. Simon, had been despatched from Paris to make known to the two armies that hostilities must now cease; these officers were detained on the road by the police, near Blois, where the Empress Louisa was holding a court; and this officious detention cost the blood of 7,000 brave men, which flowed over Mont Rave and through the streets of Toulouse.

My regiment returned to the gay city of Toulouse, where we were quartered; the officers were billeted here and there through the town. 'Tis all a lottery; one may get into an hospitable house, another may find a vinegar-face of a landlady. I was not over lucky, but my room was clean, and I lived as best I could on my *promissory note, the* six months' pay due, the great sum of about £55, deducting income-tax, which was levied from the pay of the junior ensign!

The Duke of Wellington established his head-quarters in Toulouse; there was no end to gaiety; we were out at balls, concerts, and evening parties; we had the *entrée* into all the theatres to any part of the house for a franc; the people seemed happy and rejoiced over the new order of things. The town had not suffered in the least during the killing and slaying outside, excepting on *our* side of the river, which was plundered, fired, and demolished by the French troops as they were beaten back. The Duke did not suffer a shot or shell to be thrown into the city when held by the vanquished troops after their retreat from Mont Rave, and of course gained the respect and esteem of the citizens for his consideration and humanity.

The Duke d'Angoulême made his public *entrée* into the city escorted by Wellington and his staff, and all the dignitaries of the town and country. I went out with the rest of the cocked hats and feathers to meet him some distance off, being well mounted on a spunky horse, who *would* be in the front. He carried me, *nolens, volens*, alongside of the Royal Duke, when and where I was admonished by Sir E. P——, and ordered to fall back! I never had a very thin skin, and did not torment myself at this checkmate; but I have known an officer who was so hurt by receiving a rebuke at the head of his regiment that he went deranged, was placed in an asylum, and never recovered. He was a most excellent officer, and had his regiment in first-rate order, until he met this uncouth savage of an inspecting-general.

The Duke's welcome *home* was echoed everywhere by old and young; fresh and fair, aged men in heads of snow, all pressed forward to kiss his stirrup. All a mockery. The restoration of the Bourbon dynasty did not last long, nor was it desirable; the rational character of human nature was shocked in the Protestant line by the mummery of priests and impostors in the Papist Church. Popery was soon re-established, *miracles got up*, confessions and processions and tubs of holy water supplied *ad libitum*, to wash away Buonaparte transgresions, and begin a new score of bigotry, superstition, and blasphemy,—anything to fill the pockets of greedy priests. The hearts of the poor people were expanded, and the change was agreeable to a class of mercurial bipeds who went wild for a season.

After six weeks of refreshing jollification, we got the route for Bordeaux. I was glad of the expected change of quarters; we had a few days' notice to *quit*, and lighten our baggage. I sold my three horses to raise the wind and pay my debts. I did not realize for the three so many dollars as one of them had cost me, the market being overstocked with horses, mules, and donkeys, all at a fearful discount, every officer selling off. I was not very well at this time. I suppose a regular kind of life and a feather-bed did not agree with my former manner of life on the green sod. Our doctor recommended me to go down the river with the invalids in an open boat; barges were provided for the sick and wounded soldiers, small boats for small parties of officers, the weather being charming, we required neither sails nor oars, so away we went, smoothly gliding over the silver stream, one man steering (it was hard work for the poor horses pulling up those heavy barges against the stream).

We landed every evening at some village on the banks of the fine river to pass the night. The dames from the different auberges made a rapid descent upon us the moment we landed, with such a clatter and noisy invitation to go to their respective houses,—everything so nice, so good, superior, and such moderate terms,—abusing each other all the time in the most *distingué* fashion.

We knew pretty well what was meant by moderate terms, all that they could screw out of famished pockets. After exhausting all their polite language, if it is possible to tire a French-woman's tongue, we took a peep into their respective shells, selected our lodgings, and made our bargain,—a necessary arrangement in France, and all over the Continent, to prevent disputes, overcharges, and imposition.

However, they bustled about with good humour, and made us all so very comfortable, that we would have remained there willingly for weeks if we could. The situation was so charming, so peaceful; no parades nor drills, nor a chance of one's bones being broken with shot or shell. How wonderful was the feeling of quiet; no trampling of horses, nor clashing of arms, nor tir-whit of a shell, or the *whop* of a cannon-ball, splashing the mud in one's face, or perhaps the brains of your camarado.

Three delightful days we passed on the Garonne, and then brought up in the beautiful town of Bordeaux, amongst fruit and flowers, choice wine, and nice friendly people—first stage, homeward bound—it all appeared as a holy dream. Our last run down was a short one; on landing, four of us went to a café and ordered breakfast—a good one, and no mistake. We were hungry as hunters, and were well served. We cast lots who was to pay the bill; I was the Jonas, and it just cleared me out to a cent, and left me in every sense in light marching order. Not a penny at my command—let loose in a large city, full of luxury, frolic, and fun, I searched all my pockets in vain for a single franc to get a scrubby dinner, but it was no go; so I went in search of my billet. After roving about the *city* for some hours, I found No. 2, Rue St. Colomb,—Monsieur Ducasse—knocked at the door and presented my *ticket* to the servant, who took it up for examination. After surveying me with wonder or *admiration*, never having seen a red-coat at No. 2 before, I was received kindly, and shown up stairs to a suitable room, for sitting and sleeping in combined, and left there to look out at the window, to turn over in my mind how or where I was to find my servant and my baggage, which was reduced into so small a compass that he could easily carry it on the top of his knapsack, along with firelock and the rest of his war *tools*, for I had discarded *the* frying-pan and all the other camp toggery. I made a start into the town, without money or credit—nothing but an alarming appetite. I knew that I had my rations to fall back upon, but I could not find my servant, nor could he find me—we were both lost. I rambled about in search of him for hours, and did not find No. 2 till late, when I was presented with some light supper of salad or vegetable diet. A round of boiled beef would have been more in my way, but I never saw one in France.

The kind landlord now told me that I must never be out of the way at three o'clock—it was their dinner-hour. I must always breakfast and dine with the family, and be one of themselves while I remained, or he would be very *angry*, with an emphasis on the word and a smile on his honest face—a friendly offer which I accepted with thanks. Particularly lucky I thought myself, as there was nothing in my department but the rations and a thundering appetite. I had permission to draw my rations once a week in a heap, which was sent to the kitchen of my landlord. The next morning I made my *début* at the breakfast-table, after waiting about three hours beyond my usual time. An early tasse of *café noir* keeps a Frenchman alive until the *déjeuner* at eleven o'clock. I was introduced to Madame and the fair Clementine, not out of her teens, and the son, an agreeable young fellow, who spoke English a *leetle*. We became great allies and correspondents for many years afterwards. I found my stray *cook* and *butler*, who was also a guest and lived in clover—nothing to do but clean my boots and study French in the *cuisine*. His name was *Death*, which may account for many escapes in battle, he being the destroyer never to be destroyed; but he was a stupid fellow at any foreign language!

The young lady played on the harp and piano, and was really an accomplished, pretty, bashful girl, who was sent to *mass* very often with her maid, and to confess her sins to a crafty old priest who might have excused her innocence. The absolution was required *within* the box, not from the simple child on its knees *outside*.

They had little music parties of an evening; on one of those occasions a French officer came up to me and looked at my buttons, being, as he said, familiar with the No. 34, and asked me if there was an officer named Day in the regiment, and if I knew anything of him. "Oh, yes! he was our Adjutant, but was unfortunately killed on the Pyrenees on the 25th of July last, when you paid us that most unfriendly visit." "Not so," he said, "but was mortally wounded; I found him on the battle-field after he had been plundered, and spoke to him. He gave me the sign and token of a brother of our craft; and, being a Freemason myself, I took him from that moment under my charge. I was sent to Bayonne with our wounded and many of your prisoners; poor Day was my especial care—I got him so far, and made his wasting life as quiet to him as possible. He wanted for many things that I had not in my power to provide; I got him cash for a bill on England, which I may say was duly honoured, but he did survive over a couple of weeks or so, and was buried with Masonic honours."

This was the *finale* of a good soldier; he fell into the kind hands of a brother Mason, and was not left, as we thought, on the field amongst the slain, to be devoured by the vultures. I resolved, after hearing this little chivalric story, to become a Freemason if I got safe home, and I kept my word. The Brethren are to be found amongst all nations; and if you can make yourself known, you may be sure of aid, friendship, and security; and although denounced by the Pope as *heretics* and out of the pale of the Church, I can assure his *Holiness* they are the most loyal of her Majesty's subjects, stanch supporters of her Crown and dignity, and of the Church of England as established by law, and on this subject the opinion of the Pope is worthless beyond the Vatican.

Our army was now encamped about seven miles from Bordeaux; and, as if we had not fighting enough, certain regiments were selected to embark for America, to begin a new war with people who could speak English. Our wise law-makers at home were too fond of settling disputes in those days with powder and lead. The expedition embarked for New Orleans under the command of Lieutenant-General Sir Edward Pakenham, brother-in-law to the Duke of Wellington, an able and gallant officer who passed through the Peninsular war to be killed by an American rifleman from behind a bale of cotton.

Our people found this a different sort of warfare; the cunning Yankee would not fight on open ground. He was a smart fellow at a pot-shot from behind a wall or from the top of a tree; and, if successful on this occasion, he may thank those who planned the expedition and sent our best troops to land in his marshes to be shot down before they could get on standing ground. Brother Jonathan is a boasting enemy, a deep player at brag, talks of whipping the *Britishers* and all *creation*, and so on; but sure to find his level sooner or later, even in his own country and amongst his own kin; a house divided against itself is likely to tumble to pieces.

The rest of our army began to embark for England as ships arrived; in the mean time there was much unpleasant work and bad feeling between French and English officers; both

parties being so habituated to fighting, it seemed quite out of
their power to give it up—like two game-cocks who meet on
the same path, they must have a kick at each other! There
was a feeling of deep jealousy against us; we received much
attention, and the ladies favoured the British officers with
smiles, which made things worse. There were many quarrels,
and the *Duello* came into practice; the theatres were crowded,
and some of our officers were insulted one night by their antagonists. To insult one red-coat then was an insult to all, and
so there was a general row, the French officers being driven out
of the house. The next night there was a great muster of
both parties, I believe for the purpose of renewing the war or
opening a new campaign at Bordeaux; the Frenchmen had
their swords, the English officers none; the Irish gentlemen
carried *shillelaghs*, as they do at Ballymacrack, in Tipperary.
Somehow a nice little quarrel was soon got up about some
ladies who were receiving attentions from the boys of Kilkenny,
every one of them nearly six feet high; and, indeed, the sweet
girls of Kilkenny, although not so tall, are very fine specimens
of Divine art—so fair and so fresh—

> "Their cheeks are like roses,
> Their lips just the same,
> Or like a dish of ripe strawberries
> Smothered in cream."

The French ladies, not appearing to countenance any but
those big Irishmen, sharp words were spoken against all red-
coats, a great many frowns—swords half unsheathed and
dashed back into the metal scabbard with a sort of clang of
defiance—the blood of St. Patrick was roused; those gentle
creatures, whose trade was killing and slaying, did not require
much fuel to get up their steam. One of the Fitzgerald's
"Light Division," a battering-ram of himself, drew his stick
half-way up through his left hand, and sent it down again with
a bang on the floor, looking pistols and daggers. There were
some sarcastic words; then a shove and a scuffle, which soon
increased to something like an Irish row at Donnybrook fair,
when the Frenchmen were banged out of the theatre whole-

sale. All this play began in the lobby beween the acts; and, as the last of the blue-coats went rolling down the stairs, some one above cried out, "Exeunt omnes!" and all was quiet. Next morning was fixed for the *Duello*, the general *finale* of such sports; blood was spilt on both sides very freely, and one or two gentlemen were qualified for a *wake*. Preparations were being made for a great fighting field-day on the following morning; but the whole of last night's campaign being reported to our Commander-in-Chief, hostilities were suspended by a general order, and all officers prohibited going again to this theatre, under certain pains and penalties.

The French officers were ordered by their chief to retire across the Garonne to their own quarters.

In defiance of the general order, some of our officers had the imprudence to return to the same theatre, but found a sergeant there with a book to insert the name of any who insisted on going in; with one exception they all retired, and that exception was the senior captain of my own regiment, an old officer who ought to have shown a better example. When the book was sent next morning to the Adjutant-General, Captain B—— was placed in arrest, and had his choice to stand a court-martial or quit the service. He chose the latter and gave a step in the corps, a most unfortunate *finale*, and deeply regretted by all his friends; but the first duty of the British soldier is to obey orders!

My regiment lay in camp some miles from the city. I was too comfortable myself with my kind friends at No. 2, to mix in any of these broils; their hours were early, and the family quiet and happy, nor was it my part to be out late, so I stayed at home. The good landlord used to say to me every day at dinner, "No Ros-beff, Monsieur George;" and the kind lady always gave me Benjamin's portion at breakfast *à la fourchette!*

My corps had nothing to do, so they did not want me, nor was I at all anxious to leave my town residence.

I went out one day to pay them a visit, and to see Sir Lowry Cole on a little private affair. General Cole was a neighbour of ours when at home, and always ready to do me a service, but we seldom met; he commanded the 4th Division of the army. On this occasion he got me leave of absence to precede my regiment going home; my turn for leave was far distant, so I came the old soldier over my seniors; but they forgave me after much chaffing, such as, "We suppose that General C—— is going to take you on his personal staff, and, of course, you must go home for your cocked hat and feather." "O, no doubt, old fellows, lucky enough for the man who has a home to go to; I will be happy to see you all at my château when your time comes to be quartered in our country town." And the time did come in reality, and the officers, one and all, were welcome guests at Belle-vue, when I was far away, frying in the East Indies, in another campaign, and in another regiment.

But here I am, still passing a day at the camp near Bordeaux, hearing all the news, seeing all my old comrades, the men of my company, and every one, as if I had been absent a year, everybody jolly, oceans of money, and no end to good living for man and horse! An issue of six months' back pay in gold opened the eyes, and the mouths, and the hands, and the hearts of a whole army; the matter was how to spend it. Soldiers like sailors win their money like horses, and spend it like asses. There was no lack of wine-houses and restaurants, dominoes, pitch and toss:—*Head, I win!—tail, you lose!*—anything to catch the penny; so their thirty or forty dollars did not last long.

"What about our old friend, Mrs. *Commissary-General* Skiddy?" I asked one of my sergeants. "O, be gad, sir, she's all right and fresh as a *shamrog*; there she is, sir, crossing the green, would you like to speak to her?" "Yes, I will hail her myself. Hilloo, mother Skiddy, come over here till I look at you, and see if it's yourself or your ghost?" "Oh then, Musha, God bless you my dear, sure it's myself that's glad to see your honour alive, after being kilt on the top of a house in the great battle when I was away in the care of Dan. Sure they reported down where I was, you were kilt entirely; but, my fegs, it's right well you're looking, the Lord *presarve* ye, and sure Dan was so sorry for yer honour, and said, 'how many's the mile you carried his firelock for him on the long march,' for he was sometimes bent, tired, and ready to *dhrop;* an ye know, sir, when I found him smashed up in that battle at Saint Peter's, he says to me, 'Biddy,' says he, 'I'll never march any more, for my leg's bruck in two *heves,* by that pagan that kilt me.' Well, sir, when the doctor *cum* to set his leg, it wasn't *bruck* at all, only a big hole in it, but 'twas mighty sore; an sure I have him here now as good as new. All the men as was wounded, barrin' the killed, cum up here t'other day; would you like to see Dan, sir?"

"Surely I must see him before I go home,—I'm going to Ireland soon."

"Is it to ould Ireland, sir? sure that's me own counthry, the blessin' av all the saints be wid yer honour, sure it makes me heart bounce when I think av bein' there agin." And wiping her eye with a corner of her very white apron, she ran away for Dan.

He was a very wiry piece of stuff, not over five feet three; but able to do more work than two lanky fellows all backbone and no muscle; always at his post, and a great enemy to them *vagabones,* the French!

"Well, Dan Skiddy, I'm glad to see you looking so fresh after being *killed* at St. Pierre in that big fight. You will soon be qualified for the pension, and we hope you'll get *the shilling.*" "O, then good luck to yer honour, and sure it's yourself that would make it fifteen pence if ye *cud,* for I marched a power in Spain, and kilt a good dale av the French, bad scram to them the *vagabones.*" "O Dan, avourneen, don't be cursin' the *frinch* now that we're done wid 'em; sure they couldn't help it, the crathers, bein' paid to fight for ould Bony himself."

"Well, you know how they murdered my leg, Biddy." "Sure that's their *naither,* dear, to murder every one av us, but the *pace* has made them quiet and civil now. O, me back!" "What's the matter with your back, Biddy?" "O, yer honour knows how my back was bruck on the *rethreat* from Madrid down to Portugal in the short days of winter rains, when everybody was lost; but Dan made promise niver to tell any one, and there he is *forenenst* me," giving him a sly look for permission to tell her story.

"Yer honour minds how we were all kilt and destroyed on the long march last winter, and the French at our heels, an' all our men *droppin'* an' *dyin'* on the roadside, waitin' to be killed over agin by them vagabones comin' after us. Well, I don't know if you seed him, sir, but down drops poor Dan, to be murdered like all the rest, and says he, ' Biddy dear, I can't go no furder one yard to save me life.' 'O, Dan jewel,' sis I, 'I'll help you on a bit; tak' a hould av me, an' throw away your knapsack.' 'I'll niver part wid my knapsack,' says he, 'nor my firelock, while I'm a soger.' 'Dogs then,' sis I, 'you 'ont live long, for the Frinch are comin' up quick upon us.' Thinkin', ye see, sir, to give him *sperret* to move, but the poor *crather* hadn't power to stir a lim'; an' now I heerd the firin' behind, and saw them killin' Dan, as if it was! So I draws him up on the bank and coaxed him to get on me back, for, sis I, ' the Frinch will have ye in half an hour, an' me too, the pagans ;' in thruth I was just thinkin' they had hould av us both, when I draws him up on me back, knapsack an' all. ' Throw away your gun,' sis I. ' I won't,' says he, ' Biddy, I'll shoot the first vagabone lays hould av your tail,' says he. He was always a *conthrary crather* when any one *invaded* his firelock.

"Well, sir, I went away wid him on me back, knapsack, firelock, and all, as strong as Sampson, for the fear I was in; an' fegs, I carried him half a league after the regiment into the bivwack; an' me back was bruck entirely from that time to this, an' it'll never get strait till I go to the Holy Well in Ireland, and have Father McShane's blessin', an' his hand laid over me! An' that's all the thruth, yer honour, I've tould ye."

"Well, Mrs. Skiddy, you are a wonderful little woman, you saved a good soldier for yourself and the service; all the regiment knows how well you acted on the march, where we lost so many of our gallant comrades; you have been always a most useful person, well respected, and I wish you safe home to the green Isle, and a safe meeting with your friends and Father

McShane! But where was your donkey all this time?"

"Och then, yer honour knows when that murderin' villain shot our poor donkeys. I helped on the back of my wee fellow all that he could carry, to save what I could for the poor women whose dead beasts were left on the roadside, and so I was left to walk myself, and carry poor Dan a bit; the curse av the crows be on *his* fire-finger* that shot the donkeys."

I bid this wonderful structure of humanity a friendly farewell, after squaring a long account with her for about a year's washing and darning. She was reluctant to take anything, saying, "O, sir, sure you always belonged to me own company, an' you're welcome to the bit av washing."

I hope *Dan* got the shilling, *i.e.*, a shilling a day pension for life; but the Government of the day that wasted with unsparing hand England's gold in millions, passed off with a sixpenny pension the old soldier, bearing many scars, and very often with sixpence or ninepence a day for nine, twelve, eighteen, or twenty-four months, when it ceased and he became a pauper. The sinecures held in those days by the aristocracy and their friends and relations for doing nothing would have pensioned for life thousands of brave men who nobly fought for their country and their king; but the war was now over, and as the historian, the great and gallant good Napier, said in his conclusion, "Thus the war terminated, and with it all remembrance of its veterans' services."

* Fire-finger,—the fore-finger that pulls the trigger.

CHAPTER XII.

Adieu to Bordeaux.—On Board Ship.—Welcome Home.—Hero-Worship.—
The Huntingdon Peerage.—Life in Ireland.—Sounds of War.—The
Castle Guard in Dublin.—Tipperary.—Peace.—Life in Scotland.—A
Prize in Life.—The Baby Major.—The 45th.

I PASSED six most agreeable weeks in Bordeaux, Monsieur Ducasse repeating every day at dinner, in his jocular way, " No ross-beff, Monsieur George ;" but there was always something equally good, if not better, and an honest good welcome.

My time was up now, and I had to say a very sorrowful farewell. The kind Ducasse took me aside and offered me any amount of money I wanted, saying, " When you return to England, it may be remitted at your convenience. I have every confidence in the word of an Englishman." All this was touching liberality. I thanked him sincerely and assured him I had plenty of money, more than I required to take me home. He urged me to give up a military life and come to Bordeaux; settle as a merchant, and give over fighting. I promised to think of it, and expressed an earnest desire, which I still feel, that England and France might live in peace and harmony as good allies for all generations to come; welded together they might stand against all the combined enemies in Europe.

He accompanied me to the ship, kissed both my cheeks, and we parted for ever !

I had a passage on board the *Sultan*, a seventy-four ship of war, with the 71st regiment. I took my own sea-stock for the voyage, according to the custom of those times, packed up in hampers. In the evening I went below to get something to eat and a bottle of wine out of my store, when I found my jolly friends of the 71st enjoying the contents of my hampers and laughing immoderately at the fun. " Ho, my lads ! " I said, " do you know that's my sea-stock you're pitching into ;

all I have got for the voyage. I suppose I must mess with the cook for the trip home, as you have emptied the baskets, wine and all." "Oh, never mind," they said; "come, sit down, have something to eat, and make yourself agreeable; here's your health and a bon voyage. Our mess is not yet open, so we took a dive into the first larder we met." The whole of my prog at this time was being spread out on a table in the gun-room, the fellows laughing away and drinking my health all round. The party increased in numbers and in appetite, until the whole contents were demolished in mirthful glee, for all were happy, cheerful, and elastic. Home was in every eye; families and friends just in view, and such welcomes awaiting the brave on every hearth-stone in the three kingdoms.

I was formally invited next day to join their mess for the voyage, having nothing left. Twenty-four bottles of wine I calculated enough for myself, but that only served my friends for their luncheon. However, all came right in the end, and we had a jolly party.

We all had breakfast, dinner, and beds in the gun-room, five-and-twenty of us; it was one *salle-à-manger*, dormitory, and bath-house, a very hotbed of *devilment* at night after the master-at-arms signalled "Lights out, gentlemen." The very first night, when all was quiet and the old fellows snoring, a couple of young lads crawled about in the dark with sharp knives, and cut down by the head or heels all the swing cots in their way, spilling the contents on the deck, at the risk of broken necks and of crushing all underneath.

There was a general row now, much clamour, yelling, and laughter, as they came down *smash* on the hard boards. "O my head!" "My back's broke!" "Is the ship going down?" "My eye is knocked out," says another. A fat bag of a paymaster came crash on the top of me, as I lay just below him rolled up in my cloak; the only bed I had was a *soft* plank. He nearly broke my legs. There was a deuce of a row amongst the wounded, and much confusion, the conspirators tittering in obscure corners, and screeching with convulsive laughter. Nobody being killed, this frolic caused more amusement than ill feeling next day, but to prevent a second edition we were allowed horn lanterns, with padlocks for their security, for the future.

Our voyage prosperous and the weather fine, the sea-stock just lasted our time until we reached the Cove of Cork. Let go the anchor and *exeunt omnes*. The custom-house gentry were soon on board, but missed the opportunity of inspecting my kit, I having popped into a boat alongside and gone ashore. All my contraband was a few presents from la belle France. If liable to duty or not, I made no inquiry; if I was cheating the Government, they often cheated me; so we were quits on this score. I never got any interest for my six months' back pay.

I booked myself at once by the mail-coach for Dublin, travelled outside all night to inhale the fresh nocturnal breeze, and arrived in the capital of the green isle at three o'clock p.m. next day, and found all friends well as I left them three years ago. I was a sort of a lion amongst my people and friends for some time, flattered and feasted over much, and talked to death almost day and night. I was considered a great hero, and never wanted a fair partner in the dance in the many gay evenings I passed here; but I longed for home, "sweet home," my own dear home; and away I went—the way I came, in the same old coach, with an additional pair of horses, the two guards in their new scarlet royal liveries, sounding their horns as they passed out of the General Post-office yard at seven o'clock p.m.

Next day I was met by my brothers on the way, and at the end of the long avenue by my father, mother, and sisters with such a welcome. Bonfires blazed on the hills all night, kept up by the tenants, who were regaled with whisky. Nothing of this kind is well done in Ireland without whisky! When Paddy buries his wife or his mother, or, indeed, any of his kin, the funeral would be considered a dry one without a *dhrop* of somewhat to soften *the* grief, and wash down the dust after the journey—sometimes a very long one. The women all yell together, or set up the Keenah, as it is called. They are generally divided into sections or subdivisions, and take it in turn. It is a very wild lamentation, but few tears are shed until the *covering up*, when near relatives of the woman-kind open out in concert a fearful cry of heartrending grief and sorrow until the last sod is placed on the grave. Then all is silent, and the whole party adjourn to a convenient shade to drink the health of surviving friends; a keg of whisky is broached, and *the* glass goes round until the whole is finished. They drink fair, there being only one glass for the multitude, which carries a bumper to each biped. A happy termination to any of those evening parties was of rare occurrence; there was generally a row or a shindy got up as the whisky went down, and some broken heads; or, perhaps, a very unlucky fellow qualified for a wake.

When a boy, I used to enjoy the fun, particularly when there was a fight; and I had plenty of opportunities, for the old Popish cemetery was situated in an island just opposite our house. There was no getting there without permission to pass through our grounds and having the use of one of our boats. On a wet day the priest performed the ceremony of a Mass for the dead in our coach-house *en passant*, and always used a bucket of holy water just from the pump to wash away all impurities!

I was considered a wonderful sort of a fellow just now; there was open house for a week for all friends. I was in great demand, and looked upon as a sort of Wellington; always dressed in uniform, and danced with all the pretty girls in the country. I had no doubt a great deal too much vanity, which was not discouraged; and, away from all discipline, I went wild for a season.

My father presented me with a very fine and valuable horse, and I made use of him in the Irish fashion, *i. e.* riding across the country, practising for the harriers in winter, my brother Tom always at my heels on his gallant grey, the very best steeple-chase horse in the country. He was a far better horseman than ever I was, yet I could ride well too. We formed a very nice racecourse a little way in front of the mansion, round a circle hill, and adapted it for flat races or steeple-chase. Our younger brother, William, had his horse too, and a right good one; he had plenty of pluck, but was sure to be left in a ditch on any attempt to go in for sweepstakes. The officers from the town (two miles distant) enjoyed the fun, and were our constant guests; they could ride, or drive, or come by water from their barrack gate; either way the scenery was beautiful, the whole country undulating, and the lough, or lake, "Erin" winding through a lovely country for sixty miles, studded with upwards of three hundred islands. Our home was rightly named Belle Vue. My eldest brother was too grave a character to join with us in our field sports; besides, he never could ride or dance like a Christian. He was always tumbling off his horse; but he had the *head* of us all, and was engaged at this time with the Huntingdon Peerage; and, solely without any other aid, he established Hans Francis Hastings, Earl of Huntingdon, and the third peer of the realm. The peerage was long in abeyance, and often talked of by Hastings, who was a constant visitor at our house; but he had no means to prosecute such an expensive affair as the claim to a title; when my brother took it in hand, with all the expense and all the risk, and had all the glory to himself.

It was a very romantic tale—too long to be touched on by me. The descent of the Earls of Huntingdon was from the famous outlaw Robin Hood, who played so many wild pranks in Sherwood Forest six hundred years ago. We had a grand field-day when the news arrived, a feast and a bonfire, and never talked any more with anything but respect of the gentleman who could never keep his seat in the pig-skin.

Riding along the king's high-road one day with brother Tom, our horses ran away with us at full speed; turning a corner, his horse came down with a broadside crash, splitting his rider's knee-joint open and displacing the cap, leaving a very painful and ghastly wound. "Is my horse much injured?" he said. "Very little indeed; knees quite safe." "All right; then I don't care for myself." After a painful struggle I got him into the saddle; and, reaching home, sent for our doctor, who sewed up the wound; and there he lay for six weeks.

When boys, we two always ran in couples—seldom apart in fun, frolic, or mischief—we took a lead in manly exercises. I was a little more active on foot in leaping, wrestling, vaulting, and running; but he beat me in the hunting-field, kept close at the tail of the hounds, and was always in at the death. This was his pride; he cleared fences that I would not look at; he depended on the abilities of his noble horse, brought up and trained by his own hand, and he never failed him.

How families get divided! We took different ways—army and navy. His first expedition was to the North Pole with Captain Parry, where his ship, the *Fury*, was crushed like an egg-shell between two icebergs, and went down. All hands escaped on the ice, and were rescued by the other ship, *Hecla*.

He went again to the North Pole, *cui bono?* He sailed the world around, over and over, and maintained that he was better off than I, although he lived like a *snail*. He said that he carried his house on his back, and always had a bed at night, while the soldier is so often exposed to the open air, rainy season, and sleeps on the wet sod.—*Chacun à son goût*.

It was a great many years after this that I met him accidentally on the beach, at Madras, at sunrise, while taking my morning walk, inhaling the sea-breeze. We were both amazed and charmed at this unexpected pleasure and singular adventure, neither of us knowing anything of our respective localities. Our time was short—all here is shadow—all above is substance; everything recoils at death.

My leave was nearly up now, when a friend at court offered me a recruiting district, which I accepted. It was but forty miles from home, and it doubled my pay. I kept a horse and dog-cart, took up my quarters at an Irish hotel on the coach road, where I had plenty of room and little company. I very seldom saw any recruits, and had lots of time for shooting, fishing, visiting, and hunting. I was in fair demand amongst the few gentry about, who lived in the old style of open house, and keeping the family blunderbuss always loaded with slugs. The good gentleman, proprietor of one of those houses where I was so frequently entertained for days at a time, was shot dead in his garden one evening while taking his usual walk.

I was horrified at seeing a pool of blood on the road side one morning not a quarter of a mile from my quarters; and, upon inquiry, was told it was "only the Excise officer who was killed last night!" Those murderers were never discovered. I had an old uncle living some few miles off, where I was always welcome. I rode his horses after the hounds when I found him from home; he had a splendid garden, and always wore top boots. I was a great favourite at "Mount Prospect,". the old house on the top of the hill, where he died one day at an advanced age, forgetting to leave me his heir. He had a nephew senior to me, and with another name, who inherited the broad acres. They made him happy—he lives there still and wears top boots; not quite sure if they were not the very same boots uncle Tom wore during the last fifty years of his *bachelority*.

I had a jolly time of it, until news arrived one fine morning, which spread like a grass fire on a prairie, that our old friend *Bony* had broken loose from Elba, and all the troops in the world were collecting to hunt him down.

There was wonderful excitement in every house, in every face, and soldiers went up fifty per cent. premium as the consols went down. All the ships on our coast were in instant demand to carry an army over to Belgium. I threw up my appointment and joined my regiment in Dublin. One half of the old Peninsular army, that could do anything and everything human, had been already disbanded, so quick were the wise men of the State to pull down the pillars that supported the canopy of England for so many years past. Disbanded—dispersed,—not to be had at any price, yet worth millions if got together. Raw levies took their place; brave, but feeble and undisciplined, and, as Wellington said (and he was a very good judge), "The Waterloo army was the worst I ever commanded."

All now was hurry-skurry, bustle, and get out of the way; bugles sounding, drums beating, orderlies galloping, staff-officers flying about and tumbling over each other, ammunition being packed, baggage put into store, artillery ordered out to the park for practice, grand inspection of cavalry, infantry men selected for service, all the weeds formed into a depôt, the whole of the garrison in a deranged state of war excitement, all the soldiers joyful, all the fair sex piping! Our baggage packed and placed in store, the men were snorting for the battle-field; but as luck would have it, for good or for evil, we were left behind; so long waiting for our ship, which never came, we were left behind to garrison the capital of a warlike and mercurial country, that never could be left a single day without fixed bayonets. I believe some of us cried for very disappointment and vexation, but there was no remedy, the battle of Waterloo was fought and won without the gallant 34th!

If the Duke had had his old army with him, he would have won his battle sooner and saved some thousands of men; as it was, he was saved by his allies; but his soldiers fought bravely, he did not wonder on the 18th that he gained a victory, but he said he wondered the next day that he won the battle!

At this period, a dinner was prepared for the officers at the castle-guard, with an allowance of wine and beer, ditto beds and breakfast; but a system of economy sprung up all at once, and everything was curtailed, or diminished, or pared down so much that the captain of this Royal Guard declined the honour of this banquet when announced the following day; the *subs* followed suit, and the matter was reported to the general commanding the garrison, whose bile was stirred up to wrath. An order was sent to the field-officer of the day (who always slept in the chamber allotted to him in the guard-house) to report in writing the cause, should any officer refuse dining there in future. It happened that we gave the guard the following day, which mounted at four o'clock p. m., as usual; Captain S—— told us that he intended dining at our mess before guard-mounting, as he had no idea of eating such scraps as might be provided at the Royal Guard. All backs were up, and we on duty prepared for a long fast. Dinner was announced at the usual hour by the contractor. "We have all dined," was the answer noted in the book and sent to the general.

We were supposed to be punished by sending my regiment far away from the great city, the very thing we all ardently desired, and off we merrily marched to inhale the fragrant breezes of Tipperary, where the women were very pretty and the men always fighting. Paddy is the only man I ever met who fights for fun; he is, and was at this period, very unruly; there was no persuading him to keep the sixth commandment, nor the Sabbath-day; there was a continual strife between moral law and disorder. I was often on *duty bound* to see those unfortunate wretches standing on the *drop*, with the rope round the neck, making their "Last speech and dying words" to a vast crowd in their native tongue; where there was a wild wailing and lamentation—next moment, light or darkness awaiting. They were a wicked and untamable generation of bipeds, and no mistake. Landlords were murdered for letting their farms to solvent tenants, or for ejecting those who would not pay rent; houses were burned, cattle hocked, barns fired, and girls carried off at night, per force, to be married! There was no end to this savage nocturnal play; priestcraft sealed all up with a pardon and a passport to and from Purgatory, according to payment!

I had just taken my seat at our jolly mess-table one night, with a party of friends, when the Adjutant gave me a private hint that I was wanted outside for a moment. "What's the matter now? can't you wait until after dinner?" "Come with me," he said. Old Peckett was firm; I obeyed with a growl. "A magistrate, sir, in waiting with a party; some *foreign* Tipperary service which will spoil your dinner, I fear." Old Peck, as we called him, had had his supper by this time, for he was an early bird. After tramping away in the dark for a couple of miles in solemn silence, the J. P. informed me he had information of a party of *shanavats* in the mountains, who had evaded the law too long, and he was going to *nab* them at last. "What have they been doing?" I said. "Oh, just what they have been doing the last five-and-twenty years, making whisky, and getting drunk, and burning *houseloads* of honest people, and swearing in ribbonmen, manufacturing pikes, destroying cattle, and shooting their landlords!" I believed this to be all true enough, for a very near relative of my own, a magistrate of the county, a popular gentleman and excellent landlord, was shot dead by a hired assassin when returning to his house from the parish church on the Sabbath-day, at noon, and in the presence of many people. Not one of them attempted to arrest this demon; he jumped over a ditch, got into a wood, and disappeared. A reward of £500 was offered for his apprehension, but he never was arrested. This villain did not even know Mr. B—— until he was pointed out to him as the gentleman he was allotted to murder, having come from another county, by *order*, to do the job!

We crawled up a very rugged mountain, through water-courses and brambles, with caution and silence; in the distance we could see a glimmer of light in a cabin, which we surrrounded, and closed in on the nest of hornets; the light was put out as they heard our approach; they rushed outside ready for a bolt, but received the caution, "The first man that moves, we fire a volley," and so we grabbed them all. The informer was kept out of sight, to save his ears, and we lodged the innocent birds in the stone *jug* before daylight; some of them changed their quarters soon afterwards to botanize in Australia!

There was plenty of hunting, and fishing, and dancing, and horse-racing, and all manner of fun in this golden valley. The red-coats expected to be the leading party in all amusements, their buttons being made of gold! My captain, a most liberal fellow in all things and a first-rate horseman in the hunting-field, being asked by a civilian, who was his banker and what was his income? said—"A thousand a year; 'tis very small, you know, but one can manage to spin out on it in country quarters." Turning to me, he said—"Did you ever hear such an impudent question from such an oirish gentleman? *I have* a thousand a year, but 'tis only for one year!"

Peace was once more proclaimed in all the Continental nations, which was to last for ever—*nous verrons*. Poor *Bony* took a voyage to St. Helena for the benefit of his health, and for the public tranquillity of the world, where I called to visit his grave when he was quiet under the willow. Our army at home was reduced by one-half. My dear old battalion was disbanded, broken up, and sent adrift. Some of the officers and men were drafted to the 1st battalion in India, to complete that corps; the rest of us got our congé without ceremony or thanks for past services. I was most liberally provided for with a retiring half-pay of *four shillings* a day for the rest of my natural life at the advanced age of twenty-two by the generous and liberal Government of England!! There was a grand parting dinner before we separated, never to meet again at the same table. The happy and unanimous family circle dissolved; the disperse was sounded, and Freeman, our chief bugler, might blow his loudest blast in vain to reassemble the old warriors, as he had done for years past. Alas! it was a very cloudy day, but there is a silver lining behind every cloud. Never despair, young *subs*; the spokes of the wheel of fortune follow each other so fast that all are uppermost in their turn.

The drummer of my company, Morgason—a young fellow of excellent character—came with a tear in his eye to bid me farewell and to offer his services as one of my retainers! I advised him to stick to his trade, and if we chanced to meet some other day, I might be able to do him a service; and it so happened.

I mounted my gallant steed for a 300 mile ride to the paternal home; engaged Death to follow me, and left Clonmel, our late quarters, to begin the world again, in what way or in what capacity I had formed no idea. I was not fit for anything but being fired at in the King's livery; an idle life was to me at all times a life of slavery. I had no pursuit, and needless as yet even to try back into the service. There was a multitude in waiting who had prior claims, and hundreds who had no claims at all; but they belonged to the *dress circle!* and left me far behind.

I got restless doing nothing at home, and found myself about six months after date in Scotland, fishing in summer and hunting in the winter with Lord K——'s foxhounds—a generous, kind-hearted nobleman, who kept a fine pack, and in good style too. I was frequently his visitor. There were many other lords and gentlemen whose acquaintance I made in the chase and in their banquet-halls, but they all lived too fast for me. I could not keep time with gentlemen on full-pay! so I gradually retreated from the hunting-field, and built a bungalow for myself on the side of a hill facing the sea and commanding a beautiful view of the country. I had a lease of the ground for 999 years; I asked for 1,000 years, but was refused, not being regulation. I had a pursuit now that occupied my time and attention for some time to come: a nice residence and garden. I laid out the grounds myself, planted my fruit-trees, had plenty of vegetables, milk and cream, and lived like a fighting-cock. In the winter I had troublesome visitors. The old laird would not grant any one permission to shoot, although I told him his hares were peeling my apple-trees, and the wild pigeons eating my cabbage-plants for breakfast and dinner; so I took the liberty of shooting the wild doves from my dining-room window, and caught the hares in a trap. I was seldom without hare-soup and pigeon-pie for dinner, without going out with my gun! The Earl of Douglas invited me to join his regiment of militia, he being the colonel. He looked so like an old warrior with his one arm, that I joined his corps as captain and got a handle to my name, thinking I was now at the top rank of my profession. But I did not like this service,—all honour, but no pay, except for the twenty-eight days we turned out for drill, and as I was a resident close by, I had the honour to entertain my colonel and his brother Charles, who was the major,—both excellent, kind-hearted, unaffected gentlemen as ever lived. We had established a mess at the hotel for our *lunar* month of military pleasure. With the exception of the field-officers and three captains, all the rest were in the awkward squad, and somehow could not get out of it!

I got a prize in the lottery of life about this period; a high-caste, sensible, accomplished bonny Scotch lassie for a wife. She had a charming voice, and never lost it in all our travels. Europe, Asia, Africa, and America have each heard her sing the sweet songs of her native land———

I had been reminding the Horse-Guards every now and then that I was ready and willing to be restored to full pay at the shortest notice! I never got an uncivil answer, but I never received a direct one on which I could place any reliance. It was always the same old story:—" Your application will be taken into consideration with others, &c., *when* an opportunity offers." I narrrowly watched the many opportunities that *did* offer and saw them filled up by lap-dogs who had never been across the Channel nor smelt powder. I watched the career of some of those noble fellows: they had a fine run in the service, topped the old veterans, became general officers before their time or their turn, and were pensioned for life! This system of military distinction poisoned the hearts and the hopes of good service soldiers, who died in obscurity.

"What noise is that up-stairs, nurse?" said an English nobleman to his Scotch nursery maid.

"O, *nothing* ava sir, 'tis jist the *Major screekhing* for his parrige." Just so; the major had a jolly time of it in the nursery, and no doubt was a Major-General before I got my company, for which I paid £1,100 regulation, besides——

A trifling incident often turns the events of a peaceful life into paths of trouble, toil, and danger. A party of the 6th regiment *en route* to Aberdeen marched into our town; their drums and bugles set me wild. I asked the officers out to dine at our bungalow. None of them had seen service, but expressed their disappointment, and wondered why I had retired so soon from the army. "I could not help it." "Try the Duke personally," said Captain V——; "no use in writing letters, they bring nothing." I started off to London to try my luck. The Duke of York, our Commander-in-chief, held his levees at night in the Horse Guards. He was a kind, affable person, encouraged young fellows to speak out boldly, and tell their tale. He heard me patiently, and seemed surprised that I had not been returned to the service, but gave me no promise. I went next to Sir Herbert Taylor, to ask him if I might rely upon being placed upon full-pay, as I had many private arrangements to make. He said, "You may expect your wishes realized very soon."

It was a great pleasure to have anything to ask or say to the military Secretary; for there never sat at the Horse Guards a more gentle, mild, amiable person, than Sir Herbert Taylor. I was soon gazetted to the 45th regiment serving in Ceylon, and had a month's notice to clear away out to that spicy island. Sharp practice for an indefinite period in the East. I sold my bungalow, only to rent another in perspective, and embarked on the *Warren Hastings*, one of John Company's trading ships, 1,060 tons, considered a large vessel at the time, Captain George Mason commanding. I had no choice of a ship. There was a contract for the troops, and the owners made their own charge for the ladies' accommodation; they put me in for £250 —exclusive of my own passage, free of course; but we were all charged so much *per diem* for our board.

Our masters in power professed to send us all free to our destination—13,000 miles—a long way to find a six feet home. I don't remember that *one* of our men, out of 200 rosy-faced English lads, returned from India. My share of the voyage cost me personally £240, rather a dip into 7*s.* a day full pay; a generous way of starting young fellows into an expensive trade so far away; but I had a wife and baby girl included in the bill.

CHAPTER XIII.

At Sea.—Mutineers.—Breakers ahead.—Shark-fishing.—Crossing the Line.—The Trade Winds.—Trincomalee.—Its Scenery.—Landing at Madras.—Fort St. George.—A Journey.—Palankeen-bearers.—Negapatam.—The Cobra.—Back to Madras.—The Route.—My Wife's Diary.

WE sailed from Gravesend on the 9th of April, 1825. One hundred and twenty days in a sea prison, with a plank between one and eternity, is a trial of patience; besides the usual allowance of sea-sickness which I thought would never end, and for which there is but *one* cure, and that is— never go to sea. Our troubles commenced in the Channel; there was a gale of wind all the wrong way, then a dense fog. The young soldiers lay about the decks so helpless, that the sailors were tumbling over them, which caused a bad feeling, hard words, and blows at a very inconvenient time, when every blue-coat was wanted at his post. Pigs lost all hope, and died by the score; the guinea-fowl all mutinied to a feather, and cried with one voice, "Go back— go back." The boatswain's mate fell overboard; being an accomplished swimmer he enjoyed a cold bath until picked up by a pilot boat. *En passant,*—every male bird should learn to swim. The wind came astern, and gave us a drive out of the fog into sunshine, and an orange climate, somewhere off Gibraltar, which very much cheered us all *up*, and gave us a *warm* welcome for the first time on deck; but there was a discontented crew, and mischief hatching below.

The boatswain (named Jameson), a very powerful man, over six feet, caught the idea, "in his dreams I suppose," that the ship would be a good prize, and he would make a better and bigger captain than George Mason, a dwarf in comparison as to their respective heights. He gained over two-thirds of the crew to a mutiny that he had planned, which was simply this: to batten down the soldiers in the night between decks; kill all the officers; throw the officers of the watch overboard, before any alarm; the captain to follow, and the ship to be their own. When this was being talked over in the night down below amongst themselves, one of our soldiers' wives, who was lying sick on her own side of the partition, heard the conversation, and reported it quietly, which put us all on our guard; although the little captain pooh-poohed it, the chief officer, Mr. Davis, who looked after everything as well as the navigation of the ship, was disgusted with the character of the big boatswain, to whom he looked for support in the management of a crew, not very select. They had some sharp words on deck at noon, there was a scuffle, the big boatswain could not restrain his violence, but seized Mr. Davis by the throat, and nearly strangled him, before any assistance came to the rescue. The soldiers turned up, but they had no arms, and were all ordered on the poop. Captain Mason turned out of his poop cabin in uniform, cocked hat and sword, to *awe* the whole deck, when the villain Jameson made a dash at him, took him up in his arms like a baby, and was in the act of throwing him overboard, when he was caught by the *royalists*. I held him by the leg, others clung to him by the skirts, Davis called aloud to the crew for help, but none came; the quartermaster left the wheel, the ship ran up in the wind, the sails began to flap, and I believe it was the look of the two hundred red-coats on the poop that kept the crew out of the struggle, but not one of them would obey orders. However we had a strong party of our own now, as the mutiny fortunately broke out in daylight.

One of our side, the "master-at-arms," as he is called, was a tower of strength; hearing the row, he came up, looked about, and seeing the captain and Mr. Davis both in the grasp of this tiger, made a rush at him, when all three fell on the deck in a heap, and after a long and tremendous struggle of kicks and blows, the tiger was held down by seven strong fellows until secured hands and feet in irons, and dragged up on to the poop, where he spit out his venom until a den was prepared for him below, where he was chained to the deck like what he was—a wild beast. The master-at-arms was his gaoler, and a faithful one all the voyage. He kept him in his chain, and fed him like a dog, no one being allowed even to see him the rest of the voyage. The quartermaster was disrated, tried, and flogged with some others; and so ended this act of the play. The master-at-arms was a true man, with a little of a strange history tacked to his right name—he had a borrowed one at this time. His name was Thurtle, of a very respectable family in Norfolk; had been much at sea with Lord Cochrane. His ship being paid off, he returned to London after a long service, and found that his brother had been hanged for the murder of a Mr. Weir; he felt the disgrace so much that he went into a watchmaker's shop one day, asked to see some watches, put one of them in his pocket, and walked out of the door. He did not attempt to run away, was arrested by a policeman, and brought before the Lord Mayor and was asked what he had to say in his defence. He said he took the watch for the purpose of being transported, on account of the disgrace that fell on himself and family, and that he had no other means of getting away from England, never to return. The Lord Mayor was fully acquainted with the cause of his trouble, and got him the appointment he held in our ship.

Our next adventure was an escape from a reef of almost invisible rocks far out at sea. The captain had been on the look-out all day, with his charts before him, for these ugly sharks somewhere in our path, when night came on. Supposing he had passed them on his right or left, he let the ship go before the wind. About half-past ten I heard a shuffling noise on deck, trampling of feet, and a speaking-trumpet, denoting alarm. A small craft had just crossed our bows (the first vessel we had seen since leaving home), calling out, "You are going on the Deserters;" and passed away! The helm was put down, the ship brought up, and laid to all night so close to the rocks that one might have thrown a biscuit on to them. All we could see was a cluster of jagged black points above the water, and so we were mercifully preserved from positive destruction; a few minutes more and our ship would have been inevitably lost, and most probably all hands. Not long after this we had another providential escape. It was the custom of the chief officer to go down once a week, with a lantern, into the grand store, for the supply of spirits, wine, and other stores; this place was full of combustibles, such as tar, dried rushes for the cooper business, &c. Something particular being wanted one night, contrary to rule, the captain asked his chief officer to take with him a careful person, and go into the store. Unlocking the door, they were surprised and astounded to see a light before them—a tallow candle was fixed to the mast, the wood was being charred, a tar-barrel, close by, and a bundle of rushes hanging above. A short time and there would have been an awful flare up. The *Kent*, with troops, had been burned at sea about this time, and all precaution was taken against fire, yet here was a clandestine attempt at a wholesale destruction that never was discovered; the most strict investigation brought nothing to light.

As we approached the Cape, we felt the cold, for it was the *July* winter there. April is a bad season to leave England for India. The cunning of the shark is amusing; to see him play and coquette with a four-pound piece of pork on a great hook fastened to a chain at the end of a strong rope, trailing astern. As the ship very gently glides along, he comes nearly to the surface of the water, his dorsal fin above, smells the bait, gives it a shove with his nose, and disappears below. He soon returns, sails round and round it, gives it a slap with his tail, and dives away. He now feels his appetite getting as sharp as his teeth, approaches cautiously, turns on his back, opens his huge jaws, sucks in the delicious morsel and darts away; his rapidity of motion only hooks him the faster, then comes the play; his violence has no bounds, he jumps above the water, shakes his jaws to get free, plunges and bounds with such force of strength, that he often breaks the chain and gets away to digest his iron lunch in the deep, or let it rust in his jaws. When hoisted into the ship, his play on the deck soon clears the way. One whack of his tail would break a man's leg; he slaps music out of the planks of the deck, and makes a wide circle for himself, until the carpenter comes with his axe, and puts his tail out of joint! then a crack on the head, and all is over. The sailors take a cutlet off his tenderest part; I tried and rejected its coarseness, as being neither fish nor flesh.

There was a barbarous custom in those days, when ships crossed the line, to *shave* all hands on board who had not crossed before. It was a day of mirth and glee to the old sailors, who had a fine opportunity of exercising or paying off old scores against comrades. It was a grand holiday in the ship, and conducted in the following way. The day was fine and warm, and nothing beyond a three-knot ripple to keep the vessel steady. At eight-bells, Neptune with his staff was announced by the sounding of *conches*, as coming up from the deep to pay his respects to the captain of the ship, and drink to his health. Being requested to advance, he was wheeled in his car of state from behind the scenes, with his trident in hand, up the quarter-deck, where the captain met and thanked him for his favourable voyage so far, and requested he would continue his good offices to the end. Healths being drunk in bumpers of rum, those sea-devils retired behind the curtain to begin operations. To give a descriptive account of the fashion of dresses worn at the bottom of the deep would be impossible. All we soldiers, who were arranged on the poop as spectators, enjoyed the fun with roars of laughter, in which the ladies joined.

By means of tarpaulins a very large tank of sea-water was prepared on the deck, a pole was stretched across this pond; the *barber* and his men stood by it. All hands who had never crossed the line were kept below, or out of sight, till called for. The order from Neptune went forth aloud through a conch to shave his children, beginning with his eldest sons (the officers of his good ship). Some ran down below and hid themselves; but it was of no avail; they were caught and *carried* to the barber's shop if they resisted. Some were very obstreperous, and fared the worse for it. Blindfolded and held tight by the two arms, in undress, *i.e.*, shirt and trousers, the first of many dozens was perched and held tight on the pole. The barber then dipped a large paint-brush into a bucket of tar and greese, *lathered* his chin very well, and shaved all off with a rusty iron hoop. A bucket of sea-water was then dashed in his face, and he was tumbled heels over head into the tank, to get out at his leisure. If a good-humoured fellow, he immediately joined in the fun; but the reverse of good feeling was occasionally displayed, and if the one being shaved opened his mouth in complaint, the tar-brush was sure to meet his teeth, if not his tongue. Any display of faintness was checked by the smelling-bottle, represented by a cork filled with needles, which gave one such a dig in the nose that kept him wide awake during the ceremony.

Some were rough, and kicked against *authority*. They were sure to get shaved with the *saw* side of the razor, taste the brush, *feel* the smelling-*salts*, and get half drowned into the bargain; but that was the most agreeable part of the play, for just under the line the heat was so intense one envied the fishes. By eight-bells again Neptune and his people had gone down below, and everything was restored to order but torn *breeks* and ragged shirts. A lady in the ship expressed to the captain a great desire to *see* the *line* we had crossed. " O," he said, " I will have much pleasure in letting *you* see it through my great telescope, but you must wait until sunset." In the mean time he fastened a hair across the glass, placed it on a rest, and told her to look steady and tell him if she discovered anything. Putting her finger tight over one eye she looked and exclaimed, " O dear me, I do indeed now see the line distinctly; how small it is, which explains how easy we got over!"

She was a person of great naïveté, and it saves a great deal of trouble to believe everything one hears or sees.

We fell in with the trade winds occasionally, which carried us on smoothly and swiftly; the voyage lost much of its monotony and terror, for the roughs in the ship became more civilized, having been whacked into a form of discipline. Our table was well supplied; we had little evening parties, and dancing on the deck, when I was in great demand with my violin, the only music, such as it was, on board. Then comes a dead calm; the heat intense, one's shoes sticking to the pitch that oozed from the planks of the deck; ship rolling heavily from side to side, the yards dipped in the sea right and left. This continued for three days in succession, tossing every one about fearfully. Then up starts another trade wind, and away we went before it joyfully for three weeks at a stretch until we sighted the spicy island of Ceylon. The 7th of August brought us up in the beautiful harbour of Triucomalee. The sweetest music I heard for 120 days was "Let go the anchor." What a joyful plunge, and the run out of the cable too, so harmonious.

The anchor was hardly down when a rush was made from the shore by hundreds of the natives, swimming out like black ducks, until the good ship was surrounded and taken by storm. They crawled up the sides like squirrels, and stood on the decks, on the poop, on the rigging, and got into the portholes. All the ladies rushed off and down to their respective dens at the first sight of those black devils, who had not a rag about them but the fig-leaf. They were perfectly harmless, but declined all warning to disperse and cut away home until the captain ordered a cannon to be loaded with powder, and well hammered down. Blow the match—fire—bang. Down they all went head foremost into the deep, like frogs in a well, from every part of the ship, and away to the shore. There were several of the fair sex mixed up in this water excursion, but they kept swimming about below, enjoying the warm bath like black mermaids.

Mr. Twining, master attendant, sent his boat and invited us, with the captain, to go ashore and stay at his house. Everything was charming on *terra firma;* a perfect paradise all around; a new world; a singularly strange, handsome, ebony people. I mistook the young men in their snow-white, curious folding robes for pretty girls, they looked so happy and waited with such respect and attention at table, moving about as light as fairies, and so gentle.

The lizards, green and blue, kept running along the ceiling catching flies; little birds of beautiful plumage kept flying in and out of the open windows. Outside, the tulip-trees, covered with blossom, and such a variety of lovely plants and flowers. A perpetual sunshine, and the sea-bath at your door, —the *tout ensemble* to me was no illusion, it was a paradise.

We sat down to a nice breakfast under a tree; the crows sat above on the branches waiting for a foray, impudent birds and cunning as crickets. Every person at meals has his own servant to attend. The moment one turned his back for anything, down popped a crow, like a dart, and carried off something from the table, so quickly and so neatly done, that nothing was broken or displaced. They often snapped the bread and butter out of baby's hand with wonderful dexterity. The coolies carried the soldiers' dinners from the cook-house to barracks on wide earthen vessels on their heads. The kites and crows, always on the watch, would pounce down and carry off what they could grab. It was amusing to watch their cunning. I kept a pellet bow for their service and my own amusement, hitting one now and then when on the wing, but never brought down my bird. The weather was extremely hot, but I felt in a second paradise, and continued my walks most joyfully for a time, even as far as the inner harbour, the most beautiful and one of the most extensive in all the world, feathered all round to the water's edge with trees and shrubs unknown in Europe. The cinnamon, nutmeg, pepper, coffee, calamander, and many other valuable and precious shrubs and plants were ever meeting the stranger's eye.

The sea-shells were beautiful, the variety charming, and hawked about for sale by the natives, arranged in boxes to catch the Johnny Newcomes as they landed, for every one grabbed at everything as they were released from prison and got ashore. I thought I could live here for ever, and enjoy the quiet of life, as Adam first settled down in the old garden, but there was a something near at hand to remind me that a bit of a churchyard fits everybody. I walked in and found the memorial of those whom I expected to meet alive! This world is but a training-school for the next.

My gallant corps, the 45th, a very distinguished one in the Peninsular war, had left the island, so I went on to hunt them up at Madras. It was a dark night; we anchored in the offing. I was pacing the deck, thinking where I should go next day, or what I should do. I did not know any one; there was no such a thing as an hotel or a lodging-house, then, in all India, which bothered me very sorely, when I heard a splashing about the ship. Looking over the side, I saw the dark shade of a living block of humanity, sitting on the *soles* of its feet, paddling three logs of timber tied together, about ten feet long, as much under the water as above it. "What do you want, you black rascal?" cried the watch on deck. "A chit, massa." "Come up!" and up he came like a monkey, after fastening his *craft* below, stood on the deck as upright as a ramrod, perfectly naked, and black as "Day and Martin." He took off a little conical straw or rush cap which he had tied tight on his head, and drew forth the *chit*, or letter, rolled up in a rag, quite dry. It was for myself—an invitation for us next day to the house of very kind, hospitable, but unknown friends, who heard of our coming to India. We had never heard of or known them. This Indian hospitality, so welcome at the time and so well-timed, was quite joyous, and relieved all my anxiety. Their carriage awaited our landing next day, and took us *home*.

The landing at Madras is no fun—too much adventure in it for old women or sexagenarian gentlemen troubled with gout or rheumatism. The surf is always running mountains high—no boat of England's build could live through it. The Mussula boat alone can cross those mighty billows and breakers. It is a simple piece of mechanism sewn together with coil rope, deep and elastic; no nails nor iron in the whole construction. They are dexterously managed by a dozen of native boatmen, all of them keeping up a sort of bellowing gabble, going over the billows and through the breakers; they lie on their oars, and watch the swell approaching; as it passes under the boat and increases in magnitude, they follow it up until it becomes a mountain of water, and breaks into a stupendous foam. Now is their time and opportunity. All their steam is got up; they pull with all their might, and strain their lungs with the most barbarous yells, to make all the way they can before being overtaken by the next swell; until at last the boat is washed high and dry on the sands. Now's your time! jump out and away, or the coming billow may carry you back to sea, unless the men have time to pull up their bark high on the sands.

I found my regiment in Fort St. George, my commanding officer a jolly sort of money-saving half-heathen. He gave me ten days' leave to refresh myself with our friends at their country bungalow. We were all driving on the beach the same evening, where all the fashion and beauty—white and black, brown and tawny, café-au-lait, and all the colours of the East—were assembled to inhale the fresh sea and balmy breezes, to throw life and vigour and appetite into humanity after the broiling sun had gone down; then home to dinner, the punkah overhead, with all its circulation of air, a fan beside your plate, all the windows and doors open, your wine and water cooled with saltpetre, the bottles of beer in wet flannel bags kept in a draught to cool, claret ditto;—but we griffins could not find a cool corner anywhere. All the pores were wide open, and the ladies' curls lay over their cheeks and necks in straight, wet hair. The bedding cost little; musquito-curtains and a mattress, a sheet and pillow, were all I ever required. The sun is an early riser, but you must be up before him, dressed by your lamp, and away to take your morning ride or walk, before he tops the cocoa tree. My friend, Mr. D——, a civilian, had nineteen horses, so I had no need to walk much; but I was always a great walker, and walked overmuch at times, to my injury.

The *Doctor*, or sea-breeze, falls into the deep about nine o'clock p.m., when the opposite *land*-wind comes down to the coast. All the windows and doors on that side of the house are closed against it; the exposure often causes pains in the joints, stiff neck, rheumatism, and fever; but none of those things ever gave me the slightest trouble, nor had I any fear of danger from any disease in any country all my life. I always observed that those who had, fell into a melancholy sort of despondency and dropped off the roster like leaves in October. A soldier has no more right to tamper with his life than he has to distrust the Most High, in whom he lives and moves and has his being.

The accommodation in Fort St. George barracks for a *sub* was just one room furnished with two chairs and a table—good enough for a bachelor—but many wives had to live in these dens of a fiery furnace, their meals being cooked outside the door in the verandah, from whence the savoury smell of roast meat about four o'clock, along the whole corridor, was not a perfume over agreeable to visitors. Every officer had his man-cook and the cook's mate, to make his breakfast, and roast a joint of a kid as big as a rabbit—hard work for two black innocents, who couldn't or wouldn't do anything else; then there was the butler, and the dobey, or washer-*man*, not woman, and the beastly wallah, or water-carrier, and the derze, or tailor, horsekeeper and grass-cutter, two for every horse, and with these nine I managed to get on for a while very well. I found a tolerable sort of an old house in the Fort, which I rented and furnished. It faced the sea and the cooling breeze; but we wanted the beauty of Ceylon about our doors, its woods and forests, fruit and flowers, coffee plantations and cinnamon trees, the far-famed harbour and all the island perfume; a bare, barren-looking Fort, under a tropical sun, made all the difference.

Death is written on all things; dear relatives that we expected to meet were missing. Sister L—— was called, in full preparation, at the early age of twenty-four; her husband sickened and died after our landing. My presence was required some 300 miles down the country. I answered the call — a perfect stranger in a world unknown. I suffered myself to be carried away one night in a palankeen by thirteen savage-looking black fellows, not one of whom could speak a single word of English, nor did I understand a word of their lingo. They agreed, by interpreter, to convey me in safety this long journey for so many rupees, one-half in advance, and such *buchshis* as massa please to give— *i.e.*, as what was meant, a sheep for their dinner every day! So we commenced our journey, six men under the poles at a time, the relief running alongside a stretch of perhaps seven miles or so; then a change, but never a lowering of the palkee until they all came to a stand for supper, or, as they say, to eat rice.

After a couple of hours' rest and a sleep, they swathed their loins very tight and firm in their long cloths, the torch was lighted, the palkee raised, the pads settled between pole and shoulder, and the monotonous cry of " I-hi-hee-hee, o-ho-harra-ba-ha-he-hum!" raised, and away they went all together, keeping the step well locked up until daylight, when I was put down at a choultry, or by the side of a tank under a shady tree to spend the day. The head man came to make his salaam, and boil my kettle for breakfast, and take orders. We understood each other by signs only, but he never forgot to ask for the sheep; they were not of the Leicester or Southdown breed, nor so expensive. I seldom paid more than 3s. for one on the line of march, and it was always cooked, curried, and devoured in about two hours—a little bit always reserved for *massa*. No one can boil rice like a palkee-bearer; every grain comes out of the chattie as dry as wheat, and nothing more simple; the rice is put into an earthen small vessel, with cold water, and set, covered, by the fire; when well boiled, but not overmuch, the water is poured off, and the rice still left in the vessel by the fire; give it a shake now and then till wanted, and all will turn out as dry as meal. While one man is boiling the rice, another is away to some brook or pond, with his casting-net for fish for *the* curry. Others are preparing the plates for dinner; large fine green leaves are gathered, and sown together with stiff grass fibres; the rice is divided out on those *trenchers*. A little curry and chilies mixed make up the repast, which is eaten with the hand. After this they pour some water down the throat, and go to sleep. They are honest and careful of anything left in their charge, and the most useful, patient, and ill-paid men in all India.

I strolled about under the shady trees all day admiring the beautiful plants and flowers, monkeys, birds, lizards, and all the divine works of nature, in this retired out of the world resting-place, where all was silent as death, except the chattering of monkeys and parrots, screeching beetles, and the chirping of insects in the long grass, which I carefully avoided, the snakes here being in great force.

The sun went down, and I pursued my journey; passing over several rivers and streams in the night, I heard a great excitement going on amongst my black boys; they put down the palkee, and I jumped out to see the cause. One of them had been bitten by a snake, and the rest were dressing the wound with herbs; his foot was bleeding, and the question was, whether the reptile was a *cobra*; if so, there was no cure, and they knew it. Passing on, we came to a deep river not fordable; a small raft was found, formed of reeds, buoyed up with empty chatties, one fellow fastened a rope to it, swam across, and pulled it over with the palkee on top. The raft was then pulled back, and I was taken over safe and dry, the boys (as they are called) swimming alongside like ducks; and so we pursued our journey for a week of brilliant nights, and tropical days of red heat. If you happen to fall in with any civilian station on your line, you may be sure of a good welcome to pass the day. I was thus fortunate on many occasions, and made some nice friends, for there is no country I ever found so hospitable as India. I passed through Pondicherry at this time, a French settlement, and introduced myself to the *Chef-de-port*, and passed the day with him most agreeably. He was a regular John Bull of a Frenchman, who escaped from France in perilous times, and settled here. He had a picture of King George III. over his mantel-piece, and spoke of England as the only free country in Europe, &c.; he showed me all the town and everything in it worth seeing, had a bath ready for me before dinner, packed my palkee with prog, admonished my bearers to be careful and attentive, and gave me instructions how I was to get along, and warned me to be sure to come back.

Everything comes to an end; and in every relation and situation of life there is some cross for us to bear. Love and sorrow never die. I met the living in affliction, sat upon the snow-white tomb of her so much beloved; doorless was that house, and dark it was within; there she was detained, and death had the key!

Negapatam, or town of snakes, lies on the south coast of the Carnatic, in latitude 11°, not far from Ceylon. The natives venerate the deadly cobra snake; they had a nest of them here, and fed them on eggs and milk, all from fear, and hoping

to win their affections, and keep them away from their children!
They are very fond of riggling their way into houses, and
coiling themselves up in one's bed. I had many encounters
with them single-handed; on such occasions my servants declined aiding me in the combat, for when pressed, the cobra
capella stands on the defensive, and can throw himself forward or backward; and they well knew that a nip from his
teeth was certain death. I met one of these visitors about
noon serpentining past the front door as I rode up. I gave the
alarm, jumped off my horse, and attacked with my sword, which
I found too short; after the first dash he made at me, raising
himself half his length, he opened his mouth, spread his hood,
darted out his hissing forked tongue, and showed fight; my
black fellows looking on in wonder at my folly and risk; he
got to a border of thick grass and nearly out of view, when I
got hold of a long bamboo, and pursued. Once more he stood
up in anger, when I hit him on the head, knocked him over,
and finished him off with my sword; hung him up on a tree
until nothing was left, but a skeleton of dry bones; his length
six feet one inch, which was considered a large cobra. They
have two spiral tusks from which the poison is emitted from
the bag below in the jaw.

I remained with my kind friend here for ten days, a lonely,
retired, warm corner of the globe to any one without a pursuit.
There is a little native trading kept up between Ceylon and
Madras, of coir-ropes, cocoa-nuts, and oil, in boats called
d'honies; a sort of naval architecture, primitive in shape
and make, and said to have been just the same since Adam
and Eve lived in Ceylon, supposed to be *the* Paradise, but
certainly not Eden, which signifies delight and pleasure.
(Gen. chap. ii.)

Fond of adventure I agreed for a passage back to Madras
in one of those shells going up with the monsoon, an accom-
modating sort of wind that blows half the year one way, and
vice versâ.

There was not an inch of iron in all this *ship*; they had a
wooden anchor, and one ragged cotton sheet for a sail. I had
never been on board one of those things, but supposed there

was something in the shape of a sleeping den; and so my friend sent out my palkee fastened on two canoes, to be put on board with some cooked rations for the voyage. When I embarked in the evening, I found the palankeen lashed on the top of the house, the hold full of cocoa-nuts, rice, oil, and coir-rope. It was like a country cabin thatched with Palmyra leaves, and as hot as blazes. I crawled into my den, the anchor with a big stone to it was hauled up, the rag of a sheet with twenty holes in it was spread before the warm breeze, and we boldly ventured to sea. I was baked in my kennel all the day; at night I crept out to breathe and take my supper. The captain of the *ship*, Cather També, and his crew, two men and a boy, all as black as ebony, did not know one word of any language but their own Cingalese, not a syllable of which I understood; but we got on pretty well by signs. I found on the second day my prog had all got bad and was walking away, so I pitched the contents of my hamper amongst the fishes. També seeing my hungry position, came and squatted himself beside me on his heels like a black frog, looked into my face, opened his mouth, and ran his finger half-way down his throat. I gave a nod of assent to this movement, when he crept down a hole into his store (all in my view), filled a cocoa-nut shell with cold boiled rice and oil, stirred this mess up with his finger, and presented it to me in great glee, showing his white teeth all the while; but, alas, it only made my interior boil and bubble. The generous countenance of the sable captain drooped as I gently declined the repast. He sat very thoughtful awhile, and then turned his attention to his fishing-lines, but had no bait; however after many a dodge with a red rag, he hooked a small fish and hauled it in with chattering glee, cut it up for bait, cast out his line, and caught a real good one, looked at me joyfully, and put his finger into his mouth. We understood each other; he soon made a bit of fire on a stone flag, and roasted the "poisson." I had some biscuit, and made my dinner, with a tumbler of wine, half boiled with the sun's heat. I now amused myself fishing, and got a few each day, but not enough for the *crew*. On the fourth day we fell in with some regular fishermen, and had a deal or barter,—fish for cocoa-nuts; it was a hard bargain, and it was difficult to come to terms. Three times the fishermen left us, and three times an additional cocoa-nut was held up to bring them back, with a volubility of speech that would have confounded all the fishwives in Billingsgate. However they came to terms at last, and the crew of the d'honey, had a fish dinner without sauce, that might have satisfied twenty men. The fish was picked from the bones, and mixed up with cold rice in a bucket; all hands went to work, and it was from hand to mouth until the bucket was cleared out. Também boiled my kettle, and I had my tea every evening, and lived pretty well, as I couldn't live better.

It was a six days' voyage that surprised all my friends at Madras when they heard of it, and none so much as myself when it ended.

I had hardly got back to Madras, when my regiment got a sudden call for foreign service. We were ordered to Rangoon in a great hurry, a new region of the Eastern world, to fight the Burmese, a people unknown to British soldiers or sailors. Ava was a country we seldom or ever heard of, or bothered our heads about. England, never quiet, was now forming a British army at the Antipodes, to assail and do battle with an empire of savages, armed with spears, dahs, knives, and matchlocks; the whole country, a low unhealthy jungle as we were told, where the army was sure to die off. It was only a matter of time, and so it turned out.

All was hurry-scurry in Fort George, to provide quarters and accommodation for wives and families, the military department having most kindly notified that the ladies must all turn out as soon as the troops embarked! I was more fortunate than most of my comrades, having a brother of my wife in the country who was only too glad to have her and baby with him; but the distance was far away on the south coast, and no conveyance but a palkee; that would never do. I went to our agents in despair for advice. "A brig," they said, "was in the roads returning to Ceylon, but all natives." "What sort of savages?" I said, "are they to be trusted?" "Call to-morrow, and we will have the *captain* here and make some kind of binding agreement." I did so; he looked very like a picture of the devil without a tail. I didn't admire him; but an agreement was signed, and he promised everything. All was now arranged to embark the next evening at sundown. The *ayah* must have leave to see her friends before she would consent to go *abroad*, with double pay granted. The time was up, and no appearance of this black handmaid. Three black fellows were dispatched in search of her; after a long search, she was found by the roadside as drunk as a lord, having lost her balance, homeward bound. I pressed a bullock bandy going by for her accommodation, and got her lifted quite helpless into a Mussula boat, and took her to sea. The brig was to be off the next morning, and without the black devil all my arrangements would have been defeated, no substitute could be found, and a lady and child must be left without an attendant. She was a good servant before and afterwards. This is one of the *agreeable* changes and chances in a soldier's life!

I remained in the ship all night, and left next morning, doubtful of our ever meeting again; but everything turned out with us right in the end. My wife says in her diary,"When you left us we felt desolate and oppressed, the dear child and myself unable to move out of our berths for two days from sea-sickness, the ayah unable to help us, nor had we anything to eat or drink but some fruit and rice-water. Two monkeys came in at the window, ran about chattering, and examining everything in the cabin; they opened one of the hampers, tossed out the bread, cold fowls, and all the fruit, helping themselves to a bit of this and that, and throwing the rest at their heels. I had not power to resist them or drive them away, they were a perfect torment, mischievous but amusing, and kept dear little Mary in constant fits of laughter; when one of them would sit in the port-hole on watch, the other would creep in like a thief, look all about, open a basket, and pitch the plantains to his ugly brother, and away they scampered with their mouths crammed and their *hands* full! When able to go on deck, we enjoyed the evening breeze coming over the sea, the land in sight, and everything so serene and quiet after all our late excitement ashore. We had now the whip hand of the two monkeys, and kept them out of our domicile; so they turned their attention to two *reverend* Brahmins on board, who would not be polluted by the touch of man or beast from their own caste. Those two idolatrous priests lay on the deck together, eat and drank and slept there, had their provisions in a bag and their water in a large chatty beside them. After their noon feast they went to sleep in the bright and scorching sun; monkeys on the watch ready for action. Down they come from aloft, creep all round the deck, and approach very gently the sleeping *babes*, whom they examined to see that there was no deception or trap. One of them opened the bag, and crammed his mouth full, throwing his comrade a share of the plunder. He then put his *hand* into the water-chatty and tossed it up into his mouth so quick, keeping a sharp look-out on all sides. The other one came to have a drink also, but in his hurry he upset the water-pot on the Brahmin's turban and into his mouth. He made a sudden plunge out of his sleep, roused up his companion, had just one glimpse at the two robbers running up the ropes, when they turned round chattering, showing their white teeth, and seemingly quite pleased with their frolic. Not so the Brahmins; they threw their prog and water overboard, lay down again, and fell asleep!

"There was a fine large pet cat on board, who came up on deck every day to enjoy the breeze and have a snooze; the two *robbers* used to watch till she closed her eyes for a comfortable repose, then crept gently behind and gave her such a slap on the ear as made poor pussy bounce; then away they would fly, one would suppose, laughing at and enjoying the joke.

"We arrived safe and well here, after five days' voyage; my brother rejoiced to have us with him; he has a fine bungalow, plenty of servants and horses, and lives like a small king. We ride on horseback every evening, and have a good gallop along the sands for five miles at a stretch. There are plenty of cobra snakes, which makes me nervous about our darling child going out of an evening; however, she has three attendants, one always a little in advance to clear the way with his rattle in hand. Snakes are easily disturbed and frightened; but they are too fond of coming into the house, the doors and windows being always open. The other evening, when we came in from our ride, a large cobra snake met us in the hall; my brother let him take up his position, then fired at and shot him. Indeed this Negapatam means the 'town of snakes.'"

CHAPTER XIV.

Embarkation.—At Sea.—Rangoon.—The Great Dagon.—The Burmese.—Goose Eggs.—Burmese War-boats.—Tiger-traps.—Palmyra Toddy.—Sandford and Bennett.—The Rhahams.—Sagacious Elephants.—Tactics.—Mal du Pays.

I WAS dreadfully ill from knocking about in the sun for some days, and hardly able to walk, even in the shade. A burning fever and total prostration left me *hors de combat* and hardly able to get on board with my regiment. When I got on the deck of the *Golconda*, and into my den, I rejoiced at the prospect of some quiet. No place like sea for an invalid; a bath at daylight, and the shadow—not the sun—simple remedies, soon restored my health, strength, and appetite; we had but a very indifferent table, eat up all that was put before us, and blew up the contractor every day.

Our route lay across the Bay of Bengal; we nearly ran into the Great Andaman Island, and would certainly have been on the rocks had it not been noonday, for the skipper knew very little about his trade. We put into one of the islands for water, and met some unfriendly savage fellows, who disputed our landing. They came down upon us in a rush with their bows and their quivers, let fly a shower of arrows into the water party, killing one and wounding three. This Robin Hood sort of skirmishing roused all the steam in our ranks, and a volley of bullets soon cleared off the bowmen far away back into the jungle, yelping like jackals. The officers generally slept on the poop under the awning, and even there they were assaulted by the cockroaches and had their mattresses and bedclothes absolutely eaten from under them. I remember one officer throwing his mattress overboard one morning, it had been so destroyed in the night by those nocturnal marauders; but worse still, there were centipedes in the ship, and plenty of them, full-grown, six inches long, venomous and disgusting; they crawl into your bed, and you wake up to feel one nibbling at you between the sheets, or marching across your face; next to the scorpion, they are the most unwelcome, nasty, hideous intruders one meets with.

All well on board, crowded so that few men went below at all, day or night; intensely hot weather. Made the Cocoas, a group of islands to the S.W. of the Great Andaman, not inhabited; but the natives from other islands and from Burmah visit them for the cocoa-nuts, which flourish there in abundance. Light baffling winds for the last thirteen days. A great many small ringdoves alighted on the rigging of the ship at different times, 200 miles from land. 1st November made the Preparis Island in our course to Rangoon. It came to blow with squalls. Running under reefed topsails, the look-out observed a line of low rocks running out from the island, about four miles into the sea. 'Bout ship just in time; in the dark we would have shortened our voyage!

3rd. Saw Diamond Island,—current strong against us; wind failing, we anchored in twenty-six fathoms water, 150 miles from the mouth of the Irrawaddie. Weighed anchor at four next morning, with a gentle breeze; wind soon dropped, and so we dropped the anchor in twenty fathoms. Off again at five in the morning, and anchored at twelve, wind always failing at noon; very tiresome and very hot; caught some nice fish, made twenty miles, and so we crept on from day to day contending against a strong current and baffling light winds, provisions getting scarce and limited, and the elements becoming heated like a furnace.

10th. Discovered land; appearance very low, and thickly covered with trees. Steered for the Elephant, a large clump at the mouth of the Rangoon river, ship turning up the mud with her keel in six fathoms twelve miles from land. A fair wind ran us up to Monkey Point, a few miles from Rangoon, where we anchored. Country on both sides this noble river low and covered with jungle; the Syrian and Shoé Dagon, praws or pagodas are seen at a great distance, and have a majestic appearance glittering in their golden brightness under a fiery sun. The distance up the river to Rangoon is about thirty miles, varying from three miles to half a mile wide. We dropped up to the King's Wharf on the 12th of November; and, as we turned Monkey Point, we sighted Rangoon, with its 3,000 pagodas, its stockade, shipping, war-boats, high and towering talipot and cocoa trees, Poonghee houses, and the great burnished temple topping all, and standing in the midst of this forest of fairy-like land of enchantment. On disembarking, I found it all show—nothing substantial but the great teak-trees forming the stockade; beams of massive timber as durable as oak fixed on their ends deep in the ground, and about fifteen or twenty feet high, closely put together, and strengthened inside by bars of wood, top and bottom. This *timber* fortification was loop-holed, with a stage all around the inside for the enemy to keep up a fire. The Burmese considered it impregnable, saying that the "English did not fight like soldiers, but like red devils; that they carried ladders and climbed up their stockade, and got in like cowards, without any notice or warning!"

We marched up at once to our camping-ground, about two miles of an ascent—the highest spot of ground around us for 200 miles—and in all that space there was not a stone to be seen. It became a novelty to see or to find one; but there was no end of brickmakers and bricklayers; the town of Rangoon itself was a wretched village of bamboo huts, built upon platforms, supported by teak beams along the bank of the river, the water flowing underneath. On the way up the *brick* road to the Great Pagoda, Poonghee houses, or dwellings of the priests, stand on both sides at a little distance from each other. They have but one flat, and that is without doors or windows, and is open on all sides. The rest of the house is all show, very handsomely and ingeniously carved and gilded. There was a space of an inch between the planks of the floor, so we had plenty of air—not always very fresh—where the natives kept their pigs and cattle below, all houses being built on piles. The priests all cut away, so I cut into one of these *villas* for a temporary possession; the roof was water-tight, and I kept open house, as Irishmen sometimes do, who have no doors nor windows; but it rains here occasionally, and a whole month's allowance will come down in three hours, with thunder the most terrific, and lightning forking itself into the ground, and dropping in round *balls* of fire, and exploding like a gun-shot. I never saw lightning in all its power, and at our very door, until I came here.

We had no mess; every man lived on his rations as best he could, with what else he could catch. My chum had not arrived yet with the left wing of the regiment, and he had charge of all the stores. I was thinking how and where I could get a breakfast, when I heard a band and drums approaching, and glad to find it was the gallant 87th Royal Irish "clear the way." The two oldest officers in the corps were my cousins, but we had not met for thirty years. All that time the two brothers stuck together, and were first-rate campaigners; their tent was pitched, and a first-rate breakfast on the *table* in less than an hour. They came from Bengal fully equipped for the campaign, and here I got my first breakfast in Ava. They were two distinguished, good soldiers; but I'm not going to write their history—I am making such a sorry tale of my own. They asked me to dinner, and to join their mess as a guest, and live with them altogether; but they got the *Hookum* for a voyage up the Irrawaddie, and we never met again in India.

Took a stroll to visit the Great Dagon pagoda; it stands upon the top of three square platforms, the lowest about a mile and a half in circumference. There are four grand passages up to it; the finest from the east side has seventy-five steps leading up to a long porch, supported by handsome wooden pillars, carved and gilt. The ceiling of the porch is lacquered and painted with different figures; at the front base of the pagoda there is a handsome pavilion, with an open chequered iron gate finely gilt, containing an image of Gaudma more than gigantic in size. It was much defaced and mutilated; the temple is octagonal at the base and spiral at top, with a *tee* on the summit hung all round with bells. The building is quite solid, and covers about five acres of ground, including the minor pagodas that closely surround it. Between each of them there is a figure of an immense griffin as guardian, and another nondescript something like the Egyptian sphinx. A gilt copper leaf hangs from the clapper of each bell, so that the least breeze of wind sets them all chiming, and the effect of seventy or eighty thousand bells ringing at once had a pleasing and soothing charm.

Amongst the great forest of these temples of Buddah, there were not half a dozen that escaped mutilation; hundreds were razed to the foundation for the plunder of the gods, some of them containing as many as five hundred images of gold, silver, brass, and alabaster, but chiefly silver. Colonel S——, a knowing old cove, gave his men orders not to trespass for *loot*, nor to go amongst the pagodas without leave. He was an early bird, and might be seen contemplating amongst the ruins in his dressing-gown and slippers before any one was astir, and would come suddenly on a party of his men going home with a basket of *sammies*, as they called them, from the tombs. "Holloa, you rascals!" with a voice of thunder. He had no occasion to say more; the basket was dropped, they went off at the double, and he carried home the prize. His leisure hours were occupied peeling the silver gods and putting their hides into his treasury.

The natives had a sacred bird called the henza, in carved wood, placed on high, in all directions; a long hexagon-shaped wirework gilt was suspended from the beak of this monster, and the usual number of bells were always in motion.

They had grand processions, very often to the Great Dagon Praw. Every one carried their offerings; they were of boiled rice, flowers, plantains, painted and gilt paper, bits of cloth, &c., I suppose according to ability. When they advanced to the stairs leading up to the temple, they came to a halt, put down the offerings, prostrating and bowing the face to the ground three times, after which they held up both hands in prayer, with a bunch of flowers between the fingers. In the mean time, the dogs and the crows were helping themselves to what they liked best, which seemed to be understood, for they were not at all molested until the procession advanced to the foot of the Praw, when the same ceremony was repeated. They then took up their offerings, and placed them before their favourite deities, the dogs, kites, and crows waiting anxiously for their departure to finish *their* repast; indeed, the crows were so impatient that they carried off most of the prog before the poor Burmese had done with their devotions. There are very large stone basins about the temple, where people may throw in their offerings at any time, and no sooner thrown in (if anything eatable) than a scramble is sure to take place for the contents between the birds and the beasts!

The Burmese have no *caste* like the natives of Madras and Bengal. They will not take life for food, nor kill any animal; but if you shoot an old cast horse in the jungle, they will not hesitate to cut off a rump-steak, stick it on the top of a bamboo, and carry it home for supper. They live chiefly on vegetables, rice, and fish, which they have in abundance. When the fish exposed for sale in the hot sun becomes putrid, they throw it wholesale into a wooden trough with chilies, mash it up into a pulp, call it Napee, and it meets with a ready sale for a curry!

The Burmese are a stout and athletic race of fine men, middle size, inquisitive, intelligent, and of a gay and lively disposition, seemingly without any prejudices; they will eat anything, and drink brandy without a scruple; tobacco grows in abundance, and you may always see a quid in every man's mouth, or one ready stuck in a hole in the lobe of his ear. The men are tattooed from the waist to the calf of the leg with various figures; they are very active in their games, and very strongly built. I have seen one of them carry away two sepoys to hospital, slung in two baskets over his shoulder. They would make excellent soldiers for a colony.

The women are short, stout, and well formed, but very plain; one seldom sees a pretty girl; the nose rather flat, high cheek-bones, and their teeth always black from the constant use of betel-leaf and chunam, which is disgusting to a European. Both sexes are of a copper hue. They much resemble the Malays and the *Celestials*. The dress of the fair sex is peculiar to Burmah,—a narrow piece of cloth, a kind of silk plaid tucked under the arms and across the bosom (which is pressed down), open down the front, so that in walking one leg and thigh is always exposed. They wear sometimes a loose white robe, or jacket with sleeves; their jet-black hair is combed back, well oiled, and tied in a knot behind, sometimes with flowers intermixed. Their ornaments are gold; they despise silver; a long roll of thin gold, like a carpenter's chip from his plane, is stuck into a hole in the lobe of the ear, until sometimes it hangs or is dragged down to the shoulder by its own weight, and this is their chief ornament. The men have no beards, long or short, and the ladies are sold occasionally for £. s. d. I saw an old couple one day with their daughter pass into one of our officers' quarters. I followed in to see if it was all true that I heard about the *sale* of Burmese girls. After some haggling a bargain was struck, the great fool of the party paid down the amount of sale in hard cash, the papa tied it up in a red cotton Manchester handkerchief, and walked away with his withered old spouse without saying a single word to the young *lady*, who sat like a frog, quite unconcerned, smoking a cheroot! Perhaps she considered herself a wife, the wife of a British grenadier! I said to my friend, "What on earth tempted you to buy that turkey?" "Why do you call her a turkey?" he said. "Oh, just because she was sold like a turkey to a goose," and I bolted off. I got some fine *goose* eggs for breakfast one morning, and considered myself in great luck when my butler told me I might have them often. When boiled, the yolk was very bright crimson, and the *white* very like pale starch, with a peculiar *fishy* taste; I got half through one, when I called my black market boy to explain how and where he got the goose eggs. "No goos egg, marsa; dem crockadile egg. Crockdile lay him in de sand, up de creek. Burmese hunt him up, and sell him in de bazar."

In shape and size they would deceive any one, so like were they to the dear old goose's egg at home. We got turtle eggs next day, which I did not relish either; the shell is soft, and about the size of our duck egg at home: they were cheap and nasty.

A good many Chinese are settled here; very industrious, inoffensive people; they trade in anything and everything; they changed my gold, and gave me twenty per cent. premium.

I was told that they sold it again at thirty per cent. to the native soldiers and followers, they not having any means of carrying much silver in safety about their person; for they hoarded all their savings to take back to Madras. The Chinese feasted here in the most luxurious way upon swine, which they love above all meats, bought alive from the Burmese, who could or would not even kill a pig, but had no objection to a pork chop.

Our ration was a pound of very tough buffalo beef, a brown biscuit, hard as horn, often *alive*, and a dram of arrack, per diem. I had a couple of goats which I brought from Madras for milk, knocked up a little poultry-yard, and had fresh eggs. Everything was so very dear, we required to be very economical and to keep our eyes open. Beer two shillings a bottle; butter, when we could get any, eight shillings a pound; a small leg of mutton was sold for twelve rupees, or 24s., a luxury in which I never indulged. But towards the end of the war we fared better. Venison came into the bazaar, with yams, plantains, and poultry, at a moderate price; but we had to wait a long time.

They have very fine canoes of all sizes. I have seen one large enough to carry *sixty* men, hollowed out of the trunk of one teak tree, the sides raised with planks, decorated and painted. This was called a war-boat, and well manned; they go at a rapid pace against the stream with so many oars. During the war a very little steamboat built at Calcutta was sent to Rangoon, and was of great service for communication with the chief, Sir A. Campbell. These Burmese war-boats were then very formidable on the river, and were always on the look-out for our matériel going up. On her first trip, the *Diana* fell in with one of them, that had been lying in a creek manned with sixty oars. Thinking that the steamer was one of our large boats on fire, they shot out into the stream to make a prize. Seeing this enemy approach, all the steam was put on, and a dash made at the warrior, which started off at full speed up the river, the little steamer in chase. No Burmese had ever seen a steamboat before, and a vessel running against wind and tide without sails, oars, or any visible thing but one man at the helm. They took the alarm, said it was the d——l from the deep, and while consulting what to do, the *Diana* was gaining on them so fast and so near that they all with one consent jumped overboard and swam to shore and hid themselves in the jungle. The boat was taken in tow and brought down to Rangoon, a beautiful specimen of a war-canoe.

The majestic talipot and palmyra trees suffered much hereabouts in the war. Thousands were hewn down to open the country and circulate a freer current of air. About our camp the cocoa-trees alone were spared; but indeed the whole country was one great forest for twenty miles around. The trees, plants, and flowers were rare and beautiful, foreign to any I had ever seen; plenty of cover for tigers near at hand, and dangerous neighbours they were, coming into and poaching on our grounds at night, and carrying off a goat as a cat would a mouse. The Burmese trapped them now and then. A strong teak wooden cage, built in the jungle and secured; a partition at one end for the bait, and a jolly big door to admit his royal highness the tiger when he called. A goat or a kid was placed in the *drawing*-room, quite in safety, but visible through the bars. The tiger walked in, the trap-door fell as he put his foot on the spring, and there he was without much room to dash about and break his prison, neither could he touch the poor, trembling, half-dead little animal beside him. Walking one day through this forest I fell in with a tiger-trap, and while examining its simplicity and strength, a jungle-fowl got up and flew into a thicket close by. Wishing to see this wild hen, I threw a stick into the bush to flush her out, when the frightful growl of a tiger made me quake. I cut away as hard as I could tear, and never looked behind me until I got out of the wood. The jungle-fowl is first cousin to our domestic hen, who once on a time went into the woods a little way from home, laid her eggs, hatched her brood, and let them grow up wild, and so they multiplied to become a great people. There is a wild-game caste in their plumage. They are not as large as the common barn-door fowl, but are as tender and good as any pheasant.

The natives tap the palmyra-tree for toddy, which is very nice and refreshing if drunk *before* sunrise; after that it ferments, and is used as barm for bakers, and becomes an intoxicating and dangerous drink. The tree itself is very tall, and straight as a ramrod, but quickly ascended in this way :—An active young fellow throws a girdle very loosely about his body and the tree, then throws himself back into the strap, places the soles of his feet against the tree, works himself up as quickly as you please, takes out his knife, makes an incision, and sticks in a peg, under which he fastens a little pot to catch the sap as it flows. He may have a dozen of those pots on every tree to empty the next morning, when he climbs again for his toddy, which he puts into a long wide bamboo can on his back, and then comes down at a running pace.

I took a glass of this toddy one very hot day at noon which nearly killed me; I did not get over the effects of it for three days; but I was then a *Griffin*, *i.e.* a new comer, a "Johnny Newcome," inexperienced, and tumbling into all sorts of difficulties and dangers. I met a few natives yesterday some distance from the camp while strolling in the woods; they came up to me as an old acquaintance without any ceremony or formality, and began a conversation which was all Hebrew to me. One fellow minutely examined my buttons, which had a crown and the No. 45; this amused and astonished them all very much; they felt the texture of the cloth in my jacket, and everything about me; but when I turned up my sleeve, and showed an arm tattooed like themselves, they expressed great delight, and I was their brother at once, their *father*, and their friend! I liked their off-hand, independent manner; there was a sort of gay straightforward honesty about the resident friendly natives here, that I had never seen before amongst any foreign people. But they were all *civilians*, not soldiers fighting for his Majesty of the golden foot, master of the sun and moon, king and emperor, ruler of all nations, possessor of the white elephant, &c. &c.; a great don in his secluded ignorance, a barbarous heathen, who despised his enemy, and sent his best general, Bandoolah, "to drive all the red-coats into the sea, and cut up and burn the black troops who were all idolaters." Here he was right, but only differed himself in colour, being a very gross idolater.

Two officers of my regiment coming down the river in a canoe from Prome, sick, and ordered to sea, put ashore in the heat of the day to cook some dinner, and take a *siesta*; neither of them keeping watch, nor sleeping with one eye open, like old soldiers. They were betrayed by their boatmen, taken prisoners and bound with cords, after being plundered; one was Dr. Sandford, the other Lieutenant Bennett. They were marched across the country all the way to Ava, the capital, and from thence to Amarapoora, where the king's Majesty of the golden foot then resided; here they were placed in a dungeon, in fetters, and fed like wild beasts. On three occasions, as our army gained some victory and advanced, they were taken out to have their heads cut off, or disembowelled, but after much consultation were remanded. The king fortunately took ill at this time, and was recommended to consult his prisoner, who was an English doctor. A half-caste Portuguese about the court, who spoke some of our difficult language, was interpreter, and the doctor was taken out of his den, and ushered into the presence. He found that his Majesty had been gormandizing, like many other kings and potentates, had a slight fit of indigestion, prescribed, and put him in eating order in a few days, and so got into favour, and got some additional food, but no liberty. Poor Bennett was still unthought of or seen by any one but his jailer, who took him his scanty prison diet once a day.

Towards the close of the war, when his Majesty was forced to accept the terms offered, he sent for the doctor and asked if he could be relied on to carry a despatch to the great chief of the army of red-coats.

Sandford replied, "Yes, and I will return with an answer." This astonished the whole court, for none supposed for a moment that he would be such a spoon as to come back. He arrived in the camp very like a wild savage, delivered his despatch to Sir Archibald Campbell, and returned with an answer, to the amazement of all the court, telling the king, by interpreter, that an Englishman always keeps his word of honour when pledged, even to his enemy. They were now both released, the king gave Sandford one of his best horses, which he brought home to England; but the very rough usage those two officers received shortened their days; they both died early. Poor Sandford used to sympathize with himself, and grind his teeth when he told the story about his watch "being grasped by those vagabonds; they bound me tight, and rifled my pockets, taking out my gold repeater; they heard the tic, tic, and passed it round, each one putting it to his ear, thinking it was alive; when the chief of this cut-throat gang knocked it against a stone and killed it; being sent round again, it was pronounced dead, and I saw it no more!"

The Rhahans, or priests, wear a long robe of yellow coarse cloth, reaching down to their heels; their heads are shaven, and always uncovered in the house and out of doors under the hottest sun. They neither cook their own victuals nor beg, but subsist entirely upon alms. I have seen them issue forth every morning from their kiooms with their lacquered basins in hand, to collect from the laity a supply of provisions for the day. They wander along, looking neither to the right nor to the left, never asking for anything; but are amply supplied by the charitable and religious. *En passant,* when they have collected a sufficient supply of boiled rice and vegetables for the day's consumption, they return home, teach the children to read and write, and take care of the idols. They observe celibacy. I have seen the idols manufactured by an *artist* in Rangoon, who sat in a shed, squat, like a frog, hammering out a piece of silver to get it as thin as paper; it was then shaped on a block (a model of the idol Gaudma), and when well licked into proper shape and dimensions, and polished off, it was taken off block, and filled up with a cement, which soon became as hard as a stone, and ready for the market!

I had a silver bowl made for myself by one of these ingenious artisans. I gave the fellow a bag of rupees (being first weighed), which were melted into a pretty thick sheet, then hammered into a shape on a block, embossed, with an inscription in Burmese around it, which no one can read but myself! It is used as a sugar-basin up to this 1866, and considered a curiosity by the *unlearned!* It weighed the same amount of silver I gave the *jeweller*, he being paid for his work. The native *goldsmiths* in India turn out some beautiful and substantial gold ornaments; you give the gold in advance weighed, the same weight is returned, and so much paid for the work; you are sure to have your ornaments of pure gold. Not so in England; if you dig deep enough, you will find a good foundation of copper. I believe the artisans in India are all descendants from Job; they are the most patient people on earth. You may find one of these naked fellows, black as Day and Martin, squat on his heels in the sun, with the most primitive, rude, coarse tools one could imagine, working a Trichinopoly chain of exquisite art; and there he will sit for days and weeks with the most imperturbable calmness.

A large tiger was killed yesterday near to our quarters in the jungle; he had kept the district in which he lived in constant terror and alarm, most likely the same one I had disturbed the other day, for it was near the same ground that he was surrounded by a host of Burmese, who closed in upon him with their spears and dahs. They are very expert with the spear, which is their chief weapon; they throw it a good distance with skill and certainty.

3rd December.—I was amused to-day seeing the disembarkation of twelve elephants sent from Calcutta to be used in the war. Two wide flat-bottomed boats lashed together, laid over with planks and green branches, shoved off to the ship lying in the stream. They were put in the slings below, and hauled up in great terror; when lowered on to the raft, they would not move a foot until every inch of *ground* around them was felt by the trunk to see and feel that all was safe and firm, yet still they would not move. The raft, with four at a time, was drawn near to shore by the help of a windlass, the banks being of deep mud. The Mahout urged them by coaxing, persuasion, and threats, to step off the platform and go ashore, where plenty of jack-fruit branches, a favourite dish of theirs, was in waiting for them before their eyes. They hesitated a long time; at length one of them *knelt* down, ran his long trunk into the mud, and felt the depth and solidity of the bottom, which was satisfactory, for he advanced one foot now into the mud, and felt again if he was safe, then another, and so on, feeling his way step by step till he got out of the mud. He then took up a branch, more than I could lift, and flapped away the flies with as much *nonchalance* as a lady would use her fan, seemingly very happy.

Employed myself getting up a bath in my dwelling-house, for I was melting away to bare bones with intolerable, clammy heat. I cut a bamboo in the jungle quite as thick as a nine-pounder, which I formed into a trough, and fastened up in my *bedroom*, one end passing into my *dressing-closet* through the partition. Two coolies carried up from the tank a supply of water; I sat on a camp-stool inside; the water was then emptied into the trough, and came pouring on top of me like a mill-race—a delicious cooling luxury. My bath was generally approved of, and adopted by the officers all around me. We had a parade always in the morning, which was got over by eight or nine o'clock. Our commanding officer was a great dunce at the drill, I suppose being long out of practice, living up at Kandy in Ceylon with his head-quarters, which might have numbered twenty men, band, drums, and standards. He came on parade always book in hand, in which there were manœuvres enough to bother the brains of the British army, and nine-tenths of them useless. However, he always stuck to one at a time, carefully reading it aloud before he began the puzzle.

When I come to be Commander-in-chief I shall have a grand revision of this book, and limit the manœuvres to five or six, make it less complicated, and so distinct that every *sub* may be able to handle a regiment after one year's service. If you attempted one-half of the present manœuvres in the battle-field, you would get into such a tangle with the enemy you could not escape nor re-form before the cavalry would cut down and disperse all before them, with little danger or loss on their side. You would lose your men and your reputation as a soldier. Quarter-distance column is the first, best, and safest formation in going to work; deploy on any company; form squares, simply and quickly in many ways; advance and retire in line or column. What more do you want in action upon the level? All the rest are very pretty in the Phœnix Park, or in London, if one could see the performance there, and may be useful as a drill, but nothing more. Any old soldier who has seen good, honest, fair fighting on the plains, front to front, will, I think, agree with me that those fancy movements are dangerous. However, my commanding officer at this time knew nothing about them.

After parade I dressed in light marching order for the rest of the day—that was, in my shirt and trousers, and lay upon a mat on the floor till the sun dipped into the forest. I had no books; it was a monotonous life to lead, but I could not help it. I kept my journal strictly day by day, which afforded me some help to pass the time. My chum was away up with the army, and I was expecting the *hookum* to follow every day. My corps was now a good deal detached. I had two or three dinner parties; those invited sent their servants with their rations, beer, chair, knife, fork, and spoon. I had the banquet-hall and a large pot for making broth, and with a buffalo's head along with the ration beef we had most excellent soup, plenty of vegetables, and always a curry.

We had three young officers very ill and very desponding; one of whom had a wife at Madras. I kept visiting them all, and endeavoured to cheer them up day after day, but all in vain; they could not get up the slightest assurance of any hope. I never saw three young fellows so utterly prostrated; they would say to me, "Do try and get me off to sea, then I know I should recover, but here I must die, and never to see home again—'tis cruel." They were right; had they been sent to sea I have no doubt of their recovery. I spoke to the doctor, but *he* did not think them so very ill, and was very averse to give any sick certificates, as he said "nobody likes this horrid climate, and every one with a bit of a fever wants to get away." Poor Grey and Forbes died in a few days, and we buried them under a talipot-tree near our quarters. The other lad was sent on board a ship, but too late; he also died. He was brought ashore and buried too beside his comrades, his last request being complied with, which was to "let the miniature picture about his neck go along with him to the grave." It was that of some very pretty English girl.

Our men were dying off so fast, we had no parades or any duty but the digging of graves until the best part of the regiment were under the sod. The mortality became so alarming I began myself to think we were all to be left here, although I had no dread of the cholera. I continued my walks of an evening in the jungle, and saw some of the *blood-red* squirrels with their *white* tails, hopping from tree to tree, and plenty of the flying fox, that very singular animal, half fox, half bat. The most beautiful miniature head is that of a pretty little fox, with its black eyes and nose, tiny ears, and charming *countenance*. The leather wings of one we shot were three feet from tip to tip. His wing was broken, and he became quite tame, crawling about the house and eating his dinner of plantains like a *Christian*, as the drum-boy said, who looked after him. In *bed* they sleep with their heads hanging down, suspended by the claws from the branch of a tree. There is also a very small and beautiful parrot that sleeps in the same awkward position; its plumage is exquisite.

On Christmas-day I dined with the Colonel and his messmate, the Doctor. We were always very good friends to the end of the chapter. Our dinner was soup, buffalo beef, and a marrow-bone, with a bowl of brandy-punch. Thermometer, in the shade, 82. During the afternoon, a Burmese was brought in from the jungle, very much deranged, body and bones, by a tiger. I did not learn how he was rescued, although I was told by some fifty people, all chattering at once in their unintelligible tongue.

CHAPTER XV.

Bandicoots.—Celebrated Mosquitoes.—Ants.—Rat-catching. — My Cuisine.— Burmese Customs.—The Great Bell.—Burmese Law.—Mandamar.— Jungle Fever. — Cholera. — Burmese Honey.—The Climate.—Burning a Priest.— I Exchange.—A Thunderstorm.—Adieu to Ava.

27th.—I was sent with my company to keep the peace at Rangoon, and to stay there. As there was no Q.-M. General to put us up, I selected the quarters in a long, empty shed, with a roof quite airy, having no doors, windows, or side-walls, the top supported by teak beams. I separated my share of the house with some tall, wide bamboo mats tied together, forming two square apartments quite private. At night I had some visitors who came to spy out the land and look into my baskets for supper; one fellow jumped into my bed, followed by the rear guard. I jumped out, got hold of a bamboo, and slashed about me. I never felt the want of a dog so much. Here in my own house I was assailed by a brigade of bandicoots, the largest size of the most hideous species of rats in the world, ready to eat a fellow alive. I battled with them all night off and on. There was a great shindy, too, between them and the soldiers, who contrived afterwards to have a light and a watch all night, with long bamboo canes for defence. The second night I was attacked again, and had my servants slashing amongst them every hour till daylight, when they disappear. On the third night I had a ship's hammock slung from the roof out of their reach. We got a couple of dogs tied in the shed, that alarmed this frightful and disgusting vermin so much that they took their departure; but the town was full of them.

This was anything but a lively detachment: no one to speak to, nothing to do. The other officer of my company had *bought* a *wife*, and lived in a corner amongst the rats; he came to borrow a candle from me, saying that the rats had eaten up all he had. I asked if they had eaten his wife along with them. "You wish to be very facetious," he said; "she's a very nice girl." And walked off in a huff, never to pay me another visit.

I will back Rangoon against all the nations of the world for mosquitoes that are the largest and most poisonous, penetrating, persevering, persecuting blood-suckers that ever cursed mankind. I had heard from a *traveller* that they were as large as *prawns*; but as I never believe entirely anything I hear,—in fact, nothing but what I see,—I can correct this *thumper*. They were strong on the wing, more than double the usual size, and their long *bills*, as the soldiers called them, sharp enough to penetrate the hide of a rhinoceros. They come in cloudy swarms at night from the swamps by the rivers, and spread themselves over the camp into the houses. I rolled my legs up in three folds of my cloak, and kept a large palmyra fan in hand in the evening. I had nets for my cot, of course; but somehow, with every precaution, they would sometimes discover an opening, and one single intruder would keep you awake all night, and leave you in blisters and torment. Many of the men died during the campaign from the stinging of those poisonous insects. They scratched the itching wounds into sores, the sores inflamed and mortified. Such was then the medical report.

Our next plague was the ants—white, black, and red. They were a very amusing little people, but great thieves. The white race live in the fields and build houses, sometimes five feet high above the ground, with a deep foundation and cellars below, constructed with great ingenuity. They always work under cover, tunnelling as they go along. They know, I suppose, that the birds would eat them all up if they appeared above ground, and so they keep out of danger. In size they don't exceed a grain of wheat, but their queen is an ugly monster as large as a black snail, and not half so genteel. She is guarded down below; and unless she is dug out or destroyed, her subjects will never forsake the garrison. They have made a tunnel from the compound nearly a quarter of a mile into my house in India, and finished off a pair of my *boots* before morning. They will eat anything and everything that comes in their way, from a blanket to a teak beam of timber. The black ant is much larger; sometimes takes wing and takes possession of your dwelling. I have been driven out of a choultry, of an evening while travelling, by millions of these ants. After killing loads of them, assisted by my palkee-bearers, I found they only increased and multiplied, so I turned out and left the house to themselves. So long as they were on the wing, I had no control over them.

There is another white ant of a large size that takes wing for a few hours; they cover the ponds as they fall, and are raked off by the natives to make a curry. When the wing drops off, they crawl away and die—their day is over.

The little red ant is everywhere, always on the move, and laying up something for a rainy day; nothing is safe from his claws that he can eat or carry away. They are very fond of sugar; and, to keep it out of reach, it is generally placed in the middle of a large dish filled with water; in fact, in an island. They soon scent it out, and march round and round the water. At length they assemble in a strong column, hold a consultation in their own way, a *forlorn*-hope is formed, and they take to the water. I have watched all their manœuvres for hours, and have no doubt but they perfectly understand each other and work in harmony. The *forlorn*-hope having entered the ditch round the sugar fortress, is followed by thousands, until a bridge is formed of their dead; the castle is stormed and taken now without opposition. Every one enters, takes up and carries off with him a tiny bit of sugar as large as himself, and proceeds to deposit the store, perhaps amongst the tiles, if you watch their line of march up the wall. Down they all come again for another load, pass each other on the right and left as regularly, or more so, than people do in "Cheapside," until at length I get tired, take up my sugar-basin, and put it away out of their reach for the present.

The rats, too, are very cunning. I have placed my bread and butter, and any other ration, on a tray slung from the rafter above, pulling it up or letting it down by a cord. I have watched a rat coming down the cord from above tail foremost, helping himself, and returning the reverse way head foremost. This was at night while the lamp was burning, and I was lying on my cot very quiet. The next night I laid a trap for this ugly robber; I placed a bit of meat on the tray, had a large bath of water underneath, kept the end of the string in hand, and, when he came down and got on the tray, I let go, and had him swimming about, when one of my *boys* was at hand to kill him.

All the servants are called boys, although one of these *boys* may have a grey beard, and another not be under forty years.

We went to the Pegu country, where some of the royal army of the King were getting saucy, and wanted a thrashing. We took a stockade, in which they supposed themselves to be in security, leathered them out of it, and chased them across the plain into a thick jungle. Our loss was an officer and a few men killed and wounded; the poor young fellow killed was the only son of his mother, and she was a widow. And strange that he always predicted his own death in this way; but, as for the Burmese fighting in general, it was a bagatelle— it was the climate we had to contend against, and that decimated a fine army.

I lived upon prawns for the last ten days; they were pretty large, very good, and in high condition. My head-*boy* was cook and butler, and served me well when looked after, always threatening to go home and leave me when out of humour. "Why do you want to go to Madras, chowry?" "'Cause rats eat me alive last night again; see my big *toe*, how him's bit. I want see my wife and siles."

"Never mind the wife and siles, as you call them; you have double pay, be content the war won't last, and you will go back with me." "Vera well, massa; I nebber leave massa." And away he went to prepare dinner. He cut a tiny bamboo for a spit, pierced a dozen of prawns, dipped them in ghee, and set them a roasting by the fire; when done, he served them up, spit and all, on a tin plate covered by a large, green leaf; the brown biscuit was taken out of water, where it lay for six hours to soak; no tooth but that of an elephant had a chance to make an impression on its iron circumference. I had neither table, chair, nor damask cloth; the grass was green, and I had plenty of company to pick up the crumbs. "Chowry Mootoo" was engaged with another roast, when he came with his black muzzle to inform me that one of the coolies had upset the bottle of ghee, with the hope, I believe, that I would go out and whack him; but that was always against my caste, and I told him I would get another. "Bring more prawns." I always had a second and a third course; *i. e.* I ate three dozen for my dinner; and with a bottle of beer sometimes, or some arrack, I could last over the day. Ghee is a sort of clarified buffalo butter, used for cooking generally, a nasty-looking, oily stuff, that would make a lady's lapdog sick, but never disagreed with the stomach of an old soldier. When Chowry brought in the bottle after dinner, I said, "You must go and try to get the ghee." "O, massa, plenty ghee in bottle." "You said it was spilled." "No, massa, only bottle upset; cork I always put in him, can't spill."

A big elephant was eating his dinner close by; his "mahout" was his chief butler and baker, rolling up sheaves of long grass, like a crow's-nest, filled with rice, and placing it in his mouth as he threw up his trunk over his head to receive this bundle of green forage, which he masticated with patient deliberation, then opened his ugly mug for another *bite;* when he had finished his allowance, the mahout went away, leaving a little black baby in his charge; when this little black animal would crawl away too far, the elephant would take it up gently in his trunk, and bring it back to his feet as tenderly as its mother!

I went into the villages here and there to see the natives and their simple manner of life; they were always inquisitive and eager to see anything about me. My watch amused and surprised them extremely,—I had to put it close to the ear of every old woman in the village; they would hold up their hands in amazement, as if it was alive, and they believed it to be so. There was a general shout of approval when I stripped up my coat-sleeve and exposed an arm tattooed: they all cried out,

"Kaumba, kaumba,—good, good!" I was a Burmese then, and pretty safe among them.

They bury their dead in the jungle in rather a shallow grave, without anything to mark the spot but the bamboo bier and the pillow of the deceased. The children begin to smoke as soon as they can toddle about, encouraged by their parents.

They had no coined silver or gold of their own; these metals were all in the rough. But they soon found out the use and value of our money, which they called "uñgah." They seemed fond and respectful to their parents when aged, carrying the "Paterfamilias" when tired. The old fellow would stand upright, and open his legs; his son went behind him, put his head between his thighs, and hoisted him up on the back of his neck, his legs dangling down, the *jockey* resting his hands on the young man's head; he was lowered at pleasure on his feet again, without any exertion or inconvenience.

There never was a country in which it was so difficult for a civilized army to carry on a war. There were no roads; a path through the jungle led to some place, but one never got on the right path, and the guides knew the time and place to give you the slip; then there was a countermarch, and the thing was given up, and abandoned altogether. The buffaloes that carried the baggage kicked up their heels when they got tired, and kicked it all off, or would lie down, or bolt away into the thick forest, and go plump into a pond up to the nose. Then the men would get up a *whillibaloo* in the chase, and drive them crazy. One didn't know whether to laugh or to cry with vexation, seeing his camp equipage scattered about, and half of it in smash.

But everything comes to an end, and so did this wretched war. The *Golden Foot* was whacked into terms of peace; a crore* of rupees and a ceded district were his penalty. And just about time it was all patched up, for nearly half our men were dead or dying; 3,000 had just come down the river *hors de combat*, and were sent to Madras and Bengal.

The great bell from the Dagoon Pagoda had been taken as

---

* A crore is 100 lacks; one lack is 100,000 rupees, or £10,000.

a prize on the first arrival and capture of Rangoon. It occupied our people, from time to time, six months in getting it down to the river for embarkation, and after all it slipped off the raft, and went to the bottom, just as it was got alongside the ship. It was now fished up, and presented to the right owners as a gift. It was a grand holiday with the natives; the whole population assembled *en masse*, rejoicing with their drums and trumpets, fiddles, clarions, and all kinds of music. The great bell, after wonderful exertion, was got to the shore, and went plump into a bank of mud, out of sight; this finished our English part of the play. It was now their own once more, and, nothing daunted, they got a cable into the loop from which it was always suspended to the cross-beam. At least 500 strong men in all their might went to work with a long and a strong pull altogether, and raised it to the light, when a yell that would frighten a tiger, from ten thousand voices, expressed the universal joy at seeing this treasure released from the deep. A thousand hands more went to the ropes, until it was out of danger. Then a rest for the day—music, dancing, feasting until a late hour. The orchestra was besieged by boys and girls, old men and young men, wives, maids, and widows, to hear and see the opera. The more noise and discord, the more cheering and applause. One fellow I called the "Big Drummer" thumped away with the flat of his hands on thirteen drums, as hard as he could pitch into them. A piece of blue clay was stuck to each end of a drum, to deaden the sound, varying according to size. The violins had but three strings, rude in shape and make; a few holes here and there knocked through the back, belly, and sides, made no difference in the tone; they were ornamented with bits of glass inlaid. Another gentleman knocked his part out of nine gongs and a pair of cymbals. But the great trumpeter made me jump; the first blast on his horn nearly drowned all the other musicians; one could hear him a mile off. Such a barbarous row I never heard before. The natives sat in a wide circle, like dogs, just as they sit on their haunches, enjoying everything, particularly the dancing. A couple parade upon a mat; the great admiration is in the lady, who is half-naked, twisting and turning the arms, hands, and fingers, the feet being moved slowly up and down without advancing or retiring from the stage. Sometimes she keeps time with her own voice, which would frighten the crows. The whole scene to a European eye is barbarous in the extreme. They got the bell fastened on a sledge, and made such good progress that it was placed in its original position in one week. Its height was eleven feet; weight, I was informed, nineteen tons; circumference, 118 feet; it stood, or hung, three feet from the ground, and was tolled (like St. Paul's) only on great occasions.

The punishments are severe and cruel. Two of our Lascars were caught robbed and murdered by some of their marauding parties, who were afterwards taken and given over to the Kee-Wongee, who had them tried by the Burmese law. One of them was found guilty and ordered for execution. He was tied to a sort of bamboo crucifix fastened in the ground, his arms extended, he being quite naked; the fatal instrument was presented to him, which he felt with his thumb, and replied, "Kound si" (good, all right); the executioner then stepped forward with his knife and ripped open his belly, so that his bowels gushed out; he shook and trembled exceedingly, but braved death and its horrors without a groan. He was left exposed in this situation for three weeks as an example. Corporal punishment is rather sharp work, but a blunt kind of practice or operation. The culprit is brought before the judge, who surveys him from head to foot with scornful dignity, makes a signal to his petty officer, who catches the fellow by his long hair, and pulls him on his knees to the ground; another person in office gets *his* knees on the small of his back, and with his two *elbows* pounds away at him between the shoulders and on his back until he is hardly able to rise; a punishment very severe, and which would, I think, kill any one but a Burmese.

The high-caste men wear a scarf of beautiful silk in many colours, about four yards long; it is called a "putcho," the price varying from forty-four to sixty rupees. I got a very handsome one, which is considered a *chef-d'œuvre*, worked on both sides in a sort of embroidery, colours brilliant. They are manufactured at Sillah, near Ava; the silk comes from Guman, in China, and wears better than Indian silks.

I called on "Mandamar," a chief of the district, who held his levee in a room ten feet by seven. He sat on a mat with his favourite mistress beside him squat on her heels. He seemed glad to see me, but made no attempt to rise. We shook hands, and I came to an anchor right in his front and had a full view of the ugliest-looking rascal I ever beheld. His betel-box and nut-crackers lay beside him, with a silver spittoon, also a silver drinking-cup on a chased silver stand, as well as three small silver boxes for his chunam and betel-leaves; his brawny shoulders four feet square, altogether naked, with the exception of a silk scarf about his loins. When he opened his ugly jaws to speak, he threw back his head to prevent the horrid, disgusting stuff from flowing out of his mouth. The chunam is a mixture of lime and cocoa-nut milk beat into a paste; a small bit of this is rolled up in a betel-leaf, fresh and green, and lodged in the mouth like a *quid* of tobacco; it colours the lips and tongue a blood-red and the teeth a jet-black, and gave this fellow a savage appearance.

Some natives came in and made their obeisance by bending both knees and raising both hands in the attitude of prayer, had their say and retired, the lady all the while smoking her shruit and chewing her betel. She was rather a comely woman, with a good countenance, black eyes and black teeth, very curious, like most of the gentle sex, and admired my buttons; but was delighted with my watch. "Make it speak," she said. I put it to her ear as near as I could; but the fine gold was rather in the way, which she removed, and then put up both hands in astonishment when she heard the tick-click, and proclaimed it alive and no mistake. Those gentry can have but one wife by law, but as many concubines as Solomon, if they can feed them. They all live in the same house and have their squabbles; but the wife is commanding officer, and keeps them in order. The marriage ceremony is simple enough. The bride gets some presents of silks or cloth, bugles and ear-rings; they eat together out of the *same dish*, and thus they are spliced, man and wife; no more bother about it!

I was too much in the sun—thermometer 96—and was taken seriously ill on the 8th of February, with fever, commonly called jungle fever, ague, and symptoms of cholera, which floored me all at once; but our doctor got me round again in a few weeks. Calomel was all the go then for every complaint, I believe, under the sun, and left my teeth shaking like reeds. I suppose it answered the purpose, and I had nothing to say against it; every one seemed charmed at the prospect of getting out of this fever and ague trap.

I took our Major on board a ship in the river dangerously ill and sent him to sea; he partially recovered his strength, but ultimately the climate fever, which never was eradicated, destroyed life. His wife, Mrs. H——y, was a most charming woman, very handsome, and her little girls extremely pretty. Captain F——s and his brother also died. The Captain was a most excellent, good and pious soldier, and his wife was a pattern of excellence, beautiful in person, and loved and respected by all around her.

Our people did not rally so fast as we hoped now that the campaign had virtually closed. The cholera got loose again, and made its attack always at night; before morning the patient passed away in great suffering. We lost more men by this plague in six months than by the sword during all the war. I watched it myself without any dread. It began in the night, and before morning the patient vomits the contents of his stomach, and the bowels are evacuated. This is peculiar to the disease, the canal being completely emptied of its contents, a sudden feeling of exhaustion is produced, faintness supervenes, the skin becomes cold, giddiness, and often deafness, spasmodic twitchings of the muscles of the legs and arms are felt extending towards the trunk of the body; the pulse from the first is small, weak, and accelerated, and very soon, and especially upon an accession of the spasms, becomes imperceptible; in all the external parts the skin becomes colder and colder, but is usually covered by a clammy moisture; in Europeans the colour is livid, the lips blue, and the nails of the same hue; in this state the skin is insensible to chemical agents, yet heat upon the surface is always complained of; the eyes are sunk in the orbits, the features of the face collapse, and the countenance becomes cadaverous Thirst is an urgent symptom, but the tongue is moist, whitish, and cold; a distressing sense of burning heat; the breathing is oppressed and slow, the breath becomes deficient in heat; the prison of the soul is broken up, and the shattered shell remains but a spectacle of poor humanity, reminding one that man is but a handful of dust—life a violent storm.

A dispatch was intercepted one day going from a Burmese chief to the Raywoon (an officer of distinction, or governor of a town); it ran thus:—" The Rebel strangers are strongly posted at Prome. One chief lives outside, and I would have taken him prisoner, but there was a guard close to his house. I would have surrounded the enemy in Prome, and cut them off, but they watch too well. I could not approach near enough, but I surprised some of the black strange soldiers, and have the honour to inform you that I killed three of the rebels, took six firelocks, and *one pouch*." I suspect this was the only pouch captured by the valiant general during the war.

When the treaty of peace was signed at Yendaloo, on the 24th of February, Sir A. Campbell was going to fire a salute in honour of the day, and to compliment the King, but the Woongee (Councillor of State) said, " O no!—please don't fire. If the noise of your guns reaches the *Golden Ear*, he will think hostilities renewed, and will run away and not stop, perhaps, till he gets on the borders of China."

One of the generals, who was armed to the teeth with sword and spear, said, without any shame or confusion of face, " I was four times engaged with the English, and after the first shot I made off with my aide-de-camp as fast as we could go, leaving my army to follow or not, as they pleased. It was useless to stand in front of such mad people, who climbed over our stockades, and murdered our men before they had time to collect their spears or their dahs in defence. O no, such people are worse than devils, who could not be kept back by the greatest monarch and the most victorious army in the world!"

Had a long stroll through the forest with a friend, and came upon a most beautiful opening near to the river, so secluded, serene, and novel to us; the jungle-cock crowing in all directions, the deer skipping across our path, the parrot and minna, with such a variety of the most beautiful feathered tribe chattering on the trees; the flying-fox in heaps going off to rob some garden of plantains, of which they are very fond; pine-apples in great plenty growing wild; and as for trees, shrubs, plants, and flowers, there was no end to variety and beauty—all new to us. The shady time of night, when tigers come out for supper, gave us warning to countermarch.

The Burmese, like the Malays, are great gamblers in cock-fighting; they will risk all, anything they possess, on one battle of cocks. I went into the Bazaar to-day to buy some honey, when an old stager said, "Perhaps you are not aware how the honey is gathered here." "No," I said; "but I suppose from bee-hives." "Yes; the bees make the honey to preserve the carcass of some filthy old priest. When a Phonghe dies he is embalmed in honey, which drips from the bier, and is sold to the red-coats!" I never tasted honey in Ava again.

March 17th, Patrick's day, is never passed over, where there is an Irishman, without a *dhrop av dhrink*. I got back to Rangoon, and found it full of Patlanders drinking arrack for the honour of the day, thermometer in the shade at 100°. I was nearly on fire, the elements melting with fervent heat, not a bell ringing. Lieutenant L—— taken suddenly and dangerously ill. The Doctor of the *Champion*, passing by, stepped in and *bled* him, and had him carried to my quarters, and laid on a mat. Another doctor came and bled him in the evening. He was bled a third time next morning by thirty-five leeches applied to his temples, and, wonderful to say, he recovered.

I dined *out* to-day with two very fine young fellows who had seen some good service; another joined us in the evening, sadly worn by this climate, and under medical treatment—he was dead in three days, and my other two friends soon afterwards! No man's life was worth a month's insurance; there seemed to be no hope for any one while in this fatal swamp; our daily bread was digging graves in the jungle.

Yangoon (as the natives call it) begins to smell very strong. The spring tides begin to flow through the town; when the water retires, the stench is enough to poison all humanity. I wonder how people can exist in the wet season, and it approaches fast upon us. Thermometer 100°. Heavy rains—thunder and lightning. The stockade is surrounded by a broad, deep, green, stagnant swamp; a sort of wooden bridge leading into it, 300 feet long, but useless to us; its only inhabitants now are buffaloes, snakes, and lizards.

Dined on board the *Champion* with Captain S——. It rained with such violence that I stopped all night with my kind friend—indeed, an invitation on board a King's ship was always most acceptable to hungry soldiers, and never refused, wet or dry.

I was *hors de combat* until the middle of April, and had no enjoyment—but "never say die!" I passed through the hands of the *medicos*, and protested against phlebotomy. I never was bled with a lancet in my life; it is taking life out of one's body and bones. I got some English butter, loaf-bread, and milk, and issued cards of invitation to some invalids about for a tea-party. When all was ready and handed about, the tea part of the feast was rejected, being, as my guests pronounced, made of salt water. One of my black rascals had stolen the sugar, and filled the bottle with salt—one of their usual tricks; and our best pearl tea, milk, and all lost. I called up the *butler*, "Chowry Mootoo," to explain. "Ants eat all de sugar, massa, out bottle, an Viapree black rascal coolie fill him up in salt." No use arguing any point with these fellows; there is a lie always ready, and they stick to it. I had no more sugar, and never ventured again on a tea-party.

April 20th.—I went away two miles and a half into the jungle, to see the ceremony of burning a high-priest. The day was hot as fire, thermometer 130°. I dipped my umbrella in every pool of water I met, to keep my head cool until I got to the ground. The old priest had been defunct four months, preserved in honey; he was brought home on a rude sort of car, partly gilt, and partly covered with cloth of scarlet. He was taken out of his box, laid upon some planks, and washed, and his old carcass was then covered with gilt paper, purple velvet, and scarlet cloth. After some chanting or grunting amongst an immense crowd of spectators, who looked merry and careless, the corpse was put into a coffin, and the coffin placed in a canopy twenty feet high, adorned with scarlet cloth and much gilding. A rope was stretched about 200 feet from the canopy, or golden bower, as they called it, and fastened to an upright pole in the ground. Rockets were discharged along this rope, and went bang into the bower. This play continued for an hour, until the *sarcophagus* was considerably damaged. There was yet one great gun in reserve—an immense bamboo, loaded to the muzzle with gunpowder, and placed up close to the bower. It went into the priest with an awful roar, setting all in a blaze, until his holiness, dwelling and all, was consumed to ashes; and so ended this barbarous ceremony—yet not half so barbarously wicked as the suttee in Bengal.

One of my soldiers brought me a snake this morning, twelve feet long, and as thick as my leg, with a long forked tongue hanging out of his ugly mouth. It was "charge bayonets" as the reptile was intruding into his quarters. The Cobra and the Green Pelonga snake enjoy good health about these grounds; and another reptile, something between a lizard and an alligator, resides in old walls, in the roofs of houses, and about the old pagodas, and sings out all night with a loud voice, "Petto, petto, o, o." The natives dread them as venomous, and so did I, when one of them, up in the rafters above my bed, kept me awake with his monotonous growl all night.

I saw a young Burmese girl or wife to-day, sitting at her door facing the street, with a child at one breast and a little dog at the other, both or all three enjoying themselves in the sun. The *ladies* are not particular in exposing the upper part of their body; they are always in light marching order this weather, very indolent and lazy. Rice is cheap, sixty pounds for a tickal (two shillings and sixpence); vegetables and fruit most abundant, so they have few wants unsupplied. Many cast horses of late have been shot in the jungle, which feasted the Burmese and the vultures to their full content; neither party ashamed of their meat.

The wreck of our army began to assemble about Rangoon. The Royals, 13th, 38th, 41st, 45th, 47th, 87th, and 89th regiments of British, besides many corps of Sepoys from Madras and Bengal, the latter nearly all used up, many of them literally skin and bone; I never saw such living skeletons. My fortune turned to-day on the call of a young officer of the Royals at my quarters. Talking of home, he said, "I would rather remain in this country; my regiment is going to England, and I shall be put on half-pay, being a supernumerary, which would not suit me at all." And so the matter dropped. A few days after an order came for every regiment to embark with convenient speed before the monsoon, excepting the 45th, which corps was to remain in the country— woeful news for some people! I called on my young Royal friend, and asked if he was now inclined for an exchange. "Yes," he said, "this moment; let's change jackets for surety!" We did so then and there, and sent in our papers. I became the 22nd lieutenant of my regiment, with a poor prospect of promotion; but released from Ava, and a grave under a talipot-tree, I was satisfied, and began to make fresh acquaintance with royalty.

A tiger came prowling into our cantonment last night, and carried off a small pony for his supper. Its poor mangled carcass was found in the morning amongst the pagodas, after which the dogs had their share of the feast.

There seems to be some trouble in collecting the first instalment of the *crore* of rupees to be paid as an indemnity for the war according to treaty. The ladies are called upon to contribute to the general fund by throwing their gold ornaments into the scale. How very ungallant; the earrings, or bolts, and bangles are disappearing. I suppose our collectors were a long time in scraping out of the king's treasury this enormous amount of tickals, for it was *fourteen years* afterwards before I got my share of prize-money!

The *Enterprise* steamer, the first that ever came to India, arrived here from Calcutta, and astonished the natives, as well as every one else. She was a few days after her time, to gain the reward; but the captain and owners were well recompensed for the risk, and *John Company* purchased her at a high figure. She returned to Calcutta with Sir Archibald Campbell and his staff under a salute of seventeen guns. All was now hurry-scurry to get away, the sick foremost; they were laid up in sheds in different parts of where the town stood last week, for it was nearly all consumed by fire, and it burned like a bonfire, being a city of dried bamboo. There was no carriage or transport for the invalids; some were carried down to the wharf by the Burmese, two in a basket; others crawled down on hands and knees; I saw one poor sinner going along at a snail's pace, on his *back*, feet foremost, kicking his bundle before him, so anxious to get away.

May 3rd.—Never in the course of my life did I experience such an awful and alarming night as the last; it seemed as if all the artillery of heaven had been opened upon our camp. It was exceedingly dark before the storm began; but the lightning illumined the face of the earth till it was bright as day. It came down in all shapes, in clouds of fire, in long bars, forked, in round balls in thousands, that exploded like shells as they neared the earth; if it had not been for the rain, that fell in torrents, I think the tents would have been on fire. All the thunder and lightning put together that I ever experienced was nothing in comparison to this frightful storm; it made every one in the camp quake and tremble.

The monsoon had set in. Went up to take a last survey of the great temple; it is a wonderful building of solid brick. The bells were chiming in the breeze; the great bell was in its old position; it can cover sixteen soldiers standing with fixed bayonets; a grand procession had just come up from the town, and were casting their offerings into the stone basins, very many of the Madras coolies in waiting for a feast, and to cheat the dogs, the offerings to-day being rice, plantains, melons, jack-fruit, sweetmeats, pine-apples, rice-cakes, flowers, and gilt paper. As the natives retired, there was a general rush at the flesh-pots; kites, crows, dogs, and coolies contended for the contents, and gobbled up everything, the Burmese worshippers looking on with dignified contempt and indifference.

The people are flocking into Rangoon now, and very familiar and friendly in their tone and manner. They bring poultry and venison into the bazaar, and know the value of money; but the good things are coming too late after the long starvation, very nearly up to a famine. Most of the troops are gone, and, thank goodness, my new regiment is under orders to embark for Madras.

Spear in hand I went for a long stroll into the jungle in a new direction; met Sir W. Cotton and his staff, with an escort of dragoons at their heels. He advised me to return, for there was still a very troublesome chief not far off, and I might be trapped and treated like a tiger. General Cotton was a jolly, kind, good-hearted soldier. Glad to meet him, I took his advice and gave up jungle exercise. The last Sunday in Ava was, like all the other former Sabbath days, kept unholy, a day of drunkenness and riot, swearing, singing, and debauchery. There was no church, no parson, no controlling power to subdue vice and immorality. The poor heathen people who were blind and ignorant, worshipping their images, conducted themselves with more sobriety and gentleness than most of those who professed themselves Christians.

Religion was laughed at; anything serious was turned into a jest; but the Scripture cannot be broken; all will come right in the end, the Gospel of Peace will be proclaimed here far and wide, until all shall believe that the Lord is God and Christ is the only Saviour.

CHAPTER XVI.

At Sea.—Arrival at Madras.—A Severe Tea.—Summary Punishment.—The Bag of Rupees.—March to Bangalore.—A Curious Idol.—Damul-Wallagahnagur.—Arcot-Vellore.—Pallicondah.—The Moharum Feast.—The Ghauts.—Rice-fields.—A Surprise.—Arrival at Bangalore.

May 16*th*, 1826.—I embarked with the head-quarters of the Royal regiment, my new corps, on board the *Eliza*, Captain Mahon, a ship of 530 tons. Three hundred and forty soldiers, seventy black servants, and with the officers and crew altogether about five hundred souls, packed as tight as herrings in a barrel. The black gentry stowed themselves away in the chains, or in any corner where they could freely breathe, although they were exposed to the rains and squally weather day and night.

Myself and two other officers were stowed away in a wretched little dark dog-kennel hole, without air or light and with a strong perfume of the cockroach. We lay at anchor in the river, waiting a pilot, all the next day. In the mean time I went ashore, to inquire after my poor friend, Captain J. F——, whom I had been attending for the last week on a sick-bed. The 45th had just marched into Rangoon, the baggage all lying out in the rain. The men were soaked in wet, and every one looking miserable. I met my old chum, Captain S——, and asked, "How is Forbes?" "Alas! poor fellow, he is at rest. We laid him beside poor Gray this morning before we marched off—under the clump of palmyra-trees. Cut off in his bloom, universally liked and respected for his mild, social, and gentle manners, amiable disposition, a safe friend and companion, and strictly honourable in all his actions."

"Well, S——, how do you get on, and what do you mean to do?" "Well, you see, we married fellows are all wretched

—not a bamboo to cover our heads. Our wives and families are coming to join us here, and when we applied for quarters, were told to build houses or buy them!"

"Your ship is getting under weigh, sir," said some one close by. A shake-hands, and a rapid departure. Got on board wet to the skin. Soon got round Monkey Point, and lost sight of Rangoon—I hoped for ever.

We had not been many days at sea when sickness broke out in our ship. Eight poor fellows were thrown overboard. I was one of the first attacked. Bilious fever, pains all over me, great debility, and loss of appetite. The captain took me very kindly into his own cabin, and with attentive medical skill I got over a very dangerous illness in a fortnight. Captain Bennett was also very ill, not having half recovered the vile treatment he suffered in his captivity in the donjon at Ava.

June 6th.—Since 23rd May, heavy rains, baffling winds, and hard squalls. The ship had no ballast, and every squall laid her on her beam-ends, and every tack we made the guns were dragged across the deck, and all hands followed, to keep the vessel from careening over. The estimate value of a soldier being £100 a head, by "John Company," the balance being struck between the freight of a transport and even *ten* lives, "John Company" was the loser. And so it has been the case as long as I remember, the life of a *soldier* was no consideration. Here we had 340 well-seasoned, good, old warriors, pitched into the hold of a small ship not sea-worthy, where half of them had not standing-room, and the other half always wet to the skin by the heavy monsoon rains; and this continued for thirty-four days! The weather was frightful. After the first twenty-two days, we were as far from Madras as when we left the Irawaddy river. We had a most tempestuous voyage along the coast of Sumatra. It blew so hard off Acheen Head that the captain did not hesitate to say that we were in great peril. He had to beat down all this way out of the direct course to catch a wind for Madras, where we happily arrived on the night of the 18th of June.

Went ashore next day for my letters, and to hear the news at head-quarters. All very good. Instead of my regiment going home to England, I found them under orders for Bangalore, the best station in the Presidency. I went now in search of two ladies of my old regiment, to give them very many messages from their husbands at Rangoon. I could not get any sort of conveyance, and by the time I found them out, some distance in the country, I had not a leg to stand on; I was so weary and worn and scorched by a tropical sun. I found them all well, their baggage packed, and ready for sea. A hundred questions were asked me in ten minutes. I endeavoured to find replies, but was so exhausted, that I asked for a respite till after tea, having had no dinner. I adjourned into the hall with a dozen ladies, and astonished them with my sea-appetite. Seven weeks grinding at ship-biscuit tries one's jaws; here it was all nice bread and fresh butter. After demolishing ten good slices, I begged the ladies not to take any notice of me, as I had a hungry fever, and was only going to begin my tea. A pretty young girl beside me kept my plate well supplied, until I was really ashamed of a barbarous appetite. "And now, ladies, I devote the rest of the evening to your inquiries about the land of promise." "What kind of houses have they got? good bazaar? plenty of provisions? good shops — palkee-bearers?—tell us all."

"Well, ladies, I may not deceive you, or you will suffer from disappointment; there is no house in Rangoon which any of you would inhabit from choice. There is a bazaar where you may buy betel-nut, chunam, savoury fish, crocodile eggs, plantains, pines, mangoes, jack-fruit, and young girls." "What did you say about young girls?" "Why, yes; they were tolerably cheap when I left; one could buy a good, fat, stout girl for one hundred rupees, some more expensive, according to shape and quality; they have no caste." "O, dear! what creatures they must be, if you are earnest in what you say." "O, indeed, they are," said I, "the ugliest devils without petticoats I ever beheld; but there was very little demand for them of late, the laws of Ava forbidding them leaving their own country." I kept the ladies laughing until a late hour, with some little adventures or stories like the above, which, although very true, had some tinge of fable about them. I took my leave, and made for Fort St. George, promising a speedy return to aid my fair friends in getting off to sea, stretched my weary bones on the broad red bricks in a barrack-room on a mat, and slept like a fish till dawn, when every one is up and away to ride, walk or bathe. I made for the beach, and found my company had just landed, fell in, and marched away to Codoonpankum camp, about seven miles out on the Bangalore road; here we were ordered to halt ten days, to fit out our men, who were in rags. I was introduced by Major L. McLean to our Colonel, Sir R. Armstrong, whom I had not seen before, and who was considered a great disciplinarian. I apologized for asking a favour so soon after joining his regiment: my family were at Negapatam, I wished to gather them up and follow the regiment to Bangalore. After considerable importunity, I got two months' leave and was joyful: all applications after mine were refused. I had no conveyance, no cabs by the wayside; and so I had to walk seven miles back to Madras, where I hired some servants, bought a horse and buggy, and made a beginning. I stopped at the Fort to breakfast with a young fellow there, and a very wild one he turned out afterwards. There were two bad eggs served up with some fish, that had lain in the sun too long! He called up his cook, locked the door, got hold of a big dog-whip, and asked why he bought *bad* things with his *good* money. "Take up those two rotten eggs," he said, "and eat them both, shells and all, or I will whack your black life out." "O, massa! please, I don't do it again." Crack! went the whip round his legs. "O, massa! I eat 'em." He was now driven into a corner; another crack of the whip, and he gobbled up one of them. "That will do now; the next time you won't get off so *shaper* as you tell me every day." Exit the cook, with all the savoury things, looking over his shoulder for another crack of the whip.

"Is that the usual way," I said, "of managing servants here?" "Yes, when one's robbed every day; that fellow is a great rascal, he gets things, *plenty shaper* as he says, all bad, and pockets half of the bazaar money. You will find them out soon enough. Do you know," he said, "that Lieutenant M—— of ours was robbed lately of seven hundred rupees he had saved; it was in his trunk, no one had access to the room but his head-*boy*. We got him into the hall, tried him, and found him guilty; there were only three of us on the *court*. We put a stout rope over the rafter above, fastened the door, put a loop in the rope, and threw it over his head. 'Now,' we said, 'this is your last chance: where's the rupees? or up you go!" 'Please, massa, can't tell, if you hang me, I don't know.' We then gave him a hoist, when he gobbled out, 'I tell, I tell!' Down he came. 'Well, where did you hide the rupees?' 'O, massa, I was choke, and I say I tell, 'cause much feared; don't know.' M—— was in a great rage, sir, and swore a big oath that he would now go up to the rafters and never come down alive. Blackie thought this alarming, but protested his innocence. So up he went again, and in a half-choking condition blubbering out, 'I *do* know; I tell, I tell, massa, let down.' So down he came, frightened nearly out of his black hide, took us all out into the compound and dug up the bag of rupees!" I knew all this to be very true from another party, and I knew many such things afterwards worse and worse; but still these black servants were ill used for very trifling offences, and there is no perfection.

I hastened to my two lady friends and assisted them to get on board their ship for Rangoon; they were quite alone, baggage all safe and dry, trying to be joyful; they took their departure never to return. Mrs S—— was a very excellent, good soldier's wife, and could rough it better than her companion Mrs. A——, who was a very pretty, delicate creature. Poor souls, they little knew in what a wretched place they were going to leave their bones.

Lieutenant-Colonel S—— arrived from England to take command of the 45th, but was spared the voyage across, being suddenly cut off from the land of the living in a few hours. People get short notice in this country to meet death, therefore it is wise to be always ready.

July 9th.—Took up my quarters at "Egmore Retreat," with my kind friend D—— L——n, a partner in the house of Binny & Co., and here my wife joined me with our bonnie lassie. I believe she was afraid I would have taken another coasting voyage in a *Dhony* to look after her, and saved me the journey by starting off at once for Madras, where she arrived in safety after six nights' travel over two hundred miles of a wild country. Little Mary, now but five years old, was her only interpreter speaking the Malabar language like a native, and with all their gesture; she made all my bargains for me, and was as useful as she was sweet, pretty, and ornamental. Here we enjoyed life for some weeks, always mixing of an evening with the *beau-monde* on the seabeach for our drive, and meeting our friends. There is ever an alloy to one's happiness in the journey of life; my poor wife was taken dangerously ill in the night with fever and inflammation. A long way to send for a doctor in the dark, bleeding and blistering before morning, again repeated, calomel administered, and with those remedies now in disuse a perfect cure was effected.

We commenced our march for Bangalore on the 9th August, 1826, the palkee in advance with my wife and child. I followed in my bandy, as it is called (buggy in English), the butler, cook, and waiting-boy always going forward the evening before, and having breakfast all ready on our arrival at the halting-place. The cowry-bearers kept up with the palankeen, each man carried two baskets suspended in slings from the bamboo which was balanced across the shoulder. These baskets contained changes of dress, provender, wine and brandy, plate, tea cups, &c. A cooly carried a couch on his head, on which we sat by day under the shade of a tree, and on which I slept by night; I required no covering. Another cooly carried a trunk on his head, containing my wardrobe for the march. The horsekeeper always sticks by his horse night and day, the grasscutter going on before with the heel-ropes and picketing-sticks. Women and children travel at their leisure. All these people feed themselves; they get their wages monthly, and seldom or ever touched our food. Arrived at Cunnatoor, twelve miles from Madras, encamped under some mulberry trees, sat down to a good breakfast at nine o'clock. Nothing remarkable here but the tailor-birds above head, sewing the leaves together to form a nest, which is suspended from a branch, and keeps dangling in the air with every breeze.

10th.—Got under weigh at five o'clock, and arrived at Streepermatoor at nine, a very excellent choultry, twelve miles from the last. The road was so bad and so very rough, I got knocked about from one side of the bandy to the other. I came in with a violent headache, which laid me up for the whole day. I was merely able to walk to the Brahmins' Choultry, which was close by, in the cool of the evening: it was a very large and fine building, originally built by a native for travellers of his own caste. He was a very rich man, had three wives, but no children; and as it is considered an act of great devotion to build one of these resting-places, the two mentioned were erected by him at an enormous expense; one for Europeans, and the other for Brahmins. A strong regiment might *form line* on the *top* of the latter on the front terrace, and *ten large* families might dine at the *same time* on the roof in *separate* places, without any inconvenience to each other. The interior is sufficiently large to accommodate *two* regiments; there are four wells of good water, built of hewn stones, in the different squares behind, and the whole is surrounded by a high wall; on the opposite side of the road there is a long range of stalling and a bazaar; where we stopped there was an excellent stable and kitchens detached. All kitchens are detached a little way from the houses in India.

11th.—Started precisely at four o'clock, and arrived at the Rajah's Choultry at nine, distance fourteen miles, one half of the road a deep sand, and the remainder ankle-deep with mud. Poor Bandula (my horse) had hard work pulling me along; the country was flat, and the late heavy rain made it almost impossible for a wheeled vehicle. I always carried a good feed of boiled grain with me to give him when we arrived, as it took some time to get it ready. Here, there was a very fine tank full of water, with a flight of stone steps all round, where the natives bathed, washed their clothes, and *drank*. It was a square tank, measuring 2,232 feet round, and had twenty-three steps, leading down to the water, of hewn stone, all in perfect repair. There were three choultries close by on the three sides of this sheet of water, and a small native village on the other. The one we stopped in was all built of hewn stone, and supported with pillars of the same, carved with all kinds of idolatrous figures in the rudest way. Those poor blinded creatures worship almost anything. One of the commonest idols I saw amongst them was the figure of a man with the trunk and head of an elephant. The figure was represented holding the trunk in its *fist*, so truly ridiculous I could not help laughing at it. The tank and the choultries were surrounded with very beautiful fine old trees, which gave the place altogether a very cool, pretty, and singular appearance; everything looked so Eastern. The huge elephant picketed in our place, peeling the bark off the smallest branch, having first flapped the flies off his immense body, then eating the leaves and soft tops, and throwing away the rest: when the flies get very troublesome he draws the dust into his trunk, and lets fly such a volley you almost lose sight of him for a moment; he is a most singular and sagacious creature.

At a little distance is a drove of camels, with their long necks and legs, awkward appearance and hump backs, some kneeling to have their loads packed, and others eating their chopped straw—a sorry meal.

There comes a Moor man and his wife; who ever saw *her* face? She may be plain enough; but they are generally handsome women. She rides astride on a bullock, entirely covered with a white cloth, with a small netting over her face to see and breathe through.

There are bullock carts without number of the most rude and unheard-of construction; some coming in, others going away; many of the drivers taking their rest, while the oxen are eating their straw; black fellows scolding—they have a most incessant chatter; but, cowardly dogs! they never come to blows.

There is the *farmer*, with his buffaloes and *crooked stick* tipped with iron, *ploughing* his ground, about three inches deep.

The palankeen-men squat on their heels, eating their rice, and the familiar crow stealing a *pick* out of their green dish;

the coolies with their little net drawing the tank for fish; if fortunate in catching a few little things, they will have a good curry. The day is cloudy, without rain; the thunder breaking in peals over our heads; my good wife playing her guitar, and the little one amusing herself with her dog, and conversing with the natives: all these things have a curious effect upon the young Indian traveller; but custom becomes a second nature, and if it was not to pass off my time, and bring to remembrance, at some future period, a few of those little incidents, most of them would now pass unnoticed, and be forgotten. At seven o'clock in the evening I always collected my palankeen-men and coolies for the night, and made them lie down in a circle surrounding ourselves and baggage; even then they are little protection, for they sleep so soundly. I have been kicking at a fellow for some time before I could get his eyes open. They are extremely stupid and very lazy; once they get stuffed with rice, down they drop, and are asleep in a moment; sometimes they lie on a bit of mat, but as often on the earth or hard stones; the long cloth they wear about their heads by day is shaken out, and serves for a covering by night.

12*th*.—Got my lamps lighted at half-past four, and started for Damul, eleven miles, and arrived at half-past eight. The palankeen arrived first, although I had the start in the morning. The country was flat, the roads very bad, as usual, but somewhat better than yesterday; all pasture land, but few cattle visible; occasionally you see large flocks of sheep; I bought a very good large one yesterday for eleven fanams, or about 1*s*. 10*d*. Damul is a very poor village; it could only afford us two eggs and some milk. The head-man came and made his *salam*, when I sent him to the next village to get me a fowl, which he soon brought back, having got the price of it in advance. There is a small bungalow, where we stopped, had our curry and rice early, a glass of good old English port, and a bottle of Hodgson's pale ale, and started at four o'clock for Cauverypawk, where we arrived a little before dark, put up in the bungalow for the night, and set out next morning for Arcot at four o'clock. Being only nine miles, we got in before the sun was very hot, and put up with Dr. and Mrs. Gibbon for the day. Being Sunday, I went to church, and heard Mr. Smith, a reverend gentleman who resided there for fifteen years, preach a sermon, the subject of which was very good; but the extraordinary manner in which it was put together, and the very peculiar way of his delivery, did away with the impression that it otherwise would have made upon the congregation. They were principally soldiers of the 13th Light Dragoons, and, however they might have conducted themselves formerly in a house of worship, many of them, I believe, could not help smiling.

Wallagahnagur, a town two miles east of Arcot, was the neatest I have seen in India; it was one of the best trading towns in the Carnatic for all kinds of cloth manufacture, and, perhaps, is so still. I saw the natives very busy making shawls and various other kinds of cotton and woollen goods. It had all the appearance of comfort, and seemed very clean.

Arcot is a considerable native town; the cantonment is a little distance from it, prettily situated on the side of a hill, surrounded by mountains. The officers live in bungalows, most of them neat and commodious, having a compound, with stabling and other conveniences attached to each, and surrounded by trees and shrubs ever in bloom. The night was extremely hot, and I turned into the palankeen in the verandah; but was awoke in the night by my good wife saying she was almost eaten alive by mosquitoes, and begging me to change places, which I of course was obliged to do through common politeness; but was not very much delighted at being roused out at three in the morning. I was up again at half-past three, and made a tour of the compound, kicking up my black fellows wherever I found them; for unless I collected them myself, they would never think of moving. I got my lamps lighted, and steered for Vellore; but had not gone many miles over the worst of bad roads when I was brought up by a big ditch with a stick laid over for foot passengers. My bright horsekeeper then found out he had led me the wrong road; but about daylight, after winding through the rocks, in danger of having my Tilbury wrecked any moment, some native traveller put us into the right road, and we arrived at Vellore about nine o'clock to breakfast, at the house of Captain and Mrs. Macleod, where we remained nearly three days. The country about Vellore is beautiful and romantic. The fort lies in a rich and fertile valley, which produces a succession of various crops all through the year. It is ever in a state of cultivation, and always green. The natives are constantly employed raising water from the wells and irrigating their grounds, which are thus kept in a fertile state. The valley is covered with beautiful fruit-trees, and is surrounded by steep and craggy hills, which have a fine effect. The fort is surrounded by a ditch, which was formerly full of alligators; but there are few in it at present. It is commanded by a high hill, and in consequence is not strong, at least it would not hold out any time against heavy artillery and shells. I called upon Colonel Fair, the governor, who invited me to stop and dine with him next day; but I excused myself, being anxious to proceed upon our journey with as little delay as possible, and left Vellore next morning, the 16th, at five o'clock. It had been raining very hard all night, with dreadful thunder and lightning; in consequence of which the roads were very heavy; but my little horse never made a mistake, although he had to do the work of two larger fellows than himself, sometimes up to his knees in mud, at other times up to his loins in water. The roads were only marked out through the fields, if they deserve the name of roads, for there never was a stone laid upon them. I arrived a little before nine at Pallicondah; the palankeen came in half an hour afterwards, and we seldom had to wait twenty minutes for breakfast after we came in, although the provender-baskets were never sent in advance. The country from Vellore was very well cultivated, plenty of buffaloes and sheep, and large herds of goats; provisions getting cheaper as we advanced; got two fowls for three fanams, or about $6\frac{1}{2}d$. Pallicondah is a native village, situated in a plain under some very high rocky mountains, fifteen miles from Vellore. We put up in an empty bungalow by the side of a mosque, and I had my horse picketed under some shady trees close by; a river ran near at hand; some herds of cattle were browsing about our bungalow; a great variety of beautiful large trees surrounded the village; the cocoa-nut woods, about half a mile distant, under the opposite mountains, and the tops of the native huts, cropping up through my little clump of shrubs, gave the landscape a beautiful finish.

We never could enjoy those things undisturbed, the mosquitoes were ever tormenting us, as well as the eye-flies, a small creature that ever keeps on the wing, so close to you that every moment you fancy your eyes full of them. Our ears were also assailed almost every day by some scolding black wife, and I will venture to say one of them will scold more in an hour than *seven* of the most noted Billingsgate fishwomen. We were very much annoyed for the last ten days with the Moharum Feast; it is strictly kept by all the natives through the country in honour of their prophet. It seems their new year commences on the 6th of August, and the name of the first month or moon is called Moharum; the feast continues ten days, during which time there is no end of the most discordant music night and day, noise and processions. The tom-tom is worst of all, and the most noisy; it is a sort of a drum, which they thump with a stick, and sometimes not less than a few hundreds of these are going at a time, to the great annoyance of all Europeans. On the tenth day, which ends the feast, the image is carried in grand procession, and thrown into the river, although it may have cost a great many hundred rupees; so ends this idolatrous custom until the following year.

In consequence of a swarm of black ants taking possession of the bungalow, we thought it prudent to retire, and give them full possession for the night, having just lighted some straw, and burned half a lack of them. They were the largest of the kind I had ever seen. At certain seasons they get wings, and make a flight for a few hours, when they drop off, and commence the march again. Their bite is very sore, and leaves a blister.

The night was very warm, and we slept safe and sound in the open air. *Set sail* next morning, the 17th, for Laulpet, at half-past four. I forded two rivers before daylight, and one at sunrise,—none of them deep; but the heavy sandy bottom tired every sinew of poor Bandula; he stuck several times, and I was fearful he had exhausted all his strength; however, he got me safely through them all, and brought me to the end of my stage before nine o'clock, being fifteen miles, some parts of the road being tolerably good. Our march was through a beautiful valley, surrounded by woody mountains, all the way; the scenery was delightful. I passed and repassed the palankeen several times, but arrived first at the bungalow, which stood on the side of the road on a delightful plain in the midst of the hills, a lake before the door, the green fields affording pasture for the cattle (a very uncommon thing that time of the year) and for lots of sheep and goats; some very fine old trees surrounded our quarter, and various kinds were scattered over the plain. What a paradise it might be made by Europeans; such a country in England would be invaluable. The village was very small, yet there was a most beautiful mosque, and here was the first place I saw the crescent on our march.

We left Laulpet at half-past four in the morning of the 18th, and got to the summit of the Penanadroog pass about eight o'clock, after fording the river below, which was rapid and rather too deep for *travellers*. I got my bandy over with some difficulty, and was obliged to walk the remainder of the stage; the mountains were so steep, and the roads so bad, my horse had enough to do. The scenery from the top of the Ghauts was beautiful and the view magnificent; the mountains covered with trees of the most beautiful kinds to the very top, the valleys cultivated with rice wherever there was a convenient spot; the turtle doves and a variety of the prettiest of the feathered race hopping from branch to branch without any fear from the hawk-eyed sportsman; the crow of the jungle-cock was answered by one of his own tribe far away amongst the rocks; the bells at a distance denoted a drove of oxen approaching laden with rice; the palankeen-bearers are always heard before they are seen, from the peculiar way they have of shouting as they get swiftly along. You will see a company of travelling natives with their families, the poor women carrying all their household furniture as well as a little black urchin tied on her back, also one in a basket on her head, the lazy rascals walking without anything. The whole furniture consists of a few earthen pots for cooking their rice on the roadside, and a mat to sleep on. They require no clothes, and they sit upon the ground; if they get enough to eat they are sure to sleep enough, and they are generally healthy. I have seen them sleep in the sun with bare heads, when I was frying in a *water-bath* in the house.

We arrived at Naikanairry a little before nine, and put up in the bungalow; it was very pleasantly situated on the side of a hill, a large and extensive green all around several miles in circumference, and a good sheet of water a little below; large herds of cattle grazing in the woods, and the various groups of native travellers making their fires, eating their rice, and feeding their cattle, gave the place a lively and singular appearance.

The rice-fields, I perceived, require much attention. That most useful grain, which is the staff of life to all India, will only grow on level ground, because it requires to be always kept *under water* until it comes to a certain height; it is often a precarious crop, for the rains sometimes are so heavy that the seed is swept away clean out of the earth; at other times too much drought is equally injurious, so that the crop requires the greatest care: it is always cultivated in low ground, and thus must be within wells, tanks, or large ponds of water, dammed up to be let in gently over the fields as required.

We felt a very visible change in the climate after we got clear of the low country: it was much cooler, and of course much more comfortable. Naikanairry is a miserable little mountain village, the smallest I had seen in our route. We left next morning at half-past four, and travelled through a very poor, barren country, hardly a tree to be seen and the roads almost impassable; my horse sometimes up to his loins in a rapid mountain stream, and a bank at the other side almost impossible to clamber up. Poor Bandula stuck in one of those nullahs; but with some little assistance we got him out of the mire. I could not help thinking at the time *if* there was such a road at home and a fellow ventured to drive his gig along it, he would be thought a madman or a great blockhead.

We arrived at Ventacaghirry about eight o'clock, at the bungalow, and soon after sat down to a good breakfast. It is a poor village; close by are the ruins of an old fort and ditch. We remained until four o'clock and went on to Baitmangulum, the whole distance for the day being twenty miles, a pretty long march in India with any kind of vehicle on *wheels*, the roads being so extremely bad; but our journey the day previous over the pass being only ten miles, I attempted to get on the next two stages in one day, to give me an extra one at Bangalore, to get my house in order before my leave expired; but when I got over about eight miles of the worst of possible bad roads in the world, it came on a most dreadful day of rain. I put up under a tree until I was soaked through, when I thought I might as well face the storm; and a storm in India is truly terrific; the rain comes down in torrents, the thunder is most wofully loud, and the lightning frightful. It was a providential thing I did not remain longer under the tree, for I had not advanced a mile when I found a low part of the country I had to cross completely under water. I lost 'all trace of the road, except here and there a rising ground with the mark of cart-tracks, which was my only guide. I made my horsekeeper wade on before, in case of tumbling into a hole, where I should at least have lost my horse; but thankful I was when, after a journey of about two miles in this frightful situation, I gained the high ground; had I remained fifteen minutes longer where I first took shelter, I could not have got any further for the night, and there was not a shelter within miles; what I feared most was getting capsized into one of those vile cavities that I found all along the roads, made by the mountain torrents. In one day's journey I have met perhaps twenty of these impassable cuts in the road, and was always obliged to take a circuit through the fields; however, I made my way to Baitmangulum a little after dark, my good little horse much tired and his shoulder chafed with the collar from the wet and exertion of dragging me through the mud so far; all our things were well soaked with rain, and we had an uncomfortable night. We remained next day (the 20th) until twelve o'clock, to get our traps dried in the sun. A little before I set out, a palankeen came up, and, to my great surprise and delight, who should step out but my old worthy friend, comrade, and companion, Surgeon Shean. We looked at each other like two game cocks for a little, when I stretched out my hand with, "God bless my heart and soul, Robert, is it possible I see you?" "George Bell, as I'm a living man," says Bob. "What, in India and I not know it?" Well, our hands went to work in the usual way of congratulation until both our arms were tired; then we sat down and talked over other times when we fagged it out in Spain, lived in the same tent on the summit of the Pyrenees with no money and little to eat, plenty of hard knocks and nothing for it, and how we met in a bungalow in the East Indies, after having lost sight of each other for ten years—and had only an hour together. Poor Bob was a very handsome, fine young fellow. When our regiment was disbanded, in the year 1816, he got into the 13th Light Dragoons, and six years in India had changed him much; but his bright black eye and good honest countenance will only die with himself. We had lived together almost from the time he joined the regiment until after the battle of Toulouse, when peace was proclaimed and I went down the river Garonne to Bordeaux. I do not know anything more truly delightful than meeting an old *friend* in such a manner and so far from home, when there was not a European within fifty miles around, unless a solitary traveller. Well, we again shook hands, and each took a different way in hopes to meet some other day.

Five o'clock the same evening brought me to Colar, over a worse road than ever. (But I'm tired writing about roads; I fear I shall find them no better during my journey.) The distance was eighteen miles—far enough in the heat of the day, but I judged my time well, for I was not long under cover when it came on another dreadful night of rain. Colar is a small town surrounded by a mud fortification, prettily situated at the foot of a mountain, and surrounded by pine-trees. I saw several antelopes the last stage. The country was very sterile and covered with very large stones; hardly a tree except those on the roadside. After we crossed the Ghauts and got into the Mysore country, we found the bungalows very good all the way; they were built by the Rajah for the accommodation of European travellers; and indeed it is a very great accommodation, for we should have encamped every night otherwise, for there is no place in a native village where we could have stopped. Left Colar at five o'clock, and arrived at Belloor in three hours, distance ten miles. I'll say nothing about the road, save that I stuck in a nullah until I was helped out. The road lies through the mountains, and I found it very cold; indeed, the climate had been getting colder since we came through the Penanadroog pass. Belloor is a very poor village, surrounded by a mud wall by way of a fortification; there is a good bungalow, but nothing to be got in the bazaar save a little rice and other grain. I had my gig at the door next morning at four o'clock, and left it without regret. Found a tolerably good road all the way to Ooscotta, where I arrived at eight o'clock (fifteen miles). There is a beautiful avenue of handsome trees all the way, many of them covered with crimson, yellow, and white flowers, a great many of them mulberry-trees loaded with fruit. The morning was extremely cold, which brought to mind days of yore. Indeed, I don't think I shall ever like a cold climate again, although I am aware how prejudicial the great heat of India is to European constitutions.

Under weigh by three o'clock. I had not gone far before I repented of having started before daylight, having come to a river; though not deep, nor very rapid, yet the bottom was laid with large round stones. I was fearful my horse would have either broken a leg, or lost a shoe; else my bandy would have gone to pieces. However, I providentially got safe over. My dog was tied behind my gig, and the force of the stream broke his cord and carried him down, but he landed safely at the first convenient spot, and returned to me. I very soon got into another river, which I forded also, and between heavy sand and deep mud I made my way on a very cold morning to Bangalore. On my near approach to the cantonment I was at a loss where to go to find out my house; but I soon met some of the officers, who led the way for me to a very handsome bungalow with large compound, where I found my good wife. She had received every possible attention on her arrival, and was quite charmed with her new quarters.

CHAPTER XVII.

Bangalore.—Its Garrison.—Amusements.—The Cobra.—Its Bite cured.—A Snake-charmer.—Devotees.—Sir Thomas Munro.—En Route encore.—Brahmin Women.—Naikanairry.—My Friend the Colonel.—Guzaron.—Vellore.—Mauvais Temps.—Affliction.

BANGALORE is a most delightful place, situated on the crest of a hill, half-way between Madras and Bombay. The bungalows where the officers live are all detached from each other, like so many villas in the neighbourhood of a large city in Europe, each having a large compound from one to twelve acres of ground, laid out partly in garden, grass, and walks planted with very beautiful trees of various kinds, shrubs and flowers; the fruit is generally orange, pumpella, plantains, guavas, mangoes, &c. &c.; there are also strawberries in many gardens, and all kinds of European vegetables. All houses have stabling, coach-houses, and a set of servants' apartments, with many other conveniences, detached a little way from the dwelling. Almost every house has a bath; but it was no luxury at the time I arrived there, for the weather was so cold I was obliged to put on woollen stockings and warmer clothing. I found all my baggage had arrived, and not so much as a wine-glass broken; so I gave myself much credit for packing so well. Had I left that job to any one else, I must have been a great loser, for the black fellows are so awkward, stupid, and thick-skulled, they cannot form an idea of their own; everything must be hammered into their stupid brains, for they would never pick up anything themselves; eating and sleeping is their sole delight; if one in a family can earn as much as will keep the rest in rice, they will sleep and idle away their time rather than work.

I soon made my formal calls, and was received with every attention. Colonel W—— took me to the Fort, and introduced me to General Sir T. P——, and afterwards to some of the high-caste people in the cantonment. Our arrival in one of the finest and most healthy quarters in India commenced with a most hearty welcome to the Royal regiment. Balls, parties, and other amusements gave a very good impression of the place to a stranger. Whether it may continue will be shown by the sequel. At present, I never was in a more delightful quarter, nor were we ever more happy or more comfortable.

Bangalore, 23rd Feb., 1827.—Monthly balls, private parties, amateur theatricals, mess dinners, riding, driving, horse-racing, &c., were the order of the day. All our parades and field-days were over by nine o'clock in the morning. The garrison consisted of two brigades of horse artillery, a company of foot artillery, 1st regiment Native Light Cavalry, 6th, 29th, 31st, and 52nd regiments of Native Infantry, and 2nd battalion Royal regiment. Major-General Sir T. Pritzler commanded the district of Mysore, Lieutenant-Colonel Armstrong, Royal regiment, commanded the cantonment, and Lieutenant-Colonel G. A. Wetherall the battalion. Those three officers were all just what those under their command could wish them to be — indulgent, kind, considerate, and strict. Colonel Wetherall was justly the most popular; extremely hospitable, very indulgent, he encouraged all in their enjoyments, and was a general favourite, not only with his own officers, but with every soul in the cantonment. He was an accomplished officer and a steady friend. The public rooms were handsome and convenient; we built a theatre adjoining, and commenced operations with a comedy, which was very successful. The rosy-faced slender plants, of small size in the waist, were screwed tight into stays, well dressed, powdered and painted, they made very nice girls. In a few days 1,690 rupees were subscribed for new scenery. We had first-rate scene-painters and actors and decorators, and a balance, after all expenses paid, to go to the fund. After the play the ladies were charmed with a ball and supper, music, and dancing, all included for one rupee a head!

The General resided in the Fort, about three miles from the cantonment. He had an officer's guard there, which was relieved daily, and a very pleasant sort of duty it was. The officer always dined at the General's table, and passed the evening most agreeably with the family. This old palace of Tippoo Sahib made a capital quarter, affording abundance of space for the balls and entertainments frequently given by Lady Pritzler.

This fortress fell to Lord Cornwallis in older times; Tippoo's troops fought well, keeping their ground, and defending the palace until they fell to a man. The pettah, or native village, outside the walls, has a population of 70,000, not including the monkeys, a very numerous race, who live in the trees, on tops of houses, and amongst the children, quite undisturbed; indeed, they often jump up on the back of a carriage during the evening drive, and frighten the young lady Griffins, their object being to levy a toll for passing their tope. They are first-rate active hands at robbing a garden, pitching the fruit from one to another until a tree is well nigh unloaded. I have seen a big fellow high up shaking a tree, while others below were gathering up the fruit, another being on the watch ready to give the alarm, many of the thieves at the time carrying their young clinging to them like wax.

I met a "cobra snake" to-day riggling up to my bungalow very free and easy. I shirked his near acquaintance, and called for help. All I could get was a big stick handed to me by a nervous black fist: it served me well. I made a good shot, knocked him down, and killed him for falling. No wonder that the natives run from these reptiles, whose bite is so fatal. One of our officers, returning home after his evening ride, sat down by the table, and threw up his legs on a chair to rest, his dog walking about with his back up, grumbling all the while. My friend had not far to look for the cause of this growl; on the chair opposite sat a big cobra de capella, half coiled up, half erect, *bowing* to his host. "What did you do?" I said. "Well," he replied, "he seemed very civil, and quite at home. I got hold of my gun, gave him notice to quit, and, as he left, I shot him outside, thankful I had not sat down upon my guest." Another officer, pulling on his boots in the morning, felt the cold, clammy, greasy damp of a snake under his foot. He pressed hard upon it for a moment, called his

servant, and with great coolness said, "I want off this boot."
A black fellow is always a boot-jack when you want one, very
simple and very sure. You sit on a chair, he turns his back,
and receives your boots between his legs, heel and toe in both
hands; you put your other foot to the small of his back, and
send him flying boot and all before you. "Take care," he
said, "there's something in that boot; shake it out — don't
put your hand in;" and out dropped a snake, as lively as
could be expected, at Blackie's bare feet, who made a surprising spring out of its way, and cut out of the room, leaving
his master to square accounts with the intruder. Mrs. Sandford, our doctor's wife, lying on her couch one day very unwell,
saw a mouse cross the room, and jump up on the sofa behind
her; by-and-by she heard and felt a rustling under her pillow;
she called her ayah (nurse or maid) to lift her off to another
couch, when she discovered a large cobra snake under the
pillow, who had just swallowed the unfortunate mouse.
Although these snakes are so deadly venomous, they only act
on the defensive; but the slightest assault is so sharply
returned, it leaves no man time to make his will. I only know
of one instance where a cure was successful. A horsekeeper,
running after his master, who was riding fast across our parade-
ground, trod upon a cobra, who instantly bit his leg; he
stopped not, but followed on after his master, who had pulled
up at Dr. Stodart's bungalow. The horsekeeper called out at
once that he was bitten by a snake. "Are you quite sure?" he
said. "Yes, massa, cobra, I see him; when bite me, he dive
into him's hole; I know de place." No time was lost, the piece
was cut out, and the wound cauterized. He drank brandy
until drunk and stupefied; it was then poured down his throat
to the extent of a whole bottle; it was a case of kill or cure.
The man was placed in a go-down, and left there insensible
until the next day, when he began to stir. Towards evening
he became lively, and was able to point out the hole of this
reptile. We sent for two pioneers, who dug him out of his den.
The doctor had him skinned, stuffed, and kept as a trophy of
his skill. Those snakes burrow in the earth, or live in the
grass, or in the jungle, as it suits their convenience.

My cook reported to me one day that he saw a "cobra" going into a hole at the back of his fireplace. I was going to parade, and told him to tell his mistress. When I returned, she told me there was a grand hunt after this impudent fellow, who had taken up his quarters as the cook said; but none of our servants could be induced to disturb him. She sent for a couple of men from my company, who very soon knocked down his house, and saw him escape from a *back*-door; but he was followed up and killed in the grass, leaving a large family of young ones behind him in his late quarters. An empty house is better than a bad tenant, at any time, and so we banished this colony of vipers. The great enemy of these snakes is the "mungoose," a very pretty little animal, living in the grass, and amongst the milk and aloe hedges. When he meets a snake, he attacks him with a furious violence; when bit by the cobra he lets go his hold, hurries about in the grass until he finds an antidote against the poison, nibbles it up quickly, and returns to the attack. Unless the snake gets into a hole in the mean time, he is sure to suffer death. I had often heard of serpents being charmed: it is true that they have an ear for music, ugly and revolting as they are. A snake-charmer came into my compound one day, and asked permission to "kill all massa snakes." "Yes," I said, "catch and kill them all, and I will pay for them dead or alive." He sat down by a hole in the hedge, pulled out his *bagpipe*, and began a snake concert of wild and discordant music, which lasted so long, that I got impatient standing in the sun. "Stop, massa," he said; "snake come." And sure enough one came out very quietly, without fear, and with great dignity raised himself up half-way, and began to keep time with the music by bending his head and *shoulders* back and forward. The *piper* caught him by the tail in one hand, and slipt the other quick as lightning up to his head and held him tight. After inspecting and *seeing* all this performance, and the snake put into his basket with others, I had no more doubts about snake-charming; but still I am very sceptical in believing the many wonderful things one hears of; and it occurred to me afterwards that this wonderful snake-charmer might have put one of his pets into this hole for the purpose, for they are very artful in deceit and falsehood. However, wild or tame, the beast came out of its hole and *danced* to the music!

We have a great variety of trees and plants and shrubs here, although the country about is bare enough; a small tope and a tank, the work of some religious Hindoo, is all that one sees for many miles, not far from our beautiful quarters. The trees are the "Jack," a noble tree bearing large fruit like a hedgehog, which grows from the trunk; it makes excellent furniture, resembling mahogany.

The cayaputa is valuable for its oil; the coffee-tree, as a shrub, grows in almost all the gardens; useful and ornamental, it yields abundantly. The Indian lilac, a large tree, is beautiful in blossom and sweet in perfume. The pumplemus, a very pretty tree, bearing fruit like the orange, but much larger. The liquet bears a fruit something like a small white plum; they grow in bunches, are tart, but make a nice preserve. The guava is a common tree, yields abundantly, and the fruit makes very nice jelly. The citron, not larger than a gooseberry bush, often bears fruit half the size of my head. The mango, a beautiful tree, grows large and shady enough to screen a regiment of soldiers from the sun; the fruit delicious. Peach and lime-trees, cassarina, cinnamon, cotton, india rubber, sago, talipot, cocoa; the clove, a pretty evergreen, with a small leaf, tasting strongly of the spice; the castor-oil plant. No end to the variety of trees, plants, and flowers.

I observed two devotees yesterday in the bazaar, doing penance, or something of tomfoolery. One lay on his back in the street, naked; in both hands he raised a very heavy large stone as high as his arms would permit. When at the full extent, he let it drop on his belly, which made him grunt, remaining motionless and in pain for a little; he hoisted the stone gradually and repeated the dose. The other black lazy rascal lay on his back, his head buried under the earth. I was puzzled to find out how he could breathe; he had one arm extended in the air, the other lay across his *grave*. But the *chattie* lay on his breast to receive the *pice* of the charitable and religious! These fakeers are a singular race of devotees;

one fellow will stand upon his legs for days, holding up one arm until it becomes as rigid as a poker, while another is measuring the road for a hundred miles with the length of his miserable carcass. I have seen another ragged black rascal who held one of his hands closely shut until his finger nails grew out at the back; and all this play will go on until the gospel of peace enlightens their darkness.

May 5th.—Captain Grove, H. M. 13th Light Dragoons, and his wife, died rather suddenly at an early age. I dined in his company at Colonel W——'s a few days before. Doctor A—— was of the party, and he was buried in a few days. He was the seventeenth passenger on board the ship that came out with our Colonel, who had died within six years.

The weather was so hot the last two days, that we had the windows open all night and the tatties kept well soaked with water. On the 7th the change was so great, that the windows were closed and we slept under blankets.

Sir Thomas Munro, Governor of the Madras Presidency, arrived here on the 24th. We got up a play for his amusement, and gave him a banquet and a very grand welcome. He went on to visit his ceded districts before leaving India, but died at Ghauty of cholera, a few days after leaving us. He was greatly esteemed and respected, and most deeply regretted. He was a man of few words, but of great penetration, sense, and ability, judgment and discretion. At Madras he had a breakfast-table for all who chose to walk in at eight o'clock. It was convenient enough for many young officers to have a first-rate breakfast who had nothing at home, which was very often the case when they had a row with their servants!

Sir Thomas always had his porridge in Scotch style, and enjoyed it in silence. A young griffin just arrived from England sat down beside the Governor, intending to make himself very agreeable, as he hoped, and said boldly, "Any late news from that war in Ava, Sir Thomas?" The old Governor gave him a side glance, and replied, "Eat your breakfast, sir." He was shut up at once, and no doubt wished himself in his barrack-room. I could hardly suppress a big laugh that was all ready when I surveyed the two faces, one gobbling up his *stirabout* and the other blushing like a peony.

There is a small lake at Bangalore, where the soldiers found a watery grave at times, and the officers, too, had many escapes being upset in their cockle-shell boats, which they rigged up in man-of-war style to sail round this basin, the General leading the fleet—anything *pour passer le temps*. Unless there was an adventure occasionally, it was considered a very slow amusement.

In the racing department I was at home, and we had some very good sport in a small way, more enjoyable to us all than the great *Darby*. Then there was a big dinner in the public rooms, and a ball for the ladies in the evening. And so the time passed on till the end of August, when I got four months' leave to go and visit our kindred and friends in Calcutta. 'Tis a world of trouble and bother travelling in India, and such slow work, half one's time is wasted on the road.

On the 24th of August I sent my servants and three horses in advance, passed an agreeable day, as usual, with Colonel and Mrs. W——, and left next morning at four o'clock. My wife and little one in a palkee, myself on horseback, Missalgee in front with a flaming torch, coolies and cowry coolies well laden with prog, and waiting-boy mounted on a pony; his sole charge was the kettle, and to have it boiling on our arrival at the halting-ground, with eggs and milk on the table for breakfast. Our first march was thirty-five miles; the sun frying my head, for the last hour left me *hors de combat* for the rest of the day. My bed was a mattress, carried by a coolie; my companion at night was my own little darling, who would not sleep with any one but me, although fond of her little black maid. I cannot say she was a very comfortable bedfellow, for she kicked like a young filly from dark till dawn. The mosquitoes, so very fond of English *claret*, had no mercy or compassion on our humanity, and the poor child suffered most frightfully. My wife slept, or tried to sleep, in her palankeen; two crickets had stowed themselves away carefully, one at each end; when one had finished his song, he was relieved by his relation. They sometimes had a duet, and kept up the concert till daylight, although we were miles on our way before the dawn. We halted by a tope and a tank next day, had breakfast under a grand shady guava-tree, and amused ourselves, my wife playing her guitar, and singing, to the wonder and astonishment of the natives. I filled up my note-book, while little Mary and her *blackamoor* maid gathered wild flowers. A deputation of the palkee-*boys* waited on us, and after the usual salam, commenced an oration one hundred to the dozen. I called my child, and said, "Tell me what those black gentry are saying, or what do they want?" "Yes, papa;" and a conversation was carried on with a wonderful flow of language, grimace, and excitement, for nearly a quarter of an hour, which my little interpreter explained in their own words. "Great massa, we poor boys carry great lady our *mother* safe. We, all your *childers*, and very hungry. Massa, *pleas*, give present one sheep *ebery day*, good for our *belly* to mak work. Salam!" They had the present, got the sheep, and eat it up, rump and stump, in two hours afterwards, when they all went to bed on the sunny side of the tank. They are no protection at night; you may walk over them like stepping-stones, and never disturb their dead sleep; but I always found them honest and faithful, and the hardest-working, patient creatures in the world. We passed several Brahmin women on the road the last two days, mounted astride on *bullocks*, with their heads and faces covered, merely a little netting open-work, to let these *divinities* see and breathe, their *keepers* walking alongside; comfortable sort of travelling, thermometer at 110°!

Arrived at Colar next morning at six o'clock, and found the cholera was amongst the people; had a fresh horse waiting me there, and pushed on to Baitmungulum; arrived late, half-past ten, the sun scorching hot, and my head nearly on fire, distracting headache, hardly able to get off my horse. We were all knocked up for this day, and began to think we were paying dearly for the hopeful pleasure of meeting friends so far away. A black fellow walked into our bungalow in the evening, *demanding* a present, something very unusual, and got very insolent at being told to cut away. "O yes, I'll go away now;

but I will return at night, and fire the house, and have something!" This in his own language, not knowing I had a little interpreter who understood every word he said. I sent for the cutwall * of the village, who brought him back, when I told him if he came about the bungalow at night I would shoot him. We were in the Rajah's territory, and thought it best to barricade, having no arms; and if I had, he was safe enough; but they do not like the smell of gunpowder.

Next day, Ventacaghirry. Tropical rains, which cooled the horses at their pickets; the mosquitoes came in clouds to put an end to all comfort for the night. I sat by the palkee with a viscera, or native fan, for hours keeping off these bloodsuckers; but still we got severely punished. Towards morning a stiff breeze of wind came to our relief, and cleared them all away, when I fell asleep, but was soon roused up by the loud voice of a boisterous Irishman abusing some one in his native language, mixing with it five or six words of *Tamil*.

The traveller's threats were not understood, although he plainly told the cutwall a hundred times " he would report him to Commissary B――s." At length out jumps my friend from his palkee, and away starts the cutwall and his peon— devil take the hindmost—each expecting most likely a *clip in the ear*. I thought it useless attempting to sleep any more, so I called up my various attendants, and ordered off my things, turned out, and asked the unknown gentleman what was the matter, and if I could lend him a hand. I found it was Lieutenant-Colonel W――, H. M. 54th regiment, on his way to Madras by *post* or dawk. But his palankeen had been broken the day before, and he was set down here without a single attendant, to be forwarded by the next set of bearers that should have been posted at this stage, for the fellows that brought him on made off the moment they put him down. However, I sent one of my *boys* for the cutwall, got him a fresh set of bearers, who mounted himself, palkee, and all, on their *heads*, being minus one pole, and moved off, broadside foremost, at a snail's trot instead of four miles per hour. I

---

* Headman of the village, a sort of constable.

followed soon after, and arrived at Naikanairry long before him, although I did not put my horse out of a walk. My people were all up in good time, and I had a dish of tea ready for the Colonel, who had not a single thing left. Here another set of bearers awaited him; but I advised him to get his *coach* mended if possible, before he again started, or he would not reach Madras for a month; so a despatch was sent across the country, and a blacksmith arrived in about two hours, most extraordinary to relate, with all his tools; for these animals generally just come to see what's to be done, and then they sneak away for their tools. A fire was soon made, under a scorching sun, and Vulcan commenced, and with the assistance of a carpenter they patched up the palkee by two o'clock, and the gentleman started for Vellore.

Naikanairry is a very pretty spot; the village, if it deserves the name, consists about a dozen of small miserable huts; but we were provided with all we required, such as fowls, eggs, oil, milk, and good water. I bought a very good sheep for one rupee, and we feasted on fish, for the first time for a year, which was caught in a large tank or lake below the bungalow. The afternoon was very fine, and a short march was tempting. We dined early, and started about four o'clock to cross the Ghauts, although it was very hot. The scenery was, as usual, very beautiful; birds of the most beautiful plumage chanting their sweet notes; turtle doves, so tame that they sat within a few yards of you on the road; the hills and valleys thickly covered with wood, the jungle-cock crowing in all directions; wild peacocks and all sorts of game in great abundance. We walked down the steepest parts of the pass; the river almost dry at the foot of the hills, although my horse was nearly swimming in it the year before, at any earlier period. Marched on four miles farther, to the bungalow at Laulpet, where we found our friend broken-down once more, and swearing at the black fellows because they could not understand *plain English!* " Pen and ink, bring, you stupid rascal—I want to write! Now isn't this enough to provoke a saint? See how the fellow looks at me. Get away, and coubra (bring) the pen and ink."

It was very amusing to hear a conversation between the Colonel and a Moorman about the purchase of a few baskets of oranges, one speaking English and the other Hindostanee. My child got so impatient hearing the farce that she stepped forward, with her little hands behind her back, to interpret between them; otherwise they might never have brought their bargain to a conclusion. The oranges being bought, and the palkee again cobbled up, our hero* started about ten o'clock, without offering the child an orange. We retired for the night, having first bought a few dozen of fine oranges for my sweet pet—they grow at Sautgur, near this place, the best in the Madras Presidency. We started by torch-light for Palicondah, where we arrived at a little past seven a.m. Sun very hot. The road leads through a rich, fertile, and beautiful valley all the way. Made a memorandum of the height of the thermometer in the shade, at Bangalore, from the 1st of October, 1826, until the 22nd of August, 1827. I am writing this on the crown of my hat—no table, no desk. "Curry and rice ready, sar." "Very well; I'm coming." Three plates laid upon a clean-swept floor, some cool beer, and fruit, served for our repast.

We left Palicondah about three o'clock in the morning, and continued our route through the same fertile valley towards Vellore, where we arrived to breakfast with our kind and hospitable friends, Captain and Mrs. McLeod. I found a large bath in my dressing-room, which I enjoyed extremely after my journey. I went to the Fort after breakfast, and called upon the Commandant, Lieutenant-Colonel Fain. Dined with Major Anderson, commanding the 16th Regiment N.I. Took a drive in the evening, and returned to tea with the ladies. I was surprised to find Vellore so very cool, the thermometer in the shade being only 85°, but was informed it had been raining for several weeks, although there had been none in the Mysore country, where it should have just commenced. On the 31st I went to see a new theatre, being built by subscription. It was a very poor place in comparison to our pretty little one

---

* He got 100,000 rupees in the lottery when he went to Madras.

at Bangalore. Amongst many other mistakes, they forgot the stage! Passed the remainder of the day quietly at home. Major Anderson and Dr. Fraser dined with us.

September 1st.—Captain McLeod and myself arose very early, and ascended the hill of Guzaron. It stands immediately behind the town of Vellore, or rather leans majestically over it; the ascent is extremely steep and rugged, but the view from the top is extensive and beautiful. We enjoyed a delightfully cool breeze, which is never felt in the valley; it is only from the top of this hill you can see the full extent of the pettah, or native town, which contains thirty thousand inhabitants. You have a very fine view of the Fort also, which is completely commanded by this and the next hill adjoining, called Cesaron. I was anxious to obtain a sight of the King of Kandy, who was confined in the Fort; but he seldom turned out, even for exercise. There were also in confinement a host of women, the wives and concubines of *Tippoo*, altogether, attendants included, about four hundred. They, as well as his sable Majesty, the King of Kandy, enjoyed everything they could wish for but liberty. I believe these women were all very old, except one, who was married very young. It is a common thing to see the natives marry mere children; but then they are immediately separated until they are of a proper age to live together, which is often as early as thirteen years, and sometimes younger. But to return to the top of this hill. On the very summit was a fort, about a mile in circumference, somewhat decayed, but still pretty strong. There were several guns of large size lying about dismounted, and a few piles of shot and shell. Some iron cages lay on the grass, which once contained the bodies of the ringleaders in the mutiny at Vellore, in 1806. There was a large square well full of fine clear water. The powder-magazine is kept up here, and some stores. A guard of sepoys, consisting of a havildar and six privates, are always posted there, and relieved once a week. After resting a while, we returned home, where I was glad to plunge into a cold bath before breakfast.

There was neither church nor parson at Vellore, which I thought very shameful, considering the number of European officers and the large cantonment; but I was informed the foundation of a church was laid about five years before, and there was a probability of the building getting forward in the course of time. There were several monks, a Roman Catholic chapel, and a number of idolatrous places of worship, which latter are to be seen in all corners of the country.

We left Vellore at three o'clock on the morning of the 3rd, and passed through Arcot about six. His Majesty's 13th Dragoons were at their drill as I passed, and also a regiment of the light cavalry. Marched on as far as Cauvery Pauk, where we had breakfast and dinner, but the bungalow being perfectly alive with red ants, we were obliged to leave the house to themselves and bend our way towards the next stage, having first cleared the palankeen and baskets of some thousands of those nasty wretches, for the red ants are very disgusting. Nine miles farther on we found the bungalow at Damul a perfect ruin; but two miles farther on we found a very neat new one, that had just been finished, which made up for the former disappointment. The moon shone bright, and the evening was extremely hot, so warm that the perspiration poured off us from head to foot, and all we could procure was some bad water and a little milk for little Mary. Soon after we lay down, the rain fell in torrents, accompanied by thunder and lightning, which did not much favour the poor horses that were picketed in the field; but the air became 20° cooler immediately, which relieved us very much. My wife took very ill in the night, and called to me that she was sure she was taking cholera. I jumped off my mattress to give her some brandy and laudanum, when she got a little better, and had a sleep, which restored her very much. We did not start next morning until five o'clock, and arrived at another new bungalow, same as last, beside the Rajah's Tank, —the roads from Vellore to Madras almost under water and knee-deep with mud, a disgrace to the country and the Government; in fact, it was wading through a swamp the four last days of our journey. The morning was dreadfully hot; as soon as I arrived, I was glad to throw myself down in a corner of the room on my mattress, not able to move with violent headache.

Dreadful squalls of rain, thunder, and lightning, in the night; no stables, horses picketed in a wood; could not sleep with the heat, almost suffocating; got up at half-past two, and sent off the coury, baskets, horses, &c. Mounted my little grey, and left the palkee to follow. No appearance of a road, except here and there I could discern the mark of cart-tracks up to the axle, and at one place passed upwards of seventy carts stuck in the mud; the country quite inundated. However, little Dustyfoot took me through it safe, and brought me to the best bungalow on the road (Stree Permatoor); indeed, it was an excellent house, with five very fine rooms and two verandas, good stabling, and other conveniences. Here I met with Major Harris, 6th N. I., on his way to Madras. I asked him the news, when I was grieved to hear of the death of Colonel and Mrs. Chambers. They were travelling down from Bellary to Bangalore, to make a short stay with their daughter, Mrs. Taylor, before proceeding to England, when Mrs. Chambers was attacked by cholera, at Baughpilly, which soon carried her off; the Colonel immediately dispatched a messenger with a note to his son-in-law, Captain Taylor, mentioning this trying and melancholy scene, and died himself on the evening of the same day, leaving their daughter, Miss C——, an amiable and most affectionate young lady, to weep over their dead bodies and bewail the irreparable loss of a father and mother, without a sympathizing friend nearer than sixty miles, and in a vile country overwhelmed with disease and insufferably hot. What a trial of faith and Christian patience! —a mild, delicate, sweet girl of seventeen, left in this deplorable state of affliction. Both her parents had that day fallen victims to the dreadful disease that now fastened on herself, when the providential arrival of her brother-in-law preserved her from the same grave that closed over her beloved parents, who were brought on, and interred together at Bangalore. The meeting of the two sisters can hardly be described; the most poignant and bitter grief choked their salutation; and to picture or describe the anguish of those two lovely young sisters, when they fell into each other's arms, would be impossible. Colonel Chambers was a gallant soldier; the last occasion on which he had an opportunity of distinguishing himself was against the Burmese, when he received the public thanks he justly merited. Mrs. Chambers was a very fine-looking person; and altogether they were as charming a family as I have ever met.

CHAPTER XVIII.

An Old Friend.—Affair with a Tiger.—At Sea.—Diamond Harbour.—
Land Again.—Calcutta.—Our Ménage.—Calcutta.—Fort William.—
Barrackpore.—Serampore.—A Nautch.—An Apostate.—A Christian.—
Prayer.—A Fakeer.—Kidderpore Orphan School.

WE left Stree Permatoor next morning at four o'clock, and arrived at Poonamalee about eight, after a very hot ride; the last two miles of the road was under water. We found a neat quarter and an excellent breakfast ready for us on our arrival, prepared by my friend Captain Bernard. The first thing that attracted my attention was the corpse of a soldier of the 45th (my old regiment). He had just drowned himself in one of the tanks, I understood intentionally. Poonamalee is the great depôt for troops arriving at Madras; they are immediately marched to that place after being disembarked. The recruits and young women incautiously eat all kinds of fruit, drink arrack, and expose themselves to the sun, which brings on rapid disease, and they die daily in consequence. Poonamalee lies thirteen miles west of Madras, on a flat, surrounded by marshy ground—hardly, I think, a healthy place for European troops.

Went on to Madras, got a field-officer's quarter in the Fort, furnished it for a week, collected our baggage sent in advance, and waited the arrival of our old good ship *Warren Hastings* for a passage to Calcutta. The week passed, and no arrival. *Princess Charlotte*, Captain Biden, came in, and he asked us to take a *free* passage with him, "the *W. H.* being a slow coach." Mrs. G. B. met three of her cousins, passengers with him for Calcutta. Another friend turned up just going to sail for Calcutta, and would take no excuse, we *must* go with him, his whole ship being at our service, and so we embarked, excusing ourselves to Captain B., time being limited.

One morning, during our week at Madras, I was sitting on a stone, looking at the mountain breakers and inhaling the fresh sea-breeze, when I observed near to me a naval officer intent upon an old newspaper. I looked at him as I was passing home; he caught my eye,—a sudden recognition, and a clench of hands, a joyful and unexpected meeting; it was my brother Tom, his ship, the *Hind*, in the offing, going on next day or two to Penang. I took him back to the Fort, to spin a yarn seven years long since we had last met. He would have me to dine on board next day. I went, and looked foolish enough amongst the jolly party; the ship rolling most horribly nearly rolled the life out of me, and rolled me away from the dinner-table. I was annoyed and vexed with myself; but I could not help it, poor fellow. He put me ashore, and we parted company for seven years *more*.

15*th*.—One of my horses died in the livery-stable. I sold off the others in case of "Misfortunes never come single."

There was an officer of the 1st European regiment living next room to us in the Barracks; he and our little Mary got quite intimate, for he was extremely fond of children. I asked him to walk in one day and take tiffin with us. While I waited his arrival, I took up an old magazine for August, 1819, and read the following providential escape from a tiger:—

"Lieutenant A. Calder, of the Honourable Company's Rifle Corps, who was severely wounded by a cannon-shot in the battle with Holkar's forces in India, on the 21st December, 1817, had a short time previously a most providential escape from the fangs of a tiger. On the morning of the 29th September, 1817, while shooting amongst the jungle with other officers, being separated from them by a rivulet, he came to a small opening in the wood, about the size of a door, in which, to his inexpressible horror, he perceived a royal tiger basking in the sun. He was immediately retiring, when the animal sprung upon him with a tremendous roar; but not before he had fired his rifle, and wounded him in the head, the distance, about four yards, affording only half a leap to the enraged brute. Mr. C. was knocked down, and remained some time insensible. On recovering, he found the tiger standing over him, his left shoulder being in the animal's mouth, the hairs of whose face were actually touching his cheek. At this instant Mr.

C.'s eye caught the tiger's, when, to his astonishment, it let go its hold, and ran off! Still grasping his fowling-piece, he entered the jungle about sixty yards, and was found by one of his servants, who with the officers carried him two miles to the camp. His wounds being dressed, he recovered perfectly in two months. The indelible vouchers of this miraculous escape are deep marks of two tusks and four teeth on his left shoulder, the complete print of a paw on his right hip, and slighter wounds on his arm, breast, &c. His life was some time in danger; but his having bled profusely, even to fainting, assisted in the cure."

When my friend came to tiffin, I mentioned the above circumstance, and I found *he was* the identical person who had such a miraculous escape. Captain Calder then told me the story, and, with the exception of the print of the animal's paw on his hip, it was all true enough. I found him afterwards a very pleasant gentleman-like man. We left Madras about the same time; he went to Masulipatam, and I took my departure for Calcutta on the 21st September, that is to say, I embarked on board the brig *Macaulay*.

We had a fine leading wind for the first forty-eight hours, when it fell off to a calm; the sea ran high, and the ship rolled so very much, I thought her masts would have gone overboard. The wind sprang up again fresh about nightfall, and continued fair until four o'clock the next day, when it died away, but freshened again at night. Sunday morning, the last day of September, very hazy all round, every appearance of a gale; it soon came on to blow fresh, with heavy rain, thunder, and lightning. A sea struck the vessel aft, came into our cabin, washed away my bed, and set us afloat. Another soon followed, when we got the carpenter to work, and had our windows closed up. Nothing in life so comfortless in my opinion as squally wet weather at sea, where you cannot get a dry spot to sit down; raining above, and the sea washing into every little chink below; all hands (I mean passengers) at work who are able to stand, securing their traps from the wet, hanging up bandboxes, bundles, parcels, boots, shoes, and clothes to the beams of their cabin, securing their trunks one above another to keep them dry; and, after all, finding it impossible to keep them free of the destructive element. The weather cleared up at twelve o'clock, and the day became very fine, with a stiff breeze, which unfortunately fell off about three o'clock. We dined on deck; all well. Aiken speared a dolphin, and brought him on deck; I had often heard much concerning that fish when dying, and now witnessed the truth of what I thought might have been somewhat exaggerated. I never saw anything more beautiful than the various changes of colour which it displayed during the time it was dying. The long fin, which reaches from the back of the head down to the tail, changed its colour frequently, from a dark brown to the most beautiful light blue, spotted with red, white, leaden, black, pink, and other colours; as soon as life was extinct, it returned to its original water colour, and we eat him for dinner.

All hands well, a calm all night, ship sat like a duck on a pond until morning, without giving a single roll.

October 1st.—Wind sprung up lightly from the north, hauled up close; but it soon died away, and we were again left in a calm. "Hope deferred maketh the heart sick," and so it was with us, for we had not so much wind as to stem the current, and we were daily making a retrograde voyage, until the morning of the 6th, when the wind came round to the S.W., with a fine breeze, and we walked away on our voyage most delightfully, with cheerful hearts and smiling faces; fell in with the pilot on the evening of the 8th, and made the land next morning. Anchored at Kedgeree; went on shore in the afternoon, but saw nothing worth notice. The village was small, and the bazaar could boast of little save eggs, fowls, and fruit. The natives work mats very prettily, and had a large supply for sale. Next morning, the 10th, we ran up with the tide as far as Diamond Harbour, and anchored. I went on shore after dinner, and took a walk along the banks of the river; but there was nothing worthy of notice. The country is quite level on both sides of the river, and I should think in the rainy season it would be a perfect swamp. Diamond Harbour is only a mere nook, or curve in the river; the Indiamen generally lie here; the *Minerva* was the only one then at anchor. Went on board again at half-past seven in a dingy, or Hooghly fishing-boat; they are very much superior to the Madras Mussula boats, but not built for crossing a surf. The dingy is rowed by ten black fellows, who sit upon a deck made of any kind of rough boards, and always carry their nets below. They make no noise when rowing, like the Madras men, who never cease singing or skirling the whole time they are at sea. We were serenaded by jackals all night, being close to the bank of the river: those prowling beasts cry like so many human beings in great distress.

11th.—Anchored about four p.m., the tide having failed us. I went on shore, and had a long walk. Shot some birds. Saw an alligator about twenty feet long. The country was very fertile, and the village extremely populous. The river began to get narrower, but the scenery was not remarkable; villages all along the banks, pressing through the cocoa-trees and jungle. The river winds very much, and is muddy from the Sand Heads all the way to Calcutta. We began to get extremely tired of our voyage, although Aiken was very attentive and hospitable; but as we expected to make a passage of five or six days, and had then been twenty-two on board, it was really sickening; and the weather was so hot we could hardly breathe. While ruminating on this tedious business, our brother John came alongside in a beautiful boat, and we were not long before we had our baggage removed from the ship,* and started off with him. He had left Calcutta in the morning, thinking to meet us about Garden Reach, three miles down the river, but he had dropped down with the tide twenty-five miles before we met, and as the tide turned against us at six p.m., we had to pull up against it for eight hours, and arrived at his house a little after one o'clock in the morning—a splendid mansion,

* Brig *Macaulay*. She was purchased afterwards by Aiken for S.R. 22,000, and lost on the Tenassarim coast, having struck against a sunken rock, while conveying troops, stores, and passengers to Moulmein. All hands saved. Poor Captain Aiken was lost afterwards — ship, passengers and all, wife and child, on his passage to the Mauritius. Alas! poor fellow, how kind and hospitable and generous; would not accept a shilling from me for twenty-six days' passage to Bengal—a good table included.

and elegantly furnished, in Chowringhee—indeed, all the houses in that part are palaces.

Calcutta has been so well described, and painted in such various lights and splendid colours, that I am somewhat at a loss to say anything about it, further than just to bring to my own remembrance what I saw and what I thought of the "City of Palaces," commonly so called in Bengal. My first arrival in the great metropolis of Eastern India being in the middle of the night, I saw very little, being more in danger of tumbling off the box of the coach which conveyed us from the banks of the river, than straining my eyes in search of some of the palaces I so often heard of. However, I was much pleased with the view from my window next morning, our house being on the Chowringhee Road. A large extent of many hundred acres of level ground, *green* and beautiful, intersected with fine broad roads; Fort William, the Government House, the shipping in the river, a range of splendid houses, and a great variety of equipages, horses, buggies, palkees, natives and Europeans, Jews, Greeks, Turks, Armenians, Parsees, race-horses in training, ladies on horseback, red-coats and coats of all colours, greyhounds, bulldogs, hounds, terriers, and other curs of low degree, presented themselves to my view. I liked the novelty of the sight, and I was favourably impressed with the first view of Calcutta, which is said to be half the battle, if you go there to reside, or even to enjoy yourself for a few months as I did. We were summoned to breakfast at half-past eight. Morning service having been first performed by our host, we sat down, and, after being on board twenty-six days, I confess I did ample justice to the *bread-and-butter* in particular. The manners, customs, and appearance of things struck me as widely differing from Madras. There were no less than seven or eight black rascals attending at breakfast, with their white turbans, long mustachios, bare feet, and white muslin robes, not one of whom would stir to touch my plate. Every fellow attended merely to his own business, or what work was cut out for himself. I thought it necessary to get one of these animals into my service, and I had patience enough to keep him a week, during

which time he acquitted himself in the following manner:—
He was very punctually behind my chair at breakfast, handed
his mistress her tea, and changed her plate; after which he
left the house, and did not return until half-past six in the
evening, to dinner; he changed a plate three or four times,
and waited until the cloth was removed, when he removed
himself along with it. The lazy villain would not do another
thing, and, not being accustomed to keep such gentlemen, I
requested he would never come into my presence again. I was
very much inclined to help him down stairs. This fellow is
called a *kitmagar*, and his wages are eighty-four rupees, or
about eight guineas a year. The *consumar* goes to the bazaar
to provide for the table; he sees the dinner, tiffin, &c., placed
on the table, and attends until the cloth is removed, when he
goes home (hard work); wages, from ten to fifteen rupees a
month. The *abdar* cools the wine, beer, and water; seven
rupees a month. *Sedar-bearer* takes charge of his master's
clothes, and pulls the punkar *sometimes;* eight rupees a month.
Hookah-bedar prepares the chillum, and keeps the hookah in
order; seven rupees per month. The *bearers* dust the furniture and pull the punkar, at five rupees each per month; these
are the only fellows that will keep in the house, and lazy, indolent snails they are. The *chokedar* is a sort of watchman, that
sleeps half the night, for which he gets five rupees per month.
The *molly*, or gardener, gets five rupees ditto, for clawing up
the ground with his fingers; no doubt they have four or five
tools which have not been improved for the last 1,800 years,
and those kind of poor animals do all their work squatting
down; a Scotch gardener will do more work in one day than
six of these mollys in a week. The *syce* is the groom, or
horsekeeper, at five rupees a month; if you keep twenty horses
you must keep forty people to attend them. The *durwan*,
six rupees per month; he opens the gate and shuts it at
night — mighty hard work! yet the lazy thief will not do
another single thing. The *bobbache*, or cook, the most useful
rascal in the lot, gets fifteen rupees a month; *missolga*, or
cook's assistant, gets five rupees ditto. The *frash*, or lamp-lighter, has nothing to do but clean the glasses and light the

lamps, at five rupees ditto. *Coachman* does nothing but drive the horses; he would not clean a horse, nor dust the harness; his pay is twelve rupees ditto. The *peon* carries letters, chits, &c., at six rupees ditto. The *doby* washes your clothes, and batters them to pieces on a stone for fifteen rupees a month. And here ends a list of a few of the useless rascals, and the amount of their wages in the house of our worthy host, not including the *ayahs*, or waiting-women, and *their* attendants, at fifteen rupees ditto. I often thought the servants of the Madras Presidency bad enough, but those dogs at Calcutta are a thousand times worse; they are the curse of the country. I only took one Madras man with me, and he was worth seven of the Bengal servants. I had hardly been a week in Calcutta when my syce took the liberty of thrashing my sirdar for looking after my horses. I soon got hold of the fellow, whipped off his turban, rolled it round his neck, and held him fast until I made my fellow leather him with the broomstick till they were both tired. My Madras man was never molested again.

Calcutta lies very low, on the left bank of the Hooghly, about a hundred miles up the river, and may well be called the City of Palaces—but I would add also, of hovels, of luxury, poverty, fogs, frogs, and jackals. There is a fine race-course which stands on the Green, opposite Chowringhee Road on the east. Government House, a splendid building, stands about half a mile to the north of it. Fort William, to the west; and Kidderpore to the south. There are a number of tanks on the Esplanade, large and deep, out of which is taken the water for drinking; but it is first filtered. The water for watering the roads is also taken from those tanks. The natives prefer drinking the water of the Hooghly, being a branch of the sacred Ganges. Riding out of a morning along the river, I have seen thousands of the natives, men, women, and children, washing in the river; and as soon as they had finished they filled their water-pots and carried them home, although the fluid was anything but clear or clean. I did not consider Calcutta nearly so healthy as Madras, lying so low, so far from the sea; not a rising ground nearer than 200 miles.

Smothered in a thick fog almost every night and morning, the heat during the day intense, the country round about jungle and marshy; while there was something intolerably oppressive in the heat out of doors that I never found in the Madras country, although the nights were cool enough during my stay, it being the cold weather.

The great profusion of meat that is daily cooked in Calcutta, one-half of which is thrown out in consequence of the natives not eating it, draws jackals innumerable into the town as soon as it gets dark in the evening. They prowl about all night, occasionally setting up the most horrible yelling, disturbing the nocturnal slumbers of many a fair dame. They frequently come into the verandas, and into the houses when they can. They are good scavengers, as well as the "adjutant," a bird of great size, with immense long legs, and a huge beak; it has a large bag under the throat, which hangs down about a foot in length, and is capable of holding a leg of mutton : it will swallow a rat, a marrow-bone, or a small fowl, with ease. They are innumerable, and there is a fine of fifty rupees for killing one of them, which I thought very right, as they keep the city free from filth; they rest at night on the tops of the houses. I heard of a man being killed by one of them:—as he carried a basket of meat on his head, one of those huge birds made a dash at it, and sank his beak into the man's head so deep as to fracture the skull. They are something like the heron in England.

Fort William is built close to the Hooghly, and commands that part of the river. It is a beautiful fort; but so large that it would take an army to protect it against an enemy. It is not nearly so strong as Fort St. George at Madras; the ramparts and all parts not built upon are laid out in grass, and kept in fine order. It is about a quarter of a mile from the Government House, and commands the finest view about Calcutta, and that is saying very little; but as the houses have all flat roofs, the most extensive views are from the top of them, where people walk and sit of an evening to enjoy a breeze if they can catch one.

On Saturday, the 24th, I started with Mr. D. Renny to pay a short visit to Barrackpore. We had a beefsteak at his office in Calcutta at four o'clock, and commenced our drive at half-past in his carriage for about three miles, until the sun was well down, when we found a buggy and horse awaiting us on the road; the carriage returned, and we proceeded along a very beautiful road, as straight as an arrow, with fine lofty trees on each side, more resembling an avenue or an approach to some of old England's stately mansions. On one side was much jungle, with cottages peeping out here and there, with an occasional tank, a paddy-field, or a garden on our right. The country was open, and thickly cultivated with rice, which the natives were employed in cutting down; half-way on the right side of the road is a small barrack to accommodate troops marching down to Fort William from Barrackpore, as the native troops are generally relieved there once a month. There are also fine stables and coachhouses, where the Governor-General changes horses on his way up and down. A little beyond this, at Cook's Stables, we had another fine horse in waiting, which took us along in good style to the end of our journey. Although the road is good and level, and the distance only sixteen miles, it is necessary to have at least one horse in waiting half-way.

We found Dr. Renny, 69th N.I., expecting us, and I did justice to his mutton, as well as his wine and *malt;* went to bed at ten o'clock, and slept like a fish. I got up at daylight, and found a beautiful Arab horse at the door in waiting for me. I was soon on his back, scampering through the park —and a most extensive and beautiful park it is: I never saw a finer in England. It was kept in good order, beautiful roads for driving intersecting it, serpentine rivers and trees of all sorts and sizes interspersing the grounds. I observed the tamarind-tree flourishing amongst the rest, loaded with fruit; it grows large, and the leaf and branch are very like the sensitive plant; some of the trees are of immense size, and very majestic. The scenery here is extremely fine. I rode about until the sun began to say "I'm too hot for you;" but under the shade of a banyan-tree, on the banks of the

Hooghly, I stopped a little to take a look at Serampore, on the opposite side; it looks very pretty, and has more the appearance of an English town on the Thames than any place of the kind I had seen before, in consequence of the spire of the Danish church rising from amongst the houses. I was informed this place was the *Holyrood* of Calcutta, where men escaped to and laughed at their creditors. The Missionary School is a fine building, and stands just on the opposite bank, facing Government House. The river winds here, and the great number of pretty houses, gardens, pagodas, budgerows, dingies, &c., gave a lustre to the scene which I little expected, and then the steam-packet happening to be coming down from Calcutta, and passing at the time I stood on the river-side, almost made me fancy I was looking at the Clyde; but then, here comes a carcass, and there is another, and you see a third in the middle of the stream, each bearing along the ravenous kite and carrion-crow, as they feast on the last remains of some poor blinded and once superstitious Hindoo, whose body, yet alive and breath remaining, was most likely carried from his sickly cot, and left close to the water's edge, until the next tide of the sacred river carried him away—and this is their custom. Alas! how diligent those men should be who are sent forth to preach the Gospel to the heathen. I believe much is doing in the schools amongst the junior branches; but idolatry, the most gross, absurd, and obscene, is in every place to be witnessed, more particularly amongst their innumerable pagodas on the banks of the river; but the hand of the Lord Omnipotent is stretched forth, and in His good appointed time I humbly hope the Gospel of Christ will cover this heathen land as the waters cover the sea.

 I rode home, much gratified with my morning's ramble, and, after breakfast, went to church. Divine service was performed in one of the large rooms in Government House. There was only a congregation of forty people when the clock struck ten. The Governor-General, with Lady Amherst and their daughter, accompanied by their staff, walked in from an adjoining room, and the service commenced; his Lordship was dressed in a plain blue coat, striped waistcoat, and black silk trousers.

I paid a visit to Captain and Mrs. Pearson, neither of whom I had ever seen before; but, for auld lang syne, I was determined to see a lady whose family I knew. Mr. D. Renny and myself drove down to the river about one o'clock, where we found a gentleman's boat sent for us. We crossed over to the other side, and walked down the bank to Mr. Walker's, who has a silk and cotton manufactory. We found tiffin ready, and sat down as hungry as a *gled*. The wine and beer cool and good, and I did my host's good things all the justice he could wish. His house was beautifully situated on the bank of the river, commanded a pleasing prospect, and was at that distance from Calcutta where he could run down with the tide in his boat in an hour or two. We crossed again to our own side about half-past four, found a fresh horse and buggy waiting for us, went to the park, and drove about there until dark. The only rising ground I saw during my stay in Bengal was in this park, and here and there there was a little hill and dale, which relieved my eye. We returned in time for dinner.

We left Barrackpore next morning soon after daylight; the morning was very cold, yet Lord and Lady Amherst were in the park before us, taking their morning ride. Having three sets of horses, I arrived in Calcutta in one hour and a half, much pleased with my trip; but would have liked it much better could I have paid it a visit more at my leisure, and on a weekday.

I long wished to see a fine nautch in Bengal, and an opportunity offered which I had little reason to expect, as the great annual holidays, or Doorga Poojah, were over before my arrival in Calcutta. However, a rich native, Roophaul Mullick, issued cards to *all* the gentry in the town, requesting the favour of their company to a nautch at his house in Chitpore Road, on the 3rd, 4th, and 5th of November. Mrs. B. and myself dined with Mr. and Mrs. Gisborne, and we all went together, merely out of curiosity, for once in a way to witness this festival. The street leading down to the house was narrow, and so crowded with carriages, buggies, palankeens, horses, &c., that we found it an intricate navigation; however, we at length arrived before

Mr. Roophaul Mullick's mansion, which was of great size and extent, and the whole part, outside railing, &c., in a blaze of light from innumerable lamps, being close together. As we entered the front door, I found the inside was also brilliantly illuminated with fine chandeliers.

The centre of the apartment was covered with a rich carpet, where the nautch-girls danced and sung, and the company walked in a gallery which ran all round it, elevated only about six feet; the apartments above were filled with visitors; off the galleries the rooms were spacious, and many of them were laid out with splendid suppers and the most expensive wines. Refreshments were handed about all the evening, and the host seemed pleased with those who ate and drank most. He was a good-looking, stout, black fellow, with a string of immense large pearls and emeralds round his neck; the former were better seen and to more advantage round his sable throat perhaps than on a whiter skin. The most ridiculous and absurd thing is to see the nautch-women dance and sing: those that exhibited on this evening were a set of miserable-looking wretches. They bawl and they squall and they move about so slowly, turning and twisting their hands, arms, and eyes, with the tom-tom and the small brazen jals or gongs clattering at their ears, that it is impossible to hear a word those disgusting creatures articulate; their ankles are thickly covered with silver bells, which add to the music of their inharmonious voices. They were richly dressed in their own costume, and wore many valuable jewels. I observed a character in the room dressed in a general officer's uniform, who I was informed was an apostate to the religion of the Hindoos; and it was doubtless too true, for I ascertained afterwards the melancholy and impious truth of this man's falling away, and of his having built many pagodas, or small temples of worship, and there bowed his knee to Baal. From his long residence in India, and from his general appearance, I thought his days on earth were nearly numbered, and I could have wished his hoary head had been engaged in the true cause. General Stew—t served in the Company's service for more than two-thirds of his life, and when I saw him I understood he kept a kind of harem, would not eat the flesh of an ox, and washed in the Hooghly like the natives.

We left the nautch after looking about and gratifying our curiosity for about two hours, not being at all inclined to partake of supper amongst such a motley group, for there was a crowd of all sorts of people, high and low, rich and poor. Although printed cards of invitation were sent to the gentry, no person was prevented going into the nautch who was at all decently dressed; indeed, it is no uncommon thing for a rich native to issue cards of invitation to a very large number of people for an entertainment, and put them in mind of it afterwards by an advertisement, saying " he hoped all those ladies and gentlemen who *were invited* to his nautch, would be so good as to come, as well as those who were *not* invited." I observed in one of the apartments an *idol*, lighted up very brilliantly, and General S——t coming out at the time; whether he had been paying this stick or stone a visit of ceremony on the occasion I did not see. I returned home about eleven o'clock, both gratified and disgusted. The entertainment lasted three nights (of which Sunday was one), and may have cost Mr. Roophaul Mullick about seventy or eighty thousand rupees.

A young gentleman came down the country in bad health to our house while I was at Calcutta, where he remained until he quite recovered. I was very much pleased with his acquaintance, and he has my hearty good wishes for all true happiness to attend him in his career through life. Although young in years, he had not been led out of the true path, nor was he likely to have his heart and affections weaned from his God, with all the examples of impiety, coldness, and careless disregard to the duties of holy religion. He was serious, devout, and attentive to all that concerned his eternal welfare; would that I could say so much for myself. While conversing with him one day in my room, he read to me the following extract from his sister's Journal (a beautiful young woman, who died in India, in her twentieth year), and allowed me to take a copy of it. It ran as follows:—

"Alas! how transient are these endeavours. Has a sense

of my sin been ever before me ? or have not my good feelings rather, and sincere expressions of repentance, faded from my memory ? The first accident or incident that occurs puts out the flame of devotion and zeal for the service of God. O, Lord, support me I beseech Thee! I see and feel my own weakness, and that of myself I cannot do anything that is right! Be Thou pleased, therefore, to grant me Thy grace and assistance to keep me *steady* and *constant*. Thou hast promised to give Thy Holy Spirit to those that ask it. I am, therefore, emboldened to implore its divine assistance to help my infirmities, and so to fortify my mind that I may not be seduced from my duty to Thee by the deceitful enticements of the world, the flesh, and the devil. Let me, O Lord, in all times and in all places think of Thee, remember that Thou art present with me, though invisible, and privy to my most secret thoughts, that I may be afraid to offend Thee and never dare to do but what Thou approvest, or of which I may not fear to give an account at the last great and terrible day. O, fit and prepare me for that solemn time by a virtuous and holy life! In whatever I do let me remember Thee ; be Thou ever in my thoughts, then I shall not forget Thee when I leave my closet, nor have so often to upbraid myself with coldness and indifference in Thy service. I have now attained my seventeenth year. O, Lord, how good and merciful in Thee to have preserved me, an offending worm, so long; to have so long borne with my repeated acts of disobedience and ingratitude— how merciful! when I might have been cut off in the midst of my sins. But Thou hast been patient and long-suffering. In how many things have I *knowingly* acted contrary to Thy holy will, and have neither loved Thee, feared Thee, nor obeyed Thee, as I ought to have done. If Thou shouldst deal with me according as I have deserved, I could expect nothing but the severities of Thy displeasure. But Thou art a gracious God and Father, pitying Thy children, knowing that we are but dust. Pardon all my wickedness I beseech Thee, merciful Father, for the sake of Him in whose name I dare only ask it—for Him who died for my sins and shed His precious blood that I might be accepted. For His sake receive me graciously and forgive me freely; and, O Lord, give me, I pray, Thy assistance, that for the future I prove a more faithful servant to my great Master, and that every year that He shall be pleased to continue me on the earth I may be found in the way of my duty, and may every year be found nearer that happiness which Thou hast promised to those that serve Thee. Gracious God! grant this for the sake of Thy Son and my blessed Redeemer, for whom my soul does bless and praise Thee. Amen."

The above was written by this pious young woman on her birthday, in her *seventeenth year*.

I was walking one day through the China Bazaar, when I was struck with the appearance of one of those religious Fakeers who are so often seen in India. He was a very black fellow; his hair, from its appearance, had never been cut from his head; it had been twisted and plaited like ropes, and bound round his head, forming an impenetrable jungle against the strongest horse-comb; his head was jet-black, his countenance grave and gloomy, without any expression, and his left arm was raised perpendicular above his head, and from the length of time it had been kept in this position hardly anything but the bone and sinews were remaining; the nails of his fingers and thumb had grown so long that they twisted round his wrist, so it was impossible that he could have made any use of that arm; but it seemed to me to have been so long kept in that erect position that he could not change or move it about; and this poor wretch most likely had made a vow to remain so through life to gain a place in heaven. Archdeacon Corrie told me he went amongst the mountains, while up the country, to see one of this kind of animals who had been in a cave all his life, and so wild-looking he was—more like a "wild man of the woods"—that when asked why he remained there, he said "because a person lived there before him whom he had fed until death separated them, and then he took his place." This was all the reason he could give for living in this solitary, wild den. But the people near at hand never allow these kind of folks to be in want. Some of these poor blinded pagans, who are wont to inflict upon themselves cruel and unnecessary tortures, often make a vow to sit in one position for years.

Some lie upon blunt spikes, some measure their length along the road for hundreds of miles, and others stand upon one leg, and so on.

I frequently paid a visit to my friend, Mr. Hovenden, the chaplain and secretary to the Lower Orphan School at Kidderpore, where he was very comfortably situated, having a free license and a salary of 1,300 rupees a month. Mrs. H. takes charge of the school, for which she can draw 300 rupees if she chooses. This is a very fine institution and supports many an orphan who otherwise must be left destitute and alone to the mercy of the world. I went over the school, in which there were then 104 girls, all very comfortably situated and receiving a liberal education. Most of these are half-castes. The house in which they all reside is very large, lofty, and spacious, and situated in a fine airy park. All the girls in this school are the children of *officers;* none others are admitted, and here they are gratuitously clothed, maintained, and educated, as long as they choose to remain, and if married, they get from 2,000 to 4,000 rupees to rig out for the occasion. The institution is kept up by the subscriptions of all officers in the Company's service in Bengal. There is also a boy's school in the same park, where they are brought up until they are provided for, receiving a liberal education.

CHAPTER XIX.

Mortality in India.—Mirzapore.—The Races.—Stewart's Museum.—Hindoo Deities. — Ceremonies. — Beast-worship. — Summary Punishment.—A Monster Banyan.—Converts.—Leave Calcutta.—A Night on the River.—En Voyage.—Masulipatam.—On Shore.—Football.—Madras.

9th December.—I fell in with my old friend Captain Mason, of the *Warren Hastings*, and was the first to drive him out on the course in my buggy. He had a long and tedious passage of nearly six months, being left in a calm for nearly seven weeks in the Mozambique Channel. One of his passengers, a lovely young woman, the wife of Mr. Gough, a civilian, died on board in her twenty-second year, and her body was committed to the deep. What a heart-rending scene to a husband! not one year of their wedded life together, when the awful summons overtakes her on the deep, and she submits to the call of death. Her mortal part is given to the waters, but her spirit flies to heaven. O heavenly hope, O glorious immortality! Christ is risen—the first fruits of them that slept; and through Him and by Him, the sea will deliver up its dead as well as the earth, when body and soul will again be united to praise Him eternally. In the burying-ground, which was close to my quarters at Calcutta, I have taken my morning walks, and observed the greater proportion of tenants there were young women from the age of sixteen to twenty-four, married and unmarried; and, from my own calculation, the average of deaths, male and female, according to years, was under thirty. How certain is death, more particularly so in India, where the call is so sudden to the grave; sometimes in the enjoyment of perfect health with the rising sun, which on the same day sets upon your grave. There is something so awful and heartrending in such an immediate change, that it should ever bring to our remembrance the blessed words of our Saviour: "Watch, therefore, for ye know neither the day nor the hour," &c. I never saw a graveyard so thickly crowded with monuments, nor tombs so closely united, yet the ground is spacious and surrounded by a high wall; it is intersected with gravel walks, and I think a profitable place for any person seriously inclined to take an occasional stroll. A row of cassarina-trees surround the wall outside; there is a porter's lodge at the gate, and, I believe, the inmate has seldom time to leave his quarters, from the many mournful visits paid to this " God's Acre."

14th December.—I went to Mirzapore, to the examination of the native *female* children, being the anniversary of that institution, under the patronage of the ladies of Calcutta. About 120 girls were present, divided into three classes. They commenced by singing a Bengalee hymn, after which they repeated the Lord's Prayer. The third, or youngest class, read and repeated Watts' short catechism, and Pearson's Dialogue between a Mother and her Daughter. Second class read Bible history and St. Matthew's Gospel; and first class read the Gospel of St. Matthew, Merton's Dialogues on the Creation, and Pearce's Geography, being all in the Bengalee language. I did not understand them, but Mr. Wilson, the Missionary, who examined the girls, occasionally interpreted for the audience. He put many questions to them from St. Matthew's Gospel, which they answered most satisfactorily, and in that simple, unrestrained, clear manner which showed the heavenly effect of the Gospel had begun to take root in their hearts. (God grant it may bring forth much fruit.) The questions were put by Archdeacon Corrie, through Mr. Wilson, from the New Testament, and the latter gentleman explained their answer, being a thorough linguist, which gave the assembly pleasure to find their labour was not in vain. A few of the girls read remarkably well in English. The assembly to visit this interesting examination was principally ladies, but not a very great many of them; perhaps from the distance out of town. Lady Amherst, and Lady Sarah, her daughter, and Lady Ryan were present, as well as many others *interested* in the school; but the majority were of the second class. I went to the theatre in the evening, to see the " Poor

Gentleman" performed, and saw no lack of ladies there. I have no wish, notwithstanding, to be uncharitable, as the ladies are deserving of every praise for keeping up and supporting so good a school for their own sex, and I wish them every prosperity.—After the girls had retired, there was a door opened in an adjoining apartment, and a long table displayed, covered with various little English articles for sale. Several of the ladies took charge of the table, and the sale commenced, the profits being for the benefit of the school. The articles were priced high, but made a ready sale, particularly as some pleasant married wives and pretty spinsters took charge.

A poor blind girl, about fifteen years of age, excited considerable interest. She has, from listening to the other children, got by heart many passages of the Gospel, and can almost repeat all the second chapter of St. Luke. She is led to the school by her sister, and teaches many of the smaller children to get hymns off by heart.

17th December.—The Calcutta races commenced. The morning was very fine, and free from fog or mist. The assembly of gentry was unusually great. The Stand was filled with gay, smiling, and pretty faces; although many of the young ladies had lost every tinge of colour, they seemed cheerful and healthy. The horses were of the highest Arab caste, and superb animals, and were so well matched as to make the heats very interesting. The second morning was very unfavourable. When I mounted my horse, the atmosphere was so thick with fog I could scarcely see ten yards before me, and it continued so until half-past seven o'clock, when the sport commenced. The second run five horses started, gentlemen riders, and they all went off at speed. Four of them were coming in neck and neck, when a native boy rode across the course right ahead. It was impossible for the gentlemen either to pull up or avoid him. He was consequently ridden down, and two of the horses at the top of their speed tumbled over him; but most providentially the gentlemen, as well as their horses, escaped with little injury. Colonel Gilbert had a frightful spin; I thought he was killed, but I met him at a ball the same evening! I happened to be close by at the time. I rode up, and had the native lad removed off the course under the shade of a tree. The vital spark had not fled, but he was *all but* dead when he was carried off the ground to the hospital. From his appearance and dress I fancy he was a lad of some rank, and about fourteen years old.

Third Day.—Adverse fog until eight o'clock, when it began to clear up. I only saw the horses *start* and *come in.* Sun got so powerful I was obliged to ride home before the conclusion.

20th.—I dined with the Governor-General — a large party and a half-cold dinner, with a grand state of formality; not in my way at all. Government House is certainly a most splendid building, and does great honour to the illustrious nobleman who built it.

26th.—The last night was cold, with much rain, and the thermometer stood at 63° in our veranda at breakfast-time. Got up early, and rode to the Course. It was in fine order after the rain. The races were good, horses well matched, and no accidents.

27th.—Lady Amherst at home. Went to a ball at Government House. The party began to arrive at half-past nine o'clock, and by eleven the dancing-room was crowded with many of the beauty and fashion of Calcutta. I stopped until twelve o'clock, and not seeing any sign of supper or refreshments, I took myself home.

I went to see General Stewart's Museum, commonly called "Hindoo Stewart." He certainly had the greatest assortment of heathen deities I ever saw before—all of those worshipped by the natives. The Hindoo deities amount to 330,000,000, yet all these gods and goddesses may be resolved into three principal ones — Vishnoo, Shivŭ, and Brumha. I don't say that the General has collected so many, but he has the largest collection I ever saw. Vishnoo, the first god, is represented in the form of a black man with four arms, in one of which he holds a club, in another a shell, in the third a chŭkrŭ (an iron instrument of destruction like a wheel), and in the fourth a water-lily. He rides on Gurooru, an animal half bird and half man, and wears yellow garments. The Hindoo Shastrus gives an account of ten appearances or incarnations of Vishnoo, in the character of the preserver, nine of which are said to be past.

Brumhū, the *one God*, when he resolves to re-create the universe after a periodical destruction, just gives birth to Brumha (the idol of that name), Vishnoo, and Shivu, to preside over the work of creation, preservation, and destruction. After a periodical dissolution of the universe, the Four Vedas remained in the waters. In order to enter upon the work of creation, it was necessary to obtain these books for the instruction of Brumha. Vishnoo was therefore appointed to bring up the Vedas from the deep; who, taking the form of a fish, descended into the waters, and brought up these sacred books.

Vishnoo assumed the form of a tortoise, and took the newly-created earth upon his back, to render it stable; and the Hindoos believe to this very hour that the earth is supported on the back of this tortoise.

Stone images of Vishnoo are made for sale and worshipped by those who have chosen him for their guardian deity. The offerings presented to him consist of fruits, flowers, water, clarified butter, sweetmeats, cloth, ornaments, &c. The distinctive mark of this sect of Hindoos, who worship Vishnoo, consists of two lines, rather oval, drawn the whole length of the nose, and carried forward in two straight lines across the forehead; it is generally made with the clay of the Ganges and sometimes with powder of sandal-wood.

The following is a description of the heaven of Vishnoo. This heaven, called Voikoont'hu, is entirely of gold, and is 80,000 miles in circumference. All its edifices are composed of jewels. The pillars and all the ornaments of the buildings are of precious stones. The crystal waters of the Ganges fall from the higher heavens on the head of Drover, and from thence into the bunches of hair on the heads of seven Rishees in this heaven, and from thence they fall and form a river in Voikoont'hu. Here are also five pools of water, containing blue, red, and white water-lilies, the flowers of some of which contain a hundred petals, and others a thousand; gardens of nymphs, &c. On a seat as glorious as the sun, sitting on water-lilies, is Vishnoo, and on his right hand is the goddess Lŭkshmēē. From her body the fragrance of the lotus extends eight hundred miles. This goddess shines like a continued blaze of lightning, &c.

Shivu, the destroyer, has the second place among the Hindoo deities; he is represented in various ways, sometimes as a silver-coloured man with five faces; an additional eye and a half-moon grace each forehead; he has four arms. Another image of Shivu is represented with one head, three eyes, and two arms, riding on a bull, covered with ashes, and naked. Another image of this gentleman is a smooth black stone, in the form of a sugar-loaf. This image I have seen constantly worshipped, and it is generally kept very moist with the quantity of oil rubbed over it as an offering at the time of adoration. Many of the stories relating to the worship of these images are so gross and disgusting as to be unfit for relation. *Shivu*, they say, is a worshipper of *Vishnoo*, and the disciples of the former never eat animal food; perhaps it is because they offer bloody sacrifices to him.

On the festival days, those unfortunate superstitious creatures cast themselves from a bamboo stage, as high, sometimes, as twenty feet, upon bags of straw filled with iron spikes. They are seldom killed, but frequently severely wounded. They also have their tongues pierced. It is sometimes done by a blacksmith; he rubs a kind of white stuff on the fellow's tongue, then catches a firm hold of it, and runs a knife through. I have seen an iron rod, fifteen feet long, that had been run through a hole made in this way, in a native's tongue; also, in the same manner, I have seen a thick rope, about forty feet long, that was passed through the side of one of these unfortunate worshippers of *Shivu*. At this festival they also run bamboo, living *snakes*, and various other things, through those incisions made in their flesh!

They have another ceremony called *Chŭrukŭ*, or swinging by hooks fastened in their back. An iron hook is fastened in the back of the man or woman through the flesh; the rope is then fastened to the end of a bamboo, and the wretch is hoisted up and whirled round, describing a circle of about thirty feet diameter; they swing five, ten, forty, or sixty minutes; and this in honour of their deities, or the fulfilling of a vow.

Brumha created the Brahmins and the *cow* at the same time, which is a proper object of worship, as the cow affords milk and clarified butter. Besides the images are anointed with milk, curds, butter, and cow-dung. All unclean places are purified with cow-dung, and many Brahmins do not leave the house in the morning until the door and passage-way has been rubbed with cow-dung and chalked. The cow is worshipped in the cow-house before a pot of water; yet these unfeeling rascals beat the poor animal unmercifully, although she be a goddess.

The black-faced monkey is worshipped; he is supposed to be immortal, and can grant long life and every gratification. Mr. Ward says, about thirty years ago, "The Rajah of Nudcega spent *one hundred thousand* rupees in *marrying two monkeys*, when all the parade common at Hindoo marriages was exhibited. In the procession were seen elephants, camels, horses richly caparisoned, palkees, lamps, and flambeaux. The male monkey was fastened in a fine palankeen, having a crown upon his head, with men standing by his side to fan him. Then followed singing and dancing girls in carriages, with every kind of Hindoo music; a grand display of fireworks and dancing, music, singing, and every degree of low mirth were exhibited at the bridegroom's palace for twelve days together."

The elephant, the lion, bull, buffalo, rat, deer, and goat are worshipped; also the owl, peacock, goose, and others. Trees of various kinds are worshipped; also rivers, particularly the Ganges; and in fact more absurd things than I could mention.

11th January.—Up very early in the morning, and rode with my friend to see the lions at Dum-Dum. We arrived in time to breakfast with Doctor and Mrs. Wood, of the artillery, after which I went to see the models of the various guns, rockets, carriages, &c., which are kept in beautiful order, and in the command of Major Powney. I took a look at the church and the mess-house of the artillery officers; but there was not anything else worthy of attention, except an extensive plain, where the artillery exercise and people ride and drive. There is a very neat and handsome theatre, where the amateurs carry on theatricals. Dum-Dum is the great depôt for the Bengal artillery. I returned to Calcutta on the following evening, being engaged to dine with my friends Mr. and Mrs. Gisborne.

13th, Sunday Afternoon.—I saw an immense crowd collected on a green near our house, and being desirous to know the cause, ordered my horse and rode amongst them. They were all natives of the shoemaker caste formed in a ring, and a solitary woman in the centre, who held a brass pot in her hand full of water, in which was placed a small green branch. A man stood close to her with a *bullock-whip* in his hand, and who seemed ready to commence operations on the poor woman who stood among the crowd. I inquired what was the cause, when I was informed the woman had been caught in ———, and she was brought there to be convicted in public, and flogged. I told the head man present, that if he attempted to touch her I would send to the Fort and have a guard to disperse them. He said there was not yet sufficient proof, as some said she was not guilty, and others said she was. They all spoke together, and it was impossible, I should think, to know one word that was uttered; but I was determined to dash my horse in amongst them if they had attempted to proceed to punishment; however, they kept talking away until dark, and then they dispersed.

16th.—I went to the Town Hall to see the annual show of European vegetables, and I never saw a better or a finer collection in Covent Garden Market, which speaks much for the Horticultural Society. Lord and Lady Amherst were present. Medals and premiums in money were distributed to the native gardeners who produced the best vegetables of various kinds. Some of those fellows were quite pleased when I examined their medals, which were suspended from their necks, many of them having two or three. Potatoes, peas, cabbages, carrots, turnips, broccoli, cauliflower, and various other kinds of vegetables, were as fine as any I had ever seen before.

x 2

The Town Hall is a magnificent building. I went to dine with my friend Mr. Hovenden, and in the evening drove to the Lower Orphan Schools, which can accommodate four hundred girls and three hundred boys, the children of soldiers. The schools were remarkably clean and in good order; the children looked healthy and very cheerful. The boys were separated from the girls; they have good teachers, and get a very good plain education. The former go out as clerks in offices, or to trades, or into the army, as they grow up. The latter are married at an early age. A soldier of good character who wants a wife gets a certificate from his commanding officer, and goes down to this school, where he is introduced to some of the girls by one of the female teachers, and then he selects one for a wife. If she has no objection to her suitor, they arrange matters very soon, are called in the church, and get married, although, perhaps, they never met before.

My time now rendering it necessary to leave Calcutta and return to my regiment, I sold off my four horses, not willing to risk any of them in a sea voyage to Madras.

I went down one day with my friend Gisborne to see the Botanical Gardens, which are situated on the right bank of the river, about five miles from Calcutta. They are very extensive, kept in very fine order, and contain an innumerable variety of the choicest and rarest plants in India, numbers of them being sent home every year to the East-India Company; but that which attracted my attention most was the great banyan-tree, the largest, handsomest, and most magnificent one I had ever seen before. I took the dimensions of it, which were as follows:—

Circumference of the outside of the branches .. 600 feet.
Do.   of the trunk.................. 60 ,,
From the trunk to the outside circumference .. 75 ,,
Breadth of the shade under a vertical sun .... 150 ,,

Three thousand men might encamp beneath its branches and be sufficiently sheltered from the rays of the sun. It had thirty-six pillars supporting the huge outstretched arms, each of them as thick as a moderate-sized tree. I think I have described this wonderful work of nature in some former part of my journal, and those who have been in India will allow there is no exaggeration in the description I have made. When the arms grow out horizontally, they cast down small fibres, which are at first no thicker than a fine whipcord; but they gradually increase in size and strength until they touch the ground; then they take root, and support the parent branch, and as this continues constantly, no wonder the tree grows to such magnitude.

We sat underneath its branches for some time, and the space around was so beautiful that we regretted very much we had not brought some tiffin with us; it was such an inviting spot to dine, and the truth was I had not been so hungry for many a day; but I did ample justice to the *connor** in the evening. We remained until the sun lost his daily influence, and then joined our boat. Mr. G—— and myself stripped, took to our oars, and pulled home five miles.

I called on Mr. Goode, senior clergyman of the old church, to bid him good-bye, and was pleased to hear him say that "Christianity was making some progress amongst the natives. The seed was in the ground, and there was hope, through the blessing of God, that the harvest would be plentiful in due time." He informed me that eight Brahmins at Burdwan voluntarily renounced their impure and idolatrous religion, and had openly professed to be disciples of Christ. "He that *will* have His holy religion spread through all the dark corners of the earth, opened the hearts of those bigoted people to a conviction of their error, and they were then most anxious to be baptized;" but the Rev. Mr. Deer wished to give them a thorough knowledge of the importance of the change they were about to make, before they were fully admitted as members of the Church of God.

Mr. Goode was a most worthy, pious Christian, and I believe what he preached he practised, and what he practised he preached, and that without any worldly fear of giving offence. I had the pleasure also of being acquainted with the venerable Archdeacon Corrie, and a more pious, good, and worthy man

* Connor—dinner.

I never met before; his very countenance was humility, and pictured everything that is good in man ; he was at the head of all that was being done for the kingdom of Christ, and wherever he found anything to do for his Master and the people of God, or the conversion of the heathen, there he was found at his holy work, and there he laboured with zeal for the glory of God, who will reward him eternally.

28th January.—I embarked my buggy, palankeen, furniture, and about twenty dozen of good claret, on board the brig *Macaulay*, and the following day we bade adieu to our hospitable, kind, and most worthy relatives, leaving behind us the City of Palaces and a population of 600,000 souls. My wife's brother, Mr. John D——, was one of those merchant princes of Bengal who retired afterwards with a fortune of £10,000 a year. I held on at my trade to the end of the chapter, and retired from business with *not ten thousand pence*. Such is the difference of fortune between that of a civilian and a soldier; yet, if I was to begin life again, I would go back to my old trade. Our good friend Mr. Gisborne not only lent us his pleasure-boat, but accompanied us all the way to Saugur, to join our ship, a distance of one hundred miles. He ordered his boat to Garden Reach, about seven miles down the river, and there we met it, having travelled so far in the carriage; but when we arrived at the Ghaut, we found our trunks had not arrived, neither had our prog, of which we had good store; however, as our friend had provided also a good supply, we agreed to start with the tide, having sent back my servant in search of our stores, &c., which I ordered him to bring down the river without delay. Garden Reach is the most delightful part of the Hooghly, it being the resort of the wealthy inhabitants of Calcutta, who have very fine and handsome houses all along the banks for about nine or ten miles from the city. After you pass them there is nothing very worthy of notice on the river. We had agreed to stop at Faulta, about forty miles on our way, where there is an inn, and where we intended to pass the night; but unfortunately the tide turned against us about ten o'clock, and there we were, without even a mattress to lie down upon.

We had no kind of covering except a cloak belonging to
Mr. G——, which he wrapped round little Mary, and she went
to sleep. Mrs. B—— felt the cold extremely; but my friend
and I kept ourselves warm by using the poles in pushing
along close to the shore. We continued hard at work until
about half-past twelve, when a breeze sprang up, which took
us over the river, and up to our long-expected quarters. The
night was exceedingly cold, and we bundled out of the boat as
fast as we could; but instead of stepping into a comfortable
inn, as I have done in England, the only apartment we could
find was an uncomfortable room, exposed to the north wind,
and without even a window; as for a bed or a blanket, there
was no such thing to be had. We found some crockery ware
on the table, and with some trouble we got a cup of tea made.
Mrs. B—— and Mary betook themselves to a couch, under the
cover of a boat-cloak. Mr. G—— went back to his boat, and
I stretched my bones on a ratan cot, where I was almost frozen
before daylight (notwithstanding I was in India). Next morning we all assembled to breakfast a little more cheerful, and
with better prospects of passing a pleasant day, my servant
having arrived in the night with all our traps; as there
was a good breeze, we started about eight o'clock, and
stemmed the tide until it turned with us, having on board
lots of provisions, wine, beer, &c. We took our baggage-boat
in company with us, it having come up in the morning with all
our ship furniture and heavy luggage. Our boat had three
sails and ten oars; but the boatmen are such miserable hands
at pulling, that it annoyed me more than I can express to look
at them. I almost think I could get an old woman that would
pull more with a horn spoon than any man we had. We got
on very well with the wind and tide in our favour until eight
o'clock, when we found it impossible to gain the ship, so we
put into a creek in Saugur Island, and made ourselves tolerably comfortable, the tigers roaring all the night so near it
made me nervous, for they often take the water, and swim
across, picking up a black fellow if at all in their way. To
land on Saugur Island is to go home with a tiger as sure
as you put your foot ashore. We moved off again about

three o'cock, and got alongside of the *Marquis Wellington* about seven in the morning, when we went on board. Our baggage-boat soon came up after us, and we took leave of our excellent friend, who returned to Calcutta.

February 1st.—Captain Chapman was kind enough to give us one of the poop cabins, and we soon got ourselves very comfortably settled. The *Wellington* was a very fine and handsome ship, of a thousand tons burden, and two of the officers on board happened to be townsmen of ours. The wind now came round to the north, and we were very anxious to be off; but the captain did not get down from Calcutta until twelve o'clock on Sunday, the 3rd, when he arrived by the steam-packet with his passengers.

Monday we weighed anchor, with a light breeze and the tide in our favour; but the wind failing us, we anchored after making a few miles. The following day we got under weigh again, but got no further than the floating light; but in the morning of the 6th the pilot left us with a delightful breeze, and the old *Wellington* walked away at six knots without even turning up the bile in the most delicate stomach on board; however, a daily account of a voyage is ever uninteresting unless something very particular occurs worthy of observation. The wind having died away again on the 7th, it was needless to either whistle for another or wear out our patience without a cause; for my own part, I fell into the hands of the doctor for the first time since I left my regiment, for having awoke one morning with a violent sore throat, fever, and pains in my head and back, I was obliged to take to the *medicine-chest,* which I never failed to do in India when seriously attacked; and I think if Europeans in general followed my example in this respect, they would not only save their health, but prevent the necessity of returning to Europe on " sick certificate." I was very unwell, but recovered in a few days. Nothing, perhaps, so much damps the ardour of a traveller in India as to find that he may wander league after league, visit city after city, village after village, and still only see the outside of Indian society. The house he cannot enter, the group he cannot join, the domestic circle he cannot gaze upon, the free, unrestrained converse of the natives he can never listen to. He may talk with his moonshee or his pundit, ride a few miles with a Mahometan sirdar, receive and return visits of ceremony among petty nawabs and rajahs, or be presented at a native court; but behind the scenes in India he cannot advance one step. The bars of intercourse arising from our faith are so many, that to live upon terms of intimacy or acquaintance with the people is impossible.

It is rather singular that during my stay in Bengal I never saw a *stone*, with the exception of the milestones between Calcutta and Barrackpore. The houses are all of brick, covered with chunam, a very fine and beautiful plaster, which gives them for a time an appearance of polished stone or marble.

On the 13th we anchored in the small Bay of Masulipatam, about six miles from the shore, in five and a half fathoms water; no one on board had ever been there before, so that all were anxious to go on shore, and none more so than myself. The jolly-boat was soon lowered, and the captain and six more pushed off for land to have a *three hours' cruise*. We had agreed to rendezvous at the master attendant's office, at four o'clock in the afternon, to return to the ship; but the fact was we did not know the place we were going to, as will be seen. The wind was fair, so that we got near the beach in an hour, and went bump aground on the sand, not knowing the channel of the river. The sailors soon jumped out, and with the assistance of some black fishermen dragged us into the the proper channel of the small river, which is a branch of the Kistna; it being low water at the time, we stuck in the mud more than once, and before we got up to the landing-place the boat was surrounded by black fellows, who pulled us up to the wharf. From where we anchored we could only see the tops of the high palm-trees and the flagstaff; as we approached the land, we found it a low sandy beach, without a single house visible, but after we got about a mile and a half up the winding, mud-banked river, Masulipatam opened to our view; and how shall I describe it? There is a Fort of immense extent, surrounded by a very fine deep ditch, which may be filled at high and emptied at low water by means of two floodgates or sluices.

The rampart was of brick, and very much gone to decay; a few nine-pounders in bad order lay upon the bastions at a considerable distance from each other, and as no attention was paid to the fortress, it seemed likely soon to fall to pieces; indeed the walls were then breached in several places by old age and want of care. There are barracks inside of it for two regiments, a powder-magazine, a church, a small Catholic chapel, a large pagoda, and a populous native village. The officers' quarters are separate from the men's barracks, and are very indifferent, indeed, the worst I ever saw in India, with the exception of our parade-ground. The rest of the Fort was a deep sand, very hot, and as miserable a quarter as I ever saw. But this is digression. Captain Sweeney, myself, and three of the ship's officers landed together, and sallied forth. It was then three o'clock, and the sun very hot; but a light breeze gave us courage to steer for the pettah, or native town, particularly as we were all determined to lay in a stock of the famous snuff of Masulipatam, for friends in need. I confess when I passed through the western gate of the Fort and beheld nothing but an immense swamp with a causeway through it, and a wood in the distance, I felt more inclined to return, but *curiosity* and the *snuff* prompted me to go on. After we crossed the swamp and walked a considerable distance ankle-deep in sand, one of our company (Mr. Duncan) sat down unable to proceed any further. Soon afterwards the other two sailors fell astern, and we saw them no more. Captain Sweeney and myself kept moving until we got into the centre of the village, where there was a tolerably large square, all sand, the houses small, and not a thing to be got. In the middle of the square there was a variety of the finest specimens of carving on stone I had ever seen; all I could learn of them was, that they had been brought from a very considerable distance, and they were to have been placed in a pagoda which never was built. We then inquired for snuff, and a black guide, who had attached himself to us, took us a considerable distance to the house of a native; but as he was not at home, we sat down outside the door to await his arrival, for he was a Brahmin. He soon, however, arrived and produced two bottles, which was all he had; this we purchased at his own price, and he promised to give us what we wanted the following day. It was now getting late, and as we were far from our rendezvous, hungry, thirsty, and tired, we agreed to return by the cantonment, and walk into the first house we met, introduce ourselves, tell our story, and beg a night's lodging. As it happened, the first house we came to was occupied by Mr. Lewis, the clergyman of the station, who was pruning some young cocoa-trees in his compound, when we introduced ourselves. He received us with kindness and hospitality, and after taking some refreshment, we went along with him to hear the band of the 38th Regiment N. I., which performed once a week before the quarters of the commandant, and attracted all the *beauty* and *fashion* of the place. After hearing some tolerable music, we returned with our worthy friend the parson, who gave us a comfortable supper and a good *shake down*, which I fear put him to some inconvenience. His sister appeared at breakfast the following morning, a very nice young person, with all the bloom of Old England on her cheeks. My friend and I being provided with horses, now bade our worthy host adieu, and rode off to the place of embarkation, but unfortunately we arrived too late for the boat, and all chance of getting off was then at an end for that day. I was much annoyed, but went to the quarters of Mr. Campbell and Mr. Roper, 38th N.I. I got a change of dress, and accepted a general invitation to dine at their mess while I remained.

The 1st European Regiment are almost all Irishmen, and I was not a little surprised to see nearly half of the corps kicking football at noonday under a scorching sun, and many of them without any covering on their heads. This was enough to destroy the strongest constitution, and send them all to hospital; but they are thoughtless fellows in general, and they tripped up each other's heels with as little ceremony as if they had been on the green sod of Old Ireland. A comrade passed over the ground to his last home at the time, attended by an officer and the usual party, when they all of one accord ceased from their amusement, opened out right and left, took off their hats, and stood motionless until the funeral passed through to the chapel, when one fellow gave the signal to *raise the ball;* and up it went into the air like a shot, from the foot of one Darby Kelly, and the play was renewed as lustily as ever.

A very shocking affair occurred at Masulipatam a short time previous to my arrival there. Two officers of the 1st quarrelled at billiards, when one took up his cue and struck his opponent on the head, who died a few hours afterwards. The culprit was placed in arrest, tried by the civil power, and merely sentenced to one year's imprisonment in the common gaol at Madras.

As we had agreed to go on board very early the following morning, I aroused all up betimes, and after a scrambling breakfast left the Fort, and found a large party embarking for the *Wellington,* to see some friends on board who had taken their passage home. Our boat was there, no doubt, but not a man at his post. We walked about until eight o'clock expecting them, but no appearance; so we returned to our quarters, and found a message from a young sub, saying that he had got a private boat. So off we went, six of us on board, with five black men, to sail our little barge, and after a tedious and most disagreeable run, terminated our excursion to Masulipatam, one of the most miserable, deserted-looking, dull deserts I ever witnessed in India. The following day, Captain Chapman came on board in his jolly-boat with several passengers he had picked up on shore. We weighed anchor at four o'clock p.m., and stood out to sea, and after a short passage anchored in Madras roads on the 18th, when I immediately proceeded to the hospitable residence of my friends, Major and Mrs. Macleau.

I now parted again with my good wife and little one. Her brother long anticipated the pleasure of another visit from her, and awaited her arrival at Madras. So they started for Negapatam, in palankeens, on the evening of the 23rd, being provided with every comfort they could carry with them. My leave of absence having now expired, I was obliged to apply for a renewal, which I obtained through the kindness of my commanding officer and friend, Colonel Wetherall, who not only made the necessary application, but invited me to take up my quarters in his house on my return to Bangalore.

16th March.—I passed this my last day with my hospitable friends the Macleans, whose great kindness has made the time pass speedily away. It was on this day, three years before, I left my house and friends in Scotland, to many of whom I then bade farewell for the last time. Although it was my lot to go forth into the world, and be exposed to an Eastern clime, and pass through various other dangers, yet I was spared, whilst those I left in health, and surrounded with every comfort, were cut off in the prime of life, leaving friends and relatives to lament and reflect on the instability of human existence.

CHAPTER XX.

St. Thomas's Mount.—Wallajabad.—Conjeveram.—Wild Fowl.—Arcot.—Chittoor.—Palamanair.—Moolwaugum.—The Burial-ground.—En Route.—Arrive at Bangalore.

ST. THOMAS'S MOUNT, the great artillery station of the Presidency (then the quarters of the 43rd N.I.), is only nine miles from Madras, and is approached by the best and most beautiful road in India. The cantonment is prettily situated under the hill or mount, on the top of which is a Roman Catholic chapel and a flagstaff. I walked up, and had a fine view from the summit. The sea is about four miles to the eastward; you can also see Fort St. George and the spires of the different churches. The breeze from the ocean was delightfully refreshing; the bungalows, situated in their neat little compounds, surrounded with the graceful palm, the beautiful banyan, and other trees and shrubs ever green and lovely, formed a charming landscape. There is a very fine barrack for a European regiment, also artillery and infantry barracks for the native troops, and a handsome church, a fine mess-house, a racket-court, ball-room, &c.; so that altogether it is a comfortable quarter and a very handsome cantonment.

18*th*.—After breakfast, having bid adieu to my friends of the 43rd N.I., I slipped into my palankeen, and went on to Palaveram, a cantonment about four miles distant, and put up with the commandant, Lieutenant-Colonel Fraser, an excellent fellow and an old acquaintance. He was recovering from a most severe illness, which had *all but* carried him off; his spirits were good and he was getting on well. Twenty-nine years in India have an effect upon the constitution of a European. Liver, gout, and rheumatism were his constant plagues; yet when men live such a length of time in India, they are more unwilling than ever to give up their Eastern customs and luxuries, unless they can return with a suitable fortune to their native land—and the army is not the profession for making money.

Palaveram is a neat and pretty cantonment, situated at the foot of a much higher hill than the Mount, but on the western side, so that they lose much of the sea-breeze in consequence, and suffer from extreme heat. I sat down by myself to an excellent dinner at three o'clock, drank my friend's health in a bottle of Hodgson's best, took a few glasses of good Madeira, followed by a *dram* of Irish whisky, and remained until half-past six, when with mutual good wishes we parted. I took off my boots, changed my jacket for a dressing-gown, loosed my choker, made my bed, stepped in, and told my boys to make for Wallajabad. The flaming torch was soon lighted, and I was once more on my travels. I fell asleep in a very short time; but in the course of two or three hours I was awoke by hearing my fellows splashing about up to their knees in a paddy-field. I knew they had lost their way, and would not find it the sooner by scolding them. I therefore said nothing, shut my door, and fell asleep once more. Next morning, when I awoke, I found myself on the parade-ground at Wallajabad, with a black sergeant drilling his company close to my palkee. Having travelled twenty-eight miles, I thought it was high time to get some breakfast. I directed them to the quarters of Captain Campbell, 43rd N.I., with whom I remained all the day. There is nothing to be said about Wallajabad, farther than that it is perhaps the hottest station in India, and that few comforts are to be had. There is a barrack for a European regiment, and also for a native corps. The 43rd and 9th N.I. regiments were then quartered there. The officers' quarters were in a range of low buildings, facing the Parade. The veranda in front was long and narrow, the outside black and dirty, and the inside as hot as fire. My friend dated his letters "No. 11, Infernal Dungeons, Wallajabad," and they were most certainly more like dungeons than anything else. Although I was treated with every kindness and attention, it was a weary day to me. I breakfasted, walked up and down the veranda, read a book, wrote up my journal, had tiffin, called upon Major Gwyn, conversed with my host, looked at the Parade, washed three or four times, walked about the cantonment, dined at the seven o'clock mess, and yet I think that I never passed a longer day. There are very few bungalows, few trees, only four ladies, the thermometer ten degrees hotter than at Madras, and I was very happy to start off for Conjeveram.

Conjeveram is a large, straggling native town, famed for its pagodas and festivals. Although the sun was scorchingly hot, I took a stroll through the place, reconnoitred all the pagodas, and found them similar to all others I had seen. Some were of immense height and size; in every direction they were peeping from amongst the trees, which were thickly planted in and about the town. At one of these pagodas they were holding a feast, and the usual din of tom-toms, yelling, firing squibs, all sorts of noise and barbarous merriment were going forward. Being alone, and the only European in the place, I did not like to go near them to gratify my curiosity; yet, as if I had been some outlandish animal, or some wonderful phenomenon just dropped from the elements, I was surrounded and gazed at, some staring with mouths open, others making merry, and some showing off their wit and humour at my expense. I shut my umbrella quickly, and stepped up to one of them as if I was going to give him a knock on the ear, when they all scampered off, hooting and shouting at me.

The Brahmins were very officious in their attentions, wishing to accompany me to the different pagodas, by way of opening the way to my purse. But they had no griffin to deal with—I was up to their low obeisance, their salams, and their knavery. I retired to my bungalow, tired and terribly burnt by the sun, disappointed and determined not to stir out again. For a further description of this famed place and its feasts, see "Sketches of India," by Captain Sherer.

My little apartment looked out on a fine tank, where the white and red lotus grew in the finest perfection and abundance. At one side of my door a tope of plantain-trees, and at the other areca, cocoa, and mulberry. Men and women washed, bathed, and carried away the *sweet* water. My boys cooked their rice, *stuffed*, and went to sleep; and at noon there was hardly a stir, save amongst the kingfishers on the tank and the squirrels and parrots in the garden, who were for ever making a row—I don't know which of them was worst.

A black fellow rode up to my door on an elephant caparisoned in scarlet cloth, bells, and various other ornaments. He made his salam and told the beast to do the same, which he refused, when he hit him such a dig on the head with an iron hook as would have killed any reasonably-sized animal. Mr. Elephant raised his trunk, and uttered a roar that made the woods ring, when I gave the fellow a hint to be off, double quick. I saw him afterwards at the feast, where he was taking a part in the play.

I met a great many groups of peasantry all the way from Madras, going down with game. They were a wretchedly poor set of creatures, who subsist entirely by their adroitness in snaring wild fowl. The game consisted of partridge, quails of various sorts and sizes, jungle-fowl, pea-fowl, teal, and snipe. The eyes of the pea- and jungle-fowl were sewed up, and they were placed on a bundle of sticks, balanced on the head, and did not attempt to move (this is a cruel operation, but the natives have no feeling); the other game was carried in baskets, and the women at the same time carried their younger children across their hips, which they shove out to support them, walking in a crooked posture. It is wonderful what quantities of game those people thus take to the Madras Bazaar, and the distance they carry them; whole families, heavily laden, will travel a distance of thirty and forty miles.

Even at the risk of being thought egotistical, I may say that I have been always better able to get through the world than most of my contemporaries. I always felt independent. I could do more for myself than most fellows. Officers generally get into lazy, indolent habits in India, which is somewhat excusable on account of the oppressive heat; some will not take a shirt out of their camp drawers, nor draw on a pair of trousers without the assistance of a dressing boy. I never required such assistance, nor did I ever allow a black fellow to come into my room while I was dressing. I always took charge of my own clothes, my keys, and my coin. Of the latter I never was troubled with much at a time; but always had enough, and a little to spare in case of a march or a rainy day. I never wanted a friend—never had an enemy to my knowledge.

At four o'clock I got one of my palkee boys to boil four eggs for my dinner, and with a small loaf of bread which I had brought with me, and a dust of black salt from the bazaar, I made an excellent dinner, washing it down with a tumbler of brandy-pawny. I liked a good dinner as well as any fellow; but I was ever content with a bad one when there was no remedy. I washed my plates, spoons, &c., put them up, and ordered my *coach*, and at five o'clock I paid my *bill*, being four annas, and got under weigh. Outside the town, to the north-west, there is a very fine square tank, in the centre of which is a handsome kind of pagoda, supported by carved stone pillars. The country was very barren, the roads deep and sandy, and nothing to relieve the eye but some palmyra-trees and a few paddy or rice-fields in the neighbourhood of a tank which I passed before night. I told my boys to go to Arcot, a distance of thirty miles, and to my astonishment they set me down close to the cantonment at a quarter-past one o'clock at night. I told them to go to sleep, and call me at five o'clock, which they did. I turned out, got my dressing-case, &c., down to a tank, where I shaved, washed, and made my toilet, and then proceeded to the quarters of Lieutenant-Colonel Raynsford, 3rd Light Cavalry, commanding the cantonment, where I was kindly and hospitably received through a letter of introduction from my late hostess at Madras which preceded me. The 13th Light Dragoons had just marched for Arnee, in consequence of having suffered much from cholera. Colonel R. told me he walked into a carpenter's shop some days before, and having seen a number of coffins ready made, he asked the fellow whom they were for. "Oh," said he, "I will have customers enough for them very soon;" and no doubt he had, for twenty-four European soldiers and ten natives died of cholera the same week. I left Arcot about ten o'clock at night, and arrived at the house of my old friend Captain Macleod at about two in the morning, made my way to my former apartments, and turned into bed; had a good sleep until seven next morning, when I turned out and dashed into a large cold bath, which was to me the greatest luxury. The thermometer at noon was 94°, yet I rode out to call on Major Anderson, of the 16th N.I.

I also called upon the Commandant in the Fort, Lieutenant-Colonel Brodie, and found him laid up with the gout, a disease apparently very common amongst those people who live so well.

Having stopped with my friend nearly three days, I set out by torchlight, on the evening of the 24th, by way of Chittoor, changing my route, with a desire of seeing a new country, and getting up the Chittoor Pass into the Mysore country.

On the following morning I arrived at the house of F. Oakes, Esq., Judge of the station, a most excellent, kind fellow, with a wife, a young and pretty person, with whom I remained until the following evening. Mr. Oakes was a *Man of India*, who had ample comforts and luxuries, and was ever happy to share them with his friends.

Chittoor is a retired romantic station, lying amongst numerous hills, which gradually rise above each other, while underneath is a valley of great beauty, through which runs the river. The society is limited, it being altogether a civil station. There is an old fort, a racket-court, and a jail; the latter place is generally well filled. About 800 prisoners were in *chains*, condemned for certain periods to work on the roads.

26th.—About nine o'clock I bade my kind friends good-bye, and started for Palamanair, my next station, about twenty-eight miles distant. I passed through a very hilly country in the night; but of course could not see anything. I fell asleep, and hardly awoke till about half-past five, when I turned out of my palkee, took my spear in my hand, and walked up the pass. The country was rather pretty: hills, dales, topes, and tanks, rocky mountains and paddy-fields, a very barren soil and a stony country. How the poor creatures were able to pay the collector one-half of the produce, and live upon the other, I cannot tell. They looked wretchedly poor, and their little huts were miserable. The pass into the Mysore country is neither very high nor difficult to cross; but the roads are very bad for any kind of wheeled vehicles. I found a very material difference in the climate, the thermometer being fourteen degrees lower than at Chittoer. Consequently, there was a most delightful cool breeze, and a light, pure air that gave me new life, so that I walked the rest of my stage without being the least warm or fatigued, a thing I could not have attempted the day previous on any account.

I went to pass the day with Mr. Roberts, the collector of the station or district, where I was treated with the same kindness and hospitality I had everywhere met with. He had a very handsome house, and everything correspondingly comfortable and neat; after breakfast I amused myself playing billiards with Mr. R. and Lady Sevestre.

I play a tolerably good game at billiards, but Lady S. beat me two love games to my great astonishment. I never saw one of the fair sex play so good a game before, and as she was fair and pretty, I was almost proud to have got such a thrashing from so charming an opponent.

The country all round Palamanair is such as I have just described. Barren, rocky, and unfit for cultivation, except some spots in the low grounds. Mr. Roberts chose this place as his head-quarters on account of the pure air from the hills and coolness of the climate. He has managed to make a very pretty place and a good road also, about five miles long. There is plenty of game in the country, and he makes himself very happy (I dare say most men would do the same with his income—about a sack of rupees a month). I thought there was a good deal of useless ostentation displayed in so retired a quarter; such as three fellows running after the carriage with silver sticks when we went out to drive, and on our return about fifty peons and pullie servants assembled before the door, some with silver sticks, others with swords, and many with silver knives stuck in their belts. At the sound of a horn they formed line, and bowed their faces to touch the earth three times, all making a salam at the same time with their long right hands, and then they retired. I asked what the two silver sticks were used for (they are of the length and size of a drum-major's cane), and was told they were merely carried before *his* palkee, the fellows running and shouting all the time, "Long may *Sahib* live, and may his riches and money increase daily." There are a few other bungalows upon the same hill belonging to the Judges stationed at Chittoor, where they reside for about six weeks of the very hot weather, commencing the 1st of May, at which time their court is adjourned.

My host ordered a cold fowl, some bread, &c., to be put into my palkee, and I bade him good night about ten o'clock and started for Moolwaugum, my next stage, twenty-six miles distant. I always had a happy knack of sleeping soundly in my palkee, and, after passing a pleasant day, retired as it were to bed, and found myself next morning twenty, thirty, or forty miles advanced on my journey. Some people cannot bear to travel in a palkee, neither can they sleep; but for my part I always thought it very comfortable, and preferred it to any other mode of travelling. I was a very short distance from Palamanair before I had sunk into the arms of Morpheus, and awoke next morning about six, when I turned out and walked the remainder of the way to the bungalow, to pass a very different sort of day, perfectly alone and retired; but I really never found my time heavy or disagreeable. I could always amuse myself reading, writing, strapping my razors, or even dusting out my palankeen and preparing it for the evening's march. Soon after I had dressed, I set to work about breakfast, had my kettle boiling, my tea-things laid out on the top of my writing-desk, my cold fowl produced, and made a famous breakfast. I found I was still in the same kind of sterile country—nothing to be seen but mountains of stone and valleys of hard gravelly soil; except the usual little patches of rice, and some tobacco, not a blade of green grass visible. There was a small village near to the travellers' bungalow, where he may be always provided with milk, eggs, fowls, and water, the latter being the greatest luxury when you can get it good. The natives are not very nice about their use of water, for they wash themselves and their clothes and their cattle in the same tank from which they lift the water for cooking; ay, and I have seen them wash their greasy hides and their teeth, and then drink out of the same spot, merely putting the surface of the water aside, which was cholera green in colour and stagnant. I have been obliged to drink this same kind of liquid, having it first strained and then mixed with brandy. I confess it went down with difficulty; but a traveller in India must have water, and he must put up with the best to be got; but of late I never trust to a tank: I carry my goblet of clear water with me.

I cannot say much for Moolwaugum; the country is wild and unfruitful. An old mud-fort stands close to the village, with some five or six ancient pagodas, such a fort as may be found at every village in the Rajah's territory. In this part of the country they were originally built to defend both people and cattle from the hostilities of neighbours who, in days not long gone by, were ever opposed in feudal strife.

I saw several graves, as I came along in my journey, on the side of the path, as they were generally marked with stone or wooden crosses. I supposed the inmates had been Christians, as their burying-grounds are always distiuguished in this way. There were a great many native Christians at Chittoor, and one gentleman there in high rank (Judge D——) had actually married a black woman and left her all his property, both in India and at home. He was very anxious to convert the natives, and frequently paid them to become converts to Christianity. It is a most difficult matter to persuade an adult native to give up his prejudices and the religion of his country, and I would doubt much whether the man that was bought over in this kind of way was, or ever would be, a true and sincere Christian. I am as anxious as any person to see the religion of Christ and His holy and blessed gospel spread in this heathen land, and amongst such an innumerable multitude of the most blind, bigoted, superstitious, and stupidly ignorant people in the world; but it never will be done in this way. Schools must be established, and the junior class must be enlightened by early education, and brought up as free as possible from their long idolatrous customs and their lazy, idle, and profligate habits.

Twenty minutes before five (I like to be particular) I jumped into my palkee, having first made a hearty dinner of my cold fowl, salted a leg and a wing for the following morning, and washed my plates, which I preferred doing myself; I was soon out of the town of Moolwaugum. As I passed through, it appeared larger and more populous than I expected, and there were some well-cultivated gardens and patches of ground on the west side. You hardly ever pass through a native town or village in India, but you will see one of their abominable festivals, or a preperation for one. Here they were assembled in multitudes dragging the pagoda car, dressed up in all the finery they could muster, in procession through the village. I had not advanced very far on my journey, when I perceived a black fellow suspended by a rope from the branch of a tree on the roadside. He had been hanged, and left there most likely as a terror to evil-doers. He was quite naked, with the exception of a dirty cloth wrapped round his head, his feet about a foot from the ground, and his arms extended forward, which showed he was not bound in the usual manner, but most likely held by the hands until dead. This was in the Rajah's country, where very little ceremony was used in putting a native to death; but they are very seldom, if ever, hanged, except for murder, which was likely enough to have been the crime this unfortunate wretch had committed.

The country began to improve in appearance as I advanced, fine large trees being scattered over the plain, paddy-fields, gardens, cottages, and tanks. I got out of my *carriage* and walked about five miles; it then began to get dark. My boys lighted the torch. I put on my dressing-gown, had a glass of brandy-pawny, and went to sleep. When you travel with one lot of bearers, they always halt about midnight to eat rice and take a short sleep, two of their greatest luxuries, and people are frequently obliged to rouse them up with a stick, otherwise they would be there all night; particularly when they get about half-drunk, sleep and stupidity so overcomes them, that it is almost impossible to move them. However, I have had no cause to complain, never having had the smallest occasion to say a cross word to my bearers all the journey. They put me down at the bungalow at Narsipoor or Belloor, at two o'clock in the morning, the end of my stage being thirty miles. I shut my doors, and had four hours' more sleep, when I turned out and went through the usual routine of dressing, breakfasting, and reading a few chapters in my pocket Bible, one of the best companions a traveller can take with him on a journey; when he beholds the blind ignorance and gross idolatry of the unhappy people amongst whom he lives, he should be doubly thankful that he was brought up in the knowledge of the Gospel of Christ, and endeavour to live according to that holy religion which those unfortunate people have been ignorant of for upwards of eighteen hundred years.

I started again about half-past four o'clock, to finish my journey, and arrived in Bangalore at six o'clock the following morning, 29th of March, after an absence of seven months and five days. I put up with Colonel and Mrs. Wetherall, where I lived most happily as long as I chose to remain. All my old friends were rejoiced to see me back again, and it took me ten days to visit them all. I had hardly arrived when I was generally requested to commence theatricals once more as manager, and rouse up the cantonment. General P—— and Commandant Palby volunteered to subscribe if I promised to get to work, and have a new theatre built. I agreed to make myself useful, and in my leisure hours promised to renew my poor endeavours for the amusement and happiness of a liberal and happy society.

No rain for seven months at Bangalore, rice crops burned up, tanks dry, fields that had fine crops of hay last year were parched dry and not a symptom of vegetation; the day I went away the rain ceased, and on the very day I returned it commenced again, to the great joy and satisfaction of everybody.

CHAPTER XXI.

An O'er-true Tale.—Murder.— Remorse.—Court-Martial.—The Defence.—
The Sentence.— The Criminal. — Repentance. — The Scaffold.—The
Execution.—" *Otium cum.*"—A Youthful Débutante.—Bal Costumé.—
A Durbar.—The Rajah of Mysore.—Fighting Men.—Their Presents.—
A Courtier Elephant.—Cheetah-hunting.—The Death.

THE following memoir presents a remarkable instance of
the power of Divine grace, and shows in a striking
manner the supreme importance, efficacy, and value of religion,
and its power to support the mind when placed in circumstances of the deepest distress and labouring under the most
alarming apprehensions. The narrative will afford a convincing
proof likewise that without "the washing of regeneration and
the renewing of the Holy Ghost" a well-informed judgment,
and even an excellent character, are utterly insufficient to preserve man from the grossest crimes and the blackest guilt.

Few particulars could be gleaned relative to the former life
and early history of this unfortunate man, William Boag, a
private soldier in the Royal Regiment. It appears that he was
descended from pious parents, who took all the pains in their
power to bring him up in the nurture and admonition of the
Lord. He was a native of Glasgow, and often remembered
in after-life with grateful feelings the scriptural injunctions,
holy example, and faithful counsel of his parents. At a
proper age he was apprenticed to the business of a founder,
the heat and severity of which work, together with the advice
of depraved companions, caused him to indulge too freely in
spirituous liquors. In one of those intemperate fits he enlisted
as a soldier, and was ordered to India to join his regiment.
He often regretted, when too late, the step he had taken; yet
he conceived that by good conduct and steadiness he might
be very comfortable in the army. He continued to be a good
soldier after joining the regiment at Bangalore, in 1827, and

never was in the defaulters' report or before his commanding
officer for misconduct. He read good books, and especially
the Bible, and often talked to his comrades on the importance
of sobriety, piety, and virtue. However there is reason to
fear that during this period he was not sufficiently alive to God's
holy law, and perhaps entertained a better opinion of himself
than was proper; he had most likely rested on the outward
forms of religion (as many nominal Christians do) without
placing his whole confidence in his Saviour, the only true rock
on which he could lean with safety, and rest with secure and
steady hope. But to proceed to the fatal consequences in this
instance, attending the sad crime of drunkenness. Most of the
soldiers in the regiment received large sums of money as *batta*,
given by the Government as reward for their services in the
Burmane mpire during the war. A scene of great dissipation
ensued amongst the men on one occasion, and Boag afterwards told the Rev. Mr. Reeves, who attended him during
his severe trial, that he often warned others not to drink to
excess, that *he* hated drunkenness and frequently resolved
that he would not again place himself in a situation so truly
debasing, and that he had always been sorely punished by inward disquietude, with sleepless nights and a troubled conscience
after former revelling and drunkenness. Notwithstanding this,
he was by urgent entreaty overcome, resolutions made in his
own strength were broken, and he was once more found in a
condition in which a man neither knows nor cares what he
does to others or what becomes of himself. It was during
this horrible state of inebriety that Boag, partly by human and
partly by Satanic persuasion, and being under the influence of
temporary irritation, loaded his musket, put it up in the stand
until the lights were put out and the men asleep, and then took
it down and deliberately shot Corporal John Doran, who was
asleep on a cot beside him. Doran, although a good, quiet, and
a most inoffensive man, was hurried into eternity in this
awful manner. The unhappy murderer made no attempt to
escape or to conceal the revolting crime he had committed.
He was immediately placed in solitary confinement; and when
the fumes of intoxicating liquor were dispersed, he became

keenly alive to all the guilt, the pangs, and the miseries of his wretched situation. It was in this painful state that the Rev. Mr. Reeves, missionary, was introduced to him at the prisoner's request. He had often attended the mission chapel, but was until then unknown to Mr. Reeves, who prayed earnestly that the spiritual presence might be with him while he preached "liberty to the captive, and the opening of the prison doors to him that was bound." May all the praise and all the glory be ascribed to the God of Salvation, who listened to the voice of his servant, and caused the feeble instructions which were communicated to be so cordially received, to be so firmly impressed, and to end so triumphantly. When Mr. Reeves first entered the cell of the unfortunate Boag, he found him sitting on the floor, pensive and agitated, with his folded hands resting on his trembling knees. There was nothing in his appearance bordering on indifference or obduracy; he looked a man sensible of his situation, and the few expressions he used indicated the sorrow and pain of his mind, and the general amazement with which he was overwhelmed. The prisoner for some days appeared almost bewildered in his imagination, stunned with the enormity and turpitude of the guilt he had incurred, and appalled with the frightful consequences that were to be apprehended. To use his own words, "he trembled from joint to joint;" and an estimable friend of his, who often slept in the cell with him, frequently perceived in the wakeful hours of the night a cold perspiration suffusing his whole frame, while the arrows of the Almighty were drinking up his spirit, and his terrors made him afraid. He thought his iniquity was too great to be pardoned, and he was ready to sink into a state of fixed despair. He felt that he had sent a fellow-being into eternity wholly unprepared and without warning. This greatly distressed him; he was afraid that all this man's sins, as well as his own, would appear placed to his account. In this frame of despondency he remained for a long time. However, his fears subsided gradually; darkness was dispelled, and a day-star from on high visited him and cheered the dungeon where he was confined. "God remembered him in his low estate, because His mercy endureth for ever." He was led to suppose that the fears and alarms he had entertained were occasioned by unbelief, to give way to which was both dishonourable to God and injurious to himself.

He looked forward to the day of his trial by court-martial with considerable excitement, but passed through it with as much composure and serenity as could have been expected; the following are the sentiments which he expressed when called upon for his defence :—

"Gentlemen,—I now stand before you, charged with the heinous crime of the wilful murder of a fellow-creature, a comrade in the same regiment, and my immediate superior. When arraigned before this court, I felt inclined to stand mute, but finding that an answer was required, I pleaded not guilty, because my soul revolted from the thought of having deliberately, and with right reason, wilfully murdered another, a crime than which I believe there is none more hateful in the sight of that Being who gives life, nor more abhorred in the sight of man. I will not deny the fact that I believe the deceased met his untimely end at my hands, but wherefore I committed the act I am utterly at a loss to comprehend. Two or three nights before the fatal one the regiment received their batta granted by Government for the Burmese war; and as may be supposed under such circumstances, there was much drunkenness and dissipation throughout the barracks. I did not receive any batta, not having joined the regiment till after the war was concluded, but my comrades took care I should not want for liquor, and the consequence was I was either intoxicated or stupid during the whole of Saturday, Sunday, and till the fatal night, since which time I have never been able to form any correct idea as to the manner in which I perpetrated the awful deed. All seems like a dream. From the evidence on record it is proved that after committing the act I made no attempt to escape, nor did I seek to hide myself as though conscious I had done something deserving of death; no, I was found lying on the steps of the veranda. I am now unconscious of the words I am there said to have used. It has not been attempted to prove that there was any malice in my heart against the deceased, and indeed were the whole regiment to be individually examined before this court, I do not believe there is one who would or could say I had ever used a threat against the deceased, or that I was of a malicious or quarrelsome disposition, but the very reverse will be proved. Why I committed the act I am quite at a loss to conceive, except that I was instigated by either man or devil, for it was as repugnant to the principles inculcated by a pious father and to my former course of life as the retrospect is now repugnant to my feelings while standing before this honourable court. I was in the habit of reading my Bible—I was even accustomed to reprove my comrades for swearing, but I deviated from what I knew to be right in getting drunk, more especially as it was on the Sabbath day, and this is the awful end it has brought me to. I am aware there is a twofold end in awarding punishment—one that it may be a retribution to public justice, the other an example to deter others from evil. The former I acknowledge myself amenable to, as my just desert; but could mercy be extended to me, I trust the latter would not suffer, yea, I would hope it might be more promoted in sparing my life than in my death, for surely my future days should be spent in endeavouring to deter others from the commission of crimes, the awful result of which I at this moment so impressively and awfully feel, placed as I am on the very brink of eternity.

"I beg, now, gentlemen, to throw myself on your kindness, and to implore your humane offices in recommending me for mercy. I thank you for the time allowed me in preparing my defence."

After the trial he was kept some weeks in anxious suspense, till the proceedings were sent to head-quarters at Madras; but the impression on his mind was that the issue would be death. He often said, "I know that nothing is impossible with the Almighty. If it seems fitting to His infinite wisdom, He can cause my days on earth to be prolonged, and I am resolved in His strength that if I live a thousand years they shall all be spent in walking close with God, in endeavouring to advance His kingdom and to glorify His name by a constant heavenly conversation; but my days here are numbered, I expect I shall soon be called hence. It is just that my life should be forfeited for the life which in an unguarded hour I took away, and my whole thoughts, therefore, are now uninterruptedly occupied with eternity."

He felt very grateful to Colonel W—— (now General Sir G. W——, G.C.B.) for the many indulgences extended to him during his imprisonment. He was allowed the society of all the pious soldiers who wished to visit him, and they were not a few. He was allowed to have a light burning all night, and many of the good men would remain with him from gun-fire at night till gun-fire in the morning. They read to him large portions of the Holy Scripture, and he read to them, and lectured upon various parts of the Gospel. They conversed together of Him they loved, sang the praises of their God and Saviour, and offered up fervent prayers to their Heavenly Father that he would open their eyes to behold the wonders contained in His law, and engage their affections more and more on the side of truth and holiness. He manifested much solicitude that others might benefit by his misfortune, and when his former thoughtless comrades were admitted of an evening to see him with the pious man who embraced every opportunity to be with him, he would speak to them solemnly and kindly on righteousness, temperance, and judgment to come.

During the last week he remained in this world, not only private soldiers but officers and other pious people, hearing of the state of his mind, felt it a privilege to visit him. He exhibited great peace and calmness; his manner was free and unembarrassed, but his views were truly scriptural; he talked much of the infinite value and efficacy of the atonement made for him and all penitent sinners. On Tuesday, the 8th of April, the sentence of the court-martial was confirmed, and it became the painful duty of Mr. Reeves, who had all along attended the prisoner with the greatest care and attention, to communicate to him the awful intelligence. After having done so as tenderly as he could, Boag reclined back a minute or two, shed a few tears, and then, with much composure, said, " The will of the Lord be done." When apprised of the short space allotted to him on earth (only three days), he replied, "God does not require a lengthened period for accomplishing the purposes of His mercy." He asked whether his death was to be on the scaffold, and on being answered in the affirmative, said, "That is of little moment if the soul is prepared for its dismission from the earth." His devotional, scriptural, fervent, and humble intercession truly delighted and astonished the worthy missionary who attended him. "It is a bitter cup that I have to drink," he said; "but God can support and carry me through it all." He frequently prayed that he might be able to meet his end with the meekness, faith, and hope of a Christian.

I paid him several visits, chiefly when on duty. I asked him at one time how he could have committed such a crime. He said, "O sir, I cannot tell; it was so contrary to my nature. I would not throw a stone at a dog, nor allow it to be done if I could help it." I asked him how he felt in his awful situation. He said, "I thank God, sir, I feel well supported through Christ; His blood cleanseth from all sin." I said, "I hope your whole confidence is in God through Christ the Saviour." He answered, "O yes, sir, *there* is my confidence fixed, I have no other hope; indeed, there is no other hope whereby a sinner *can* be saved." I asked if I could do anything for him. He thanked me, and said, "No, sir, I believe I now do not want for anything." I then bid him a last farewell, with a fervent prayer, as a poor sinner could offer to God, to strengthen and keep him steadfast to the last. I went down about eleven o'clock at night to his cell, while on duty going my rounds; long before I reached the prison I heard many voices united in singing their Maker's praise. His prison-house hardly deserved the name; it was a cell in one of the *conge-houses* in the Barrack Square, where men were confined by the commanding-officer for offences of drinking, &c. On coming to the prison door, I found it open, as was usual at night (from the great heat), with sentry outside; it was crowded with men of the regiment, as well as several women. The prisoner gave out many of Watts's hymns, which were sung by all present with much fervour. When they saw me at the door, they wished to make way; but I beckoned to keep quiet, when they sang some more hymns. Then one of the soldiers said, "Let us pray." In the most humble posture they all knelt down, their heads to the very ground, and a more eloquent, pious, fervent prayer I never heard uttered than by that private soldier; it was chiefly relative to the unfortunate prisoner, giving thanks and glory to God for His grace in supporting their brother in affliction. They sat up all night singing hymns, and praying for that mercy which I have not the smallest doubt was extended to the prisoner through the merits of the Saviour in whom he trusted.

A pious friend says:—"I went up to him at noon on Thursday, and stayed till one o'clock; then it was I saw how clearly all was the work of the Holy Spirit. Soon after I went in, he proposed singing one of his favourite hymns; his simple reliance in Christ as the only foundation, and his sure hope in Him, were truly delightful. The Bible had charms for him which no other book possessed; his prayer before we parted was indescribably beautiful, and his whole countenance after he rose from his knees was irradiated as if indeed it reflected the beams from the Sun of Righteousness."

Mr. Reeves says:—"I am constrained to acknowledge the last few times I went to converse with him I felt that I was going rather to enjoy a privilege than to discharge a duty; there was something so devout in his manner, so spiritual in his converse, and so heavenly in his appearance, that he appeared evidently, under the influence of the Holy Spirit, to be rapidly growing in grace, and becoming 'meet for the inheritance of the saints in light.'"

On the evening prior to his execution he partook of the Sacrament with several other pious men, and seemed greatly refreshed and strengthened by it. The few remaining hours of his earthly course were occupied almost incessantly in praying, reading, and singing; his fervent cries for mercy and pardon ascended to heaven with incessant importunity. He gave out the hymn which commences with these lines:—

> The hour of my departure's come,
> I hear the voice that calls me home."

Before this hymn was concluded, the officer of the guard came to take him to the place of execution, of which he was informed by the Rev. Mr. R——. He asked whether there was not time for another prayer. He was told not; but there would be opportunity when he arrived at the place. He said, "Very well, let us go." He now went out dressed all in white, and placed himself at the head of the guard, Mr. Reeves by his side. As the party marched across the Barrack Square, he remarked on the serenity and calmness of the morning as an emblem of the state of his mind. He walked all the way to the fatal place; but his observations were few. He said to Mr. Reeves, "If I do not speak much to you now, it is because I wish to have my whole soul absorbed in Christ, and my whole attention fixed on eternity," and this was the reason he declined speaking the address to the spectators which he had prepared. It was as follows:—

"My fellow soldiers,—I now address you, situated as I am on the brink of the eternal world. I here acknowledge the justness of the punishment I am about to suffer. The crime I committed was very great; the more so as it was committed without provocation. I am desirous, therefore, to be resigned to the will of the Lord, who hath said, 'Whoso sheddeth man's blood by man shall his blood be shed;' and to Him do I now pray that the awful warning this day placed before your eyes may have its full effect in deterring others from those ways that lead to death. Beware, my fellow-comrades, of *drunkenness*, the fruitful mother of all other evils: it is it that has brought me to this untimely end; but I trust there is mercy with God, and though my body of sin is to meet its due desert, my soul, my never-dying soul is safe. Yes, I trust I have sought for pardon with a contrite spirit, and that my soul is washed from all sin in the blood of my Lord Jesus Christ, which the promise of a faithful God assures me cleanseth from all sin. Yea, though my sins were as scarlet, this blood can make them white, and I trust has made them white as snow. I have found during my imprisonment, and do now find in the immediate prospect of death, that Jesus Christ is a sure and never-failing refuge for all who truly believe in him. Oh! flee to him, and you are safe. Many here can witness what support I have found in the Gospel of the grace of God; and now with my dying breath I implore you to seek salvation in this way, the only sure way, for there is no other name given under heaven among men whereby we must be saved. Into Thy hands, O Lord, I commend these my last words; bless them to others. And now into Thy gracious care, O my blessed Redeemer, I commit my spirit; bear it to those mansions Thou hast prepared for them that believe in Thee. Amen."

In taking his seat on the scaffold he manifested the utmost composure and placidity, and joined very devoutly in singing the 17th Hymn, 1st Book of Dr. Watts.

> "O! for an overcoming faith
> To cheer my dying hours."

After praying again, he prepared for the executioner to do his office, and when all was in readiness he presented a few supplications to Heaven; the last words he was heard to say were "Lord Jesus, receive my spirit!" when he gave the signal himself by dropping a white kerchief behind him, and he immediately entered into eternity on the *morning of the twenty-third year of his age*, in the humble anticipation of a blessed immortality. Although his arms were tied behind his back, his hands were clasped together as if still in prayer while in death. I thought him long in dying, for his whole frame trembled some moments after I supposed him dead. The whole of the troops in the cantonment were witness of this awful scene, and God grant it had the desired effect on their hearts and minds, which was earnestly prayed for by the deceased.

His body was taken down afterwards, and buried in a mango tope by a few of his pious comrades who attended him during the preparation towards a happy eternity.

The man who urged the unfortunate Boag to commit the

dreadful crime for which he suffered, was turned out of the regiment. Had there been *sufficient* proof against him, he would have been tried by the same court-martial. He was a man of bad character, and the feelings of every soldier in the same company were incensed against him and glad to be quit of his company for ever.

I enjoyed myself very much in my old quarters again; invitations came without number from all my old friends. I went on several shooting parties with General Pritzler, but we never were very successful. Florokin is the bird mostly sought for, but they are not easily approached, being very wild; they are about the size of a barn-door fowl, with a long neck, nearly the colour of a partridge, and very delicate eating. I always thought the best part of the fun was the General's dinner and good wines, and always enjoyed my dinner in a tent in this kind of way, on a wild heath, or by the side of some sequestered tank, hearing the jungle-cock crow, and seeing the wild antelope bound along with surpassing fleetness, more than in the finest house and at the best-supplied table in India.

My wife and child having now returned from a three months' leave of absence, I rented a very nice bungalow, with compound and garden. I amused myself daily making improvements, building pandalls with trellis-work fronts; preparing my ground for a hay crop, sowing grain, planting potatoes, &c. &c.—in fact, my time was so much occupied between regimental and garrison duty and attendance to my little farm, that I never at any moment found myself unemployed, nor did I ever pass a dull hour. I managed my income with economy, lived very well and comfortably, saw my friends, and was glad to see them. No creditors stared me in the face, and I never knew what it was to be in want of a bag of rupees. My house was well and neatly furnished; my servants behaved well, for they never asked their monthly wages in vain. Our little country residence was well and cheerfully situated, commanding a view of the country for thirty miles, at which distance, in our front, stood the lofty and majestic hill of Nundidroog, towering in the clouds, with a strong and entirely perfect fort on its summit, like a crown. A little beneath our bungalow was a small lake, or tank of large size, almost surrounded by very handsome houses, each standing amongst lofty mango-trees, and thoroughly fenced by the graceful bamboo or impenetrable aloe. Four or five very pretty sailing boats were on this tank. I often sat under my pandall to see them try their skill, sailing almost in the wind's eye up to Collett's* Gardens, wearing round, and dashing off before the wind to the Pagoda Rock. It was merely a puddle, after all this grand description! My garden was stocked with the coffee, lime, guava, lequot, cotton, custard-apple, mulberry, and plantain trees, various kinds of vegetables, Indian and European, also the pumplemuss or shadock-tree, and the pomegranate. The pumplemuss is a large fruit in shape like an orange, and very good and juicy to eat in hot weather. We had also pine-apples and European apples, but of a very diminutive size.

Sir Theophilus and Lady P—— gave a splendid ball and supper on the 4th September, in the Palace. Amongst the beauty and fashion of Bangalore, my daughter M. A. B—— (aged seven years) made her *début*, or first appearance in public society, and in the palace, too, of the famous Hyder Aly and Tippoo Sahib! The house was well lighted, and had a very splendid appearance. It was a building somewhat in the Roman or Gothic style, with two open fronts supported by double gilt columns, three double rows in each front; a long gallery divided the suite of dancing and supper apartments; at each end of the gallery there were double music-rooms, one to each front, so that the music had only to *countermarch* when supper was announced. The royal band and the band of the 29th N.I. played alternately, one at each end of the gallery; in the centre there was a projecting box, the seat of former black royalty, occupied upon this occasion by the Fursdar, Governor of the province, Collector of Revenues, and brother-in-law to the Rajah of Mysore. He was a large black monster of an Indian; the white of his eye, which contrasted with his sable countenance, gave him a very stern and forbidding appearance.

* Colonel Collett, 1st N. Cavalry, who had a beautiful place on the bank of the lake, and a splendid garden.

The dancing was kept up with spirit until twelve o'clock, when we retired to a most *recherché* supper. The representative of black majesty countermarched, and looked on at the cheerful table, but would not join or sit down to supper with us. It must have been a great contrast to himself and his numerous attendants to see the ancient palace of their most renowned generals occupied by a few British officers dancing and carousing with as little ceremony, as little fear of danger, and with as much safety as they would have done in Old England, although the Royal Regiment was the only corps of Europeans in the circumference of 300 miles. The outside of the palace was well illuminated, and water-works played all night. The evening was cold and dry, and altogether it was the best party I had ever seen in India.

30th September.—The officers of the Artillery gave a fancy ball, which surpassed any other I ever saw at Bangalore for splendour, good taste, novelty, and mutual good feeling. About 150 persons appeared in fancy dresses; the costumes of all countries were displayed, from the old apple-women at Covent Garden to the Nabob of the Carnatic, the old Dervish, Turk, and Parsee, the Dutchman and Moonshee, Oliver Cromwell and Queen Mary of Scotland, Sportsmen and Blind Fiddlers, Highland Lairds and Lowland Lasses, the Tyrolese Peasants and Alpine Robbers, Sailors and Arabs, Queen Elizabeth and Henry the Fourth, Sepoys, Jews, Frenchmen, and Spaniards, Friars and Chinamen, Mandarins and Irish Ballad-singers, &c. &c. &c. The ladies were dressed with much taste and elegance. Singular to say, there were not two people in the room dressed alike. I was well disguised as an old *apple-woman*, and created much fun, selling my fruit to the ladies, until the sailors got too much grog, when they upset me in a corner of the room, robbed me of all my fruit, broke my spectacles, stole my basket, and otherwise abused me! During the evening I danced a Scotch reel with a cripple beggar, a lame fiddler, and an old ballad-singer, to the mirth of all the motley group. Quadrilles were given up, and people of all nations surrounded us; but so well were we disguised, and so nimbly did our heels fly about, that unrecognized we kept the mobility at a respectful distance till we finished a reel that lasted twenty minutes, at the end of which time the risible faculties of the assembly were nearly exhausted as well as ourselves and our fiddler; so we bolted off to our tents, and changed our fancy dress for something more genteel, and played our part at a magnificent supper.

Having received an invitation from the Resident of Mysore to pay him a visit during the Dussurah festival, Mrs. B. and myself left our home on the 8th of October. The Rajah having posted bearers for us, we ran the whole distance of eighty miles in twenty-three hours.

The terrace on the top of the house which we occupied was a very extensive one, and commanded a beautiful view of the Residency, Fort, the Rajah's Palace, Mysore Hills, the French Hills near Seringapatam, and a fine sheet of water close to the handsome park below, all the country about which was very pretty. We were entertained by our worthy host in the most splendid way; everything was of the very best, and a more superbly furnished table I never before saw spread for so many guests.

About half-past four o'clock the horn always sounded to dress for the Durbar. At five two troops of cavalry formed in front of the house, and a company of Sepoys. The Resident's carriages, *Tom-Johns*, and palankeens assembled to convey the guests, and in we scampered to any vehicle we fancied most. The cavalry led the way, then the palkees, with the spearmen and the carriages, brought up the rear. In this way the procession advanced every day to the festival. As the Resident entered the Fort, a salute was fired from the battery by order of the Rajah, and the same on his return. I shall now find it a difficult matter to describe what I saw, and how I was struck with a scene so novel, so imposing, so grand, so barbarous, so orderly, so noisy, so humiliating, so foreign to anything I had ever seen before or may ever see again. I proceeded in my carriage through some dirty, narrow streets in the Fort until I reached the square, which I found crowded with natives. It was railed off, however, with iron chains, to keep the centre clear, where the exhibitions were to be seen. We proceeded to the Palace, which occupied one side of the square, and, alighting, we were conducted through the passage underneath into another small one, ankle-deep with mud and dirt, up a dirty narrow staircase, and into a very splendid apartment, which occupied the whole length of one side of the building, and was supported with columns very handsomely carved and gilded, studded with square and oblong pieces of mirror, and fancifully painted; the roof projected considerably, and was tastefully and magnificently painted and ornamented. The whole gallery was open to the front, and in the centre his Highness the Rajah sat on his musnud, or chair of state. We were severally introduced by the Resident, made salam, and shook hands; then took our seats on either side of him. He was elevated above the other seats, sat cross-legged like a tailor, on an embroidered cushion, another supporting his back, and one at each side for his arms. Over his head hung a very beautiful canopy, in shape like an umbrella, studded with precious stones, and covered with gold. I observed a great number of precious stones in the musnud, and two strings of pearls, about two feet long, which were suspended from each arm of this chair of state, each string about as thick as my wrist. The chair altogether was valued at upwards of a lac of rupees, or about £10,000.

His Highness the Rajah was about thirty-five years of age, of the middle size, very black, but rather a good-looking man. He wore large mustachios, and in his *cheek* the usual *quid* of betel; but of larger size than I ever saw stuffed into the mouth of a subject. He was richly dressed, and round his neck wore a string of pearls and emeralds of large size, and very costly. I was informed by the Resident that his jewels were of more value and more numerous than those of any other native prince in India. He wore a new dress every day, and whenever he sat on the musnud a salute of five guns was fired from the Fort where he resides.

The jetty, or fighting men, first advanced into the square below, looked up to the Rajah, and made salam by prostrating themselves at full length upon their belly and face on the ground, then arose quickly, threw up some yellow flowers in the air, and placed themselves in a position of attack and defence. They have a horn, which is fastened between the second and third joints of the right hand, with nobs or sharp points for the more speedy drawing of blood. They do not use the left hand for blows, all the work being done with the right hand, on which the pointed horn is fastened. The head is always the object of attack, and every blow draws blood; but they have none of that science which our English bruisers are skilled in. They are extremely active, and stripped naked, with the exception of a little pair of short, tight kind of breeches about the loins, and they jump about like antelopes. I observed they always made a dash at the leg or thigh, and if they succeeded in tripping up the heels of the adversary, the fellow underneath sometimes got a severe combing; but they twisted about like eels or snakes, and so rapidly that I thought their necks would be broken; I never saw such nimble fellows. Their guards were very good, and the blows well parried; but sometimes, when they got enraged, they hammered away pell-mell, both heads hanging down, so that their blows were mere chance work; then they would come to close contact, and it became a wrestle between them for a considerable time. The fellow who was thrown always brought his antagonist with him, and they would tumble over and over, each endeavouring to disengage; but they held each other so firmly, that it was a difficult matter for the uppermost man to get away, for the moment he got his right hand clear, he pegged away at the other fellow's head, so that he left him streaming in blood. The Rajah was somewhat merciful on these occasions, for when he held up his hand it was enough; the combatants were separated, or gave over themselves, with perfect satisfaction, and apparently without the least animosity. The fight (such as it was) seldom or never exceeded five minutes, and half of that period seemed to be quite enough to exhaust many of those who were extremely fat, and others very old men. I saw one man fight who was seventy-five years of age, and I was sorry to see the poor old fellow bleeding at that time of life; his engagement was very short, for the Rajah held up his hand, and as all eyes below were ever fixed upon him, the slightest signal was sufficiently understood by the superintending people below. Every fighting man got a present before he left the square. Some got handsome shawls, others silver-gilt bangles, and others necklaces. The higher caste, and most scientific men, got the most valuable presents. The shawls were all English, the other presents were native articles. One very active, able fellow who fought the last day, got his adversary down, and secured both his arms by placing his knees upon them; he then pounded away at the fellow's head, and would have killed him had not the peons hauled him off. This man got the most valuable present of any who fought; he received a very handsome shawl; a pearl feather was placed in his turban, and he also got a necklace and bangles—total value about 900 rupees.

When the presents were placed about their necks, they prostrated themselves at full length on the earth, first towards his Highness the Rajah, then towards the right side of the square, the apartments of the Ranee. They were hardly out of the square when a pair of fresh hands were at work in their place.

I went to the schools to see them practise and spar, and was surprised to see their agility. They would make a summerset head over heels, and fall flat upon a hard floor, to show their condition; run up a wall four feet high, and tumble heels over head; put large stones in shape like a quoit round the neck, and jump about; I could hardly lift those stones. They used very heavy bats of wood, which they twisted and turned round their heads in all shapes and ways. They lay on the ground upon their backs, and rolled a large heavy bag of gravel (which I could not lift), and which was placed across the breast, down to their loins, and sent it back with their knees to its original position. A large post was stuck in one corner of the house, about seven feet high, upon which they practised a good deal; a fellow would look over his shoulder at it, make a spring, catch it by the top, and twist himself into all shapes, supporting his body by one leg or one arm, twisting and turning in all directions like a snake. These men are in the Rajah's pay. His elephants, horses, and camels were below in the square every night, covered with their finest trappings.

As soon as the fighting was over, all ranks of people, commencing with the torch-bearers, paraded in the square below, and made their most humble submission to his Highness by prostrating themselves to the earth; then, turning to the Ranee's apartments, made the same obeisance; his own sons were not excluded from paying this mark of respect, for they all went down to the square, made their salam, and returned again to the gallery, and squatted down in front of their father. The state elephant was then brought into the square, with trappings of scarlet cloth embroidered with gold in the richest manner; his trunk fancifully painted, and his ivory tusks covered with brass rings. He had bangles on his legs, and seemed to be quite proud of his ornaments. He was attended by an advance and rear guard of sepoys with fixed bayonets and music playing. He stopped in the centre of the square, made salam to the Rajah by raising his trunk above his head, and lowering it slowly; and, after performing the same ceremony to the Ranee side of the square, he retired.

A very fine band belonging to the Resident played every night; but the discordant, shrill, intolerable native music and the row below completely overcame it; the fire-works, rockets, squibs, fancy-dressed black fellows going through something like a pantomime, guns firing, and a most horrid noise amongst the fellows below, resounding the titles and honours of his black Highness. The *tout* gave a fair idea of the nether regions.

I was always glad to see the Resident rise, when we all made a salam, shook hands, and returned to a magnificent dinner. The Resident kept a much better table than the late Governor-General, Lord Amherst. Everything was good, well cooked, and of the best description, and never did I see a man so anxious to please his guests, his attention being equally divided amongst all classes.

A wild elephant was caught, and brought up to the house chained to four tame elephants by the hind leg, and by the neck. The wild ass of the desert was also brought from the Rajah's stable to gratify our curiosity; it was the only beast of the kind we had ever seen, and I believe the only one in the south of India. It had the appearance of a mule, colour dun, with a long black streak down the back, and was quite untamable. It was considered as fleet as a race-horse; but never was backed. Jugglers innumerable came to the house every day, some of whose tricks were really wonderful. A black fellow, with a pole about ten feet long, and a cross piece of wood merely to rest his feet on, balanced himself by holding the top in his hands, and jumped up and down the road and round the house as fast as I could run. Another fellow held a round stone, about twelve pounds weight, between his feet, threw it up over his back, and caught it on his shoulder; from thence he would roll it down his arm to the back of his hand by a kind of jerk; from that he would throw it off, and catch it on the back of his neck, and so on; he could do anything with it. Another fellow suspended himself in the air, and all the support we could see was a staff on which he leant his left arm.

I was out cheetah-hunting twice, and was rather disappointed with the sport. These animals were very well trained, considering their savage nature. The evening before we started they were sent forward to the ground, also men to watch the deer all night. In the morning at daylight we set out, and, after a ride of seven or eight miles, came close to a herd of antelopes. The cheetahs were hooded and sitting on a light cart (drawn by two bullocks), on a couch of network; they were chained by the neck, and had a strap and buckle round the loins. Two men attend each cheetah; one to drive the cart, the other to unhood and let him slip; the latter keeper to-day was an old sportsman, long ago in the service of Tippoo Sahib, with a very white head and moustache; a very hale old man with a bright eye and many wrinkles, and most anxious to show us some sport. The watchmen came up to say there was a herd of antelopes on the plain near to the common cart-road, and all *sahibs* were requested to ride up the hill and look out, but not to follow the cart, or the deer would be all off. We took our station accordingly, had a fine view, and waited the event. As the common carts of the country are frequently passing in this way, the deer do not take any notice, and so our two *pirates* steered along.

When within one hundred yards or so, Old Tip (as he was called) slipped the hood, unbuckled the strap, and let the *tiger* loose. In an instant he fastened his eye upon an old buck, and that one was the *individual* doomed amongst the herd. He now slipped gently down from his perch, got behind a big stone, and peeped over it. No go yet. He crawled gently to another cover, aud looked over—not near enough. A little farther on there was a bush, just within the reach of this cunning half-wild, half-tame, treacherous fellow, which he gained by creeping along at a snail's pace; here he made up his mind for the spring. The first bound surprised the herd; they hesitated a moment; the next bound they were off. The old buck was the last, perhaps to cover the retreat of his family, but too late—before he had time to turn about and fly for his life he was in the grasp of a tiger. We all rode up to see the finale. This beautiful creature was seized by the throat, the cheetah growling like a cat, and rolling over him with flashing eyes of fury and delight. Old Tip now took out his knife, cut the throat of the noble buck, and caught the blood in a dish, which was lapped up like cream; and with a lower joint of the leg cut off and thrust into his mouth, the cheetah let go his hold, and permitted himself to be hoodwinked, and took his former seat in the car.

The other cheetah was slipped in the same way when we found another herd; but he was unsuccessful, and so angry that it was a long time before the keeper could appease his wrath. He sat with his eyes on fire, growling fearfully until he got a slice of venison from the *deceased* buck. They get very savage when they miss their game, and give up the chase after a few bounds; they never follow up the deer, knowing their speed.

I went to see the Rajah's *black* tiger. It was kept in an iron cage along with another of the common kind. I put my sword into his prison: he caught it directly with the most savage fury, his eyes sparkling with rage, and his mouth open, showing his enormous teeth.

A ram was turned out one day before a lion; but he merely looked at it, wagged his tail, and lay down very quietly, putting his head between his paws.

CHAPTER XXII.

The Rajah's Carriage.—A Procession.—Seringapatam.—Tippoo's Tomb.—Hyder's Palace.—A Pagoda.—The Dussorah Festival.—A Drunken Donkey.—Novel Tiger-hunting.—The Rajah's Review.—A Durbar.—Falls of Cauvery.—On the March.—A Canny Elephant.—Fine Waterfalls.—"War" Tiger.—Burned Alive.—Closepet.—Welcome Home.

13th October.—Rajah sick. No Durbar. He sent his state coaches and elephants up to the Residency for our amusement. Twenty-two ladies and gentlemen went into the state carriage to take a drive, and myself amongst the number. The body of the coach was hung on three crane-worked perches, was of an octagonal shape, and open at all sides; but there were rods all round for curtains; the roof or canopy was supported by twelve double pillars, carved and gilt. Above each pair of pillars there was a silver spiral ornament, and on the top of the sloping roof a single one of the same kind, but much larger; in the centre of the carriage was the royal seat, which held six people, three on each side, with two passages into it, and one step leading up to it from the great body of this extraordinary vehicle. This separate apartment has a beautiful canopy, also lined with scarlet velvet, beautifully and closely embroidered in gold. It was supported by gilt pillars; there were lamps attached to these pillars, as well as the double ones outside; the large canopy was lined inside with green velvet embroidered in gold; silk tassels hung all round, and the floor was covered with English oil-cloth; the coach-box held three people. We ascended by a ten-foot ladder. The hind wheels were eight feet high, and splinter bar ten feet long; six huge elephants were harnessed and yoked to this carriage; two elephants walked behind to push it along with their trunks in case of emergency; altogether it was a rare, novel, and most extraordinary spectacle. Each elephant has his own driver, who sits on his neck with his feet in a pair of stirrups, and an iron gourd with a spike and hook to it for guiding him. They are the most docile creatures in the world amongst their keepers, and the most sagacious. I saw one going to water in the river, but he evidently was not very thirsty; his driver having urged him much to drink, he at length put his trunk to the water, made a splashing noise, put it up to his mouth, as if emptying it into his huge carcass, and then walked away, well knowing he had deceived his guide, who could not see whether he had drunk.

Elephants are much used in the field with the army. General Pritzler told me he had occasion to use them for raising guns out of the deep bad roads on the march, and one day, when one of these creatures was at this work, he was punished for being, as his keeper thought, slow in his business; he took offence at his bad treatment, got into a rage, smashed the gun carriage to pieces, and scattered it about the field! But to resume. Another state coach came behind us, drawn by another state elephant. He was almost covered with a scarlet cloth, beautifully embroidered in roses of gold, which entirely covered the harness. This coach was of a pyramidical shape at top, hung lightly on four springs, had four wheels, canopy supported by eight gilt pillars, each having a lamp attached; inside lined with scarlet embroidered velvet. The body of the coach was octagonal, a spiral gilt top above each pillar, and a large one on the summit; it only held three people—the Rajah, who sat in the chair placed in the centre, and two attendants, who stood always behind him. Two more elephants with houdahs were in our procession, carrying musical instruments of a very curious shape. The music sounded something like the Æolian harp; four more elephants with houdahs brought up the rear, some of them carrying four, six, and eight of our party. It was a sight that would have drawn millions of spectators in any other country. After proceeding some distance through the grand arch leading into the Residency, we halted, got out, some into their carriages, some into buggies, and others on horseback, and drove to the garden, where I saw little to speak of except one long avenue of black cypress-trees.

14*th*.—Lieutenant Chalmers, 22nd N.I., and myself started

at six o'clock in the morning to visit Seringapatam, having sent on a spare horse to carry me home, the distance being only ten miles. We travelled quietly through a fine fertile country; about half-way there is a small wood called Wellesley Tope, where the Duke of Wellington had a brush with Tippoo. Seringapatam is a large oblong fort built in an island in the Cauvery, which river washes its walls on both sides. Two 32-pounders mark the spot where, on the 4th of May, 1799, the storming party forded the river on the right bank, opposite the breach which was made at the extreme end of the Fort where the river divides. I passed up and down the breach, where twenty-two officers were killed and forty-five wounded. The walls at that point were built of brick, and the mark of cannon-shot was conspicuous in a hundred places. I saw the spot where Tippoo first fell; he was afterwards put to death by a grenadier in the Water-gate. The fort is about two and a half miles in circumference and one mile long; it was very strong at one period, but it is now going to decay; there was only one battalion of Local Native Infantry and four or five officers in the cantonment, which was a few miles from the Fort at the French Rocks. Lieutenant-Colonel Cullum, of the Artillery, was the only European in the place; he had charge of the gun-carriage manufactory, which was on a very extensive scale; he had 700 men working in Tippoo's palace, which once contained Hyder and all his host, and close to which the sultan fell when he was hastening (it is supposed) to put his women to death. I read Sir Arthur Wellesley's order of the 6th May, 1799, two days after the place fell. I then went up to the top of the minarets of the fine mosque, and had a most extensive view of the country, fort, river, &c. There are 154 steps to the top. When we came down, the Mussulmans presented us with flowers, grapes, plantains, and limes, which they had prepared for us spread out on a tray. We rode to the *Lol Bog*, or Red Garden, to see the tomb of Hyder Aly and his son Tippoo. It lies in a rich valley about two miles from the Fort, and is a very handsome building. On our approach to it the natives commenced with their horrid music, which at any time is sufficient to deafen a European;

however, they did not advance further than the gate which leads down to the tomb. The gate, or entrance-way, is handsome. You pass through an archway leading down some steps into a garden, and, at the extreme end of a walk lined with the black cypress-tree, you behold the tomb of the Sultan. It is a very handsome building with a large dome, and on the top a crescent. There is a flight of steps leading up to the base, and an open veranda all round supported by forty columns of very beautiful black polished granite; three doors open into the square space which contains the ashes of Hyder, his wife and son; they all lie in a row, with a small pyramid over each, three and a half feet high and seven feet long; they are each covered with embroidered cloths of different colours, and above a broad scarlet cloth is suspended as a canopy. On each side of one of the doors there is an inscription on granite slabs fixed in the wall; one is the following verse, which is inserted in the tomb of Hyder and Tippoo at Seringapatam, showing the date of the death of the former to have been, in the Mussulman era 1195, and that of Tippoo to have been in 1214.

فلک زیر دستش بود در عکو	نه ی گنبذی کذ شکوه بنا
فلک داغ گردید از رشک او	تو خواهی مه وخواه خورشید خوان
خبر یانت ضومی تطلیم از او	بود چشمش نور چشم فلک
گروهمی زکرو بیان گرد او	تراوش کنان بحر رحمت زخاک
گرنشتم از این خواب گ نکو	سحر گ یی کب فیض و شرف
نمودم چون روحانیان جت وجو	چون این معمع نازه امر بحبچشم
که تاریخ رحلت نموده است از او	که این دسته آسوده راچیت نام
که حیدر علی خان هبادر بگو	یکی زان گفت تاریخ و نام

چون آن مرد میکان نهان شد زدنی
امی گفت تاریخ شثپر کم شد

The tomb was built by order of Tippoo, and placed over his father in the space of one year. There is only one window, which is carved out of a long, square, solid slab of black polished granite. The workmanship is exquisite; the doors were once very fine, being inlaid with ornamental ivory in flowers, wreaths, &c.; but were much destroyed by picking out the ivory when the Fort was taken by Lord Harris. On one side of the tomb there is a very handsome Mussulman place of worship, extremely neat and very clean; the roof is supported by three rows of pillars. The people were very civil, and offered us fruits and flowers. My companion being an excellent Hindostanee and Persian scholar, explained to me every thing my curiosity demanded.

Of all other places of interment, those of the Mussulmen are the neatest, the most clean, and the handsomest. In England you seldom see anything but long grass or nettles in a graveyard. In India, in the Mussulman burying-ground, you see the whole space brightened like polished stone, except where a white, handsome, oblong hillock marks a grave, with a cypress-tree, a jasmine-bush, or some fragrant flowers growing around it. A plan of Mecca is hung upon the chapel wall, and to this point they always turn their faces in prayer. We went after this to see the ancient palace of Hyder. It was falling into ruins very fast, but showed the remains of much splendour; from this we returned to Seringapatam, again through the populous town of Gangam, famous for the manufacture of fine clothes and embroidery, and arrived at the Residency at five o'clock, where I was not very sorry to hear that the Rajah had been too unwell to see us at the Durbar that evening; for knocking about in the sun eleven hours very nearly knocked me up.

Next morning my friend Chalmers and self started at six o'clock to take a view of the country from a hill about three miles from the Residency, a thousand feet high. We rode to the foot of it, leaving our horses below; we ascended a *zigzag* path, which led us to the top; the difference of climate surprised us much, having found ourselves in a sharp cool breeze that we never felt in the low country. It was very refreshing and reminded us of home, sweet home. The difference in the thermometer was 10° on the very summit. There is a very handsome fine house, where the Resident lives for three months in the hot season. There is a large pagoda on the top of this hill, where the natives formerly sacrificed human beings. They call the hill Shumundah, it being dedicated to a goddess of that name who was one of the wives of Shivu, or the destroyer. There is a superb view from the top of it; we saw the Neilghery Hills, Seringapatam, the winding Cauvery, and Tippoo's tomb from it. There are several tanks of water on the top, but they would not permit us to enter the pagoda, the Brahmin priests being very busy receiving the offerings of the poor blinded people, it being a high day amongst them. We descended another way, where there was a flight of steps from top to bottom, and met numbers of people going up to make *pughe* and leave their offerings, which consisted of cocoanuts, ground and hard rice, oil, and fruits. Half-way down the hill there is a figure of a bull carved out of a solid rock; it is in a lying posture, with the left fore-leg erect, as if about to rise. Women who are barren pass under this leg and make offerings to the bull, that their wishes may be gratified. I saw several people stop and worship it, on their way up to the pagoda, and give the man who had the charge of it a few pice. Its height is seventeen feet, length twenty-three feet, by fifteen broad, not including the base.

I went to the Durbar in the evening, and repeated the usual ceremony of making salaam and shaking hands with the Rajah; his shake of the hand was usually merely a touch, but this evening I took the liberty of catching hold of his black fist and giving it a real shake; he looked me full in the face, but said nothing. I returned and took my seat; was presented with the usual quantity of betel-leaf, &c. The white wreath of flowers was put round my neck, a small bunch placed in my hand, sprinkled with sandal-wood oil, and then a little rose-water on my handkerchief.

Some of his children were introduced this evening, and walked round to all the English ladies, to make their salaam. They were young, and very pretty, and their necks, arms, ears, noses, and ancles, were loaded with jewels. They had immense large pearls on their small black noses, set in large hoop (gold) rings. Their dresses were superb, elegantly embroidered with long trains, and their eyes and eyebrows stained black as jet with some kind of dye. The square was surrounded this evening with a double strong netting, about nine feet high, and the cheetahs, or leopards, were chained, otherwise they are so active that they would have made their way through the netting and perhaps killed some of the spectators. Three cheetahs were chained in the centre. After six or eight pairs of men had fought, bled, and received their presents, two immense, strong, wooden, box-wheel cars were drawn up close to the netting, which was partly drawn aside and fastened tight, leaving one end of the cage facing the inside of the square. When this operation was concluded, the doors were raised, and we beheld two large Bengal tigers looking fiercely and wildly amongst the immense concourse of people that crowded the square. I had been down below this time, outside the netting (it was about ten feet high), closely viewing these savage animals, whose mouths were open, showing all their hideous teeth, and yearning to have a grasp at somebody. The Bengal tigers kept close in their boxes till the keeper threw in some burning cinders at the top, and when the box became filled with smoke one of them made a most terrific bound across the square, to get amongst his enemies, but the netting kept him safe. The other one now came out doubly savage, and being larger and stronger than any of the rest, I wished to survey him as closely as possible. He was on the opposite side of the square, and I walked down quietly to the netting, when he uttered a horrid roar, and at two bounds he was within half a foot of me, making the bamboos crash and me think that I was in his clutches. The great spring he made, the force with which he came against the netting, and the savage fury of his nature, I thought more than sufficient to make a breach in the net, but it was slack and yielded to his mighty and furious rage; my knees shook, I ran off as fast as I could, the tiger roared, and the Rajah laughed at the adventure, pointing to me (as I was afterwards told), saying, "See, see, how that officer is alarmed!" When I found there was no danger I returned, and was horrified to see a poor little *donkey* turned in amongst them. I expected every moment they would have torn him to pieces, and was surprised they had not fought amongst themselves long before; but no, they did not even touch the poor donkey, who little knew the company he had joined, being made quite *drunk* before he entered the arena. The Bengal tigers roared and dashed and bounded at the people. It was really terrific to stand so close to them; but, as the evening was closing, bows and arrows were distributed amongst the officers, and also double-barrelled guns, to put those creatures to death, according to custom. They were very soon full of darts, every arrow going at least an inch into their flesh. This made them doubly savage, and increased their efforts to break through. It was a cruel, cruel sight to witness. Although I am no friend to the tiger, I did not, nor could I, thus torment them. I felt for them more than I can tell, and altogether I never beheld such barbarous cruelty. They had been all now wounded, and I thought the poor donkey would have escaped without loss of blood. But no, he was the greatest jackass, in every sense of the word, that I ever saw; for by this time he was recovering from his stupor, and he went up to one of the tigers, who wished to shun him, but Mr. Donkey was pot-valiant, and gave him a kick on the head, which insult the tiger refused to notice. But the donkey was not thus to retire from the field. He returned to the charge, and actually jumped upon the top of the tiger, who now seized him by the ear, and hit him a slap in the eye with his paw, holding him firmly to the ground for a considerable time, until the tiger was again struck with a dozen arrows, when he uttered a tremendous roar, and let him go. The donkey shook his head, and ran at him again, kicking him right and left, until the tiger seized him by one of the hind legs, and stopped his kicking for the present. Some more arrows were now fired into his body, which made him roar and let go his hold. The donkey was now lame and bleeding, but he was determined to fight it out, and ran at his enemy again with fury, when he was seized exactly by the nose, and *pinned* to the ground. About a dozen more arrows were again fired through the netting, at the risk of poor donkey, whom the tiger now gradually let go, from loss of blood, and who walked away quietly, very little the worse of his combat, seemingly quite satisfied at his many escapes, and I thought quite *sober*. Four or five barrels were now discharged at the tiger, which put him out of pain. The other four fellows were springing about the square, wild and savage, tearing the arrows out of their flesh with their teeth. Double-barrelled guns were now loaded with shot and discharged at the head of one of these beasts at a distance of three yards. He gave a tremendous roar, sprang off the ground four or five feet, and ran off, apparently little the worse. He met with a similar discharge at the other side of the square, and there was now a heavy fire upon them until they were all disabled, when the spearmen climbed over the netting and gave them the *coup de grâce* by running them through the body with a dozen of long spears. I think I never beheld a more barbarous spectacle before, or anything so cruel. The state elephant now came into the square, made his salaam,. and retired; then the standard-bearers and people of every caste, according to rank. The fireworks were set in motion, blue lights hoisted, the Rajah's honours and titles resounded by a thousand voices, music playing, elephants roaring, rams and buffaloes fighting, horses prancing, buffoons dancing—altogether I never heard such a row in my life, and was glad to get into a carriage, and drive home.

Saturday.—This was the last day of the Dussorah Festival, or ten days' annual feast. At four o'clock in the afternoon there were horses, carriages, buggies, palkees, and elephants at the door, to convey the guests to see his Highness review his troops. I chose an open carriage, and went on to the ground, which was rough and rugged, the road very bad, and partly covered with loose stones. The population was 150,000, and I'm sure one-half at least were there to witness this *grand* review, as they thought it. The Rajah was preceded by a band of the most discordant musicians I ever heard. He himself on an elephant, in a silver houdah, with two of his relatives, and his nobles and gentry in the rear. Two large, brown, triangular flags were flying in a field opposite the road he travelled, and a little farther on the flag of Old England towered above all the procession. As soon as his Highness halted, a circle was made by his Rifle Corps to keep off the crowd, and two unfortunate tigers were in readiness for death; they were brought there in the usual strong cage; chains had been fastened round their loins, and bound to strong wooden pillars in the ground, so that when the cart was drawn away the tiger might be drawn out of his prison. Bows and arrows being in readiness, the Rajah generally fires the first shot. When they were pulled out of their cages they made some desperate efforts to escape. The Rajah's uncle and another of his friends pierced them with a score of arrows, and soon put them out of pain.

Torches were now lighted, and his sable Highness went a little farther to review his troops. There were about 2,000 ragged foot soldiers, whose coats once were red, but at this time all in shreds and patches. They were drawn up in line, and presented arms the best way they could, no doubt; then fired a salute by three divisions; right division and left fired to the front, but the centre division went to the *right-about*, and fired in the air; then fronted and loaded. This is a precaution lest the Rajah might have any enemies in the ranks, who might give him a sly-shot. This was the first review I had ever seen by torchlight, and I was glad to get off the ground as soon as possible.

We dined at seven o'clock as usual, and went to the Durbar after dinner, being the last night. We found his Highness this evening in a long, narrow, low gallery in the interior of the palace, facing the inside of the court-square, where his state elephant stood, with all his trappings. Music playing; his fine English horses saddled; his standards arranged on each side of the square—they were many in number, and of different shapes and sizes, all either gilt or plated. People shouting out to his praise. The smell of oil lamps, confined air, tobacco, and betel, were suffocating. We went upstairs, and being introduced in the old way by the Resident, sat down. His nobles sat squat, like frogs, on the floor, along the wall. His Highness sat on a silver couch, covered with embroidered velvet cushions; and when we English people had been all introduced, his nobles advanced one by one with their presents, and each offered a rupee laid upon a neat red cloth, presenting it in the most submissive way with both hands. He returned their acknowledgments more or less, I suppose, according to their rank and services; he made salaam with both hands to some respectable old men, while others he scarcely noticed; then he took each offering with his right hand, and gave it to a person who stood behind him, who collected the whole sum in this way; but what was done with it afterwards I cannot say. Our ladies were now informed that the Ranee would see them, and they went off to another part of the palace where no *man* ever entered but his Highness and his eunuchs. Mrs. B., who was one of the party, told me that the Ranee was a good-looking, stout woman, but not handsome. She sat on a kind of throne with her maids of honour, one of whom was very pretty and very graceful, and had a lovely figure; they spoke very little, and, after sitting a short time, each lady received a present of two handsome shawls, which were put over their shoulders, and they made their salaam and retired. The Rajah in the mean time made his presents; he put a diamond ornament of large size with a pearl chain round the neck of Mr. Casmajor, the Resident, and shawls were distributed to many other people of our party, which was a great mockery, for they were not allowed to keep them; doctors and doctors' wives were the only people allowed to retain them. The Resident presented the Rajah with a diamond star and pearl chain, also an ornament of pearl for his turban, and an English horse; altogether valued at 3,000 pagodas. He kept it on his neck a few seconds, took it off, and gave it to his treasurer, who received his minor presents, and who always stood behind him. Four very handsome boys sat near him, superbly dressed—his sons-in-law, betrothed to his four only daughters. He has only two sons and no legitimate children; he has six wives, and concubines innumerable. I got my usual *present* of betel-leaves, *sandal-wood*, oil, and the white wreath of stinking flowers, all of which I threw away immediately, bade his Highness good night, and got home about twelve o'clock. The ladies, on retiring from the drawing-room in the Residency, were requested to leave their fine shawls behind them, which were taken charge of by the Assistant Resident and put into store on account and to the credit of the Honourable East India Company—a woful disappointment to the fair sex, and the only blank in the ten days' enjoyment and hospitality.

My good wife left Mysore on the 19th of October to return home, and travelled as far as Seringapatam in one of the Resident's carriages, in company with two other of the officers' wives, they having forwarded their palankeens to await them there. I left the Residency after tiffin on the same day, as the guest of Major-General Sir Theophilus Pritzler, to visit the Falls of the Cauvery. We made a snug party of eight, viz., the General and Lady P.——, Mrs. Wetherall (their daughter), Captain C. Wetherall, A.D.C., Major Farquharson, Lieut Hill, Lieut. Lucas, and myself (of the Royals). We had about 200 servants of one kind or other, four elephants, two camels, seventeen horses, six palkees, nine bullocks, two orderly Dragoons, and a Sepoy guard. We crossed a branch of the Cauvery over a long stone bridge with about *sixty* arches, small and narrow; and, having proceeded for about two miles further along the banks of the river, we halted for the night in a very fine house belonging to the Resident, beautifully situated on the banks of the river.

20th.—We prepared for a day's shooting, but the morning was so misty that I would not turn out, and those who did go early got a wetting for their pains. Lieut. Lucas and myself went out with our guns about twelve o'clock; the day was hot, but a good breeze kept us alive; the country was finely wooded, and the under jungle fine cover for game, but we saw little except deer and wild hogs; we roused up a herd of the latter and fired into them, but without effect; small shot would not penetrate their thick skins unless they were very near; the deer were too wild, and a few pigeons and turtle doves was all we got. The flesh of the wild hog is excellent food and very tender, particularly when roasted and cold. We tiffed at three, and at four the ladies mounted their horses, and we all set out to a cheetah hunt. We soon found large herds of deer, and got as close as we could, when the cheetah was slipped. One buck was soon caught; another cheetah was slipped, but missed, which I was not sorry for.

21*st.*—We left Nundidroog about four o'clock in the morning, and had an uninteresting march of eleven miles over roads impassable for any kind of a wheel-conveyance to Kugunda. There was nothing worthy of remark at this place. We now took the common paths across the country, which were sometimes extremely bad, and in many places impassable in bad weather.

22*nd.*—Marched about five o'clock to Moogoor, a distance of fourteen miles, and encamped under some fine shady trees close to a tank. This was a neat and tolerably clean village; the head man spoke English very well, and presented us with limes and flowers. Here we entered the Company's territory. We had a fine view of the Nielgherry Hills as we marched along. Lucas shot some wild ducks on a large tank where we went to have a swim, under the shade of some trees in the heat of the day—a luxury which I always enjoyed much.

23*rd.*—We marched to Culligull, about fifteen miles, or five coss distant, and encamped in a tope. The country was flat, fertile, and rich with grain and cattle. The Coondour Hills in the distance had a fine effect; they were covered with wood to the very top, and extended along our right flank for several days' march. In the evening we walked to the top of Muddigoodah Hill, from whence we had a most extensive view over a beautiful country. The valleys were filled with cattle and grain, principally rice; the trees were large and well placed; the hills were now closer, and looked magnificent, and our tents on the tope below finished a very pretty picture. I went down to the stream to look at the elephants drinking; after which they were washed and *scrubbed*. The sagacity and docility of these animals often surprised and delighted me;

the keeper merely told this huge monster, twice the height of himself and four times the size of a dray horse, to lie down, and down he lay very carefully on his broadside in the water, with one half of his head above the surface. *Blackey* then threw water over him, took up a big stone and scrubbed him all over, seemingly to the elephant's great delight; he then turned over the other side of his enormous carcass for the same operation; when that was over he arose, drew some water into his trunk, and washed himself all over quite clean; and then walked away, reserving some gallons to assault the first insect that touched his hide. They are very sensitive to feeling; the smallest fly annoys them much, and they carry water for the purpose of drowning those perpetual tormentors. They will break a large branch off a tree, and flap themselves from head to the tail, kneel down to be loaded, and assist in putting up their burden. I have seen one hand the man on his back a stick, a rope, or any little thing he asked for, with as much nicety as it could be handled by the finest fingers; and I have seen them help the drivers up on their necks by bending a joint of their legs, and assisting them with their trunks to get up. They used frequently to be brought down to be fed at our tents.

24*th*.—We marched to Sittigull, a small village, and encamped amongst some shady trees on the banks of the Cauvery, passing through a very beautiful country, surrounded by magnificent hills, covered with wood to the very summit. We tiffed at two, and set out a little after three to see the Little Fall, a distance of five miles. Our course lay along a beautiful road for about two and a half miles, till we arrived at a stone bridge *three hundred* yards long, leading into the island. This bridge is supported by stone pillars, and has eighty-three arches, or passages for the water. It is built in the form of a crescent, and, considering the great length (*nine hundred feet*), and the vast pressure of water against it, it must be amazingly strong to resist such a current. The river divides here right and left round the island. We rode on about two and a half miles farther, when we alighted, descended the face of the bank by some steps a few hundred yards, and this magnificent waterfall opened to our view quite suddenly. We heard the roaring of the waters at a little distance; but the spray, which arose in a pyramidical cloud, we discerned very distinctly sixteen miles off. The river runs along a very rocky bed with an easy descent, dividing above this fall in three distinct parts, making three distinct and separate falls, about three hundred feet high; the largest of those three fell below us over a rock almost perpendicular with a terrible roar; the other two fell from the opposite bank. The beauty of these cascades was increased by the number of fine trees between them, along the banks and down to the very bed of the river. I descended alone, and after some difficulty got upon the rocks close to the cavity which received the great body of water. The guide would not accompany me at first; but when he saw me leap over a rapid stream between the cliffs, he followed me, missed his footing, and tumbled in. I caught him by the hand, and saved him from going over the precipice; we were near the edge of the rock, the channel deep, and running with great velocity. I then crept on my hands and feet, and looked over into the awful chasm into which the foaming waters never cease tumbling: it was a sight majestic and fearful. Before I got to the bottom, in the first instance, I was tolerably wet with the spray; but now I was soaked to the skin. The rocks were as slippery as ice, which caused me a terrible fall upon my back. I cautiously traced my way back without shoes or stockings, and got safely to the top of the hill again, where I saw a fine elk just killed by the hunters. They caught him in a net; but were not able to take him alive, so were obliged to kill him with their spears. We feasted on him for two days, and found him excellent venison.

Next morning all our tents were struck, and our camp removed to Ballikuwaddy, on the other side of the river, and we all started again for the island to see the other fall. The ladies rode on horseback to-day, and, after traversing our former road, we struck off about a mile further to the right, and obtained a fine view of these seven magnificent falls.

The island had been a thick forest a few years ago; but the proprietor (Ram Saumey, a native) had expended a lac of rupees in improving and clearing it. It was presented as a gift to the above native by the Madras Government for some service rendered to them.

I observed the cattle on the island were in better condition than any I had seen before in India; but the inhabitants seemed miserably poor, wore no covering on their heads, and were of a more deep and sooty black than their neighbours. We returned to breakfast about eight o'clock, and found two of our friends from the Residency had just arrived on the same errand as ourselves—Captain Stodart, R.N., and Mr. Brinsley Sheridan. After a hearty repast the General gave us notice that tiffin would be ready at two o'clock, and at four we should commence our march again. Lucas and myself set out with our guns at eleven a.m., to make our way to the end of the island, if possible, and see the junction of the river. We travelled along the bank of the rolling stream a few miles, when I discovered the print of a tiger's paw quite fresh in the sand, close to a pool of water, and by the side of a thick jungle. A shower of rain a little before would have erased in some measure the marks of his paws, had they not been very fresh. I therefore proposed a retrogade movement as soon as possible, keeping our guns cocked, and a sharp look-out. However we got up safely to the high ground without seing his Royal Highness. We saw a few specimens of those fellows' acting at Mysore, so short a time before, I knew we had no chance in case of an attack. We were informed afterwards that there were plenty of tigers on the island. We pursued our way, although the day was insufferably hot, but found ourselves so done up that we could not go farther than the falls which we first visited.

We returned in time to dress for dinner. A cool bottle of hermitage, some good venison, a glass of beer, and some cheese, appeased my craving appetite, and at four o'clock we all got under weigh. I observed a new tomb in progress, and upon inquiry who the deceased had been, was informed, that a Mussulman had dug his own grave on this spot about *seven hundred years* ago, and wished to be interred in it; but fearing his wishes might not be fulfilled, he walked in alive one day, requesting to be covered up, which was accordingly done, and they were *now* raising a handsome tomb over him, he having been a great saint in his day.

We left the island, and crossed the river, about six miles above, in boats nine feet square, made of bamboo, and covered outside with buffalo-hides, swimming our horses alongside. On landing we were met by a troop of the Rajah's horse, having again entered his territory. The horses were very good, but the men were like all his other troops, badly clad. They saluted the General as he passed, and then got leave to retire. The head man of the village was in waiting with his *trumpeter*, as usual; and the dancing girls, accompanied by their tom-toms and horrible music (if it deserves the name), met us on the way to our tents, which were pitched at Ballikawaddy, about a mile and a half from the river. We took some tea and supper at eight o'clock and retired for the night, all pretty tired after our day's roaming.

26th.—Started at five in the morning and marched to Maravilly, thirteen miles, and encamped in a small bad piece of ground amongst a few trees. The town was surrounded by a very old wall and a ditch, but nothing to be seen interesting, either inside or out.

27th.—Marched at the usual hour, and while jogging along with Lucas before daylight, our horses suddenly commenced a regular fight on the bund of a large tank; with a sheet of water on one side and a deep ravine on the other. We thought it safest to jump off and let them decide the quarrel, but my friend's horse galloped off and left us in the dark. However, he was caught again soon after daylight, and we proceeded on our journey. As it happened we had lost our way, and the delay gave us an opportunity of finding out our mistake, none of the followers having passed that way. We arrived at Nelloor after a pleasant ride of thirteen miles across the country; a very poor village, but the country rich and fertile.

28th.—Marched to Chinnapatam, 14 miles distant; a small town, no doubt, but it was surrounded by a very extensive fort, with a high stone-wall and embrasures for some hundred guns: but I did not see one. It had four entrance-gates, and a ditch round the walls, in which the cattle were grazing. The country about was fertile and very pretty, but there were lots of tigers in the jungle; it was at this place, in the previous year, that a young friend of mine went into a large plantation of tall cocoa and underwood to see the process of killing a tiger. As soon as the brute was roused, and the general cry set up to *beware*, my friend ran into a tank up to his chin, having got a glimpse of him through the jungle, and there awaited the result. The tiger was, however, killed by the hunters, and Master W——t walked out of his bath, determined not to go tiger-hunting any more.

29th.—Our next march was to Closcpet, only seven miles, where there was an excellent bungalow, beautifully situated. The river passed below the house, winding through a fine sandy bed, with gardens on both banks; the town lay in front of us, on the opposite side, surrounded with hills, which were covered with wood to their very summits. It was a lovely and romantic spot as any I had ever seen in India, and I would have fain taken a stroll in the beautiful woods; but, alas! they were inhabited by numerous tigers, and not having any inclination to pass the evening with such gentry, I satisfied myself gazing at the evergreen haunts and shades.

30th.—Marched early for Biddiddy, about fourteen miles distant. Nothing to be seen worthy of notice, except a large banyan-tree, which was *seventy* feet in circumference.

31st.—Our leave of absence having terminated to-day, we started off all our troops early, and marched for Kingeary, about eleven miles. After a good breakfast we saw the natives making their earthen vessels, which they shape upon a wheel, turning round with great velocity in a horizontal position, going on a pivot. As the wheel goes round they press the prepared earth, which is stuck in the centre of the wheel, with the hand, which rises to any shape or size they require, and with a bit of thin bamboo they give them a few notches round the edge to make a sort of finish, cut them off, and put them aside a little to harden in the sun; then bake them, and send them to the bazaar.

We tiffed at two o'clock, and all rode into Bangalore in the evening, distance twelve miles; found my little family ready to greet me with a hearty welcome home.

END OF VOLUME I.

www.ingramcontent.com/pod-product-compliance
Lightning Source LLC
Chambersburg PA
CBHW030405230426
43664CB00007BB/757